Orange Journalism

The Florida History and Culture Series

Florida A&M University, Tallahassee
Florida Atlantic University, Boca Raton
Florida Gulf Coast University, Ft. Myers
Florida International University, Miami
Florida State University, Tallahassee
University of Central Florida, Orlando
University of Florida, Gainesville
University of North Florida, Jacksonville
University of South Florida, Tampa
University of West Florida, Pensacola

Orange Journalism

Voices from Florida Newspapers

Julian M. Pleasants

Foreword by Gary R. Mormino
and Raymond Arsenault, Series Editors

University Press of Florida

Gainesville · Tallahassee · Tampa · Boca Raton
Pensacola · Orlando · Miami · Jacksonville · Ft. Myers

Copyright 2003 by Julian M. Pleasants
Printed in the United States of America on acid-free paper

08 07 06 05 04 03   6 5 4 3 2 1

Library of Congress Cataloging-in-Publication Data
Orange journalism: voices from Florida newspapers /
Julian M. Pleasants.
p. cm. — (The Florida history and culture series)
Includes bibliographical references.
ISBN 0-8130-2653-9 (cloth: alk. paper)
1. Journalism—Florida. 2. American newspapers—Florida.
I. Pleasants, Julian M. II. Series.
PN4897.F6O73 2003
071'.59—dc21 2003042633

The University Press of Florida is the scholarly publishing
agency for the State University System of Florida, comprising
Florida A&M University, Florida Atlantic University, Florida
Gulf Coast University, Florida International University, Florida
State University, University of Central Florida, University
of Florida, University of North Florida, University
of South Florida, and University of West Florida.

University Press of Florida
15 Northwest 15th Street
Gainesville, FL 32611–2079
http://www.upf.com

For Mandy

Contents

Columnists and Investigative Journalists

Editorial Cartoonists

Sportswriters

Series Foreword

Orange Journalism: Voices from Florida Newspapers is the twenty-fifth volume of a series devoted to the study of Florida history and culture. During the past half-century, the burgeoning population and increased national and international visibility of Florida have sparked a great deal of popular interest in the state's past, present, and future. As the favorite destination of countless tourists and as the new home for millions of retirees and other migrants, modern Florida has become a demographic, political, and cultural bellwether. Unfortunately, the quantity and quality of the literature on Florida's distinctive heritage and character have not kept pace with the Sunshine State's enhanced status. In an effort to remedy this situation—to provide an accessible and attractive format for the publication of Florida-related books—the University Press of Florida has established the Florida History and Culture series.

As coeditors of the series, we are committed to the creation of an eclectic but carefully crafted set of books that will provide the field of Florida studies with a new focus and that will encourage Florida researchers and writers to consider the broader implications and context of their work. The series includes standard academic monographs, works of synthesis, memoirs, and anthologies. And, while the series features books of historical interest, we encourage authors researching Florida's environment, politics, literature, and popular or material culture to submit their manuscripts as well. We want each book to retain a distinct personality and voice, but at the same time we hope to foster a sense of community and collaboration among Florida scholars.

Orange Journalism presents a vivid portrait of the colorful world of Florida newspapers. Compiled by Julian Pleasants, an accomplished regional historian who serves as director of the Samuel Proctor Oral History Program at the University of Florida, this groundbreaking book represents the first attempt to survey the full range of modern Florida's journalistic memory. Offering substantial excerpts from interviews conducted with a wide range of print journalists—including USA Today's Al Neuharth and noted Florida writer Carl Hiaasen—Pleasants takes us on an extended tour of one of the nation's most media-saturated states. Pleasants's probing questions about local and regional history, journalistic and political philosophy, the evolving role of newspapers in the growth and promotion of the state, and the changing nature of newspaper editing and writing as a profession often lead to revealing answers that enrich our understanding of both the text and context of Florida journalism.

One of the great strengths of this collection is an inclusive approach that encompasses the experiences of journalists at small, medium, and large newspapers, as well as the special circumstances and enthusiasms of African American, Hispanic, and female editors, investigative reporters, editorial and feature writers, cartoonists, and sportswriters. The result is a complex and sometimes contradictory picture of what it means to be a newspaper man or woman in a state undergoing massive economic and cultural change. From the Florida Keys to Pensacola, print journalists have faced the daunting task of producing the first draft of history, but that history has never been conducive to a single story line or point of view. The varied experiences and perspectives in Orange Journalism are as diverse as the state in which these journalists write, and the individual sagas of Florida journalists are often as powerful as the best prose of the writers themselves. In the end, these two revelations are Julian Pleasants's greatest gifts to the Floridians (and non-Floridians) fortunate enough to read this fascinating book.

Raymond Arsenault and Gary R. Mormino
Series Editors

Preface

In January 1999 the Florida Press Association, thanks to the leadership of executive directors Dick Shelton and H. Dean Ridings and president Ed Barber, voted a sum of $7,500 to fund a project to interview as many Florida newspaper pioneers as possible. Ultimately, the association provided some $23,500 for the completion of this project, and the Proctor Oral History Program is very grateful for their support.

The Florida Press Association, housed in Tallahassee, Florida, was founded in 1879 as a nonprofit corporation to protect the freedoms and advance the professional standards of the press in Florida. In specific terms the mission of the association includes the promotion and encouragement of higher standards of journalism to the benefit of the industry and the public, the aid and advancement of the study of journalism, the encouragement of better understanding between the public and the press, the encouragement of better business methods and practices within the industry, and the representation of the common interests of the state press on issues of general welfare and mutual concern. The FPA includes in its membership all of the daily and most of the weekly newspapers in the state. It sponsors the Florida Newspaper Hall of Fame, founded in 1988, to honor individuals, currently numbering twenty-nine, who have rendered outstanding service in the field of newspaper journalism in Florida.

The Samuel Proctor Oral History Program at the University of Florida observed that, in recent years, the state had lost many of its pioneer newspaper publishers and editors. These individuals played pivotal roles in the history of Florida journalism, but, unfortunately, their lives and stories went undocumented. While the career achievements of these individuals were well known, their personal reflections, opinions, anecdotes, and goals, as revealed through their own voices, were not. Thus, the Proctor Oral History Program and the Florida Press Association joined forces on a three-year project to document the significant role of daily and weekly newspapers in Florida's history by chronicling the lives of distinguished Florida editors, publishers, reporters, and columnists through tape-recorded interviews.

The overall purpose of the project was to help readers understand the extraordinary impact that newspapers have had on the lives of citizens of the state. Probably no other state in the country can boast of so many distinguished and successful newspapers, and we felt it important to preserve their contributions to reform and progress in the state over the last fifty years. The transcribed interviews will be available to scholars, journalists, students, and other interested parties. We hope that this collection of interviews might entice historically important press figures to donate their personal papers to university libraries to provide the materials necessary for the writing of a much-needed book on the history of newspapers in the state.

The FPA designated the Proctor Oral History Program (POHP) as the organizer and coordinator of the project. The program agreed to supervise the interviews, provide the necessary equipment, and do all the transcribing and editing of the interviews. Through the auspices of the College of Journalism at the University of Florida and Dean Terry Hynes, the Florida Newspaper Oral History Project Committee was established. The committee met several times to select the persons to be interviewed, to select the appropriate person to conduct the interview, and to formulate a series of questions to be asked of each interviewee. The committee had seven members: Dr. Bill McKeen, professor and chairman of the Department of Journalism; Jean Chance, professor of journalism; Dr. Ralph Lowenstein, former dean of the College of Journalism; Dr. Julian M. Pleasants, professor of history and director of the Proctor Oral History Program; Dr. Samuel Proctor, emeritus professor of history and former director of the Proctor Oral History Program; Dick Shelton, executive director of the FPA; and Ed Barber, president of the FPA and general manager of the *Florida Alligator*.

During the past three years, there have been numerous interviews conducted with important leaders in the industry, including Tommy Greene, David Lawrence, Allen Neuharth, Fred Pettijohn, Anne Saul, Diane Mc-Farlin, James Jesse, Carl Hiaasen, Tippen Davidson, Lucy Morgan, Garth Reeves, Al Burt, Ed Barber, Ralph Lowenstein, Don Wright, Loyal Frisbie, Edwin Pope, and Jesse Earle Bowden. These recent interviews are housed in the Proctor Oral History Program's Florida Newspaper Collection along with copies of thirty-six additional interviews done at various times by many different interviewers.

The series of questions asked each respondent included these examples: Would you comment on USA Today as the newspaper of the future? How have reporters, readers, and letters to the editor changed in the last twenty years? What specific goals did you have, and what changes did you make as editor, publisher, etc.? What are the most important functions of a newspaper? How much independence did you have from your parent company in writing editorials? How has new technology changed the way newspapers cover the news? What did your paper do to encourage the hiring of minorities? What were the sources of media competition in your community? Other questions were designed to elicit details about each respondent's career in journalism and to glean information about how they practice their specialties, such as sports, columns, or editorial cartoons.

These interviews supplement the Newsleaders Videotapes held at the Poynter Institute for Media Studies in St. Petersburg, Florida. The Poynter interviews include such national figures as Ben Bradlee, Malcolm Forbes, Katharine Graham, A. O. Sulzberger, Vermont Royster, John Chancellor, and Otis Chandler. The collection also includes videos with distinguished Floridians James Knight, James Batten, Alvah Chapman, Al Neuharth, Nelson Poynter, and Eugene Patterson.

Once the interviews had been completed, I decided, with the advice of Sam Proctor, Ed Barber, Ralph Lowenstein and others, to produce a manuscript featuring an edited version of the best interviews. I, not the committee, made the decision on which interviews to include in the book. I found the final choices to be difficult because of space limitations and the large number of extensive interviews from which to choose. The first priority was to include a variety of newspapers (African American press, weekly papers, medium-sized dailies, large dailies, and USA Today) and a good cross section of journalistic specialties, such as sports writing, editorial writing, editorial cartoons, investigative journalism, and columns. I also tried to give some geographical diversity to the mix so that I did not dwell merely on South Florida.

Obviously there are many newspapers and important individuals not included in this book. The main considerations were space, material from the interviews already completed (additional interviews will be conducted in phase three of the project), and the quality of the interview. I have not included anyone from some of the very fine papers in the state, such as the *Tampa Tribune* and the *Florida Times-Union*. Perhaps these can be included in a second volume. Attempts to contact Edna Buchanan of the *Miami Herald* for an interview were unsuccessful. Other possible interviewees were in ill health or otherwise unavailable.

Six Pulitzer Prize winners are among the group selected (Don Wright won two Pulitzers), and all the individuals chosen are recognized as leaders in their field. Two (Pettijohn and Neuharth) are in the Florida Newspaper Hall of Fame. The independent newspapers are represented by the *St. Petersburg Times*, owned by the not-for-profit Poynter Institute; the *Daytona News-Journal*; the *Miami Times*; and the *Madison County Carrier*. The major chains are also represented: the Chicago Tribune Company's *Ft. Lauderdale Sun-Sentinel* and *Orlando Sentinel*, Knight-Ridder's *Miami Herald*, New York Times Regional Newspapers' *Gainesville Sun* and *Sarasota Herald Tribune*, and Gannett's *USA Today*. In addition to some of the pioneers in the development of Florida newspapers, I added some younger members of the profession to get a better sense of how journalism has changed in the last half-century. All interviewees had a great wealth of knowledge and experience to share. Their stories are candid, relevant, often eloquent, sometimes inspiring, frequently amusing, and always insightful.

In editing these interviews, I have chosen approximately 30 to 40 percent of each interview, hoping to get the most relevant and interesting parts of the extended document. Ellipses indicate where material was omitted from the original transcript. For space reasons and to avoid an excessive number of ellipses, I have omitted them at the beginnings and ends of sentences. Occasionally, sentences have been repositioned to make a passage more comprehensible and the transition smoother, but I did not change the actual wording. Also, on occasion, I have modified the questions asked, both for space purposes and to clarify the question for the reader. I have tried to identify important individuals and to clarify indefinite terms. The factual material supplied by the editor is placed in brackets. On rare occasions I have had to change the tense of a verb or to supply a capital letter at the beginning of omitted material, to make the passage more readable, but not at the cost of changing the context or meaning of the interviews. Quotation marks are not used in these excerpts except when an interviewee quotes another person or a recognizable document.

Each interview is preceded by a biographical sketch of the featured individual. Much of this material comes from a vitae or articles supplied by the interviewee or from biographical references such as *Who's Who in America*. A short summary of each interview delineates the major issues discussed by the participant. The summary is presented primarily to give the reader some sense of the range and topics of the material presented.

The Samuel Proctor Oral History Program, the coordinating and organizing unit of the project, was founded in 1967. The repository, located at the University of Florida, currently has approximately 3,600 interviews and more than 80,000 pages of transcribed material, making it one of the major collections in the country. The purpose of the program is to preserve for future generations an eyewitness account of the economic, social, political, religious, and intellectual life of Florida. Oral history is an invaluable method of gathering and preserving history through interviews with participants. These "spoken memories" constitute both the oldest type of historical inquiry, predating the written word, and, with the advent of tape recorders in the 1940s and now digital technology, one of the most modern. These transcribed materials are available for use by research scholars, graduate and undergraduate students, journalists, genealogists, and other interested groups. Researchers have used our oral history resources for theses, dissertations, articles, books, and plays.

The program's major collection consists of more than 900 interviews with Native Americans, including Seminoles, Choctaws, Creeks, Lumbees, and Cherokees. The holdings include such diverse subjects as African Americans in Florida, Florida Olympians, civil rights activities in St. Augustine (1964), growth management in Florida, women supporters of George Wallace, black veterans of the Korean War, pioneer settlers and Florida "Crackers," and Italian immigrants in Ybor City.

We continue to work on our major projects: the Everglades restoration project, the presidential election of 2000, Florida politicians and business leaders, and the Civilian Conservation Corps. We are currently completing histories of the Levin School of Law, the J. Hillis Miller Health Center, the U.F. College of Medicine, and the School of Nursing. In addition to the interviews in this book, the Oral History repository features interviews with such distinguished Floridians as Dr. Robert Cade, one of the inventors of Gatorade; all of Florida's living governors except for the current incumbent; all of the former presidents of the University of Florida; U.S. Senators Bob

Graham, Connie Mack, and Paula Hawkins; Walter L. "Red" Barber, sports announcer; and business leaders including Wayne Huizenga and John Dasburg. For additional information, contact the program at our web site: http://www.clas.ufl.edu/history/oral.

In completing this work, I have incurred debts to many people. Obviously I want to thank all of the participants and other interviewers for their time and their expertise. Ben Houston and Melissa Mayer provided significant and untiring assistance with research, biographical sketches, summaries, and editing. Danielle Vance and Emily Wolfarth did their usual superb job of transcribing the interviews. Shane Runyon and Craig Dosher also assisted with research and fact-checking. Roberta Peacock, the office manager, made a major contribution by organizing the travel, coordinating the interviews, finalizing the manuscript, and keeping everyone on task.

I am also grateful to the three readers of the manuscript. Jeff Klinkenberg of the *St. Petersburg Times*, Leland Hawes of the *Tampa Tribune*, and Jean Chance of the College of Journalism at the University of Florida made valuable suggestions. Dr. Gary Mormino, professor of history at the University of South Florida, read the manuscript thoroughly and improved the book immeasurably with his insights and helpful comments. Sharon Damoff did a superb job of editing the manuscript. I also thank Meredith Morris-Babb, editor-in-chief of the University Press of Florida, and the staff, especially Judy Goffman, for their support, encouragement, and professionalism.

Newspapers in the Life of Florida

Good newspapers are essential to the functioning of a democratic society. As Leonard Downie, Jr., and Robert G. Kaiser explain in their insightful book, *The News about the News: American Journalism in Peril,* "good journalism makes a difference somewhere everyday. Communities are improved by aggressive, thorough coverage of important, if everyday, subjects like education, transportation, housing, work and recreation, government services and public safety. Exposure of incompetence and corruption in government can change misbegotten policies, save taxpayers money and end the careers of misbehaving public officials."[1] In Florida, for example, the *Miami Herald* exposed campaign fraud in the 1997 mayoral election, and eventually the election result was overturned in court.

Newspapers, according to Downie and Kaiser, also hold communities together in times of crisis by providing updated information that constitutes a shared experience: "Good journalism . . . enriches Americans by giving them both useful information for their daily lives and a sense of participation in the wider world. Good journalism makes possible the cooperation among citizens that is critical to a civilized society."[2] As Sandra Mims Rowe, editor of the Portland *Oregonian,* concludes, newspapers have to be the "high-quality provider" of information. A good paper is "essential to readers in terms of providing news they can't get anywhere else, or providing it at a depth or a detail or with the sophistication they can't get elsewhere. . . . There are lots of different ways to be essential. We do that by being authoritative, which means we actually have to know what the hell we write about."[3] On the other hand, Downie and Kaiser conclude that bad journalism misinforms, trivializes, and fails to report important news in a fair and accurate manner.[4]

Fortunately the state of Florida is home to some of the nation's best newspapers. In 1984 *Time* magazine named the *St. Petersburg Times* and the *Miami Herald* as two of the ten best papers in America. David Lawrence, Jr., former editor of the *Miami Herald* and a knowledgeable source on newspapers in the state, commented, "If you go around the state and you look at newspapers today, then I think we have some pretty darn good newspapers. I could easily name ten newspapers in this state that were outstanding, and others that would not fall that far behind. What other state could do that?"[5]

Earle Bowden, former editor of the *Pensacola News Journal*, agreed with Lawrence: "I do not see any weak papers in Florida anymore. I think Florida is really blessed with some great newspapers. You know, the *Miami Herald*, of course, and the *St. Pete Times*. You look at all the others, the old *Fort Lauderdale News* and the *Sun-Sentinel*. . . . The *Tampa Tribune*. Then you get into . . . the medium-size newspapers: Tallahassee, Gainesville, maybe Ocala. . . . They are all attractive newspapers."[6]

Currently Florida has nearly 900 weeklies and 375 dailies printed in the state, with several of the metropolitan papers earning a national reputation. There are 280 Spanish-language newspapers, three dating from the last century. Fifty-two African American titles have been identified, as well as forty papers representing the religious press. The diversity in the state's newspapers is illustrated by such titles as *La Estrella de Nicaragua*, the Nicaraguan newspaper in America; the *Florida Catholic*, printed in Orlando; the *Hi-riser*, which serves condo communities of Fort Lauderdale, Pompano, and Boca Raton; the *Kreyol Connection*, a trilingual newspaper (Haitian Creole, French, and English) in Palm Beach; *La Gaceta* in Tampa, America's only English, Spanish, and Italian paper; the *Seminole Tribune*, official organ of the Seminole Tribe of Florida, Inc.; and, finally, the *Palm Beach Daily News*, known as the Shiny Sheet, which keeps locals abreast of the social activities in upscale Palm Beach. Publications outside the mainstream include online papers, free weeklies that feature film and restaurant reviews and a list of local activities, and penny savers.

Campus newspapers also fulfill an important function in informing a select clientele. The University of Florida first held classes in September 1906, and shortly thereafter the first school newspaper, the *University News*, was established. Today the *Independent Florida Alligator* claims to be the largest college paper in the country, with a circulation of around 40,000. As of 2001, there are forty-seven college newspapers in the state, catering primarily to the student population.

If Pulitzer Prizes are any indication of the excellence of journalism in the state, then Florida has attained a position of national prominence. The first one was awarded to the *Miami Daily News* in 1939 for meritorious public service, and subsequently state newspapers have earned a total of thirty-seven Pulitzers. The awards have often been for meritorious public service, but also for editorial writing (John R. Harrison of the *Gainesville Sun* won in 1965, and Buddy Davis, writing for the same paper, in 1971); international reporting; editorial cartooning (Don Wright of the *Miami News* in 1966 and 1980); spot news photography; feature photography; feature writing; national reporting; criticism or commentary (Dave Barry of the *Miami Herald*, 1988); and investigative reporting. The 2001 Pulitzer for breaking news reporting went to the *Miami Herald* staff for their work on the Elian Gonzalez saga. Most of the awards have been for reporting, and the winners have included Lucy Morgan (1985), Gene Miller (1967 and 1976), Edna Buchanan (1986), and others. Although no female Florida journalists won a Pulitzer prior to 1980, since that time ten women have been honored. The *Miami Herald* has harvested a total of sixteen Pulitzers since 1939, an extraordinary achievement. The *St. Petersburg Times* has earned six awards, and the now defunct *Miami News* won five awards. The winners were not limited to large city papers, as the *Panama City News-Herald* won for meritorious public service in 1962.

Newspapers have had a long, distinguished history in Florida and have often had a dramatic and powerful impact on the history of the state. The publication of newspapers began before Florida became a state. The *East Florida Gazette* was a Tory paper published in St. Augustine as far back as 1783, while Florida was ruled by Great Britain. There is some evidence that a Spanish-language paper, *El Telegrafo de las Floridas*, was published at Fernandina in 1817.

After Florida was ceded by Spain to the United States and became an American territory in 1821, the *Floridian* became active in Pensacola the same year. These territorial papers busied themselves advocating immigration and statehood. James Owen Knauss, author of *Territorial Florida Journalism*, estimates that there were forty-four newspapers published during the territorial period of 1821–45.

By 1845, the year Florida became a state, its population stood at 66,000. In the years prior to the Civil War, the number and influence of newspapers gradually increased. Most papers held highly partisan political views, including the *Florida Whig* in Marianna and the *Whig Banner* in Palatka. By the beginning of the Civil War, there were substantial Democratic papers, such as the *Southern Confederacy* in Jacksonville. Their views were later countered by Jacksonville's Republican paper, the *Florida Union* (1864), which continues today as the *Florida Times-Union*. The first African American newspaper was started in 1873, when Josiah Walls, who served in the Union forces with the U.S. Colored Troops, purchased the *Cotton States* paper from a former Union general and established the *New Era* in Gainesville.[7]

Editors during the Civil War era were heavily involved in politics, and their papers were usually organs for the promotion of a political party. Although there were only twenty-six weekly newspapers, with limited circulation, the editors of those papers played an influential role in the defense of slavery and in creating support for secession and war. The Tallahassee *Floridian and Journal* called for secession shortly after Abraham Lincoln was elected, and Florida papers urged citizens of the state to form local militias and prepare for war. Their viewpoints often legitimized the people's support for the Confederate cause.

Some state papers, including the *Key of the Gulf* (Key West), were taken over by Union forces and replaced by pro-Union editors. Confederate newspapers nonetheless continued to support the rebel cause until the conclusion of the war. Once the war ended, several of the surviving papers urged residents to accept defeat and comply with federal orders. State newspapers, which grew to a total of twenty-seven by 1870, slowly resumed their position of leadership in the state.[8]

The period from 1879 until 1929 saw the economic boom and a dramatic increase in building, expansion, and tourism. Newspapers during these years provided detailed coverage of the Spanish-American War and World War I, the tragic yellow fever epidemics, and the automobile age. They hailed the building of a statewide network of roads, including the Tamiami Trail from Miami to Tampa, which opened up the wild and uninhabited Everglades to traffic. The era ended with the collapse of the boom economy in the mid-1920s and the onset of the Great Depression in 1929.

John Paul Jones, author of "Ink in the Sand," a history of the first fifty years of the Florida Press Association, concludes that the editors during this transition period in Florida history were usually highly educated men of "vision and versatility." Some had been businessmen, others writers, educators, and lawyers. Most had been heavily involved in politics. These men were, according to Jones, "builders." They not only built the newspaper empires that became the *Miami Herald*, the *St. Petersburg Times*, and others, but they also labored incessantly to promote Florida's climate, recreational facilities, and opportunities for economic growth. The first state journalism organization, the Florida Press Association (FPA), was founded in 1879 to coordinate the campaign to promote growth in Florida and to advance the interests of professional journalism.[9]

As the newspaper industry began to expand (*Tampa Tribune* in 1893), concern about the financial stability of papers developed. Charles Jones, editor of the *Jacksonville Times-Union*, made it clear that a "newspaper that was really a newspaper . . . is purely a business enterprise, just as a hotel or a steamboat line is a business enterprise. The public has not yet learned this. Newspaper men are not as fully convinced of it as for their own interest they should be."

George R. Fairbanks, of the *Fernandina Florida Mirror*, addressed another issue that concerned newspapers of the period. He denounced the press for filling its columns with accounts of crime. He saw this focus as a detriment to society, "yet it goes on without diminution, this daily spreading for the people their feast of bloody food." He also decried the excessive amount of sports news, "which takes the place of more judicious reading. . . . It lowers the standard of the paper which devotes undue space to baseball, horse racing and pugilism."[10]

In 1888 L. C. Vaughan, editor of the *Orlando Sentinel*, commented on the state of journalism in Florida. He discussed the responsibility that editors had for presenting the truth and concluded that technology had a powerful impact on Florida newspapers: "The invention of the cylinder press did as much for the profession, which now rules the world, as the discovery of gunpowder did for the savage profession, which ruled before." The development of the telegraph and ocean cables enabled newspapers to report on world events almost immediately, and a reader could learn what Queen Victoria had said to Parliament the previous day. Newspapers now had the world as their province and assumed a greater burden in providing accurate news: "One does not desire to have great masses of undigested news thrust upon him, but expects the editor to select the salient points and present them in readily comprehensible form."[11]

In the 1890s the Florida Press Association encouraged editors to refrain from writing and working for political parties and to get involved in the law-making process. The editors needed to do a better job of explaining to their readers what transpired in the legislative sessions in Tallahassee. Frank E. Harris, editor of the *Ocala Banner*, declared that the good editor will be noted for "his honest criticisms of officials, his advocacy of measures and his refusal to be led and used." Harris also discussed the responsibilities of the press: "If public office is a public trust, how much greater the public trust of a newspaper because its power for good or evil is so much greater, and it is in a large sense the custodian of the public morals, the character of the people and the life of the nation." Newspaper editors, he continued, "should be the most just and tolerant. It should be our constant aim to protect the weak from the strong."[12]

By 1905 the state of Florida had 566,885 residents and 173 newspapers and periodicals, including 19 daily papers. Thirty-one towns had two or more newspapers, and Miami, with a population of only 1,681, had seven, including three dailies.[13] As Florida continued to grow, especially after World War I and during the prosperous times of the early 1920s, the number of daily newspapers increased from thirty-three in 1921 to fifty-three in 1925. However, when the Florida land boom collapsed in 1925–26, newspapers lost real estate advertising, and the number of papers declined to forty-six in 1927.

As Florida began changing from an agrarian to an urban state, daily circulation increased, especially in Jacksonville, Miami, and Tampa. The papers began devoting more space to national news, in particular features on President Franklin D. Roosevelt and the impact of the Great Depression. For the first time since World War I, they began featuring foreign news on a larger scale.[14]

Since the 1930s Florida newspapers have been responsible for informing and providing guidance to Floridians on a number of important topics. Newspapers led a patriotic outpouring of support for World War II and displayed a firm commitment to retooling the economy and fighting the threat of Communism at the end of the war. They also played a key role in the civil rights movement, editorializing both for and against protests and legal challenges to the entrenched system of segregation. The papers reported extensively on the 1957 interposition resolution adopted by the Florida legislature, which denied the right of the U.S. Supreme Court to end segregation in Florida's public schools. News writers, including James A. Clendinen of the *Tampa Tribune* (who gave rural North Florida politicians the appellation of "the Pork Chop Gang"), crusaded against corruption and favored open records laws and the policy of one man, one vote. In 1968 most papers hailed the rewriting of the outdated 1885 state constitution.

Florida newspapers constantly kept their readers informed about world events such as the Korean War, the "New Look" foreign policy of Dwight Eisenhower, and the overthrow of Fulgencia Batista in Cuba by Fidel Castro. Pivotal events, including the Bay of Pigs invasion and the Cuban missile crisis, were covered in great detail by the state's papers, while the press often published favorable information about Joe McCarthy and the notorious Johns Committee in Florida.

From 1950 on, a dominant source of news was the space industry, which had a large impact on world politics and transformed the economies of many counties on the Space Coast of Florida. In 1950 the first missile was launched from Cape Canaveral. In 1957 the Soviets put up *Sputnik I*. The first U.S. satellite was sent into space from Cape Canaveral in 1958, and in 1961 the first manned spaceflight occurred.

In October 1971 Disney World opened, the key factor in ultimately making Orlando the most visited tourist city in the world. The *Orlando Sentinel* and its owner and editor, Martin Andersen, played an important role in encouraging Disney to come to Florida and in persuading the legislature to provide additional infrastructure for the new tourist destination. During the same time period, state papers issued numerous warnings about some unwelcome visitors to Florida, the omnipresent hurricanes, from Donna in 1960 to Andrew in 1992. In the 1990s killer tornadoes and wildfires garnered much attention from the press. By 2000 Florida had almost 16 million residents. The most widely reported news stories at the turn of the century were the saga of Elian Gonzalez and the disputed presidential recount of 2000.

Many important changes have taken place in Florida newspapers since 1945, beginning with the demise of the afternoon paper. Tippen Davidson, in his oral history interview, explained why afternoon papers had ceased to exist. He said the decision to close the *Daytona Beach Evening News* was made purely for economic reasons. Circulation had dropped from around 55,000 to near 25,000, and advertising went way down: "People were just not buying the combination [rate] anymore. For a long golden time, from the end of World War II on, very seldom did anybody buy any single-paper advertising." The combination rate, for both the morning and afternoon papers, was a good buy, but eventually advertisers quit the combination rate and refused to advertise in the afternoon paper. "It was a tough decision. All hands cried a lot. A lot of the people around had come up through the afternoon paper."[15]

Down the coast in Fort Lauderdale, Fred Pettijohn concurred: "The fate of the afternoon paper in the average city was pretty well spelled out. We thought instead of dying a slow death, why do we not manage our own demise? We have another newspaper [the *Sun-Sentinel*]; it is not like we are going out of business. Why not stop circulation, division by division, and slowly back out of the afternoon field, heavily recommending the morning [paper]."[16]

Earle Bowden in Pensacola had a similar experience. He noted that in the 1950s the morning paper (*Pensacola Journal*) and the afternoon paper (*Pensacola News*) had about the same circulation. It was a different time, Bowden recalled, until television began to dominate news distribution: "Then, you began to see the decline of the afternoon numbers. Advertisers preferred the morning paper because they had more circulation. I fought for years to keep the afternoon paper alive. . . . [But] by 1985, when we were forced to close out the afternoon [edition], the circulation [had] dropped to about 12,000 or 14,000. It was not viable anymore."[17]

Mergers and consolidations have had a major influence in the newspaper business in Florida. Over a period of years, national chains (Gannett Company, Knight-Ridder, the Chicago Tribune Company, the New York Times Company) purchased daily and weekly papers in the state and thus changed the face of newspaper ownership as well as their product. In the 1960s Cowles Communications moved into the state; in 1965 the Tribune Company purchased the *Orlando Sentinel*, and Knight Newspapers bought the *Tallahassee Democrat*. Gannett bought the *Pensacola News Journal* in 1969; Cox Enterprises acquired the *Palm Beach Post* in 1969; and in 1971 the New York Times Company took over the *Star-Banner* (Ocala), the *Gainesville Sun*, and the *Ledger* (Lakeland). By 2001, large chains owned 80 percent of the newspapers in the country. Nationwide, Gannett owned ninety-nine papers, with a combined daily circulation of almost 8 million, and twenty-two television stations. Knight-Ridder had thirty-two newspapers, with a circulation of nearly 4 million.

Downie and Kaiser discuss the significance of this shift in ownership: "For most of the first two centuries of American history the country's newspapers were deeply rooted local institutions. . . . Some were public spirited, others merely provincial, but everyone in town knew who the owner was and where to find him." With the growth of chain ownership, control moved from the local communities to "distant corporate headquarters." Typically editors and publishers moved about from one paper to another in the chain, never staying in one community for more than a few years. Increasingly, decisions about budgets, hiring, and news coverage were made from corporate headquarters.

Individual owners used to be willing to sacrifice some profit for public service and good journalism, but large media corporations are subject to business trends and have been under intense pressure to increase profits. In order to keep profits high (22–25 percent for Knight-Ridder and 29 percent for the Tribune Company in 2001), decision makers ordered significant cuts in both news staff and news stories.[18] Downie and Kaiser see this as a dangerous trend that reduced money for investigative reporting, limited space for national and international news, and in effect imperiled the future of newspapers in the name of profits.[19]

Some newspapers, primarily the *St. Petersburg Times*, the *News Journal*, and some weeklies like the *Polk County Democrat* and the *Madison County Carrier*, managed to fend off overtures from the national chains. Tippen Davidson related his special method of rebuffing offers from conglomerates: "It has to do with a trick you do with your head. You move it gently from left to right and back. . . . A week does not go by that somebody flies by with an offer. There has never been any drop in people's interest in acquiring this paper." Davidson noted that Cox Enterprises owned a large minority of the stock, but he added that "they have been good partners ever since they came aboard." When asked how the paper would change if taken over by a large chain, Davidson replied, "I am sure they would cut the expenses pretty drastically. This paper is heavily involved in the community. It gives away a lot of money. . . . I feel sure they [a conglomerate] would not do it as much as we do."[20]

Loyal Frisbie, a Bartow newspaperman, when asked how he avoided being incorporated into Knight-Ridder or Gannett, agreed with Tippen Davidson: "Just say no. . . . Ten or twenty years ago, when there was a frenzy to buy up newspapers, we would get a serious inquiry every few months. It was terribly tempting to take the money and run, but to some extent I think the nature of community journalism, certainly the nature of the Frisbie family, is that we have always wanted to be independent. We were more interested in working for ourselves and making our [own] decisions than we were in getting rich."[21]

Companies controlled by a single family have tended to provide excellent resources and have supported "aggressive, intelligent journalism." Downie and Kaiser cite the *St. Petersburg Times* as one of the best metropolitan newspapers in the country and the best paper in Florida because it was owned by a nonprofit media institute. This institute, created by its original owner, Nelson Poynter, and controlled by the publisher of the paper, was formed with the proviso that the paper be forever run for the public's benefit.[22] Paul Tash, editor of the *St. Petersburg Times*, concludes that his paper would never have been one of the largest and best in the state if it had been restricted by the business requirements of a modern chain. Because of the Poynter Trust, the paper had the freedom to invest profits back into the operation: "All those moves of expansion would have been impossible under the current climate of public ownership, because they would have diminished [profit] margins in the short term. And yet, in the long term, it has been . . . an enormously successful business strategy."[23]

Former governor Claude Kirk, Jr. (1967–71), believed strongly in the importance of independent newspapers: "Let me tell you about the *St. Petersburg Times*. Mr. Poynter who owns it, is a man who is liberal beyond words and who hated my philosophies. And I, in turn, probably hated his, but I respect his paper because the *St. Petersburg Times* is the finest paper for data and for honest presentation of facts. Now philosophically, they may yell and scream against you, but if you want to know something anywhere, that's real and basic . . . in Florida, his paper is a source. Not only that, the gentleman arranged to have his paper maintained independently. Which I think is marvelous, not the big chains who don't give a damn about Florida."[24]

Views differ among publishers and journalists about the benefits and liabilities of corporate ownership. Carl Hiaasen, best-selling author and columnist for the *Miami Herald*, had harsh words for the excessive profits demanded by corporate headquarters: "[For] the vigorous free press in this country today, the big enemy is Wall Street, or the big enemy is the corporations that own these newspapers, who are now putting out newspapers for shareholders, not for readers, who are much more concerned with pleasing the stockholders than they are with meeting the real day-to-day needs of readers. So these papers are being shrunk by attrition. They're getting thinner. All this is being done without telling the readers, and they're just not supposed to notice that there is nobody covering the city council meeting for a few weeks because . . . somebody quit, and they're not going to replace them, to save money."

Hiaasen noted that Knight-Ridder wanted a 25 percent profit margin for the current fiscal year: "It's absurd. I always tell people I know heroin dealers who would be thrilled with that kind of profit margin. It's completely obscene. It's unrealistic. It will have a devastating effect on the quality of the journalism that is being produced, because it means getting rid of older experienced people to whom they can afford to offer buyout packages. It's very sad, and it's shortsighted. And it's not by any means unique to Knight-Ridder. The *L.A. Times* is going through it. Gannett has been famous for it for years."[25]

Other publishers and editors took a different perspective. Diane McFarlin of the *Sarasota Herald-Tribune* recalled the immediate benefits of a corporate buyout: "Our press was . . . old and decrepit when we were privately owned. So as soon as the New York Times Company came in, we got a brand-new production facility, all new presses. This building was expanded and remodeled. We started opening bureaus so we could do a better job of serving the communities in the outlying parts of our market. So it works both ways, and I think the real key is to maintain the business strength of your operation without undermining the editorial integrity. That is a difficult balancing act, but as a publisher, I have to look both to the short term and the long term."[26]

Similarly, Earle Bowden was pleased when Gannett took over the *Pensacola News Journal*: "They were good for [our] company, a large corporation provid[ing] resources for a medium-sized newspaper. They built a new pressroom, expanded the building, began to put in computers to replace the hot-type operation . . . [with] all new equipment."[27]

Since 1945 both large media corporations and independent owners have embraced the technological revolution and have experimented with a variety of concepts in adapting to rapidly changing innovations. The breakthrough technology allowed publishers to produce a paper more efficiently, using color, bars, and graphs. By 1975 most papers had replaced their typewriters with computer front-end systems that included video display terminals and cathode ray tubes. In the early 1980s the Knight-Ridder Company and AT&T launched their Viewtron videotext system. In 1995 the *St. Petersburg Times* inaugurated its first online web project. Some newspaper and television stations began working together on news stories and shared multimedia newsrooms. In 1995 the *Sarasota Herald-Tribune* began a 24-hour cable television news operation called "Sarasota News Now" (SNN). And in

April 2000 the concept of convergence and synergy came to fruition when the Media General corporation opened its New Center building in Tampa for the *Tampa Tribune*, WFLA-TV, and TBO.com. The television station benefited from the investigative journalism and stories created by the many reporters from the newspaper, while the *Tribune* had a greater audience for its news reports and was helped by the immediate presentation of breaking news on television as well as online.[28]

One of the most astute innovators, Al Neuharth, acknowledged that newspapers had to recognize that "they are dealing with a generation who grew up on television and who are now wed to the web. . . . I think they will have to make sure that they, in print, can supplement what people get on the tube or on the web, in interesting and more complete ways and in an easier-to-get fashion. . . . If newspapers recognize that newspaper journalists are the best gatherers of news and information in any profession . . . ; nobody else can match that. . . . We have to be even more diligent in seeing to it that the best gatherers of news, newspaper journalists, have more avenues in which to disseminate that news—on the tube, on the air and radio, on cable, on the web—so that people can get . . . their professionally gathered news, when they want it, where they want it, and how they want it."[29]

Diane McFarlin enthusiastically endorsed the idea of experimenting in the electronic realm and using television to expand the paper's reach, primarily to attract those consumers who do not read newspapers to the extent that they did in the past. The *Sarasota Herald-Tribune*, with the approval and financial backing of the New York Times Company, "launched the first all-digital TV operation in the country, the first twenty-four-hour cable news channel in Florida, and the first cable channel to be produced out of a print newsroom." McFarlin operated a "blended newsroom," and SNN was able to reach approximately 175,000 households. She explained that the organization could now cover a compelling event by producing a complete story in the paper, having an SNN reporter walk the viewers through the crime scene on the air, and then providing pictures, updates, and additional details on the web site: "It is a classic example of why multimedia makes so much sense for news organizations and why multimedia really is the key to our future, because if we limit ourselves to one means of distributing information, of telling the story, then we run the risk of some people saying, 'Sorry, I can get it just by going here.'"[30]

However, as Downie and Kaiser point out, technology is merely a delivery system. Although technology has made more and more information available via the Internet, "facts become useful to people only when they are organized, put into context, evaluated and digested." Consumers will still need professional journalists to sift through the raw data, "check its accuracy and display it in a manner that reflects its importance." In the end, argue the authors, "journalists make sense of things—that is their function."[31]

From the publication of the first newspaper in Florida, the news industry has played a vital role in informing, persuading, and entertaining the citizens of the state. As the number of newspapers expanded, their influence increased. On World War II and Vietnam, civil rights and higher education, the environment and pollution, growth and transportation, and Disney World and political races, Florida newspapers have had their say.

In addition to informing the public, they have contributed to many causes over and beyond their responsibilities as purveyors of news and opinion. For example, the *News Journal* (Daytona Beach) sponsors a Medallion of Excellence to recognize superior academic achievement by high school seniors in the area. It also provides funds for Bethune-Cookman College and is one of the sponsors for the London Symphony Orchestra's appearances. The *Sarasota Herald-Tribune* started a fund called Season of Sharing, targeted toward homeless children. Earle Bowden in Pensacola has been a pioneering advocate for historic preservation in the city and is known as the father of the Gulf Islands National Seashore.

Other writers featured in this book have had a major impact on statewide developments, including fighting for the Government in the Sunshine law, which led to the opening of public meetings and public records. Carl Hiaasen has been a strong and active proponent of saving the environment; Lucy Morgan has exposed corruption in the state and constantly monitors the activities of state legislators; Don Wright, with his biting editorial cartoons, has skewered politicians and called attention to numerous problems; Garth Reeves has fought the good fight for civil rights in Miami; and Edwin Pope has chronicled the development of professional sports in the state.

The key to the future of newspapers in Florida centers largely on preventing papers from cutting news coverage and quality to maintain profits. Daily papers remain a critical part of American culture, and only great newspapers can provide the information, commentary, and interpretation that are necessary for a democratic society to function. The *Washington Post* and the *New York Times* have demonstrated that excellence and profitability go hand in hand. One would hope that other newspapers, rather than aiming for excessive profits, would follow the lead of the *Post* and the *Times*. Cost cutting often leads to a diminished paper and undermines traditional journalistic standards.

Despite readers' carping about too many ads, not enough or too much coverage of the Gators, Seminoles, or Hurricanes, disagreement with editorial policy or choice of comic strips, and impatience with typos and factual errors, what would we do without our morning papers? One sign that readers still treasure hearing the thump of the paper on the driveway (what Ben Bradlee called "the morning miracle") is the number of complaints when the paper arrives late or wet. As the following interviews demonstrate, the newspaper industry in Florida is flourishing, and the people of the state are blessed with highly educated and competent newspaperwomen and newspapermen who strive daily to bring them accurate, up-to-date news and editorial opinions on issues of consequence.

Notes

1. Leonard Downie, Jr., and Robert G. Kaiser, *The News about the News: American Journalism in Peril* (New York: Alfred A. Knopf, 2002), 4.
2. Ibid., 6.
3. Quoted ibid., 103.
4. Ibid., 6–7.
5. Interview with David Lawrence by Julian M. Pleasants, July 27, 1999, Proctor Oral History Program (POHP), 10.
6. Interview with Earle Bowden by Julian M. Pleasants, May 20, 2000, POHP, 32.
7. "A Brief History of Newspaper Publishing in Florida," Florida Newspaper Project, University of Florida, 1.
8. Lawrence J. O'Keefe, "Florida Newspapers in the Civil War Years: A Leadership Press," paper, University of Florida Journalism School, 1973, 1–20.
9. John Paul Jones, "Ink in the Sand: The First Fifty Years of the Florida Press Association, 1879–1929," *Florida Living*, August 1992, 40–41.
10. Ibid., 46.
11. Ibid., September 1992, 63–64.
12. Ibid., February 1993, 40.
13. Ibid., September 1993, 41.
14. John Pendleton Gaines, *A Century in Florida Journalism* (Gainesville: University of Florida Press, 1949), 132–42; Rembert W. Patrick, *Florida under Five Flags* (Gainesville: University of Florida Press, 1945), 105.
15. Interview with Tippen Davidson by Julian M. Pleasants, November 15, 2000, POHP, 9.
16. Interview with Fred Pettijohn by Julian M. Pleasants, August 18, 1999, POHP, 19.
17. Interview with Earle Bowden, 12.
18. Downie and Kaiser, *The News about the News*, 22–26, 83.

19. Ibid., 97.

20. Interview with Tippen Davidson, 10.

21. Interview with S. L. Frisbie by Julian M. Pleasants, October 23, 2001, POHP, 23.

22. Downie and Kaiser, *The News about the News*, 29, 76.

23. Ibid., quoting Paul Tash, 95.

24. Interview with Claude Kirk by Julian M. Pleasants, October 29, 1998, POHP, 86.

25. Interview with Carl Hiaasen by Julian M. Pleasants, August 15, 2001, POHP, 11.

26. Interview with Diane McFarlin by Julian M. Pleasants, August 15, 2001, POHP, 11.

27. Interview with Earle Bowden, 22.

28. Downie and Kaiser, *The News about the News*, 199–201.

29. Interview with Al Neuharth by Ralph Lowenstein, July 23, 1999, POHP, 42–43.

30. Interview with Diane McFarlin, 18–19.

31. Downie and Kaiser, *The News about the News*, 256.

National Newspapers

chapter 1 **Al Neuharth**

Al Neuharth was born in Eureka, South Dakota, on March 22, 1924. He grew
up amid rural poverty and at age two lost his father in a farm accident. At age
eleven he took his first job as a newspaper carrier and, in high school, began
writing for the school paper. He eventually became editor of the school paper and worked in the composing room of the weekly *Alpena [South Da-
kota] Journal*. After graduating from Alpena High School, he enlisted in the
army. Assigned to the 86th Infantry Division, he was shipped to Europe to
join General Patton's Third Army racing toward Germany. He earned a
Bronze Star and the Combat Infantryman's Badge.

After the war Neuharth returned to South Dakota, married his sweetheart, and enrolled at the University of South Dakota. He majored in journalism, graduated in 1950, and took a position in Sioux Falls as a reporter
with the Associated Press. In 1952 he and a friend launched a statewide
weekly tabloid, called *So Dak Sports*, devoted to high school athletics in
South Dakota. After raising $50,000 to start the paper, Neuharth and his
partner went bankrupt in two years because of lack of advertising and poor
management. Neuharth learned from his failure and, in 1953, looking forward to a new start in a different part of the country, accepted a job as a
reporter for the *Miami Herald*.

In the next seven years, Neuharth worked his way up from reporter to
assistant managing editor. While supervising the state coverage for the *Miami Herald*, he fell in love with the Cape Canaveral–Cocoa Beach (Florida)
area. In 1960, however, he moved back north, to the *Detroit Free Press*, part

of the Knight-Ridder newspaper chain. Then Gannett, a chain of small-city newspapers, called. Recognizing an opportunity to eventually take over the company, he accepted, in 1963, the position as general manager of its two Rochester, New York, newspapers. He assumed the role of vice president of Gannett and president of Gannett Florida and in 1966 started a new paper, called *Today*, later *Florida Today*.

The idea for a national paper came about because of the innovations of *Today* in Florida, which featured new designs, shorter articles, and color. Neuharth then established the national *USA Today*, which published its first issue on September 15, 1982, at a start-up cost of approximately $400 million. The paper gained 1 million circulation in seven months, and in five years had turned a profit, despite the jeers and criticism of more traditional papers. In 2002 the paper is firmly fixed in the national consciousness and is the most widely read paper in the country.

When Neuharth became chairman and CEO of Gannett, he dramatically expanded its holdings. In 1991 he founded the Freedom Forum, a nonpartisan, international foundation dedicated to free press, free speech, and free spirit for all people. The Freedom Forum funds and operates the Newseum from an endowment worth more than $1 billion in diversified assets. He was honored for lifetime achievements by the National Press Foundation with the Distinguished Contributions to Journalism Award. He still writes a weekly column for *USA Today*, and his autobiography, *Confessions of an S.O.B.*, was a best-seller. He currently resides in Cocoa Beach, Florida.

In this interview Neuharth relates his background in journalism and how he opted for newspapers over radio. He recalls his meeting with General George S. Patton in World War II. He speaks about the lessons learned from his first failed business venture, his time as a reporter and editor at the *Miami Herald*, and how the advent of *Florida Today* paved the way for *USA Today*. He speaks at great length about the genesis of the latter paper, particularly his inspiration from the Space Coast area of Florida, "where there is more vision per square mile than anywhere else on earth." He also shares his thoughts on how future technology will coexist with the traditional newspaper.

Allen H. Neuharth was interviewed by Ralph Lowenstein on July 23, 1999, in Cocoa Beach, Florida.

Q: The beginnings of journalism for you started in high school, did it not?

A: We had a weekly paper at Alpena [South Dakota] High School. The paper was *The Echo*. It was not really a paper by itself, but it was part of a page, half a page, in space donated by the local weekly paper. I began writing for that and became the editor of that paper in my junior year in high school.

Q: Did you have any association with the newspaper itself?

A: Yes, I worked there part-time sweeping up, cleaning up. I even got to play with the Linotype machine a little bit, but I never became a skilled Linotype operator.

Q: Did you go into the military right out of high school?

A: I went to Northern State Teachers' College in Aberdeen, South Dakota, for one quarter. I was eighteen. After the first quarter, a bunch of us in that freshman class enlisted and went into the army.

Q: What year was that?

A: I went in January of 1943. I enlisted in the fall, December of 1942, and went in January of 1943. After training, I was with the 86th Infantry Division. We were in Europe, and then we were one of the first two divisions that were shipped back to go to the Pacific. We landed in the Pacific after the atomic bomb was dropped, so we were spared any service there.

Q: I was especially interested in your encounter with General Patton [George S. Patton, Commander, U.S. Army Third Corps].

A: He was a hero of mine. He was a great guy. He was a go-go guy. Our 86th Division was part of his Third Army for a period of some weeks, and I was a sergeant in a reconnaissance platoon. On one day, a corporal of mine and I were marching a bunch of captured German soldiers through an encampment. We were resting at a crossroads, resting ourselves and them. Patton, whose jeep had stars displayed on it, was everywhere, close to, sometimes at, the front lines. This was, of course, when we were coming back from the front line. He stopped and wanted to know who was in charge. I was the sergeant in charge. He wanted to know what the hell we were doing there. So I told him we were taking a break, and he said, "Get the hell back on your feet, and [get] those Krauts moving. . . ." But I enjoyed the encounter. I enjoyed the chance of having him talk to me.

Q: Did anything about this man affect you in your later life?

A: Oh sure. A lot of people have affected my later life, but he was a person I looked up to, because he was the senior commander of the unit I was in. He believed in moving and getting things done. He was not a guy to make excuses or to fool around, and I thought his results-oriented approach to life was pretty good.

Q: As soon as you came back, did you go right away to the University of South Dakota?

A: No, I waited through the summer. I got out of the army in May 1946; it might have been late April. I got married in June and spent the summer waiting for the fall term to start. My new bride and I worked as carnies and traveled to one- and two-night carnivals and fairs around the states of South Dakota and Minnesota. I went into the university in the fall term of 1946.

Q: How did you first go to work for the university newspaper?

A: I was interested in broadcast or print, and I went to work for KUSD, the university radio station, in sports. I broadcast the sports games. I was broadcasting the homecoming game my freshman year, and my older brother Walter was sitting in the stands and had the radio on, listening to me, and had it turned up real loud. Some people in front of him turned around and said, "Would you turn that damn thing off?"

He said, "Don't you want to hear the game while you are watching it?" One of them said, "Not with that damn idiot broadcasting it."

So my brother reluctantly told me about that. I listened to some of my tapes, and I realized I was pretty bad. I quit broadcasting and went into print. I became sports writer, sports editor, and then editor of the *Bolante*, the school paper.

Q: Looking back at it, as objectively as you can, would you say that your interest in journalism, starting in those days, was because you realized you had a talent for it and you could do well with that talent?

A: I did not really know what I had much talent for when I went into college. . . . I think I felt primarily that it was fun [and] it was interesting. As the editor, I really did have, maybe, more influence on campus than someone my age or with my not-very-mature judgment should have had. I liked all that. I also felt that I could do some good. We did some campaigns on behalf of students that got me called into the university president's office three or four times, but I still felt it was important. I liked the fact that you could have a voice and sort of have a window on the world, even though the world was not very big at that time.

Q: At that time, did you think about spending the rest of your life in South Dakota, or did you have wider horizons, even then?

A: I think it was doubtful that I would have expected to spend my whole life in South Dakota, but I thought I would get rich and famous there before I moved on. That did not happen; instead, I went broke and ran away from home.

Q: Out of college, you went immediately to work for AP [Associated Press]. How did you get the job?

A: I went to work for the Associated Press, [but] . . . I had in mind starting this venture called *So Dak Sports*. The business manager of the *Bolante* and I decided we were going to do that to get rich and famous. . . . *So Dak Sports*, yes, as in South Dakota Sports. We spent much of that two years planning and plotting to start this venture, which turned out not to work. I worked for the AP for the two years while we were getting ready to launch *So Dak Sports*.

Q: And you borrowed money from?

A: We did not borrow. We sold stock. We formed a corporation and sold stock. . . . Our biggest investor invested $700. Most of them were doing it as a donation. They were sports fans or former jocks who thought a state-wide sports paper would be good for South Dakota. Nobody invested a lot of money and did not expect to make any, but that is how we raised about $50,000 to get the thing off the ground.

Q: How long did you run that paper?

A: Two years. We went broke after two years. We were going broke regularly. We never made any profit. We got pretty good circulation and no advertising, or very little. So we had to fold it after two years. It was the fall of 1953. [So] I ran away from home, went all the way to Miami, Florida, and got a job as a reporter on the *Miami Herald*.

Q: How did you happen to choose the *Miami Herald*?

A: Well, [for] one thing, I was ashamed. I had offers for jobs around there [South Dakota] and in Minnesota, but I was so ashamed at having gone broke that I wanted to get as far away from home as I could. I wanted to work on a big paper, and the *Miami Herald* was one of the leading papers in the southeast, along with Atlanta. [It was] certainly the leading paper in Florida then. . . . I got a telephone interview with the, then, managing editor of the *Miami Herald*. His name was George Beebe. I sent him a bunch of stuff, propaganda and factual stuff, and he looked it over. He had a lot of applications then from snowbirds, or Yankees, who wanted to work down there. He called me and offered me a job at $90 a week as a general assignment reporter.

I did not know Miami, so I suggested that maybe he ought to interview me first, and he said that was not necessary, and they were not paying for trips like that. So I asked him if I could come down at my own expense, which I did. I rode the train two nights and a day. I went down and looked around and got the interview with him and other people, and then I decided I was lucky to have the offer, so I grabbed it. I went back to South Dakota, took my car, rented a trailer, loaded up everything we owned, and came to Miami.

Q: When you went to work for the *Miami Herald*, how long were you a general assignment reporter?

A: I started on December 31, 1953, and I was a reporter for two or three years. Sometimes I substituted on beats. I was on the police beat a while, the court beat a while, but, basically, general assignment. I was offered a chance to go to the *Herald*'s Washington bureau for a period of three months, which they did with some of their reporters. I grabbed that. I was up there for three months and loved it. I had an opportunity to move out of reporting into editing, and I became the assistant city editor and then the executive city editor of the *Herald*.

After I left the city desk, I became assistant managing editor, and part of my job was to supervise the state coverage of the *Herald*. The *Herald* was very much a statewide paper at that time. George Beebe was the managing editor, . . . but Lee Hills was the executive editor. They were the two whom I really owe my training. In supervising state coverage, it was pretty clear that the *Herald* needed to be covering what was then Cape Canaveral, as the space program developed. That resulted in my making a number of trips back and forth and really falling in love with the Space Coast area, the Cocoa Beach area. I became kind of a space nut because I got to know all the early astronauts.

Q: With your trips up here, did the idea begin to gel a little bit that this place—I think it only had weekly or semi-weekly papers at that time—might be able to support a state paper?

A: Yes, there were three weeklies here, one in Titusville, one in Cocoa, and one in Melbourne. The daily papers that came in here were the *Miami Herald*, the *Tampa Tribune*, Jacksonville, Daytona, but primarily the *Orlando Sentinel*, which was, by far, the leading circulation here. As the area grew, it grew by leaps and bounds then. It went from a little fishing village to a space village with people pouring in. It seemed to me that it could support a daily paper of its own. Others had that idea. The *Melbourne Times* went from a weekly to a five-day-a-week daily not too long after that.

Anyway, that is how this area, Cape Kennedy/Cocoa Beach/Space Coast area, got my attention.

Q: Did you try in those days to get anyone interested in starting a paper?

A: Yes, I did. I mentioned to Jim Knight, who was then the general manager of the *Herald*, that I thought the *Herald* ought to do something exciting up here. He asked me what, and I said, "Like start a new daily newspaper."

Understandably, he kind of laughed and said, "Well, we are doing pretty well where we are," which was quite understandable because the *Herald* was the dominant paper in Florida, doing extremely well with circulation, financially, and otherwise, and it had a pretty good presence in Central Florida.

Q: I assume that you kept that in mind later on, right?

A: Well, sure. You know, having started *So Dak Sports* and having gone broke with it, I hoped that sometime in my career, I would have an opportunity to start another little paper somewhere that might work, rather than just having a failure on my record. I thought then, and even more so a few years later, that the Space Coast area was an ideal place for a new venture like that.

Q: Then, from Miami, you went to Detroit. Why did you make that move?

A: I was asked by Lee Hills, who was the executive editor of both the *Miami Herald* and the *Detroit Free Press*, to take the job of being his assistant in Detroit. [The] *Free Press*, which had been number one in a three-paper town, was number two in a two-paper town. So Lee Hills, who is a very, very brilliant and dynamic guy, said he had to figure out how to get it back to number one. He wanted to bring some new talent in.

Q: Your title there was?

A: I was assistant executive editor, which was assistant to Lee Hills. . . . I was fortunate because he had me do a lot of things outside of the newsroom as well as in the newsroom.

Q: Then you got a call from Gannett [New Jersey newspaper group], right?

A: Yes, I did. I was asked by them whether I would be interested in joining their organization. I told them I was happy where I was, but I interviewed with a couple of their top editorial people and, then, Paul Miller (who was the president, the chief executive, and chairman of Gannett). He offered me an opportunity to come in and run their two Rochester, New York, newspapers. I was very happy at the Knight organization. I had been with them almost ten years, learned a great deal, had the greatest respect for Jack Knight and Lee Hills, particularly, but others as well. But I also felt that someone in the family, probably, would ultimately inherit running those papers. At Gannett, there was no family member in the business. It was run by an outside professional, Paul Miller, and it was pretty clear that would be the pattern. I decided to make the move at age thirty-eight and see if I could not carve out a new career with another company.

Q: Then, while you were working for Gannett, did this idea of the paper in Cape Canaveral/Cocoa/Melbourne come back to the surface?

A: Sure. It did not take me long. In fact, during the interviewing process, I had told Paul Miller that I had a strong interest in and knowledge of the state of Florida and that Gannett ought to be in business in Florida.

He told me, "Well, I have tried several times to buy a paper down there, but somebody always beats me to it or offers more money."

I said, "Well, maybe you ought to start one." So I told him about my experiences here, in the Cocoa Beach area, and his interests piqued pretty quickly, even though, then, people were not starting new newspapers because the newspaper industry was not doing all that well.

Q: What is interesting about this is—I think since World War II—no new daily had ever been successfully started in the whole country, right?

A: Yes, I think with the exception of *NewsDay* on Long Island in New York.

Q: So there was a lot of resistance to trying to start a paper from scratch?

A: There was a lot of skepticism on the part of the people in the industry, and there was a good bit of resistance within Gannett. But Paul Miller was the boss, and if the boss wants to do something, he can overcome resistance.

Q: So how did you go about starting a paper here? You actually acquired another paper first, right?

A: Yes, I suggested to Paul Miller that we ought to try to buy one or two or all three of those [local] papers and use them as a base for a new newspaper. We made an effort, first, to buy the *Cocoa Tribune*. . . . She [Marie Holderman, the owner] had all kinds of offers from other people to buy her paper, and she turned them all down. She turned our people down, showed them the way to the door; it was not for sale.

Having been rebuffed there, I said to Paul, "We just have to go ahead with our plans to start a new paper, but why don't you let me have a shot at Mrs. Holderman," because I had known her from my days at the *Herald* coming up to the Cocoa area.

I came down to visit her and told her that I wanted her to know what Gannett's plans were: that we were going to start a new daily newspaper in this area, serving the Brevard County area, and that we thought that it would be pretty tough competition, that we were prepared to spend quite a lot of money, [and that] we did not want her to get hurt. We loved her, admired her, and respected her. We were willing to make a generous offer to buy the *Cocoa Tribune*, to keep publishing it as an afternoon newspaper, which it was, and we were going to start a new morning daily for the whole area.

She was only lukewarm at first; then . . . I called her and said, "We would like to fly our Gannett plane down and bring you . . . up here to spend a weekend. You can see what kind of company we are and get to know the people, and we are prepared to make you a good offer."

So she accepted that, and we flew the four of them up in the Gannett plane to Rochester. She . . . thought the paper was worth $1,900,000.

I looked at Paul. Paul looked at me. We both shook our heads, and Paul said, "Well, that seems like a fair price; why don't we shake hands on it?"

It happened that quickly. Of course, the lawyers fooled around for a while to get the job done. That is how that came about. Once we had that base—we owned the *Cocoa Tribune*—we used that as a kind of a background in many ways, [as] kind of a veil to hide our plans to start a new daily.

Q: The *Titusville Star-Advocate* was purchased by Gannett, was it not?

A: Yes, after we announced the *Cocoa Tribune* purchase, I went to see the Hudson family, Bob Hudson and his father, and told them what we were going to do and why we had bought the *Cocoa Tribune* and that we thought there was a chance that they would get hurt some by having a big new daily newspaper in the area. [I told them that] we were prepared to make them an offer for their paper to keep it going as an afternoon paper. Like was so often the case . . . we ended up with them agreeing to sell us the *Titusville Star-Advocate*. My recollection is that price was $1,000,000.

Q: Was the agreement between Gannett and these two families, the Holderman family and the Hudson families, that they would continue to have some involvement with the papers?

A: Sure. We did not have any contracts, but we told Mrs. Holderman that she could continue to run the *Cocoa Tribune* as long as she wanted to, and we told Bob Hudson that he could run the *Titusville Star-Advocate* as long as he wanted to. Mrs. Holderman did that until she became ill and died. It [the *Cocoa Tribune*] continued until after her death. Then, all three papers—Melbourne [*Times*], owned by the Perrys, and Cocoa and Titusville, owned by us—suffered in circulation because *Today*, as it was then called—it is now called *Florida Today*—began to take over most of the readership. *Today* was a morning paper. The other three were afternoon papers.

Q: You did not really start that paper until you had done a lot of research?

A: We were concerned, particularly, that Orlando might come in. Martin Andersen, a very, very aggressive, successful publisher, we thought, might come in and start his own Brevard County paper. He already had a section for Brevard County in the *Orlando Sentinel*. He had at that time, I think, 29,000 in circulation in Brevard County, the biggest chunk of circulation they had outside of Orange County.

Q: Tell me a little bit about the research that you did here that was a little bit unusual, before you really got that paper under way.

A: We had used Lou Harris and Associates. Lou Harris was a famous pollster back in the 1960s who first made his reputation in political polling and then in newspaper polling. He did some very, very extensive and expensive research in this area to see how people felt about the papers they were reading, the big papers from out of the area, like Miami and Orlando and Jacksonville and Daytona and Tampa, and the local papers and what they [were] interested in, in a paper. . . . [T]hese were people from all over the country, some from all over the world, but mostly from all over the country, heavily from the upper Midwest, Northeast, central part of the country. Most of them were well educated. They were what was then considered high-tech people, and their interests went well beyond the city boundaries of Cocoa or Titusville or Melbourne or wherever they happened to be living. They were more globally oriented.

They wanted . . . a more sophisticated daily newspaper that would emphasize heavily space coverage, since that is what most of them were doing for a living, but also emphasize coverage beyond the Space Coast, coverage in Florida, the U.S. generally, and around the world. It was that research that convinced us that if we could put together a paper that was interesting in design and had content that would appeal to those people, then it might work.

We spent many months putting the staff together, and we did a lot of dry runs. In fact, for a period of thirty days, we published it, actually published a paper every day. During not all, but most, of that thirty-day period, we printed them, and we hauled them to distribution points around the county to test out our circulation, the whole thing, and then dumped them.

Q: *Today* got a reputation, almost immediately, for innovative design.

A: Yes. It was designed to appeal to people who were in a hurry. Everybody at the Cape was in a hurry. They worked hard. They played hard. We had young people design it, and there were no sacred cows: the newspaper had not done anything before that you could not do differently. So they designed a breezy-looking paper, breezy in content and appearance, based on what the research said the people in this area wanted. It looked a little different, and it was a little different in content from the traditional newspapers of those days.

Q: Was it an immediate success, financially and in terms of circulation?

A: It was an immediate circulation success. These numbers can be verified—this was a long time ago, over thirty years ago—but I believe our circulation projections were for about 20,000 paid at the end of a year, and we had about 32,000 at the end of three months.

Q: The first paper was published when?

A: March 21, 1966. So circulation far exceeded our expectations right away. The advertising came somewhat more slowly but not bad[ly]. But because we had low advertising rates, we lost money as the circulation grew. We did not want to increase the rates too quickly—advertisers would think we were trying to gouge them, so we lost money for almost two years. We had projected that we would be profitable after three to five years. It turned out that we were profitable a little after two years, and the newspaper has done very well for thirty years since.

Q: Whose idea was that for the title?

A: The title was the work by a fellow by the name of Maurice Hickey. He was the general manager who we brought down for the newspaper. We had been kicking around all kinds of titles, all of the old standard ones: *Star*, *Tribune*, *News*, *World*, everything. I did not like any of them. I wanted something different.

He came to me one morning and said, "I got it. We ought to call it *Today*."

I thought he stole it from the NBC Today Show, but he claimed that he woke up in the middle of the night and thought of it. I think what happened was, he was a carouser; he usually closed all the bars in town. I think he did not wake up in the middle of the night; it probably hit him when one of the bars closed at two or three in the morning. But anyway, I thought it was a great idea.

Q: Was it his idea to do it in all caps?

A: No. We had design people work on that. He just thought it ought to be *Today*. We took the little sphere with the *O* and put satellites around it.

Q: So were you the publisher of *Today* here?

A: No, I did not have that title. I had the title of president. I took the title of president because we established a corporation called Gannett Florida, which would include *Today*, Cocoa, Titusville.

Q: What kind of competition did you have in those early days?

A: Well, the *Orlando Sentinel* [and] Martin Andersen . . . were very, very aggressive. They considered this their territory, so they put in a lot of cut-rate circulation programs. They increased their coverage for their Brevard [County] section. They had a very good local Brevard section. They were tough competitors. The other newspapers—Miami, Tampa, Daytona, Jacksonville—really did not react very aggressively, but they all assumed that we would fail sooner rather than later. The *Miami Herald* had the second biggest circulation here. I think they had 9,000 or 10,000 daily, and Orlando had 29,000. So Orlando had a big chunk of its business to protect. We had a lot of fun with that. They were the big guys, and we were the little guys. So we picked on them. I manufactured a few feuds with Martin Andersen. I liked him personally and respected him a great deal, but I had to pick on him. I called him the highway man from Andersenville and said all he wanted to do was make all his money in Brevard County and run with it back to Orlando, that kind of thing.

Q: Suppose you had been Martin Andersen? What would you have done in those days to really grind this new paper under?

A: [Laughs.] I would have prayed a lot. I am not sure I would have done anything all that different from what Martin Andersen . . . did. I might have done it with a little more power, a little more money. They basically took a very good existing, established product and tried to improve it and sell it at more attractive rates. I do not know that they could have done, or that I would have done, much more than that.

Q: So there was just room for one new newspaper in what amounted to a new population.

A: I think so. I think anyone, the Orlando ownership, could have come in here and started a newspaper. I think the *Miami Herald* ownership could have. . . .

Q: Were there any other newspapers in the state that you were influential in acquiring? I know you owned some weeklies as well.

A: I was chairman and president of Gannett, and I was very disappointed that we were not able to acquire . . . [the *Jacksonville Journal*]. The biggest disappointment to me was the Gainesville [*Sun*] paper. We were among a number of people who were hoping to acquire the Gainesville paper and the Tallahassee paper, and the *New York Times* was involved. We had a lot of conversations with them, and we thought we had the inside track. It ended up the *New York Times* was successful, and we were not. In Tallahassee, the same thing. We thought we had the inside track, and the Knight organization was successful, and we were not. So . . . Gannett was very fortunate in acquiring Pensacola and Fort Myers and, then, Cocoa and starting *Today*.

Q: Largely because of you, I believe, the Gannett Foundation, as it was then called—it is now called the Freedom Forum—has a great relationship with the University of Florida College of Journalism.

A: Once we were in business in Florida, we felt that we should be active in supporting, financially, certain institutions and certain endeavors. Jim Jesse [publisher of *Cocoa Today* and the *Pensacola News Journal*] is the one who was instrumental in convincing us that we should make a major contribution to the University of Florida, because they were in hopes of building a new journalism building. They had terrible quarters. They were producing good journalists. We were hiring quite a few of them. We had conversations with the president of the university, Stephen C. O'Connell [president, University of Florida, 1967–73], and the dean of the school. He was convinced and convinced us that if he had a lead grant, of something like one million [dollars], he would be able to use that as leverage in Tallahassee to get some real money from the state. So that is what we ended up doing, giving one million to the University of Florida, which I think helped get that project under way.

Q: What you did from that point on [was] you started the paper *Today*. Then, having been successful in doing that, you also had the idea of starting not a specialized newspaper but a general circulation, national newspaper, which was a first also. Was *Today* the seed of *USA Today*?

A: Sure. If *Today* in Florida had gone belly-up, there would be no *USA Today*. Remember, I had one failure in *So Dak Sports* and one success in *Today*, here in Florida. That was the thing that led me to believe that this might be attempted on a national scale. Because we had a very young staff at *Today* in Florida, there were a lot of those people still around who had played a role in Florida and the starting of a successful new newspaper that I was able to tap. . . . So the germ of the idea for *USA Today* was born because of the success of *Today* in Florida. So a lot of that Florida background and experience—and there were many others in advertising, circulation, and news who had been through the experience in starting the paper in Florida—helped us make it work with *USA Today*.

Q: You sent the original task force to think about this newspaper and its possibilities right down here to Cocoa.

A: Yes, we put them up for six or seven months in a little cottage in Cocoa Beach, kind of locked them up, and had them do their thinking and the developing of their plan there. They traveled all around the country and the world and came back here. They did it all here. I wanted them to do it here for three reasons: one, I wanted to be where I could check on them every weekend or get with them every weekend; two, I wanted them to be where *Florida Today* reminded them of the success of a new newspaper and where they could see how it was done and go back and retrace some of that; three, I wanted them in the shadows of the launch pads at the Kennedy Space Center, where I think there is more vision per square mile than anywhere on earth. It was true then, and it is still true today. I think that environment, that combination of things, is what helped those three young kids—I say young; their average age was thirty—come up with a blueprint for starting *USA Today*.

Q: When you started *USA Today*, you put a lot of your own reputation on the line, because everybody said you were crazy. I know every editor and publisher in Florida said that you were going to go broke doing it. They ridiculed it, really. They laughed at the attempt to start a nationwide newspaper.

A: Of course. I knew all about the laughter and the ridicule, and I was laughing at the laughter. I was having more fun than they. I had the advantage.

Q: You were not worried? You were not concerned?

A: No, I was not worried at all. I knew that it was a high-risk venture, but I was never worried about it because I knew that we were privy to much more information than our critics. I knew we had done it in Florida on a small scale. It was my feeling then, and is now, that whether it is a newspaper or anything else, if you want to go into a smaller venture than what you have been doing, you divide; if you want a bigger venture, you multiply. That is somewhat of an oversimplification, but at *USA Today*, we multiplied many times over the things that had worked at *Today* in Florida. So our people knew what they were doing.

Q: I think there was no other newspaper person in the United States who could really make USA Today a success but Al Neuharth. Because it took more than an idea, I think, and it took more than vision. It took someone who was a risk taker and who had power and who was willing to bull this through, because did you not face a lot of opposition from the Gannett board on this?

A: First of all, you are overly generous, you are very kind, and you are wrong. There are other people who could have done this. I happened to be in the right place at the right time. There was opposition within the Gannett company to the idea, initially, but all board members, all of them, ultimately came around. When we voted on the decision to do it, it was unanimous. During the days when we were bleeding about ten million a month, nobody ever wavered because they knew what the mileposts were along the way: that if we get x circulation by x time, we were on target. They knew that advertising would come slowly. They knew that it was going to cost us a lot of money. It cost a little more than we thought it would.

Q: Fifty million is the amount usually bandied about. Is that conservative?

A: That is very conservative. No. I think it is no secret that the after-tax investment at USA Today, until it became profitable, was about four hundred million, which is eight hundred million before tax. We were using fifty-cent dollars, remember, because of the government. You know, it was money we earned elsewhere. So that was a lot of money.

Q: And the bleeding kept up for how many years?

A: It was five years before we had profitability and a little longer than that before we had a full year of profitability. We had several months of profitability in the fifth year. But now it is making more money than the law allows. When you look at that four hundred million to four hundred fifty million price tag, it is not much more than we paid for some individual newspapers, like Des Moines and Louisville. So if you looked at it in terms of the investment in a major newspaper, it was a bargain. But if you looked at it as something that might possibly end up being worth zero, then it was kind of risky.

Q: Were there any suggestions from the board during those five years that you throw in the towel and junk the whole thing?

A: Never. No, there was never any hesitation or nervousness on the board, either expressed to me privately or expressed at board meetings, because, again, they were privy to the information. See, we knew when we hit the magic number of one million in circulation, which happened in seven months, we knew that was the end of the ball game, that then it was just a matter of time until those geniuses on Madison Avenue, the advertising geniuses who claim that they are the most creative people in the world but who are really the most conservative on earth and who do not want to invest their clients' money in a new publication or a new idea, because they are afraid if it goes belly-up that they will be blamed for it. We knew that the one million would get to them and that it would just be a matter of time.

If we had not gotten that kind of circulation, if we had lingered for a year or two at four hundred thousand, five hundred thousand, six hundred thousand, seven hundred thousand circulation, then we could have had a problem. But once that circulation breakthrough came clear, and it kept growing and growing, then everyone was convinced that we had a winner.

Q: What date did USA Today publish the first [issue]?

A: September 15, 1982.

Q: How many years of preparation went into that, would you say?

A: Probably five or six years of thinking went into it, but we organized formally—we set aside some research money, one million—three years in advance. We put the task force together about two and a half years in advance. So I would say three years of full-time planning on the part of a lot of people, and another two or three years of thinking and talking about it.

Q: Was USA Today your idea?

A: Let us say that it was generally agreed that if USA Today failed, I had to take all the blame.

Q: When did you really conceive the idea that there was room for a national newspaper?

A: In the mid-1970s, Gannett had grown to where we were in thirty-six states. We had newspapers in thirty-six states, and I traveled to all those places all of the time. I went to every place once a year. Then, I became chairman of what was then the American Newspaper Publishers' Association, 1977 to 1978, and I went to all fifty states in that role. We had our own Gannett plane. I would load it up. I read every newspaper everywhere, studied them. I talked to editors about how they thought they were doing. I talked to readers. My conclusion was that most of the newspapers in the country, including Gannett newspapers, were pretty good but not as good as their editors thought they were and that, in most cases, newspaper readers had a hunger for something more or something different than what they were getting and that more and more of them were turning to the tube more, to television more, particularly the younger ones.

At that time, we had quite a few newspaper deaths and no births; there were very few births. I was convinced that we had to do something rather dramatic with our newspapers. Because we had so many Gannett newspapers, over eighty dailies at that time, that was a great concern to me. That was how Gannett made its money. So, as a result of that feeling that we had to change the way newspapers looked and what was in them, I said, "I wonder if we could not only change what we have but if we could start something totally new and totally different." That is why it developed.

Q: In the fifty years since you first entered the newspaper business, how do you believe the audience has changed, not just the newspaper audience but the news audience?

A: Certainly, the audience has changed dramatically in fifty years, in terms of its interests. When I grew up in South Dakota and graduated from the University of South Dakota in 1950, there was not much global interest. By global, I mean national or international. People were interested primarily in their community, their city, their state, or their region. Sure, they would be interested in the president of the United States and a few so-called national sports teams, but not strong interest. That changed, I think, for two reasons. One, it changed because so many millions of us traveled around the country and around the world in World War II. We came back to our home base, and we had a somewhat broader vision or clearer vision of the world. Secondly, it changed because of television. When it became possible for everyone everywhere to get, on the tube, quick information and entertainment, they became more reluctant to fight their way through dull gray newspapers.

When Lou Harris did the research for us on *USA Today,* I remember he sat down with us in the news room . . . to talk about the survey results. He had a copy of the *New York Times* and the *Wall Street Journal,* and he said, "I am absolutely convinced, based on this research, that the television generation will not continue to fight its way through dull gray newspapers." He leafed through the *Times,* and he leafed through the *Wall Street Journal.*

Well, he was right, because it was the television generation. So those interests had changed dramatically from 1950 to 1975 or 1980. That is why we sometimes get more credit than we deserve for creating all these things at *USA Today* that were different. We did not create very much; we stole.

We stole most of it from the tube or from magazines, and we adapted it to a daily form of print. . . . Do you like the weather map? We stole it right off the TV screen and put it on a piece of paper. And the color and the graphics. So they were not new, but they were done to adapt to how the public had changed in its interests.

Q: How have newspapers changed?

A: I think it is fair to say that the appearance and content of newspapers have changed dramatically since 1980, for better or worse, depending on your point of view. But it has changed. We have a smart-aleck guy who I admire very much on the *USA Today* named Taylor Buckley, who said, when we were labeled McPaper—everybody called us McPaper, the fast food of journalism. *Newsweek* and the *Washington Post* coined that, and I laughed; I thought it was a nice label.

Q: There is a book about the beginning of the paper, called *McPaper*.

A: Right, and Taylor Buckley said, "Well, they call us McPaper, but more and more, they are stealing all of our McNuggets," as they were. Now, you can go to any city in the country, and the color, the graphics, the brightness is there. There are no longer any dull gray newspapers, with the exception of the *Wall Street Journal*.

Q: How do newspapers need to change to compete with the Internet and television?

A: I think newspapers in the future, first of all, will have to continue to recognize that they are dealing with a generation who grew up on television and who are now wed to the web, or many members of this generation are wed to the web. I think they will have to make sure that they, in print, can supplement what people get on the tube or on the web, in interesting and more complete ways and in an easier-to-get fashion. Everybody on television came in and said, "That is the end of newspapers." Well, it did not happen.

Now, a lot of people are saying, "Well, the Internet is the end of newspapers." I think that will not happen for these reasons. If newspapers recognize that newspaper journalists are the best gatherers of news and information in any profession, the best gatherers, they are trained gatherers of news; nobody else can match that. Television cannot match it. Radio cannot match it. Certainly, the Internet cannot match it. Also, recognize that most of the news that we have gathered traditionally, that our newspaper people have gathered, never sees the light of day.

So it seems to me [that] now, we have to be even more diligent in seeing to it that the best gatherers of news, newspaper journalists, have more avenues in which to disseminate that news—on the tube, on the air and radio, on cable, on the web—so that people can get their news, their good professionally gathered news, when they want it, where they want it, and how they want it.

The two key things are that they [newspapers] are the most affordable way to get the most news and information and advertising—because cable costs more money, and you have to make an investment to be on the Internet—and they are the most portable. I have said this, and people think I say it facetiously, but I mean this: you cannot take the computer to the bathroom with you. Newspapers are so portable that our research shows that newspapers are read everywhere: living room, bathroom, bed-room, bar room, office. So it is not a chore to take the newspaper with you and read it. For me, the web is not a bore, but it is a chore. You have to sit someplace. You know? I do not think that the mass appeal of newspapers will vanish. I think it will still be the biggest, single most affordable way for news and information in the broadest sense, including advertising, to be distributed, but that those who gather that will have to take advantage of other ways to disseminate it as well.

Large Newspapers

chapter 2 **David Lawrence, Jr.**

David Lawrence was born March 5, 1942, the second oldest of nine children. His father was a newspaperman working for the *New York Sun*. When his parents decided to move to a warmer climate in 1956, Florida was chosen in part because it was the winter broadcast home of Arthur Godfrey's television show, which they liked to watch. In Florida his father sold real estate and later was employed on the now-folded *Sarasota News*. He ending up working for the *Orlando Sentinel* for the last seventeen years of his life, was dean of the Florida Press Corps in Tallahassee, and earned a spot in the Florida Journalism Hall of Fame. Lawrence admired his father and decided to go into journalism.

After graduation from the University of Florida, where he was editor of the *Alligator*, David Lawrence went to the *St. Petersburg Times*, where he had worked as a summer intern. After three and a half years at the *St. Petersburg Times*, he transferred to the news desk at the *Washington Post* and became news editor of *Style*. He next accepted the position of managing editor of the *Palm Beach Post* and held it from 1969 to 1971. In 1971 he migrated to the *Philadelphia Daily News* as assistant to the editor and then became managing editor. In 1975 he became executive editor at the *Charlotte Observer* for three and a half years, before moving on to Detroit as the executive editor for the *Detroit Free Press*. Promoted to the job of publisher of the *Free Press* in 1985, Lawrence left in 1989 to come to Miami, when Knight-Ridder hired him to run the *Miami Herald* and *El Nuevo Herald*.

After ten years at the *Miami Herald* and thirty years in the newspaper business, Lawrence decided to leave the profession because he felt that it had become far more of a business than it should be. He became interested and involved in early childhood development and education after Governor Lawton Chiles asked him to be on the governor's Commission on Education. His friends formed a foundation that allowed him to remain in Miami, and the Early Childhood Initiative Foundation was born.

In this interview, Lawrence describes the newsrooms that he inhabited at a young age and the feeling he got when he saw his first byline in print. He discusses the conflicts he had as editor of the *Alligator* at the University of Florida with President J. Wayne Reitz about his views on student unrest, the Johns Committee, and the civil rights movement. He describes in detail, and with great feeling, his work as editor of *Style* at the *Washington Post* and his experiences and coworkers at the *Charlotte Observer, Detroit Free Press, St. Petersburg Times, Palm Beach Post,* and *Miami Herald*. He also discusses the role of women in journalism, the impact of ethnic minorities in Florida, and the need for newspapers to understand their audiences.

David Lawrence was interviewed by William McKeen on August 7, 1999, in Miami, Florida.

Q: Were you from a large family?

A: A large family. One of nine children. I am the second oldest of nine. Eight are still living. All of us graduated from either the University of Florida or Florida State.

Q: Could you tell us a little bit about your parents?

A: My mother came from, really, a New York Social Register family, one of ten children. My father came from a Long Island real estate family, the youngest of eleven children. My mother's family came over in the *Mayflower*, originally. My father's family came over in the wake of the Irish potato famine in the 1840s. As a little boy, I was living in New York City and on Long Island. My father was a newspaperman at the then *New York Sun*, now defunct.

[O]n my sixth birthday, on March 5, 1948, our family, then five children and a mother and father, moved to a farm in upstate New York. My father's vision was that he would work on the farm and have a vegetable garden and a cow and maybe a goat and then work on the weekly newspaper. Of course, farming did not work like that, and my father never did go to work for the *Sandy Creek News*. But, for the next eight years, we lived on a farm in the least glamorous form of farming, which is chicken farming. So if I know anything about hard work and doing it with other people, it is from growing up on a farm. I literally drove the tractor when I was nine years old and sold vegetables to neighbors. It was a wonderful way to grow up.

Well, in 1956, when I was fourteen—this is eight years after this grand experiment—my parents decided that farming was none too profitable. My parents decided, "Let us move to somewhere warm; we are tired of these frozen winters, and let us go somewhere else and make our fortune."

So we literally used the 1952 edition of the *World Book Encyclopedia* and looked up Arizona, New Mexico, and Florida, none of which any of us had ever been to. We looked them up, and I think the final telling thing was that my parents were great watchers of Arthur Godfrey on Sundays. Arthur Godfrey, in the winters, brought the show to Miami Beach, and that is how Florida came to be selected.

So toward the end of the winter in 1956, we moved to Florida. So my father ended up selling real estate, subsequently going to a paper now dead, a daily newspaper in Sarasota, Florida [*Sarasota News*]. . . . [M]y father worked there for several years . . . [and] then ended up the last seventeen-plus years of his life working for the *Orlando Sentinel*, . . . most of the time in Tallahassee, where he became the dean of the press corps. The House press gallery is named for him today, and he is in the Florida Journalism Hall of Fame. So I ended up going into journalism, purely and simply because I admired my father, and I wanted to be in the same business that he was.

When I was fifteen years old, I started working in the composing room during the summers, at the *Sarasota News*. Then I was sort of off to the races from there. I was editor of the high school newspaper. I worked summers during college at the *St. Petersburg Times*.

Q: Describe what the *Sarasota News* was like.

A: Well, it is almost certainly idealized in my mind. At age fifteen, I would go into the newsroom, and I would beg to rewrite press releases. So I rewrote those while I was waiting for my father to go home. He was then the managing editor and the general manager of the newspaper. The back shop . . . was a hot-lead operation in which there are terms like *bank* and *turtle* and so forth. We have a whole generation of journalists now who have never heard any of these terms. The printing craft was a very peripatetic kind of profession. These folks had worked at lots of different places. They were sort of crude and loud and tellers of dirty jokes, but they were warm people at the same time.

Q: You were able to go from the back shop to the newsroom and do some rewriting. Do you think that technology has changed so much that there are none of those early types working in the business?

A: These days, it would be unusual for a newsroom to hire a person who did not graduate from college. That was not true back then. Of course, pay was slightly less than mediocre, but the cliché was sort of true, that you were not doing this for the money anyway. You just paid your dues, and when somebody gave you a chance to write something or report something, that was a huge deal. I can still remember, as an intern for the *St. Petersburg Times*, the first byline I ever got. I was in the Bradenton bureau of the *St. Petersburg Times* that first summer. It had a two-column headline, and it was about the tomato crop in Palmetto, Florida. Why should I remember that all of these years? It was that big a thrill. To this day, I think it is a thrill to have your byline in the paper or your column to go in the paper. It is still very personal.

Q: Since we have you in a reflective mood, do you want to make any other observations about the changing nature of the species *journalist*? Are they too elitist?

A: It has some tendency toward that. Too many [newspaper people] are out of touch with most people. I always thought one of the big perils in the newsroom was that too many had all their friends in the newsroom. You do not learn an awful lot from people like you. You have to learn from people with different ideas and different ways of working. For all the good I still see in newspapers, there is real peril in being out of touch with most people around you.

Q: Something else that you have probably noticed in your career is that all of a sudden, a journalism degree became something like a union card, as the entrée to the business.

A: As much as I love, which I truly do, the University of Florida, if I could do it over again, I wish I had majored in history. I actually was in political science. Because I was expending so much of my energy on the *Florida Alligator*, night and day, I said, "Well, let me go over to journalism, which will be easier than political science." And that is how I came to graduate in journalism.

Q: Prior to your matriculation at the University of Florida, you worked on the high school paper in Vincennes, Indiana, did you not?

A: I had a remarkable journalism advisor, a woman named Jo Berta Bullock, a legendary figure. A tiny woman, badly crippled. A beloved figure, not a softie. A person of great intensity. The paper was printed offset. A young woman classmate of mine worked in the newspaper and did something really dumb. In those days, it was not unusual for even "good kids" to pen swastikas on their hands. It was not that many years after World War II, and, clearly, the swastika stands for the ugliest form of racism and hatred. I can remember kids who did that, and other kids would not say, "Ah, they are anti-Semitic or haters" or whatever else. Anyhow, this young woman ends up doodling a swastika on the flat, which therefore, because this is photographic process, ends up appearing as an ad. I remember Jo Berta Bullock—who was four feet, eight, or something like that, a very small person—taking her crutch . . . , swinging it up over her head atop our worktables and saying, "My God, do you know what you have done? Do you know how many people died because of this symbol?" It was an extraordinary moment. And so the power of symbols—and the power of the press, your enormous power to damage—has been a lesson that has always stayed with me.

Q: What was the University of Florida campus like when you got there, in terms of racial makeup?

A: Very white. The university was not desegregated in its undergraduate divisions until the fall of 1962, and, in my recollection, the university's student body was sort of divided between pro- and anti-civil rights. I remember vividly the university being segregated. I remember being active in the *Alligator* and covering it. I remember taking pictures. I remember writing about it. I remember asking the state NAACP to write a column, which got me into significant trouble with the university at that time because J. Wayne Reitz [University of Florida president, 1955–67], whom I came to respect a great deal, was not particularly fond of the student newspaper telling him what to do.

Remember, again, this was the time when some people thought the ADA [Americans for Democratic Action] might be a communist organization, however ludicrous it looks now. So this was a very divided campus on that subject. You know, I did not tell you an enormous strength in my parents, which was in imparting a sense of fairness. So I have always instinctively pushed civil rights, and lot of other rights, because this seems to me a fundamental matter of fairness.

Q: Did you not feel odd coming from a fairly liberal family and going to a segregated institution?

A: Remember, everything was segregated. We would go into major grocery stores, and there would be "Colored" and "White" drinking . . . fountains.

My high school was totally white. So, while the University of Florida was essentially an all-white institution, it was also an institution trying to, sort of, come to grips with itself. This is in the immediate wake, you recall, of the Johns Committee, the sickness of Charley [E.] Johns, senator [Florida state legislature, 1934–66] and [acting] governor [of Florida, 1953–55] for a while, trying to figure out who the homosexuals were at the University of Florida.

Q: When you arrived in the fall of 1960, you saw yourself as a political science major who would work on the *Alligator*. Would that be your pathway to a career?

A: I did not actually even contemplate working on the *Alligator*. . . . In the second semester, I sort of wandered over to the *Alligator* and wandered in. I was quite sure that something as important as the *Alligator* would not accept second-semester freshmen. It turns out, of course, they were looking for anybody they could get.

Q: How long did it take for you to assert your authority and declare yourself editor? [Laughter.]

A: Well, I started in my freshman year, and the paper moved from twice a week to five times a week in my time. By the second semester of my junior year, I was editor of the paper.

Q: Did you serve one or two terms as editor?

A: I served two terms, the second one cut short. I was editor the second half of my junior year and then all my senior year, except for the last month. I was frequently in trouble. Part of it had to do with civil rights, and the university administration seeing me as being intemperate and radical. Part of it was I had run a letter to the editor that really pissed off the university president. A student had written advocating free love. It all sounds relatively stupid now, or at least that part does. So the university was not particularly pleased with me. And the Board of Student Publications was controlled by the administration and faculty. Anyhow, I had written a front-page editorial that feels appallingly stupid now, an editorial that criticized the choice of my successor as "political." The person chosen is now the first-rate editor [Walker Lundy] of a Knight-Ridder paper in St. Paul.

The editorial appeared on the same day [President John F.] Kennedy was shot [November 22, 1963], so we put out an extra on the assassination. The Board of Student Publications calls a meeting for the following Monday, which would have been the 25th, to consider this action on my part. I almost certainly knew that my goose was cooked. I refused to come to the meeting on the basis that I would not dignify their proceeding by being there on a day that the president of the United States was being buried. The assassination was the one extraordinary event in my lifetime that everybody remembers where he or she was. So they simply fired my ass.

I . . . spent the next month getting married, going off on a honeymoon, and then, December 30 that year, I went to work for the *St. Petersburg Times.*

Q: Did you leave the newsroom much the weekend that Kennedy was shot? Did you have a television in the newsroom that you were watching?

A: I do remember being absolutely glued to the television, watching Jack Ruby shoot Lee Harvey Oswald. It was extraordinary. I remember Howard K. Smith [ABC newscaster] and all these folks with mournful intonations. I have a fairly good size less respect for many of the people on television now than I did then. These were very somber journalists who knew that something terribly tragic had happened to the whole country. I do not remember a more serious time.

Q: Let us backtrack a little bit to your relations with university administrators during your time as editor. You said that J. Wayne Reitz was not a big fan of yours. Do you want to talk a little bit about that?

A: Well, remember that the university was sort of under siege then. Desegregation was coming about. And what is a university president's job? To some degree, keep . . . a lid on it. Then you have the student newspaper, which, remember, was a creature of the university, so, at least in theory, Dr. Reitz is the publisher of the paper. In subsequent years the university resolved this by saying, in effect, "Let us get this paper off the campus, and they can have their own independent structure." Anyhow, 1963 on campus was a contentious time and a tough time for him and the university.

I say with sweetness in my voice now that Dr. Reitz was not looking for help from me, and he certainly did not want the kind of help I was giving him in what the university ought to do. A big word used then in Florida was *agitator.* What many even good-hearted people wanted was that people not talk about this. Maybe then the problem will just go away. There is probably a lesson for us in all of this, because if we did not have people speaking up, society simply would not make the kind of progress it should. It was just a very tough time, and Dr. Reitz was not looking for troublemakers, and I was perceived as a troublemaker, an agitator.

Q: You had some journalism courses, which, when you talked about them earlier, sounded like a necessary evil to get out of college?

A: Oh no, and I do not want to give you that impression. I came to have, incidentally, an enormous affection for Rae [O.] Weimer [dean emeritus and professor of journalism and communications, UF, 1949–73]. I never had him as a teacher, but I came to believe that he was one of God's decent people. I had two exceptional teachers. By legend, they disliked each other intensely and competed with each other—Hugh [W.] Cunningham [professor of journalism and communications and director of university information, UF, 1955–90] and Buddy Davis [Horance Gibbs Davis, Jr., Distinguished Service Professor of journalism and communications, UF, 1954–86]. They were both extraordinary teachers in my opinion.

Q: Buddy Davis was legendarily punitive. Did you ever suffer any of his wrath in class?

A: If I did, I do not remember it. He was in charge, so he was not going to take any smart lip from anybody. Also, in my view, he was somewhat of an actor playing a game. Part of it was exerting control. Part of it was to teach. If he thought you gave a damn and worked hard, you were just fine. He could spot a shirker, though. He could spot who did not care that much about journalism, and you were in deep doo-doo then. . . .

Q: What was the newsroom at the *St. Petersburg Times* like when you entered it as a full-time employee?

A: The *St. Petersburg Times* was a fabulous place for a young person to work as a reporter. Making ninety-five dollars a week, I was taking home something considerably less than that. Our dream was, if we make ten thousand dollars a year by the time we are thirty, we are going to be just fine. The *Times* was a place where you could have all kinds of responsibility at a very young age, and it was a place that, while it had a pretty sizable newsroom staff, you certainly knew everybody there.

Q: Comment on Nelson Poynter's [president, Times Publishing Company, 1953–69, and chairman of the board, 1969–78] impact on the paper.

A: I do remember Nelson Poynter vividly, and his then wife, Henrietta, as well. At one point, I succeeded Bob Haiman as telegraph editor. *Telegraph editor* now sounds beyond antiquated. Ultimately, they changed the title to *news editor*. But the A section of the *St. Petersburg Times* was not for local news. It was for national and international news, which deeply reflected Nelson Poynter's feelings about what was news and what was not, and what was most important and what was not.

I remember Henrietta Poynter, who was an interesting, intimidating, and somewhat fabulous figure in her . . . own right. . . . I can remember her going down the bank of wire machines; the *New York Herald Tribune* wire, the *New York Times* wire, the AP wire, the UPI wire, the state wire. She would look at each of them, rolling up the wire stories in her hands. It was pretty intimidating, because here is one of the owners, making up her own mind about what is news.

Meanwhile, Nelson Poynter used to call every night, about 8:30 or so, to ask, "What is going on?"

And you better know what was going on. If you said, "Not much, Mr. Poynter," it would not have been smart.

He would start a conversation, "Do you know about such and such; have you heard about such and such; have you thought about such and such?"

This was a man who breathed for his company, a visionary man. He was a man of total integrity, a man who had the newspaper foremost at heart, a man who had taken a lot of crap himself. People referred to him, which he was not, as a communist in conservative St. Petersburg. He was a man who I thought had all the right values and cared deeply about the newspaper. He was . . . a man of the world, not just St. Petersburg, not just Pinellas County, not just the State of Florida, not just the United States of America, but of the world. A great man of business, too. He was the man who set up the process that keeps the paper in its rare and independent status. He is the man who had profit sharing before people were talking about profit sharing.

He was a man who was not provincial in any way. He understood the importance of local news, but he also understood the news in a global context, which is exceedingly rare. Look at how the paper did over the years, which I think, in part, is because it had a larger view of its mission in the world. At the time I was there and, I think, always since, it was one of Florida's best newspapers.

Florida has been particularly blessed because of the economic underpinnings to the particularly good newspapers. If you go around the state and you look at newspapers today, then I think we have some pretty darn good newspapers. I could easily name ten good newspapers in this state and others that would not fall that far behind. What other state could do that? I am not sure there are any other states that could do that. Part of it was fueled by Florida [being] such a boom place, a relatively easy place to make money.

Q: We have not really talked about the role of women in journalism. You have mentioned Henrietta Poynter, who was a very strong-willed person.

Would you say the *St. Petersburg Times* was ahead of its time in treatment of or regard for women?

A: Well, I would say yes, but not so far ahead of the time that it was a world-beater. There were people there who were women who had substantive responsibilities, but for many years their responsibilities were very much connected, most of them, to women's news, softer kinds of things. A very smart woman named Anne Rowe, later Anne Rowe Goldman, was in charge of the women's and feature sections. She clearly could have been the editor of the paper. The whole business was sort of shabby on the subject. Women made distinctly less, had lesser jobs, and did not have much of a path to get more responsibility and more money.

Q: Aside from the nightly phone calls, what were your dealings with Nelson Poynter?

A: I always felt enormous warmth about him, particularly because when I left for Washington, which is where I went to from St. Petersburg, I was a member of the Newspaper Guild, and Washington was frightfully expensive. We then had two children. There was a strike. Benefits were then something like thirty dollars a week. This was a big deal in our house. How long would the strike last? I went over to see Nelson Poynter at *CQ* [*Congressional Quarterly*, a periodical owned by Poynter's Times Publishing Company], and he said, essentially, "Whatever you are making at the *Washington Post*, I will match that for the duration of the strike." Now, I actually never exercised this, because the strike was over quickly, but that was a remarkably decent gesture.

Q: Discuss some of the most important and interesting experiences in your career.

A: I would say that one of the interesting experiences that I had in my working life was being managing editor of the *Philadelphia Daily News*, the number-three newspaper facing the *Bulletin* and the *Inquirer*. Each of them had hundreds of newsroom people. At the *Daily News* we had fewer than one hundred people. It tests every competitive part of you as to how to use your resources wisely when somebody has three, four, five times more people. And who are your readers, really your readers, and how do you genuinely reach them?

Another important moment for me was going to the advanced management program of the Harvard Business School, not because I learned a lot about finance, but because I was in a class with people from thirty-three countries, not counting the United States of America. That was in 1983.

Ever since, I have made it a practice every year to go somewhere else in the world to learn. Ours is a frequently isolated country because it is so big, so powerful, so self-sufficient in many ways—though much less than it used to be, of course. It is very easy to have your whole life in this old American prison.

Q: How did you see your career developing? Did you eventually want to be a publisher?

A: Well, I never said to myself, "I want to be publisher." I was twenty-seven years old when I was a managing editor of a newspaper. So I . . . woke up when I was thirty and said, "Well, I have done this; what do I do now?" So I had a good deal of responsibility at a very young age. I left St. Petersburg when I was twenty-five, worked two years in Washington, first on the news desk and then, when *Style* was formed, I became the news editor of *Style*. Then I became managing editor of the *Palm Beach Post*, because I really wanted to run something. Cox [Enterprises, Inc.] had just bought it from Perry Publications. I only worked there for a couple of years, from 1969 to 1971, and went to the *Philadelphia Daily News* for a couple of months as assistant to the editor and then became managing editor. I worked there until 1975. Then I went to Charlotte to succeed Jim Batten as executive editor [at the *Charlotte Observer*], and I was there for three and a half years. Then, to the *Detroit Free Press* as executive editor in 1979. I then become publisher of the *Free Press* in 1985, leaving there in 1989 to come to Miami.

Q: So you were there for the creation of *Style* at the *Post*. What do you want to say about that? That is considered such a defining moment.

A: Well, I had been asked in 1968 by Ben Bradlee [executive editor of the *Washington Post*] to go back and work as the night women's editor, because he had a lousy leadership struggle there, and give him a sense of what was going on and what he needed to do. So I went back there and worked for six or so months. That was a time in this country when newspaper people were reconsidering women's pages. A lot of people were joking about the feminist movement, but there clearly was a serious feminist movement. Starting up *Style* was an extraordinarily intense time. It had a collection of really bright people, people [like] Judith Martin ["Miss Manners," syndicated columnist], a writer for that section. I remember editing Sally Quinn, who was a brand-new reporter there covering the embassy beat.

Later, in 1969, Nick Von Hoffman, the columnist, was sent to Haight-

Ashbury [the then hippie district of San Francisco, California] to do a series. Haight-Ashbury was a big deal then. He did not like my editing, and he quit. I do remember Bradlee saying, "Oh, do not worry about that. That is Nick; he will be back, no big deal," and that is exactly what happened. But it was a very heavy time for me, as a young person working with a star columnist.

Q: What did you do after that?

A: I left in the summer of 1969 to become managing editor in West Palm Beach.

Q: What was the *Palm Beach Post* like when you joined it? Was that before its Pulitzer for the migrant workers?

A: It was a paper that would not have dreamed of winning a Pulitzer. It made a great deal of money, as a monopoly of sorts. Here I was twenty-seven. The editor of the paper was, maybe, thirty-four, Gregory Favre. We practically hired the staff new, added an awful lot of people. We were so young that we did not know all the normal roadblocks to doing good things. We hired people like Dallas Kinney [Pulitzer Prize recipient, 1970, for "Migration to Misery"] and Kent Pollock that led to the Pulitzer with the migrants. But there were lots of other awards and lots of other things done. But for an extraordinary number of people, it would be a once-in-a lifetime experience. Enormous energy, enormous enthusiasm, a sense you can do anything, and, again, the economic underpinnings to do a bunch of things.

Q: At the *Palm Beach Post,* now that you were the managing editor, what policies did you institute that had not been in place before?

A: Remember, this was a newspaper owned by a man named John [Holliday] Perry [Jr., owner of Perry Publications], a legendary figure who was deeper into miniature submarines than he was into newspapers. There was not a good paper in the lot, and Perry newspapers were money machines all over the state. I had never been an editor or a managing editor for a newspaper before, so . . . I had to learn on the job. Remember that this was not your normal situation. You have a lot more money to spend, maybe not enough, but a lot more money to spend, and you have a good market to do it. It is a place with plenty of good stories, most of which have not been touched for years and years and years. The paper had not been aggressive about anything.

Q: For example?

A: The migrant labor movement was in the paper's backyard.

Q: Palm Beach is such an odd county. Such wealth. Such poverty.

A: And migrant laborer conditions that were the modern equivalent of slavery. The paper's new aggressiveness made a lot of people nervous. Nor had the paper traveled anywhere to do stories. We did some extraordinary projects. I remember one on drugs, a very sophisticated, tough piece of reporting on a vital subject. We did not hesitate to do things like sending Kent Pollock to Vietnam.

Q: After a couple of years there, was there an irresistible offer from Philadelphia, or did you just want to get out?

A: The *Philadelphia Daily News* was just an awful paper at the time, a tabloid, principally street-sold. I ended up going there far more for reasons of the quality of Knight newspapers [Knight-Ridder, Inc.] than I did because of the *Philadelphia Daily News*. The paper had a wonderful sports section, but nothing much else that was self-respecting. The paper improved dramatically over the next several years.

Its crucible came at a time when Frank Rizzo was the mayor [of Philadelphia, 1971–79], a legendary figure in American mayoral politics, larger than life, former police chief. Rizzo was in a terrible feud with a guy named Pete Camiel, who was head of the Democratic Party, about who was lying about something. I have forgotten the issue. Rizzo, who was very charismatic, was headed toward potentially being governor of Pennsylvania. People either hated him or loved him, but he had a big "love him" backing. We convinced Frank Rizzo to take a lie-detector test with Pete Camiel. Rizzo, a longtime and tough cop, was pretty sure he could beat it, but he clearly ends up failing it. The headline was "Rizzo Lied," with a picture of Rizzo strapped to the lie-detector machine with a quote alongside that says, "'If this machine says a man lied, he lied'—Frank Rizzo." Of course, it blew him up. He never was a significant political figure subsequently.

Over those few years, the paper became far more aggressive, far more into real coverage in the community, including people who frequently never got covered. It was a paper that stood up for people. It was known as the "People Paper." It was a tabloid and willing to have outrageous headlines, but it was a tough, aggressive, straightforward newspaper in everything it did.

Q: Did you see that as a key moment in your career?

A: It was significant in my beginning to understand what newspapers needed to do to get close to readers and keep your own soul.

Q: What drew you away to Charlotte?

A: Jim Batten, the executive editor in Charlotte, was going to headquarters in Miami. He was one of the sainted people in my whole life. If I had to pick the single best person I have known in this business, it would be Jim Batten. He was a man of instant integrity and the fullest decency and the greatest possible human and journalistic values. Jim was leaving to go to Miami because Knight-Ridder wanted him to play a larger role in the company. He eventually became chairman and CEO [of Knight-Ridder]. They needed his success as executive editor.

Q: At this time, did you think of yourself as still an independent, or did you see yourself as more of a Knight-Ridder man?

A: I have never felt [like] a company man in the way that some people do. While the attraction to go there was, then, Knight-Ridder and its quality, I never thought that I worked for Knight Newspapers or Knight-Ridder. I always thought I worked for the *Philadelphia Daily News*, the *Charlotte Observer*, the *Miami Herald*, the *Detroit Free Press*.

Q: In Charlotte you went from managing editor to executive editor. What does an executive editor do?

A: The definition changes from place to place. Generally, the managing editor is the day-to-day operational boss of the newsroom. The executive editor might be the person who is the managing editor's boss and the person who is ultimately in charge of the newsroom, or it could be the person who is in charge of the newsroom and the editorial page. In Charlotte, as executive editor, I was ultimately in charge of the newsroom. Later, as editor, I was in charge of the newsroom and the editorial page.

Q: What changes did you institute in Charlotte?

A: One of the things we did, in my estimation, was to try to get a far fuller picture of what existed in that part of the world. Most of the people who worked for the *Charlotte Observer* had never been in a textile mill, which was the principal industry in that part of the country. I dragged people all around the Piedmont of North and South Carolina, trying to understand the small towns surrounding Charlotte, from where an enormous number of readers had come. You have to get out of the office. You are not learning anything at the office. You better get out and see who is out there, who the readers are. You have to walk around a lot. You have to go see a bunch of different people in different settings.

Q: What impact did you have on the *Detroit Free Press*?

A: The newspaper, when I came there, had a total of four minority professionals on the staff, one of whom insisted he was not a minority. I insisted that the paper move toward being representative of the community it served, not for a social engineering experiment but to be able to cover and reflect the community far better.

Q: What did you come up with to retain good workers?

A: Well, what you come up with is some monetary incentives, but beyond that, people want to be where they trust you, where they think you care about them, where they think you care about their careers.

Q: What persuaded you to move to Miami?

A: Knight-Ridder wanted me to do something else. They wanted me to run the *Miami Herald* and *El Nuevo Herald*. I was significantly skeptical about it, because why would I want to be in the headquarters city?

Q: You felt they would be breathing down your neck?

A: Even good people would be breathing down your neck. Mine would be the paper they get at home. It is their community. They have their ideas. I would always rather be fifteen hundred miles away, even with good people. I emphasize that these are good people, and I was never asked to do anything immoral.

Q: The staff at the *Herald,* when you joined it, was a pretty amazing group of people. Would you talk a little bit about it?

A: The *Herald* had so many strengths. It was very aggressive in what it covered and did. It had wonderful writers. It had as good a set of columnists as exist in the country, and that only got stronger over the years. On the minus [side], it also had a reputation for being unfriendly to minorities and as a newspaper pretty significantly out of touch with a changing community.

During the 1990s the *Herald* won five Pulitzers, in as changing a community as there exists in the United States of America. This is a community here that is fifty-five percent Hispanic, twenty-two percent or so African American and/or black, and the rest non-Hispanic white. So folks like you and me are a pretty distinct minority. It is also a community with enormous promise to people in the Americas. It is also significantly under-educated and under-skilled and, in many ways, growing poorer. It has had a significant problem of corruption, some of it petty and some of it big. The *Herald* won a Pulitzer in the past year for coverage of exactly that.

Change is very threatening to people, so change over the years has been very threatening to people at the *Herald*. For years the *Herald* was, to some degree, inattentive to its own community and quite attentive to, oh, "people like us," who are up in the Treasure Coast, who are in Palm Beach County and Broward [County] and wherever else. Meanwhile, the community continued to change, and the *Herald* was relatively ill-positioned for this. Today, for instance, there are a half-million people in Miami-Dade County who either can only deal in Spanish or much prefer to deal only in Spanish. The *Herald* comes in the English language, the last I looked, and that is a significant problem.

Remember, as well, that the exile population that came here from Cuba in the early 1960s is significantly different from the refugee immigrant community coming here now. The people who came here in the 1960s from Cuba were generally educated people who once had money even if they did not have it now. They were often educated people, prepared for success. And they had a newspaper-reading habit. Havana had a half-dozen daily newspapers in the 1950s. Today there are no real daily newspapers in Cuba.

The *Herald* made its . . . first foray into Spanish-language journalism in the early 1960s in translating a couple of columns one day a week. Not until 1976 did *El Miami Herald* come about, and that was, more or less, the translated version of the *Miami Herald*. To use the vernacular, we "just did not get it." These people wanted "my own newspaper." Anyhow, it was not until 1987 that *El Nuevo Herald* came to be. My point is that it was not until 1987 when we began to say, "These folks need their own newspaper with their own set of editors and reporters, thinking their own way." To this day, people are struggling with what is the smart way to do this, and what are we willing to do?

Q: After nearly ten years at the *Herald*, you chose to leave the paper, but you stayed in Miami.

A: It is interesting. Increasingly, after more than three decades in newspapering, I came to want to do something in public service. But I never could figure out what to do. About three years ago, I got involved in early childhood education and development, and started to understand it. Governor [Lawton] Chiles asked me to be on the governor's Commission on Education, and then I was asked to chair its readiness committee. That is how I came to be involved in this issue. And I wondered whether I could psychologically survive not being a big shot and not making a whole bunch of money.

And there are other things involved in this [decision to leave the paper], including that the [newspaper] business became far more of a business inexorably over the years and, thus, a lot less fun to me. I never missed a day of work, so I would always be up for the next day. I just needed to do something else. So, I resolved, the only way to do it was to leave. Now, because I had no other "job," I simply announced on August 4th of 1998 that I would leave at the beginning of the following year, which I did, and that gave me some time to look.

The following Saturday, a man named Jerry Katcher calls. Jerry Katcher is a man in his seventies. He owned a bank in town with a number of branches and therefore had a lot of money. I have known Jerry over the years . . . and he called up from Aspen, Colorado, and said, "Some of us have been talking, and we do not want you to leave town; if you want to work full-time on children and readiness, in which I know you are interested, we are willing to set up a foundation [the Early Childhood Initiative Foundation] so you can do it." This was, and is, terribly humbling to me, so I have sort of committed myself that I will work hard on this for at least the next couple of years, and see what comes to pass and what difference we can make.

Q: Do you miss the newspaper business?

A: I never look back. I love newspapers, always will, and think they are important, but it was time for me to do something else. How many years do we have in this world? My father was sixty-four, and he gets cancer. He ends up retiring early and dies at sixty-six. He had all sorts of plans, and he got to do none of those. I do not know how much time I have, or how many years, and I do not know what I will end up doing. Maybe I will do this for years. Maybe I will do this for a while. Maybe I will do something else. I do not know.

Q: Do you think that your work in this area is going to send you into politics, as a lot of people thought you might?

A: There was a moment there where it was sort of heady to be asked by a bunch of people, including the attorney general of the state of Florida and other people, to please consider this and so forth.

Q: You are speaking of running for governor?

A: Right. But it never really seemed real to me. I raised a lot of money for other causes, but I do not really want to raise money for myself if I can avoid it. Part of me says, "This is a job you could do; you care a lot about the issues; you know how to get people together; you are an inclusive person; you would be fair." But the timing made no sense. I do not say "never" to anything, but I do not focus an ounce of my energy on that subject. What I do know is, that if we could ever get children started off better in this world, we would have a profound impact on society. I am excited about all of this. I love my new life.

chapter 3 **Fred Pettijohn**

Fred Pettijohn was born on May 11, 1917, in Baltimore, Maryland. When he was four months old, the Pettijohn family moved to Tallahassee, Florida, where Fred completed all of his public schooling. He worked on the school paper and developed a desire to pursue a career in journalism.

His first newspaper job was as assistant sports editor for the *Tallahassee Democrat*. He then worked as a general assignments editor for the *Florida State News*. He graduated from the University of Florida in 1941, after writing for the yearbook and the campus newspaper, the *Alligator*. While waiting to be drafted for service in World War II, Pettijohn moved to Washington, D.C., where he was employed in a variety of jobs, including as an ad salesman for the phone company and a reporter for the now-defunct *Washington Times Herald*.

In 1942 he was drafted and served three years in the U.S. Army. He earned three battle stars in the China-Burma-India campaign as a first sergeant in airborne artillery. He was twice nominated for a Bronze Star and received his honorable discharge in December 1945. He returned to Tallahassee after the war and was appointed sports editor of the *Tallahassee Democrat*. While at the *Democrat*, he won the Associated Press's sportswriting award for two consecutive years. In 1953 he moved to the *Fort Lauderdale News*, where he was named sports editor.

He quickly rose through the ranks of management, taking the position of managing editor of the paper in 1954 and executive editor in 1960. When the paper became the *Sun-Sentinel*, he was elected vice president and by 1968 was appointed general manager of the paper. Pettijohn served as first vice president and editorial director until his retirement in 1982.

Pettijohn has been active and prominent in community affairs, including membership on President Dwight Eisenhower's Committee on Higher Education, service on the board of directors of the greater Fort Lauderdale Chamber of Commerce, and participation as a member of the board of trustees of Holy Cross Hospital. He was also on the board of directors of the University of Florida Foundation, the Salvation Army, and the Fort Lauderdale Historical Society. In 1970 he was president of the Florida Press Association.

Pettijohn has garnered many awards during his distinguished career, including a Distinguished Service Award from the Florida Press Association and the University of Florida Distinguished Alumni Award. In 1991 he was inducted into the Florida Newspaper Hall of Fame, with the citation for his membership praising both his career and his character: "He earned a reputation as a tough editor with an unerring instinct for quality, and an expectation of commitment and dedication from his reporters and editors. Yet he was equally well known as a warm, humorous, caring gentleman truly interested in the well-being of his fellow man. Pettijohn was deeply committed to his community, civic organizations and higher education."

In this interview Pettijohn talks about his early career as a sportswriter, his war experiences, and his career in Fort Lauderdale. He discusses R. H. Gore, the conservative owner of the paper, and the sale of the paper to the *Chicago Tribune*. He explains his impatience with errors, the successful development of an advertising section, investigative journalism, letters to the editor, use of columnists and cartoonists, technological changes, and the paper's contribution to the community. He includes an assessment of governors Reubin Askew and Claude Kirk, Jr., along with an amusing story about Kirk. He concludes with an anecdote about John F. and Jacqueline Kennedy.

Fred P. Pettijohn was interviewed by Julian M. Pleasants on August 18, 1999, in Fort Lauderdale, Florida.

Q: How and when did you decide to go into journalism?
A: I had decided when I was in, about, the eighth grade that I wanted to be in newspaper work. We did not have a school paper at the time, but we had an energetic high school student who had a mimeograph machine and put out his own high school newspaper once a week. To show you what

kind of a paper it was, he called it *Ye Weekly Snooze*. He was quite proud of that title. I ended up as the reporter for my class. After a year I thought, "This is really what I want to do."

I talked to my father about it, and he said, "Well, I am sure it is interesting, but I can tell you now, you will never make any money in the newspaper business."

For a number of years, I thought my father was brilliant. He could see far into the future and see you would not make any money out of it.

Q: You also worked for the *Florida State News*. What was that?

A: It was an opposition daily paper to the *Tallahassee Democrat*. I do not remember how long it lasted—from the mid-1930s, I would say, until shortly before World War II. World War II probably finished the *Florida State News*, a pretty good newspaper. Comparing it to the *Democrat*, they did a pretty good job. Like most underdogs or newcomers, they were good hustlers.

Q: Why did you choose to go to the University of Florida?

A: I remember we talked to the dean of men, and my mother said, "This is the first time that Fred will ever have been away from home, and I am concerned about him."

The dean looked at my record and said, "Mrs. Pettijohn, I think we can tell you that we will have your son home by Thanksgiving."

She had a great sense of humor, but that did not strike her as funny. It did me, and I thought, "Well, it does not hurt to laugh in front of the dean of men." He obviously had used the line before with varying amounts of success. I wanted him to know he had someone who was quick on the uptake. It turned out he was not right, but it was close there for a while.

Q: Where did you live on campus?

A: I lived right by the old, I think it was, College Inn. It was a den of iniquity. Obviously, the good locations had long been gone, and had I been a little keener, I would have known there was something wrong with the availability of a room right across the street from the campus. All-night card games. They had a bunch of former athletes who had graduated and either were not able to find work, or it had never occurred to them to look for work. So they played poker mainly at night and fleeced the freshmen who were coming in.

Q: How did working for the campus newspaper, the *Alligator*, help you in your journalism career?

A: Well, I thought at that time, and I am still pretty much married to the idea, that any time that you had the opportunity to write under some degree of pressure—and obviously pressure for a college publication is not the same as it is for a daily, and the *Alligator* was a weekly at that time—and have somebody go over your copy and either talk to you about it or tell you it was all right or bounce it back at you. I thought there was a great benefit in that and the more I could do of that, the more eager I was to do it.

Q: Talk about your army experience. You were in the China-Burma-India campaign, and you were in an artillery unit. How did the war experience impact your life?

A: I felt that I had demonstrated to myself that I could handle people and could lead people. I was used to being in uncomfortable and dangerous situations. I had pretty good control of my emotions. The army is a great leveler. If you have trouble with humility, they can do a lot for you. I thought it would have been tragic had I not gone in the service, because I felt I had benefited so much from it that it was almost a totally selfish outlook. But I enjoyed the feeling of knowing that I could go into almost any situation. I certainly could survive the early part of what tough-going there [was], [which] might be learning what the routine was, and then I would progress from there with whatever I was going to do.

Q: You were with the *Tallahassee Democrat* for six years. What, specifically, did you do all that time?

A: I covered the class D baseball team. I covered the birth of Florida State University in all sports. I had a lot of success with the *Democrat*. I had won the state's AP sportswriting award two years in a row, the first person who had ever won a writing award for consecutive years.

[The] *Fort Lauderdale News* had decided to go back into the Sunday field. So they were going back in the first Sunday in June, and the editor who was doing the hiring was impressed by people who had won writing contests. He sent his political writer by the *Democrat* office to talk to me.

He told me that Jack Gore wanted to talk to me, and I said, "About what?"

He said, "He was not specific, but [about] a job with the *Fort Lauderdale News.*"

So I called Jack and talked to him on the phone and asked him what kind of money they were talking about. We [my wife, Elaine, and I] discussed it . . . [and] we decided to take the offer and drove down here. I got here with about a 102 or 103 [degree] fever, talked to the people at the

News, took the job, had a month's issue of back papers to look at, and promised them I would come to work the next Friday.

Q: Tell me the difference between the Fort Lauderdale paper and the *Tallahassee Democrat* at this time.

A: There was not a great deal of difference in circulation. The *Democrat* was up around eighteen thousand to twenty thousand. *Fort Lauderdale* was about twenty-two thousand in the summertime, but about thirty-five thousand to thirty-eight thousand in the season. It was more sophisticated. It was a privately owned newspaper.

Q: Who owned it?

A: R. H. Gore, Sr. He had been a newspaperman himself and was, by far, the most colorful creature I had ever met. It looked like the *Fort Lauderdale News* was a growing paper, and Tallahassee was pretty much limited to the growth of the state government. There were not any other large industries there.

Q: Were you competing with the *Miami Herald*?

A: Oh, yes. In our minds, we were. In the *Herald*'s minds, I do not think we were much competition. They had a bureau. They had a Broward section in the *Herald*. Just taking alone the people on a beat or on the street working, they probably had as many, if not more, people than we did, in their basic office. Old man Gore was a lot of things that are good. Throwing money around was not one of them. He liked to keep most of the money that came in, which meant that he did not want to pay anybody much. He owned a television station, he owned a radio station, and he owned the only newspaper in Fort Lauderdale, which gave him a leg up, for sure. I worked for all three.

The *Herald* had the morning field to itself. We had the afternoon field to ourselves. We moved the Saturday paper, which, in the way of income, was never a good one. We moved it from Saturday afternoon to Saturday morning. It gave us a leg up covering Friday's sports. The University of Miami played all of its games on Friday night. Advertising built up very quickly. Before I left [1982], we had the largest Saturday newspaper in the United States, in the number of pages, helped by a real estate section that was gigantic.

Q: You went, almost immediately, from sports editor to managing editor. How did that happen, and why did you decide to do that?

A: It happened because the man who was managing editor was a good newspaperman but a sensitive newspaperman, and that is a difficult thing to live with. Old man Gore was too roughshod for him to live with comfortably. He had occasional attacks of ulcers, and he finally reached a point where he just could not take it. He was nearing retirement.

Me taking the job was a little more difficult. I was bothered by several things. Was I ready to leave sports? You know, it was 1954. I was thirty-seven years of age, and that seemed fairly young for me to be leaving a field in which I had demonstrated I could do pretty well in, against any competition. Was I ready to come under the direct fire of R. H. Gore, Sr., who was a factor? Did the newsroom job scare me? No, not that much, not that part of it. I was more concerned about Gore, Sr., than I was [about] the people I was working with. I worked well with most of them. . . . Another factor which was important from the first is I now had a family that was growing along, a five-year-old and a three-and-a-half-year-old. I needed more money, [which] I was not going to get [doing] sports in Fort Lauderdale.

So I had told Mr. Gore, Sr., [that] I was afraid I did not know enough about the city. I had only been here about six months. [I said,] "I do not know enough about the city; I do not know much about the people; I do not know much about the politics. I do not know anything about your hand in all of this, but what experience I have had in life tells me that you have a very large hand that is not seen in this, and that is of some concern to me." I said, "If you will give me six months, I will study the news end of the paper as much as I can; I will talk to as many people as I can; I will learn as much about the job as I can; and, at the end of six months, I will either take it, or I will move on and get out of your way." So he thought that was fair, and that was what transpired.

Q: Explain to me, when you took over as managing editor, exactly what your duties were.

A: The managing editor of the *Fort Lauderdale News,* if he is really the managing editor, does the hiring and firing of the entire staff. He buys all the features in the newspaper. He oversees the production of every news page, with the exception of the editorial page and the op-ed. He is responsible for getting the paper closed up in the pressroom or to the pressroom on time. In my case the managing editor also wrote a column five days a week. This was Mr. Gore's suggestion, which was more than a suggestion.

Q: Six years later you were promoted to executive editor. How did that transpire?

A: We went into a second newspaper. I became executive editor so I would, in effect, be the person that ran the news pages of both newspapers, the *News* and the *Sentinel*. I continued to buy the features for both newspapers. [The *Sentinel*] was now the morning paper, located in Pompano. When we got set to get the *Sentinel* started, the reason we started it was [because] a family in Indiana wintered in Pompano and noticed there was no daily paper in Pompano, so they decided to come into Pompano with a five-day-a-week afternoon newspaper. Well, the old man [Gore] could not stand the thought of that, so we beat them out on the street by a week or two.

It was called the *Sun-Sentinel*, and the Associated Press never would accept that. They said it had to be attached to a city. I do not see that *USA Today* is attached to a city. Until [the] *Fort Lauderdale News* folded, the AP forever referred to it as *Pompano Beach Sun-Sentinel*; to hell with the people who own this newspaper. We did not have it on the masthead.

All of the department heads and the leading managers of news departments [were] in this meeting, and R. H. Gore is running the meeting, and he says, "Does everybody agree that the newspaper should not come into Fort Lauderdale?"

I said, "No."

And he said, "What?"

And I said, "No."

He said, "No what?"

I said, "No, I do not agree that the paper should not come into Fort Lauderdale." He punished me; for several weeks, he did not speak to me.

But now, I had a new assignment with my job. I had to meet with R. H., Sr., at 5:30 every morning [and] discuss with him what our news play looked like for that afternoon. The *Sentinel* was a baby to a lot of us. He never had much interest in the *Sentinel*, to tell you the truth. He got it started, [and] it looked okay, [but] the *Fort Lauderdale News* was his child. He wanted to know — and we went through the paper page by page — why the *Herald* had this story that we did not have, and if I said, "Well, we had that story, but you missed it," he said, "Where was it?"

I said, "It was on 3A."

He said, "It was not properly displayed, or I would not have missed it."

So it was a cannot-win situation, and you learned to live with it.

Q: What was the ideological base of the newspaper?

A: Ultra-conservative. We were much to the right of Barry Goldwater and looking for room to move further, but further out in that direction was pretty much a wasteland. We were one of the few papers that declared early and strongly for Barry Goldwater. We were a paper that could not tolerate the mention of Eleanor Roosevelt.

R. H. Gore had been governor of Puerto Rico under Franklin D. [Roosevelt], and, as such, he wanted English to be the primary language in Puerto Rican schools. Eleanor [Roosevelt] . . . wanted Spanish. To no one's surprise, Eleanor prevailed, and he wrote a letter to FDR, typed it himself . . . and told FDR very plainly, "If you want Eleanor to be governor of Puerto Rico, I suggest you appoint her; if you are going to support her in what I think is the most important decision that involves the people of Puerto Rico in the United States, then there is no place for me here." The old man, as I have indicated, was not careless with the nickel. There was a gunboat coming in to Puerto Rico, and he arranged to move his family back to the mainland on that gunboat. It was a freebie, and he took advantage of it.

Q: What ultimately happened to the *News*?

A: The fate of the afternoon paper in the average city was pretty well spelled out. We thought instead of dying a slow death, why do we not manage our own demise? We have another newspaper; it is not like we are going out of business. Why not stop circulation, division by division, and slowly back out of the afternoon field, heavily recommending the morning. A lot of people did not like it. A lot of people said, "No, if you are going to fold up in the afternoon, we are not going to go with you in the morning. We are going to go with the *Herald*, who we know will be in the morning for the rest of our lives."

Q: When did the *Chicago Tribune* purchase the newspaper?

A: The *Tribune* bought us in 1963. It was a natural marriage. The *Tribune* was one of the few papers the old man would consider selling to. He sold it for $18.1 million, and in 1963 nobody in the newspaper business believed that the *Tribune* had paid $18 million for that shitty little paper in Fort Lauderdale, Florida. They did not know that having the *Fort Lauderdale News* press running was a lot like having the United States Mint running. You know, we had a small compact circulation. We had a growing advertising rate. We had a popular newspaper with people. It was well read, which had been demonstrated many times. It was rolling in money.

Q: How did the purchase by the *Chicago Tribune* impact the *Sun-Sentinel*?

A: The difference between a home-owned, family-owned newspaper and part of a chain, you cannot measure. It is too wide, and it is too deep. It gave me a certain amount of freedom that I had not had, in that I did not have to go to the office at 5:30 [A.M.] any more. I did not have to undergo a daily grilling. I could look to making sizable increases in the overall payroll. I could look to adding people to the staff. We thought we would get a ton of suggestions from them. We did not. We were new to the newspaper family, too. We were their first acquisition. They did not quite know what to do with us. They were happy they had us.

Q: In 1968 you became the assistant general manager. What duties did you have in that position?

A: Well, I was overseeing all of the departments in the newspaper, editorial less than any of the rest of them. I felt editorial was in good hands. I thought it was an opportunity to know better the rest of the departments in the newspaper. The [position of] assistant was [at] Gore's insistence. He was not ready to make anyone general manager. The agreement . . . was that when I showed him I could handle the job, I would be the general manager.

Q: What financial, editorial, or circulation problems did the newspaper have when you took over as managing editor and first vice president?

A: The newspaper itself had no financial problems. As we have already indicated earlier, it was literally a gold mine, an unadvertised gold mine. Mr. Gore, by design, gave a limited amount [of information] to editor and publisher. He said, "Why should other people know how good things are here? It will just attract them to the area, and we do not need competition of any kind."

Q: When you took over as general manager, what specific goals did you have for the newspaper?

A: We were trying to improve the pressroom, which involved new presses, mainly. We had to reduce running time . . . [because] the weekend paper run was heavy. We were trying to always increase circulation.

Q: How did you go about increasing circulation?

A: You try to tell people what a good job you are doing and do all the marketing devices and all of the tools. I wanted to change the attitude of the people at the *News*. I wanted them to respect what they were doing here, [that] they were a winner in Broward County. Like anybody else who had been in the newsroom, I wanted to improve the reporting. I wanted to improve the editing. I wanted to improve coverage overall. I wanted to eliminate, as far as possible, the stupid mistakes.

Q: What errors most upset you?

A: The dumb ones. Dumb geographical errors: they do not know where the airport is located, [or] they do not know the difference between the Fort Lauderdale, Hollywood, and Greater Miami airports. You know? It seems nonsensical to say that, but that will come up in a story. [When] somebody gets confused in a story, I am irked that they got confused. I am irked when somebody sells them a little bit of con, and they go for it. I want them to be better than that. But I got mad when they just made dumbass errors.

Q: What would happen, normally, in a case like that? Would you, the next day, rectify the mistake?

A: Not unless somebody asked for it. I did not believe in correcting errors that nobody was interested enough in to correct me.

Q: Would you put the correction on the same page that the story was written on?

A: I would not promise that, but I would say we would come as close to that page . . . as we could.

Q: In your view, what are the most important functions of a newspaper like the Fort Lauderdale paper?

A: I think, overall, it should represent the needs, the desires, and the dreams of the people whom it serves, the area in which it serves. I think it has to provide some leadership. I do not use the word *strong* leadership because I do not want to go overboard in extremely strong recommendations for political offices, which is the first thing people usually zero in on when you say "leadership."

Q: Did you make recommendations in political races?

A: Yes, we did. Always, from the time I came until the time I left. We sometimes recommended a man we knew had no chance, to prove that we were looking for people of quality, not recommending winners.

Q: Should the newspaper reflect the thoughts of the people, or do you try to persuade the people as to what their dreams should be?

A: That is an old [question], and there is no right answer. My thinking is that it should reflect. I do not want to build their dreams for them. I do not have any idea how many different dreams are out there. If I can settle on one important one . . . if you want better schools, yes, I will help you with that, and I will take a strong hand in that. Reduced crime? Everybody wants to reduce crime.

Q: As you look at the paper from, say, 1953 to 1982, how did the readership change?

A: It became more liberal. It was more diversified. The flight of the white person from Dade County was underway, and we were the beneficiaries of a great deal of that, mainly . . . west of Interstate 95. They brought with them a liberal touch, and they demonstrated it in almost every election that we ever held. By this time, there was a strong Jewish vote. They demonstrated that in elections.

Q: Did the newspaper take a strong position on the growth of the area, in terms of traffic, overcrowding, overpopulation, pollution?

A: [We] recognized these problems, brought them to the table, and discussed them in some detail. If it was something like traffic, you could get your hands into it with some hope of success. If it was something like pollution, which very few people understand, I have not found [that] many people give a damn about it or are against it. Again, it is kind of a selective thing. You are not trying to pick winners and losers, but you have to husband your strength. You cannot just scattershot and make people think you are against everything. You have to pick out the things you can attack and approach intelligently. If you cannot do it in that manner, you better stay the hell away from it until you educate yourself enough to be able to go back into it with a basis of leadership and education and an intellectual approach if you have to.

Q: Is there less investigative journalism these days?

A: I do not know. I cannot answer that. There is much more in Fort Lauderdale. They have had for ten or twelve years a team of a man and a woman who lead almost every investigative situation they have, who do it well, who have been contenders for a Pulitzer several times. They have tackled [and] have had some success with state issues. Reform in laws governing pawnbrokers was one of their most recent. We did not have the manpower to do that in my time.

Q: How would you rate your paper compared to the other major newspapers in the state, in terms of the quality of the paper?

A: We would have been behind the [Miami] Herald. We would have been behind the [St. Petersburg] Times. We would have been level with Orlando. We would have probably been ahead of Tampa. We would certainly have been ahead of Jacksonville.

Q: Over a period of thirty years in the business, did you see any change in the letters to the editor?

A: Yes. The professional letter writer was born during that period. I did not know he existed, though I read the letters to the editor every day and read a number of them before they appeared in print. But I was [at] a party one night, talking to a man whom I had just been introduced to, and I asked him, if he worked, what did he do?

And he said, "I write for the *Fort Lauderdale News.*"

And I said, "That is interesting; what area do you cover?"

He said, "Oh, I do not cover an area." He said, "I write letters."

And I said, "And they pay you for that?"

He said, "No, they do not pay me for that."

So I said, "In actuality, you do not work for the *Fort Lauderdale News.*"

And he said, "No, I do not."

I said, "The reason I am questioning this so hard is [because] I am the executive editor for the *Fort Lauderdale News* and *Sun-Sentinel,* and your name was strange to me; I have never seen it on a payroll, and I just had to pursue it."

And I started paying more attention. I asked the people who handled it, and they said, "Oh yes, there are people who write six, eight, ten letters in a six-, eight-, ten-month period. If we do not get a letter from them in three or four months, we think, 'Have they died? Have they moved?'"

Q: What is the benefit of these letters? Do you think people read them very often?

A: [They are a] high readership item on every readership study we ever took. People want to know, without the newspaper trying to tell them. They want to feel the pulse of the public, and this is one way they can do it. If [the paper] was overwhelmed by letters to the editor on one subject . . . we would try to make more space available and do it quickly so those letters could be accommodated, so the letter writer would get the feeling that we are trying to keep up with what the public is asking. We were always accused of only printing letters that favored us or favored our stance. Most of the letters we received were against us and against whatever we proposed. They ignored this completely when they were reading it. Oh, well.

Q: Did you use many syndicated columnists?

A: Yes, three or four is a pretty good number, and it depends on your space situation, too. If you have a completely open op-ed page, three good columnists along with a cartoon or two will pretty much eat up that page. We would run a syndicated columnist in sports. We ran Ann Landers. We ran Dear Abby. We had a tough syndicated situation, in that people with something good always went to the *Miami Herald* first. Why? The *Herald* would pay them forty-five [dollars], while we would complain about seven.

Q: Would your editorial cartoonist, Channing Lowe, be free to write or draw whatever he wanted to?

A: He has been given a great deal of freedom. He was the first full-time editorial cartoonist the paper had, so we were late getting into that game. Your syndicated cartoonists are excellent. If you can find one who is anywhere close to your philosophy, the temptation to grab him for eight or nine dollars per week is overwhelming.

Q: Where did most of your advertising money come from?

A: We had the biggest classified section in the state. Bigger than the *Herald?* Yes. Producer of results? Positively, or it would not have remained the biggest. I think it is still the biggest in the state. Why? A good, tough question that I never have answered to my satisfaction. We had at that time a strong element—and still have—of elderly people who shop the classified pages. I always thought they were probably responsible for the response you got with a lot of ads. I ran a couple of classified ads during my time, and we were overwhelmed. People would start calling early, and they were still calling late, long after it had been sold.

Q: Have you had any problems of advertisers canceling ads due to a controversial editorial? And if so, how did you react to that?

A: The first thing I do is marshal the best people whom I have, from the overall newspaper standpoint and from the advertising standpoint, and ask the head of the local store, or whatever it is, if we can take him to lunch and talk about the situation in which he is violently opposed to something we have done. We would like to have a chance to give him our side of the story directly, and, just as important, we would like to get all of the details of his opposition to it. We understand [that we may] offend somebody with a stand that we take. But we would like to be able to live with you and still maintain our standards and still express our feelings in areas that we think are important, and if you are included in that, we are going to have these situations. It does not mean that the answer to them is to boycott us, because you do not ever want to get into a contest with a man that buys ink by the barrel. You will lose.

Q: What about the issue of changing from Linotype to computers? How did new technology affect the newspaper?

A: You were able to produce a much better newspaper, and you could do it in less time. You did it cleaner, you did it in a healthier environment, and, gradually, you got a different class of people . . . better educated, better type of person. The pressmen and some of the old Linotype operators were pretty crusty, salty people. They would do things that could be embarrassing. I remember the head of our production department was a man named Floyd Piles, and they would slip in a classified ad that read, "Floyd Piles eats cow puckies." We had a hard time explaining to Floyd how that got in the paper.

Q: Did you work to improve the number of women and minority groups on your staff?

A: In the later stages of my career from minority groups, yes. From the time I was in authority in the newsroom, always women. I found that if I had fifteen people, eight women and seven men, six of the women were probably superior to six of the men. There was a good man that was better than any of them. There were two women who were not worth a damn, probably, at the end of the line. Of course, there were a couple of men down there with them, too. . . . They had a black columnist when I came here. Directly, when I was doing the hiring, I hired four blacks and more Hispanics than I could count. None of the blacks panned out at all, although later on we hired some who were, I think, very good.

Q: What was your relationship over the years with the Florida Press Association?

A: I was a strong supporter. I sold them on the idea of the newspaper members of the Florida Press sending a person to the campus for a week as a "visiting fireman," attending classes, answering questions, [and] meeting with people. I saw the Florida Press as a means of accomplishing a number of things statewide that you could not do on your own.

Q: Give me your impression of some of the governors of the state of Florida. Let us start with Claude Kirk [Jr., Florida governor, 1967–71]. You have a good story about Claude, I believe.

A: Well, it is a story I have always liked. He was thinking about running for vice president of the United States, and he thought that he would capitalize on his introduction to Don Maxwell, the editor of the *Chicago Tribune* and pay Don a visit to see if he could garner some support from Don. Don knew him; I do not know how favorably, but he knew him and knew of him. Claude showed up in Don's office one day, accompanied by a Florida highway patrolman. Claude, during the course of the conversation said, "You know why I have this highway patrolman with me who is packing a six-shooter on his hip?"

Don says, "I have no idea; why did you bring him with you?"

He [Kirk] said, "If you do not agree to back me for vice president, he is going to shoot you."

Don, in a very disgusted manner, said, "Get out of my office, and do not ever come back, and take your Florida highway patrolman with you."

Claude went into his usual serenade, "Why, I am just joking."

Maxwell said, "I am not; I am very serious, and I do not suffer clowns during my working hours."

So Claude left, never to be vice president of the United States.

Claude was such a flamboyant guy that he was interesting and certainly was good copy and a man, who, if you followed him around that day, you would have a fine story or two. It would not always glorify Claude, but you would have a good story.

Q: Your view of Reubin Askew [Florida governor, 1971–79]?

A: Reubin brought a real feeling of sincerity and honesty to the office. Reubin, at one time, credited us with the biggest push he got in going for governor. We endorsed him when no other paper in South Florida was interested in him. He felt that was a turning point for him in that campaign, and he went on to be governor and a good one. He was effective and, I think, honest, sincere, a hard worker [who] led an exemplary life. [He has] never been touched, to my recollection, by the slightest breath of scandal. [He is] a rather colorless man. He had a little charisma, but he sold you on his sincerity and his honesty. God bless him. I was always thankful for him.

Q: During your tenure with the newspaper, what was the greatest contribution that your newspaper made to the community?

A: The greatest contribution we made was [regarding] the Ferre brothers from Puerto Rico, who wanted to build a cement plant at Port Everglades. Except for the ocean side, it would have been completely surrounded by high-priced homes of happy and contented retirees who certainly did not want to get up and face a gob of cement dust blowing onto their beloved patios every day. Ferre was intent on doing this [and] was not particularly concerned how much it was going to cost him. No one could understand why he was so bent on locating it in Fort Lauderdale . . . but he did not understand the demographics of it and did not seem to give a damn. We spent a lot of time and a lot of money sending reporters to locations of cement plants. When we could find one of Ferre's, we went there first. We did a good job on it. We had the city commission, as well as the county commission, fully apprized as to what we were letting ourselves in for, and Ferre never could get in. That was early, a triumph.

Our greatest loss—and thank goodness we lost—we were bitter opponents of the tunnel on U.S. 1, and I am afraid that it amounted to no more than the fact that Mr. and Mrs. Gore, Sr., were victims of claustrophobia. He would never let you drive him through the tunnel, and woe be unto you if you were at the wheel and went ahead anyway and drove through the tunnel.

Q: Why was John S. Knight significant as a publisher?

A: Because he was a shining light in the field of news coverage. He was a man who had been in it, done it. He used to tell the story that he loved, that his father told him that he would never amount to anything in the newspaper business, and he immediately started to bust his ass to prove his father wrong. He was somebody who, regardless of what business you were in, I think, if you met him at a meeting or a party or listened to him, you were impressed with him. He had seemingly done a little of almost everything. He worked to raise the level of the *Herald* in every respect.

Q: Who were some of the other journalistic giants during this period?

A: The man who owned the *St. Petersburg Times* [Nelson Poynter] was an outstanding figure. Certainly Al Neuharth, without any question I think, was a leader in Florida journalism. I think he was a leader in the national field, first in Florida.

Q: What do you think about the idea of a national newspaper such as *USA Today*?

A: Well, it is pitched to the traveling man. It is a smart pitch. As long as men travel, *USA Today* will be a success. The traveling man cares nothing for local news. The average one does not care about what happened in Belleville, Illinois, last night before he got there, but he does want to know what is happening around the nation. He only travels five days a week. They only publish it five days a week. That is not accidental; [it is] very smart. They picked out a good target, they zeroed in on it, and they never flinched. They had some tough times, I am sure. They had a lot more tough times than anybody has ever admitted.

Q: What about the criticism of *USA Today*, that it is McNews, that it is all brief news summaries, that it does not have thoughtful analysis?

A: So is TV. People are now accustomed to getting their news in little bites. At one time they were not, but TV, by necessity, cannot stay on a subject too long without losing.

Q: What does that say about our society?

A: It says our society has changed a great deal. We are not nearly as interested in details as we once were. We are not interested in devoting a lot of time to any one little subject as we once were. People once sat and pored over a newspaper, read every story. My father was an omnivorous newspaper reader, read everything in it. [Readers today] are very selective. I think the day will come, and it may not be as far away as you would think, when people will be able to subscribe to sections of a newspaper rather than take the whole thing.

Q: Do you think the newspaper as we know it today in its physical form is going to die out and that everything will be on the Internet?

A: At some time, yes. Quicker than I once thought, yes. I think the Internet has made tremendous strides.

Q: Is there an intellectual decline here?

A: I do not know how much of a decline there has been. I think when you get into heavy reading, there is always a heavy mortality rate. My guess would be that it is probably true that there has been a decline. I do not think it is a monumental one. I think it is a shift rather than a decline. I think that, mainly, you find that the heavy readers are heavy readers in spots. They have things that they really concentrate on, and if there is anything about that on the editorial or op-ed page, they are going to read it, [even] if they have to go to some trouble to track it down.

Q: Is there anything that you would like to say about either your career or some unusual incidents that occurred while you were in the newspaper business?

A: I am tempted to mention the most interesting story I was involved in. It involved JFK. His father [Joseph P. Kennedy] was reportedly dying in Palm Beach. I went to work on a Saturday morning. I was the executive editor, and I was in Saturday morning just to see that things were going okay. We had a report from our entertainment editor that Jacqueline Kennedy was doing the dance of that time at a nightclub in Pompano Beach, while her father-in-law was lying on his deathbed. She was not accompanied by her husband, who had stayed with his father. Our newsroom was excited by this.

Q: This would have been when, 1961?

A: 1961 or 1962. . . . I did not think the story made sense to me. Everybody else, including the managing editor, thought, "We have got one hell of a story going here."

I said, "I think we have a lot of work to do on this. We have to get hold of the entertainment editor, and we have to find out if he saw Jacqueline Kennedy on the dance floor with this instructor. Who was she accompanied by? We have to talk to the instructor. . . ." I said, "I am bothered—I am not a Jacqueline Kennedy fan, but I do not think she would do this. It does not make a lot of sense to me." So I said, "The first thing we are going to do is, we are not going to give anything to AP [Associated Press] at all, nothing, period." I said, "If AP asks us about this, we are working on it; we are not at a stage where we might print it, but we are looking into it, and if we get anything, certainly they will be the first to know."

So we started out touching all the right bases, and suddenly somebody said, "Hey, look here," and he brought a tear of the AP wire over to me, and the AP wire said that Pompano Beach says and the *Sentinel* and *News* say that Jacqueline Kennedy was dancing at a nightclub with a young man, doing the blah blah blah, while her father-in-law was lying at death's door in Palm Beach. Well, somebody who thought that I was afraid of the situation had determined to flush me from cover and had called the AP.

It had to be a staff member. Nobody else knew we were involved in it at that time. Well, this pissed me off considerably. I talked to a couple of people and asked them if they had made the telephone call. They were people who ordinarily called AP with some frequency. Naturally, I got a lot of innocence.

So the man (the dance instructor) got on the phone, and after a great deal of badgering, he said, "No, it was not Jackie Kennedy; it was a person who looked like her." Jacob [K.] Javits, the New York senator, had a daughter who looked a great deal like Jacqueline and could make herself up to look even more like Jacqueline. She and three or four men who posed as Secret Service thought they would have a game to play, and it would be fun.

Suddenly, we got a call from Kennedy's press secretary. Pierre Salinger said, "The president of the United States would like to talk with you."

This [brought me] to full wake. I said, "Fine."

[JFK] said, "I understand you are publishing a story about my wife, and I want you to know it is completely false."

I said, "First, let me say that we are not publishing it, per se. We are still working on the story, and at the moment we are speaking, I do not think the story is legitimate either, but there is still a possibility that it is, and I am not going to be able to tell you, 'No, we are not going to publish it.' But," I said, "the odds are very strong against our publishing it."

So he said he appreciated that, and he hoped that we would continue working the story until we found the right answer, which was [that] his wife was home with him, and she was near her father-in-law, as she should be.

He was neither insulting nor threatening. He was logical. I thought, "This man handles these things pretty damn well. He should be president." The story fell through. It was Jacob Javits's daughter.

Medium-Sized Newspapers

chapter 4   **Herbert M. "Tippen" Davidson, Jr.**

Tippen Davidson, currently the publisher of the *News-Journal* (Daytona Beach) was born in Chicago, Illinois, on August 10, 1925. His grandfather, Julius Davidson, and father, Herbert M. Davidson, jointly acquired the *News-Journal* in December 1928. The paper was a small evening paper with a circulation of only 4,400. Davidson's parents were both graduates of the Columbia School of Journalism. He attended the local schools in Daytona, but did not work on the paper until he was in college.

Davidson attended the Juilliard School of Music, with the intention of becoming a classical musician. He then married Josephine Field, decided not to be a professional musician, and returned to Daytona Beach in 1947 to work as a reporter for his father. He learned the business quickly and worked as city editor, managing editor, general manager, and, from 1985, as publisher and coeditor with his wife.

In 2001 the Daytona Beach paper employed around 850 people and had a daily circulation of approximately 100,000, with 119,000 on Sunday. It is, after the *St. Petersburg Times*, the second largest independently owned newspaper in the state.

In this interview Tippen Davidson talks about how his grandfather and parents took over the newspaper and the difficult times they faced during the Depression. He mentions his father's impact on the county's decision to adopt voting machines and signature verification to cut down on graft and corruption at the voting box. He also explains that the paper was the first to use offset printing, was innovative in its use of color, and constantly invested in the latest technology.

Davidson takes pride in the fact that the *News Journal* has managed to remain independent despite many offers by chains to buy it. In discussing his career, he fondly remembers the challenges of being city editor, "my idea of a really great job," and delineates the paper's strong financial support for community activities—the Daytona Playhouse, the Museum of Photography, Stetson University, Bethune-Cookman College, the Ormond Beach Museum, and the biannual visit of the London Symphony Orchestra. In addition, the paper gives a Medallion of Excellence to 30–40 outstanding seniors in the county's public schools.

Davidson makes insightful and often tart comments on *USA Today*, environmental concerns, Bike Week and other events that draw tourists to the area, letters to the editor, crime, Governors Reubin Askew and Bob Graham, the 2000 presidential campaign, comic strips, Jackie Robinson's integration of baseball, editorial cartoons, and labor unions. He contends that his newspaper is the conscience of the community and did great service for the city by advocating cooperation between the races during integration of the schools and also by improving sanitation at local restaurants and opening hospital board meetings to the state Sunshine Law.

Tippen Davidson was interviewed by Julian M. Pleasants on November 15, 2000, at Daytona Beach, Florida.

Q: Talk a little bit about your early background and your schooling.
A: My parents brought me here in 1928, when they came to manage the *News Journal*. My grandfather and my father jointly acquired control of it and took possession of it in December 1928. I grew up here through the Depression. I am a product of local schools and was underfoot at the newspaper all during my formative years. I did not have anything actually active to do with the newspaper until after high school. While I was in college, I worked in the newsroom in the summer. I was not intending to be a newspaperman. I was intending to be a professional musician, so I was really just making the most of a summer job. Then when I left school, I wanted to get married, so I gave up the idea of being a professional musician and hit my old man up for a full-time job and became a reporter here.
Q: Explain why your grandfather bought this newspaper.
A: He bought it because my father wanted him to. My father was the newspaperman. My father and my mother were both graduates of Columbia School of Journalism, both great newspaper people. My grandfather was a

businessman. His training was in the import/export business. My father always wanted to have his own newspaper, as many newspapermen have. They looked around. They looked at papers in California and New Mexico and other places, and then this one became available, and they bought it.

Q: Discuss the difficulties your father faced in the early years of the paper. During the Depression, I suspect, it was difficult for everybody in Florida, since the Depression here started a little bit ahead of the rest of the country.

A: Yes, actually, that little dip after the Florida boom. The bust of the Florida boom was really responsible for the existence of the *News Journal* as it is today. The boom shattered, leaving two small papers in Daytona Beach, the *Journal* in the morning, the *News* in the afternoon, both in desperate straits. Somebody with money arrived, Mr. Eugene C. Pullium, . . . and he and a partner bought the two little papers and combined them and proceeded to try to build them back. During the boom, they [the two papers] ran pages and pages . . . of full-page advertisements of the real-estate speculators, and nobody ever thought of asking anyone to pay for anything. Their credit was good. Then their credit suddenly was not good . . . and I think that both of the papers were really up against it when Mr. Pullium arrived. At any rate, he acquired the properties and put them together and . . . did succeed at putting it back on its feet.

When my father and grandfather showed up, it was a going concern — not a rich one, not a gold mine, but a going concern. Of course, they had an excellent [year in] 1928, made money. That was the last profit they saw until after World War II. It was pretty desperate.

Q: How did they keep the paper going all that time?

A: They kept it going on that money that my grandfather made in the bulk-materials business in the Midwest. He had a few hundred thousand dollars put away, and that sufficed to keep them going. They had a competitor starting in 1933. The politicians here convinced Mr. Robert Gore, the proprietor of the *Fort Lauderdale Daily* [sic] *News*, that this was a fertile field and that there would be no trouble running us out of it. There was a great deal of trouble running us out of it.

Q: Discuss your early years on the paper as a reporter and how you developed your skills as a newspaperman.

A: You have to understand that this was a newspaper family. My father and mother both worked on the paper. My father was the editor, wrote the editorials, and when that was done, he sat at the desk and served as news editor and, in fact, did everything in the newsroom that needed doing, with a very small staff of help. My mother was everything else. She was the Sunday editor, the women's editor. . . . But newspaper was talked incessantly at home. It just became a language. It became an atmosphere in which I was included.

Along with everyone else who has ever learned to be a reporter, I had to learn the rudiments. I was not given any special treatment by my mother, who did most of the early training. She was tough, but fortunately I was brought up speaking and writing pretty good English, and I managed to survive. My late wife took up reporting, . . . she was absolutely delighted to find out there was a job in which the main thing you did was stick your nose into other people's business. That was her idea of heaven. She became an absolutely marvelous reporter. I mean, one of the great ones, one of the intuitive ones.

Q: One of the things I have noticed about this newspaper is that you have reinvested money over and over again into new technology. Perhaps you could explain your decision to go to offset printing.

A: Yes, indeed. We were one of the first newspapers in the country to do that. We started up the first four-plate wide press in a daily newspaper in the Southeast.

Q: When did you go to color?

A: We went to color back in the letterpress days. As I told you, we were doing processed color by curving the photo engravings and Scotch-taping them to the blanks, printing color that way. We had been doing color separations in this place since the early 1960s.

Q: Let me ask you about the expansion. You began purchasing some weekly newspapers.

A: Let me put these in order for you. We had an offer of a shopper in west Volusia [County], the *DeLand Pennysaver*, a very well run, profitable shopper. The man came to see me and said he would like to sell. He wanted to get out and write novels. So we met this man's price and took over the *DeLand Pennysaver*. It did well from the very first. At that time, we bought the *Flagler Tribune* from them [*Florida Times-Union*] and the *Halifax Reporter*. We started the *Palm Coast News*, in competition with the *Tribune*. The *Halifax Reporter* . . . served no useful function at all, since it was not a very good newspaper and did not carry that much advertising and was losing money. So we laid it to rest, but we took the little shopper . . . and put a little fertilizer and a little water, and it has done fantastically well, the *Daytona Pennysaver*, and now that has branched out and we have a *Flagler Pennysaver* as well.

Q: How do the *Pennysavers* make money?

A: It is fairly profitable. It makes money very nicely. The problem, of course, . . . when you own both the shopper and the daily is to find some arena of agreement that will permit them to coexist, and we just have sort of a gentlemen's agreement. We do not knock each other. Everybody is free to do as he pleases. We do not destroy the value of *Pennysaver* advertising, and they do not have anything to say about daily newspaper advertising. We have gotten along fine. Both sides have been able to sell. The only part of our operation that has perhaps been affected is liner classifieds. The *Pennysaver* does vacuum those up somewhat.

To finish up the *Pennysaver* story, we started the *Pennysaver* in New Smyrna Beach. That did not do well at first, [although] it is doing fine now. We started a *Pennysaver* in St. Johns County, and that had a long period of limping, and it is doing fine now.

Q: How many weekly papers do you now own?

A: That are not actually associated with the *News Journal* itself, there are six little weeklies. They are Daytona, Flagler, New Smyrna Beach, DeLand, Palatka, and the St. Johns.

Q: Are all of those profitable?

A: Five of them are. The Putnam one [Palatka] is in and out, but we feel it is a worthwhile property to hang onto.

Q: Are those run separately from the *News Journal*?

A: Those are [a] complete[ly] separate corporation. They are printed here, their plates are made here, and the technical computer stuff is all supervised from here, so there is a good deal of interlock. But the staffing, the sales, the management, and so on is completely separate.

Q: At one time you owned a printing company. Is that still part of the corporation?

A: No. We had to close that. We were losing so much money at it that we closed it. The loss, generally speaking, was because . . . we were doing all right in the printing business, no great shakes, and I, the great businessman, employed a nationally known consultant to come in and advise us to what we should do. They came down and spent a week and charged us an arm and a leg and wrote us a report and told us everything we should do. We did it, and it was all 100 percent wrong—equipment selection, market selection, staffing, everything wrong, wrong, wrong! So we got in difficulties, and we finally closed down.

Q: In 1985 you were named publisher and coeditor with your wife. Why coeditor? Isn't that rather unusual?

A: Yes. That is a good question. I guess it was just that we thought I should have some standing in the editorial part of the paper. I mean, having come out of the editorial side of the paper, I have always been a thorn in the side of the editorial department whenever they split an infinitive. My being coeditor really meant that when she wanted somebody to help her say no, she could call on me. That is essentially it.

I have to tell you that my home was just like my parents' home. A lot of newspaper got talked over the dining-room table, and witness the fact that both of my children are working here now. My daughter has a graduate [journalism] degree from Columbia University, following in her grandparents' footsteps, and my son is running the Internet part of it.

Q: When you started as publisher in 1985, what were your goals, and do you feel, in retrospect, you have met most of those goals?

A: I think so. We have a five-year plan and a ten-year plan and that kind of thing, but, essentially, our goal planning is like a Persian carpet unrolled in front of you. We planned some territorial expansion. Well, we have done that. Also, when I became publisher, we had some cutting to do. We had some areas which were not working out, and those had to be closed down. We have done that. I had a complete newsroom to build because we had gotten behind on pay scales and whatnot, and we needed some front-runners in the newsroom. We had a couple of years of intensive search and hiring and building staff back. Then we needed to completely redesign the product. It was just one thing after another. I cannot say I had any grand overall goals. We always looked for the day when we averaged 100,000 in circulation. We have done that. The next one is 200,000, and I will not be here for that.

Q: Why did you eliminate the afternoon paper and move to just a morning paper?

A: It was for purely economic reasons. Remember that the afternoon paper was quite a serious paper. It had its own staff; it had its own editorial page; it had its own areas of distribution. It was costing money, and circulation descended from the 55,000 area down to the 25,000 area. Advertising, also—people were just not buying the combination anymore. For a long golden time, from the end of World War II on, very seldom did anybody buy any single-paper advertising. We made the combination rate very tempting, and people would just buy the combination rate [meaning the advertising ran in both the morning and the afternoon paper]. It got to the point where people would say, "Well, I know it is only twenty percent more, but I am going to save my money and spend it on inches."

So the advertising in the *Evening News* went way, way, way down, and it was quite obvious we were losing money on it, as well as readership. It just came to the point where we had to make a decision. It was a tough decision. All hands cried a lot. A lot of the people around had come up through the afternoon paper, me [too]. I started as city editor of the afternoon paper. But we made a business study, and like every good business study, it says what happens if you do and what happens if you do not. What happens if you do was so much more promising than if you do not that we decided to go ahead.

Q: Explain how this newspaper has remained a family-owned newspaper, when practically every other newspaper is owned by a conglomerate like Knight-Ridder or Gannett.

A: It has to do with a trick you do with your head. You move it gently from left to right and back, like that. A week does not go by that somebody flies by with an offer. There has never been any drop in people's interest in acquiring this paper. We have a big chain minority here. The minority stock is owned by Cox, and it is a large minority. We are very fortunate it has been Cox, because they have been good partners ever since they came aboard. When John Perry owned the minority, he had buzzards flying around this place, trying to trick us into selling the stock or get us in the position where we would be forced to sell the stock. It was a relief when the Cox people took it because they became good working partners and have remained good working partners.

Q: Do they have much influence on your editorial decisions or running the paper?

A: No, no influence whatsoever, nor do they seek any. Such influences they may have has been to help us. There was a special rate on the Cox wire. When they were negotiating low prices of newsprint, they just included us in.

Q: How would this paper change if it were taken over by, let us say, Knight-Ridder?

A: I have no idea. I am sure they would cut the expenses pretty drastically. This paper is heavily involved in the community. It gives away a lot of money. It gives away a lot of time and attention to community things. We not only countenance, but encourage, staff to participate in community things. I feel sure they [a chain publisher] would not do it as much as we do, anyway.

Q: They would be more interested in the bottom line.

A: Yes. But it is not their habit to do this kind of thing even in cases where the bottom line is not affected, as, for example, employee participation in community affairs.

Q: Discuss your days as a city editor. What is the most difficult job of a city editor?

A: City editor is my natural home. It is the best job on the paper, the most fun, the most excitement, the most challenge. You have to know the city, geographically and personally, like the back of your hand. You have to have a sense about what is going on. You have to understand the movers and shakers and just who they move and where they shake. You have to have your staff deployed in such a way that things do not escape you. You have a constant problem, especially on an afternoon paper—which is what I was doing—with the clock. I just enjoyed it. Every day was better than the last.

Q: There would be a tremendous amount of pressure, I would imagine.

A: Yes. Thrived on it. I thought it was great. I am not sure at my age now if I could take the pressure.

Q: I would like for you to talk about some of the issues with which the paper has been involved. For example, the paper has supported the annual music festival and has brought the London Symphony Orchestra [LSO] here, and you have supported the Playhouse and the new auditorium.

A: Having an orchestra like the LSO here every year was a feather in the town's cap. . . . The community has really rallied around this magnificently. [The] News Journal has not been heavily involved, . . . we are just . . . one of the contributors. The community raises this enormous sum of money, one million dollars, every other year to bring the orchestra. We support all the arts. We also support the museums, the Museum of Photography at the college, the Ormond Beach Museum. We have a . . . list [that] fills up an entire page in eight point with the names of all the charities to which we have given. Small gifts and large. We support Stetson University in a meaningful way and also Bethune-Cookman College.

Q: Discuss your relationship with Mary McLeod Bethune [African American education leader, political activist, and founder of the college that bears her name].

A: I did not have any relationship with Mary McLeod Bethune except that she once stepped on me when I was a little kid. I walked in front of her, and she bumped into me. She was a personal friend of my mother's, turned to my mother for advice. [M]y father was on the Bethune-Cookman board. He was a very strong advocate of Bethune-Cookman College and the work she was doing. Helped them tremendously when they had Mrs. [Eleanor] Roosevelt here. I remember that, and I was just a child.

Q: Did the paper take a position on Jackie Robinson's attempt to integrate baseball?

A: Oh, yes. That is an interesting story. Bernard Kahn, our wonderful sports editor, was practically Robinson's PR [public relations manager]. He wrote stories, and because he had many friends in the sportswriting business, he tipped off a lot of people to come and talk to Robinson. He was heavily supportive of Robinson. He was one of Robinson's pals when Robinson was first here. You can say that we had a hand in Robinson's success, mostly because of this one sportswriter.

Q: Was there a strong negative public reaction to the integration of professional baseball in Daytona Beach?

A: No, there was not a strong public reaction. I have to tell you this about the community. My father always did interracial work, not only Bethune-Cookman, but he was [also] the director of the Southern Leadership Conference and was considered a leader in interracial work. [He] hosted and chaired many interracial activities in the community, with the result that, at times of crisis—for example, when the school integration became the rule of law—the day came when the courts ruled that the schools had to be integrated, . . . the schools in Volusia County were integrated without a murmur. The buses ran, and the new kids showed up. They did not even have a playground fight in Volusia County because the principals had been so thoroughly briefed and had briefed their staffs and had briefed the student bodies as to what was going to happen and what they could expect. Everything went smoothly. In St. Augustine, they had riots on the same thing.

Again, the rule was passed that hotels could no longer discriminate. That was a huge relief to Daytona Beach because the hotels here had not discriminated for years. They quietly took black business, and they lost, sometimes, a convention or something because somebody would go in a motel and see a black guest.

The difference between us and the counties to the north and to the west is striking in terms of the peaceful way in which these integration movements took place. I am very proud of that. Of all the things that he did, I think maybe that is the greatest.

Q: Was there any backlash in terms of advertising?

A: Our community had come to recognize us as hopeless radicals. There was not any backlash.

Q: But this is still considered, in political terms, a liberal newspaper, correct?

A: Yes, unashamedly.

Q: Another important development was the increase in the military stationed in Daytona Beach in World War II. There were a lot of WACs [Women's Army Corps] stationed here . . . and a naval base. How did that change Daytona Beach?

A: Kept it from starving to death. Claude Pepper [D-Florida, U.S. senator, 1937–51, and congressman] was the fellow who wangled the WACs for Daytona Beach because my father told him that the town was going to dry up and blow into the ocean. It was a little winter tourist town, and what was going to happen to tourism during the war was, it was not going to exist. So we got the WACs and the NAS [Naval Air Station], and when the WACs were finished, an army convalescent hospital.

Q: What do you think are the most important functions of a newspaper today, and why?

A: I do not think the newspaper's function, which is to inform the public, has changed a bit. It is still the only function we have. We do it a little differently in the light of our electronic competitors. We are more thorough, and maybe we are a little less hooh-ha than we would be if we did not have this competition. But we cover so much news that the broadcast people do not cover. You know, like twenty, thirty stories to one, daily, every day. We do a really thorough job of informing our public, as the very best we can. . . . Our job is to do the best we can to note the sparrow's fall in our area. No one can be God, but we have to try to do the best we can.

Q: What is your view of USA Today?

A: I will tell you, I think it is a brilliant idea. The idea has [been] perhaps the most imitated thing in the last ten years. Every newspaper has some USA Today ideas in it. From that standpoint, from the design standpoint, from the mass production standpoint, the way it is mass produced all over the country, [it is] admirable in every way. My objection to it is that in doing this, they have made it a little vapid, a little uninteresting. It has been predigested like these patent cereals that have no taste at all anymore, they have been ground and reground so many times. *USA Today* is so good in so many ways that it is a shame it cannot have a little flavor.

Q: How has your audience changed over the years, your readers?

A: The town has become increasingly retired. The average age is getting older. For a newspaper, that is probably a good thing, because even as they curse us for being so liberal, they renew their subscriptions. They do need their newspapers, use their newspapers, respond to their newspapers, which is very gratifying. We have the same readership pattern as every paper in the country, the dip in the eighteen to twenty-fives and the mysterious rise in the twenty-five to thirty-eights, as though people got to the age of twenty-five and started reading newspapers. It must be. And then the fairly satisfactory readership figures when you get to forty-five and up. The newspaper evidently is a tool of maturing people.

Q: Do you think the readers are less sophisticated? Do they read for television listings or ads or sports? Is there a reader who concentrates on news and editorials?

A: Oh, yes. There is a reader who concentrates on news. There is no question about that. What is more, there are readers who concentrate on local news. Our paper is highly local. It is our lifeblood. We got the *Orlando Sentinel* as a competitor to the west, [with] more pages, more sports, more color, more this, more that. People take our paper because we run their socks off on local news.

Q: Do you see an end to printed newspapers? Will people get their news off the Internet?

A: No, I do not think so. I tell you what, I see . . . a possible end to printed newspapers. When the large advertisers lose confidence in us and stop using us, we will fold. It cannot live without advertising.

Q: But you do not see that anytime in the near future?

A: I have not noticed any trace of it so far. Certainly, some types of advertising have exited the papers: groceries. I have a Thursday food section that has no food advertising, not a line.

Q: How would you rank this paper in comparison with other papers in the state?

A: I have to say it is the best. This paper, in doing its duty, which is reporting the news of its area, it is the equal of anybody. I think it is very good. Otherwise, I would say the paper is well in line with its size. It is ninth or tenth in circulation in the state. I would say that it is excellent for its rank.

Q: What makes an outstanding newspaper?

A: I guess good news coverage and some sort of sense of honesty. This package goes together. You have to have a certain amount of moral standards to do this job. It is not like selling peanuts in the park. You buy the peanuts from a wholesaler for fifty cents, and you sell them for a dollar. It does not require any morals to do that. It takes a certain amount of moral energy to keep this engine going. One has to think it is worth doing. One has to have a sense of accomplishment and a sense of duty in order to really make a newspaper valuable to its community.

Q: One other standard might be accuracy. Do you believe that newspaper reporters and newspapers today are less accurate in reporting the news than they used to be?

A: In some ways, but most of the inaccuracies are technological ones. . . . Most reporters, I hope, when they actually understand what is going on, are as accurate as it is humanly possible to be. I know my people care a great deal about it.

Q: What happens when you do make a significant error? How do you correct it, and where in the paper is it corrected?

A: It depends on the nature of the error, and, to an extent, whose ox is gored. We try to make corrections at least as noticeable as the errors, and we always try to explain what happened, and we always apologize.

Q: When you look at Florida in general—and I realize you concentrate on local news—but in your fifty years, how would you evaluate the changes that the state and Daytona Beach have undergone?

A: Everybody has grown, grown, grown. Everybody. Go to places that were crossroads, and they are metropolises. Fly over to Naples sometime. Fly over those acres of new housing—miles of it. Unbelievable. One of my innovations as the general manager was to buy an airplane for the company and arrange to have a pilot. We used it to fly people to and from football games, the reporters and photographers, and used it for business trips and sales trips.

Q: You mentioned that Daytona Beach has changed. The population is older. How else has it changed, in terms of the environment, in terms of crime, in terms of education?

A: I should say we are a little better than average here with respect to the environment. There is a lot of environmental consciousness. Of course, there are always . . . developers, and there is a constant conflict, . . . but you are speaking to the editor of a paper in a county which has just passed an eighty-million-dollar bond issue for buying endangered lands and protecting the watershed—with our enthusiastic approval, of course. It passed by a sixty-two-percent vote, of which we are very proud.

Crime, we had a bad few years here when we were having early motorcycle troubles. But, actually, the last two or three years, the violent crime statistics have been going down. There is still too much violence here. A lot of it comes out of this so-called event tourism that we have, where thousands of people come to the town for the weekend, [like] at this thing Biketoberfest, a weekend without an event. It is an invitation to all the motorcycle people to come to Daytona Beach and raise hell. Four people were killed in three days in motorcycle accidents. To that extent, violence is unchecked, [but] violent crime is better [has decreased].

Now, education. We have been very, very fortunate in this county. We have had a very determined and enlightened school board for a good long period of time and three very good school superintendents in a row, all . . . different in outlook and different in method, but all determined to improve the quality of the schools. I would say our school system is pretty good. It is not world-shaking. We did for some reason have some schools that did not quite pass the recent tests, schools [in which] I know very excellent work is being done.

Schools are one of my enthusiasms, and I keep an eye on this part of it. The newspaper, by the way, is a big booster of public schools. We give an award, called the Medallion of Excellence, every year to those seniors in the public schools—the public schools only—who show remarkable excellence. We invite them to apply. We put out a poster and applications . . . , and they do apply, through their principals. Their principals recommend them, and then we have a really bad day and a half when we have to go over the several hundred really terrific applications and choose thirty or forty. Then we give it a big play in the paper, and that is a big boost to public education because it shows the quality, fabulous quality, of youngsters who come out of the public school system.

Q: Let me go back to something you said earlier that intrigued me. You mentioned that, in running the paper, you have a moral obligation to the community and that the newspaper was the conscience of the community. Could you give me a specific example of that?

A: I think the things I told you earlier about the way the community responded by its actions on integration. The newspaper's insistence that it was the community's duty to obey the law was the voice of conscience reminding the community what the law was. That was why, when push came to shove, the people in this community obeyed the law. That is what I mean by the conscience of the community. It is a lot more than just sticking your nose into public accounting and catching shortages at the dog pound and that type of thing. It means that the editorial board [and] the editorial board supervisor have to be conscious of what is going on in the community and whether it is beneficial or not. We have to comment, and we do comment. It is our stated policy to keep comment as heavily positive as we can, to push rather than pull, to use the old phrase.

Q: Do you do a lot of investigative journalism?

A: Sure.

Q: What would be some of your more successful investigations?

A: Successful? We did a shocker a couple of years ago that resulted in a shake-up of the way restaurant sanitation is handled in this community. Restaurant sanitation used to be handled by the department of public [health], the county health officer and his people. Now it is done by the state. The county health officer has no power to do it anymore, and the state, we found, has not closed a restaurant in years and years and years. Some of the ratings were awful. We went and visited the restaurants, . . . but they never got them closed. So we ran an exposé on that and made every restaurant in town sore at us. Lost a lot of restaurant advertising. I think it did some good because I think people went to these restaurants and said, "You better clean up, because until we see that A [superior health rating] on the window, we are not coming back." I think that is an example of the kind of thing that we can do.

We are suddenly and explosively interfering when it comes to violations of the Sunshine Law, so investigative reporting has been carried out in the sunshine around here for a long time. We carried out a case against our hospital, carried it all the way to the Supreme Court twice, in order to force our public hospital to open its board meetings. They were having token meetings in the sunshine and then doing everything else privately, so we called them on it, brought the suit. They defended the suit, [and] they lost. They lost all the way up to the Supreme Court. Now we have a lot of hospital board meetings open.

Q: How often would you have subscribers cancel the paper or advertisers cancel because of a stand you took, an editorial you wrote?

A: Not more than two or three times a day. Right in the center of election time, we got a lot of stir. Canceled, a handful, six or eight. Letters and telephone calls, just incessant. Dear Ann [Larson, Davidson's administrative assistant] gets most of the brunt out there. She picks up the phone carefully to see what flames are steaming out of the receiver.

Q: Well, if you did not get any complaints, you figure you would not be doing your job, correct?

A: That is right.

Q: But advertisers would not cancel?

A: I have not had any problems of that kind in many, many years, and then it was a personal thing, an officeholder whom we opposed for reelection pulled his advertising when we opposed him. It was not a very large amount of money, and we thought to ourselves, "Well, it is too bad, because he needs the advertising to keep his business going." But those breaches often are healed within a matter of weeks after they take place.

Mrs. Kaney and I both answer a lot of complaining mail, and we find that if we write a person back and say, "Well, we disagree, but this is how we arrived at our conclusion, and that we would like to hear how you arrived at your conclusion, and please stay with us because thinking readers are our most important possession." I have turned away an awful lot of wrath with letters of that kind: . . . thank you for your dissent; it keeps us on our toes.

I have to write pretty often to defend our editorial practices, which are strictly ethical. I have to defend the work of the editorial board and our practice of endorsing political candidates. The standard defense is that we have the chance to put these people on the griddle and talk to them, explore not only their campaign promises and their appearance, but also the way their greedy little minds work. This is a chance that a voter seldom has. When we endorse somebody, we have looked at him pretty closely. Occasionally, that argument will turn away wrath from somebody who is objecting to an endorsement. Not often. That is where the pie is thinnest and the skin is sorest, when it comes to your political spaces.

Q: Do you get many letters to the editor, and will you publish unsigned letters?

A: We never would publish unsigned letters. We always required identification of the writer. In my father's day, we permitted people to use pseud-onyms, provided they gave us their real name and address. In my time about ten years ago, we quit doing that. We just said, "Okay, if you have something to say, sign your name to it." We do not give out letter writers' addresses except the city. That seems to please the readers. We have more readers than we can say grace over, and readers' editorials, certainly no shortage.

Q: How have letters to the editor changed over the years?

A: They are all signed now, [and] . . . it is my impression that we do not get nearly as much hate mail as we used to. We used to get stacks of it. As a matter of fact, we had a file, a box at the back of a file drawer, which was called the nut hoard, we would drop these letters in. Every once in a while, the FBI guy would come by and ask to have a look, and once in a while, he would find a familiar face, a familiar typewriter, or something in there. I think we still have the nut hoard, but I do not know how full it is. I hope we are not becoming less exciting.

Q: Do you think when you recommend candidates and issues that the readers respond favorably?

A: They obviously do. Our endorsement is worth a chunk at the polls.

Q: I read the editorial in your paper today about the Florida secretary of state, Katherine Harris. What is your general assessment of the vote counting [for the November 2000 presidential election; this interview took place on November 15, 2000, in the middle of the recount issues in Florida] in Volusia County?

A: In this particular election, it was excellent. The mechanism that we have now, which is a fairly sophisticated electronic mechanism, worked very well, is understood and trusted by the public. That did not prevent our elections office in DeLand from making a bunch of stupid errors, losing ballots, and you saw it all. I think this is just loose management.

Certainly, we are not in any of the desperate trouble that they are in West Palm Beach with that strange ballot. In one, they have many tens of thousands of wasted ballots and people who punched twice. If you punch twice on our system [optical scan], the collector and the tabulator in the precinct will spit the ballot out and say this is not a legal ballot. Then the elections board points out the error to the voter before he can move, and he has the privilege of having a fresh ballot if he wants it. That saves a lot of trouble. We could not get into the kind of thing they had in West Palm

Beach with that chad and whatnot. We had that for two years, in two elections—drove everybody insane.

Q: Is it possible to recount all the votes in Florida?

A: Sure. Somebody said the other day on how long it would take, about eleven days, I think it was. An objective that we seek in designing a better election system should be the truth. We really want to know how people voted. This Democratic bias or Republican bias, the motives of Mr. [Ralph] Nader [consumer advocate and Green Party presidential candidate in 2000], all of those things are secondary. We have to have a system which will create a truth, a dependable truth. I think that one of the penalties of this whole presidential election nationally is going to be an erosion of public confidence in the electing process. I hope that will help people swallow the cost of modernizing their vote-collecting systems. . . .

Q: How do you choose your syndicated columnists?

A: Well, we look for a variety of outlook and a variety of style. Syndicated columnists tend to run around like scared ponies, all in the same direction. We try to find some who will not shift that way, who will write about different things. Our mainstays are the best in the business, people like David Broder, and Molly Ivins for laughs.

Q: What about comic strips? Who chooses those, and what part do they play in the paper?

A: I do not know what part they play. They amuse everybody and create a considerable amount of contention. I like to have a certain amount of sophistication. I like to . . . carry the popular things, and we do. I also like having a couple of sophisticated ones to keep the people who like that sort of thing from being bored.

Q: Do you mean like *Doonesbury*?

A: Well, yes. *Doonesbury*, of course. A lot of people read *Doonesbury*.

Q: I notice you have an in-house editorial cartoonist, and I looked at his editorial cartoon today, which I thought was quite good. What is his basic purpose, and do you tell him what to do or approve what he does?

A: He uses the old classic format. His purpose, of course, is to give us a chance at cartoons on local area and Florida subjects, which we cannot get from the syndicate. But he does national subjects as well. He comes to the morning editorial meeting with three ideas, which are passed around, and they sort of agree. He has a favorite. Almost always that is the one they agree on. With supervision of the editorial page editor and the executive editors at that meeting, too, and the news editor, they sort of agree on one. Then he goes back and inks it. If we like two of them, we may give him a day off the next day and run the second one.

Q: How do you decide main stories, headlines?

A: There is a preliminary editorial conference at eleven o'clock in the morning and another one at four o'clock. That is when the paper is laid out and the space allocated, and the bad news about . . . circulation department problems and whatnot is passed out, and then each of the interest editors has a chance to speak up for his requirements and what is coming up [in the] world, what is coming up nationally, what is coming [up] local. That is a newsroom conference.

[T]he editorial writers meet at ten o'clock every morning to talk about what they want to write about. Matters of policy, generally. That is under the supervision of the editorial page editor. Writers come in with their own ideas. If you come in with an idea and defend it with the others and they approve, then you write it. There is no question about that. The editorial writers generally, in a vague sort of way, develop areas of interest and expertise. One person finds himself doing more of the foreign ones and national ones, and then another finds that he is concentrating on De-Land. . . . We let those things happen naturally, let the editorial writers sort of find their own sea legs.

Q: Do you use a lot of local columnists?

A: As many as I can. . . . We have an old-timer. She is not so old, but she has been with us a long time on the desk. As a little girl, she was a Cracker kid running around barefoot and half-naked. She has an interesting local point of view, and she does columns about what it was like in the old days. We had a most marvelous [columnist], rest his soul, John Carter. Referred to himself as the jug-eared kid and wrote an absolutely marvelous column about Cracker Florida, with a lot of humor in it.

Q: Explain how the role of women in newspapers has changed. Obviously, in your case there was a female coeditor at a very early time, but what about the role of other women in the newspaper?

A: Since World War II, if you are talking about reporters and editors, they have expanded from a limited range of things to an unlimited range of things. There is not anything that women do not do around here. Nothing. I even have a lady sportswriter, and she is tops.

Q: How have you encouraged minority participation?

A: All I could. They are hard to get. You find that you get a talented kid . . .

but most of the really talented ones will find themselves on the *Atlanta Constitution*, or some [place] like that, for twice what I can pay them.

Q: How would you evaluate Reubin Askew as a governor [1971–79]?

A: I thought he was okay, very good. He knew his own mind and was a very moral person. In those days, he was not highly sophisticated; [he is] much more so now. But it is nice to have somebody in the governor's mansion whom you feel is really honest and really a good person.

Q: Your views of Bob Graham [governor, 1979–87; U.S. senator, 1987–present]?

A: Bob Graham is a person I like very much, personally. It is so hard to judge. Certainly, his heart is in the right place. He did a good job as governor. It is hard to judge a Florida governor on the basis of performance, because his performance is so hedged in by the antique cabinet system. I think Graham has showed up well in Washington, too. I think he is an intelligent senator. Lawton Chiles was an enthusiasm of mine from the first. He was a remarkable, remarkable man. Not unflawed, but a remarkable man.

Q: When you look at the history of this paper—you, in some ways, have already discussed this, but I would like for you to focus once again on your greatest contribution to your community. You talked about integration, but I am sure there are other areas where you feel you made a significant impact.

A: There are a number of things that we have interfered in. I think my father's major role in bringing voting machines into this county, and then fifteen years later, was it, we got the signature recognition. In promoting that, that certainly had a profound influence on local politics. The signature recognition, we finally got it where they cannot vote the graveyard; they cannot steal the election. When my father came here, there was one precinct down in New Smyrna Beach that always came up with enough votes to carry the county for the County Ring candidates, the DeLand political ring, even if it was more votes than there were registered there. The election machinery at least is keeping it honest—pretty well stamped [voter fraud] out. I do not know, maybe there is a new technique of diddling with ballots in DeLand. But as far as the precincts are concerned, it is fairly hard to do the kinds of things that were done in those days.

Q: One of the images of Daytona Beach in the past has been sex, sand, and suds. Do you want to change that?

A: Oh, desperately. Terrible, terrible image. The event mentality which hinders the entire working life of the tourist community on bike week and motorcycle races and spring breaks and auto races and that kind of thing—huge crowds which come and go. I am talking about the big events that bring in people in the six figures, leav[ing] a sea of trash and broken hearts behind them. A segment of the motel industry thinks this is the way to live. They do not care how badly their hotels are torn up. The insurance company pays for that. Our city council is getting to be very irritated about this. The bill they got for cleaning up Biketoberfest has come . . . to several hundred thousand dollars' worth of damages and garbage collection and the biggest mess you ever saw.

Some people are getting disenchanted with this. That is one reason that we have worked so hard on cultural things. They serve as a kind of counterbalance for that, and quality-of-life things serve to persuade a different type of person to migrate here to live. It is a continual argument that goes on between the event people and the nonevent people.

Q: The events provide a mass infusion of money into the community, but the cost of police overtime and all that makes it much more problematic, does it not?

A: Yes, so the city says. They are now pointing out that these two-day events with the disaster figures in the $200,000 or $300,000 level are hardly worth doing, as far as the city is concerned. The city gets very little, cannot charge admission, and gets a bill for $230,000, or whatever Biketoberfest cost them.

Q: Other than your newspaper, what would be the best newspapers in Florida?

A: I think it has to be St. Pete [Times] haute concours [highest contest, best in a public competition]. I do not see anybody else . . . in the picture. There are some other people doing pretty good work. Sarasota is doing some good things. Florida Today does some good work. I guess if I had to pick a second paper after St. Pete, probably West Palm Beach [Palm Beach Post]. That is a pretty good newspaper. I do not think the others are outstanding. I think the wonderful Miami Herald of twenty years ago is now just a ghost of itself.

Q: Is the tendency of newspapers, then, toward the Miami Herald, which is owned by a chain, rather than the independent St. Pete Times?

A: You are only going to have a St. Pete Times when you have a management which is really trying to do something. It is hard when you have a chain which is handed over to a CPA to run. It is hard for him. The whole idea of spending money on improving news coverage, spending raw money to add sports pages and add local pages and that kind of thing—just waste, production waste. He is brought up to make widgets square and no rounded corners, so a lot of things that have happened to a lot of the [newspaper] chains are perfectly logical from the business standpoint. You make them all as alike as peas.

Q: Have you ever had any difficulty with unions?

A: I had unions for a considerable period of time. I have had some difficulties with unions. No one has unions without some difficulty. But I would say that our union relations have been peaceful and constructive, largely, even when we had the typographical union, and they were rambunctious. They were always susceptible to the argument that we were in it together. My father, who dealt with them in the early stages, and I, later, always took the attitude that whatever they asked for that we could give them, we would give them without argument, and that they were entitled to a share of what we made, what we were. So that was a little bit disarming for some of these guys who came in with their fangs bared. The only one I was never able to figure out was the Guild [American Newspaper Guild]. They are so aggressive and so abusive. We had an awful time with them. It only lasted thirteen months. Employees voted them out.

Q: Is there anything that we have not discussed or I have not asked that you would like to comment on?

A: We covered a wide field. No, I do not think so. I think it is most interesting that we will hear this kind of narrative from every paper in the state. That will be interesting. I will be interested to know what some of my colleagues say, and I will be interested in other cases to know what excuses they have for what it is they put out.

chapter 5   **Diane McFarlin**

Diane McFarlin is the publisher of the *Sarasota Herald-Tribune* and has held that position since November 1999.

She began her journalism career during high school, when she worked for her hometown paper, the *Lake Wales Daily Highlander*. After graduating with high honors from the University of Florida with a degree in journalism, McFarlin began working for the *Sarasota Herald-Tribune* and became managing editor in 1985. She moved to the *Gainesville Sun* as executive editor in 1987, and three years later returned to the *Sarasota Herald-Tribune* in the position of executive editor. She was also named director of broadcast for the paper's 24-hour news channel, SNN-6.

McFarlin received the Journalism Education Association's national Media Citation for outstanding service to scholastic journalism in 1993 and served two years on the national accrediting council for colleges of journalism and communications. She has taught at a number of institutions, including the American Press Institute and the Poynter Institute. In 1997 she addressed the World Editors' Forum. She has also been a judge for national and state journalism award programs, including the Pulitzer Prize. She has been named an Alumna of Outstanding Achievement and received the Distinguished Alumnus Award from the University of Florida. McFarlin served as president of the Florida Society of Newspaper Editors and will serve as president of the American Society of Newspaper Editors in 2002–03.

McFarlin begins this interview by describing her first experiences in the field of journalism during high school and college. She then talks about her subsequent jobs at the *Sarasota Herald-Tribune* as city editor and managing editor. She discusses the role of gender in the newspaper business and her admiration for Katharine Graham. She explains why she moved from Sarasota to Gainesville to work as the executive editor of the *Gainesville Sun*. McFarlin then describes working under the ownership of the New York Times Company and how that company affects decisions at the *Herald-Tribune*. She explains how the different editions of that paper are produced for the different surrounding communities.

McFarlin compares her job as executive editor of the Gainesville paper with her job as executive editor of the Sarasota paper. She describes the formation of the Sarasota News Network (SNN), the role of newspapers, and competition from other newspapers and other multimedia outlets of news. She discusses her job as publisher of the Sarasota paper, community involvement, and the changes seen in reporting and readership during her tenure. She also briefly presents her views on European newspapers, Nelson Poynter, and *USA Today*.

Diane McFarlin was interviewed by Julian M. Pleasants in Sarasota, Florida, on August 15, 2001.

Q: You are, I believe, a third- or fourth-generation Floridian.

A: Fourth generation on both sides. [It] makes me a very rare bird in Sarasota, because everybody here is from somewhere else.

Q: How did you first get interested in journalism?

A: I had been interested in newspapers and in writing for a long time. We didn't have a newspaper in my high school, but I joined the yearbook staff when I was fifteen. I went down to a little local newspaper. It was called the *Lake Wales Daily Highlander*. It was probably the smallest daily in the state of Florida. It was the first newspaper to go to cold type, to use offset [printing], as its publishing method.

But, anyway, I went down to interview for a summer job. I had not yet turned sixteen. John Marsh was the owner, publisher, and editor, and I went to talk with him . . . and he said, "Come with me," and he took me back into the newsroom. He handed me a press release, and he said, "Rewrite this."

So I sat down at the typewriter, because I knew how to type, and I rewrote this press release and handed it back to him.

He said, "There is a youth commission meeting Monday night at City Hall; do you want to cover it?"

I said, "Sure, I do."

So I did, and then he hired me for that summer. I ended up working there every summer in high school and college.

The summer after my junior year, the summer that I turned seventeen, I was actually left in charge of the paper. . . . [I]t was a very small newspaper, because he had a managing editor [and] one was on vacation, and one had to go off on business. At the time I was in charge, the sports editor got into some trouble. He was charged with molesting Little Leaguers. It was a horrible story, but there I was faced with this and having to deal with it. I got through it—everything went just fine—and that was it for me. I knew what I wanted to do. So I never looked back. It was always journalism. So it was in my blood from the first day that I started working at that paper. It was a great experience because I got to do everything.

Q: That is the key, isn't it? At a small paper, you learn the business from top to bottom.

A: It is the key. You learn every bit of the business. I actually would set headlines. I would go back after we had written our stories. I would go back and actually help set the headlines. I got to take my own pictures and process and print the film. . . . I got to learn to lay out pages—just everything, not just reporting. It was wonderful.

Q: You graduated from the University of Florida with a degree in journalism in 1976. What is your view of the importance of a journalism degree for newspaper work? I have talked to several editors who say it is just as good to major in English and learn on the job.

A: I think that it is just as good for a lot of people. For me, journalism education really means a head start. It positions you to hit the ground running. Generally, journalism graduates have had a lot more practical experience. So when I was in the hiring mode . . . , as I became the city editor and managing editor, I leaned toward J school graduates if it was sort of a general assignment position or governmental beat position, and I wanted somebody who could plug right in, who knew what to do. For positions that are maybe more specialist positions, like a medical writer or a business reporter, I think an education on that track in that realm is possibly better—in fact, I am sure it is—than a journalism degree. To me, the perfect combination is an undergraduate degree in English, political science, social sciences, [or] health services, and then a master's in journalism, so they get that really great educational base and then go on and get more of their career training.

Q: When you finished journalism school, what was your first job?

A: There was a job at the *Sarasota Journal*, which was the sister paper of the *Herald-Tribune*. It was the afternoon paper. They had a position for a reporter/copy editor. Of course, I had done both jobs, so I was hired. After a year, I became assistant news editor, and then the second year I became city editor. So my head start at the *Daily Highlander* really paid off handsomely, because I moved into an editing position fairly quickly. In hindsight I wish that I had spent more time as a reporter because I always wished that I had more experience as a reporter.

Q: What makes a good reporter?

A: You know, a lot of qualities make a good reporter. I think curiosity is a real important quality, the ability to think critically, to have an analytical mind. You have to know what questions to ask. You cannot just take at face value what someone tells you. You have to know what follow-up questions to ask. Obviously, they have to be good writers. You can teach somebody to write, but you can't teach them to be a great writer, so that innate ability is extremely valuable. But I have had a lot of average/mediocre writers who are great reporters. In fact, some of the best stories that have ever been done at this newspaper were done by people who weren't our best writers, but they were persistent, they were courageous, meaning . . . they could be in some really difficult situations, but they didn't give up, and they weren't afraid to ask the tough questions. So there is a force of personality that makes a journalistically great reporter.

Q: I have talked to several people who have had similar experiences, and almost everybody I have talked to says that city editor was the most exciting job that they had.

A: It absolutely is the best job I ever had. I was city editor for five years. I was city editor when the Skyway [bridge] fell [1980]. I mean, my gosh, there I was. You are the maestro; you are in the middle of everything; you are at the center of the action. I think maybe the most frustrating thing about being city editor is you aren't often able to go to the front lines, but you are directing it all—the eye of the storm, if you will. You are kind of in the calm center, but you still have so much to say about what is going on in the newsroom that day. You know, I think that the managing editor's job may be the best job in a newsroom, but it is not nearly as much fun as the city editor's job.

Q: Is that not a pressure-filled job?

A: Yes, it is very much a pressure-filled job. You have to work from your gut, and that can be scary, but I think that is why the best city editors are people who were really great reporters. They develop that instinct.

Q: You were city editor for five years. Then you became managing editor?

A: Not quite. I spent a year . . . as assistant to the editor, but it was really systems editor. I installed the first computer system at this company for both the *Herald-Tribune* and the *Journal*. During that year while I was doing that, the *New York Times* bought the *Herald-Tribune*, and the *Journal* was closed. So once this system was installed, then I moved into assistant managing editor, and then after that, deputy managing editor, then managing editor.

Q: Talk about your time as deputy managing editor and managing editor. What were your major responsibilities in those jobs?

A: As assistant managing editor, my major responsibilities were sort of the advanced sections of the paper—the feature section, the Sunday paper, things like the TV book, and so on. Then when I became deputy managing editor, I resumed being responsible for news. I was very happy about that because I had really missed that when I was over on the feature side. Essentially, you are really running the newsroom day to day. The managing editor technically is running the newsroom, but the managing editor has quite a lot of administrative responsibilities. So as deputy managing editor, you are running news meetings, coordinating special projects, working with the city editor on . . . what is going to be in the paper tomorrow, and then looking a little longer term to the weekend editions and any kind of investigative series.

Q: One question that has come up periodically in the newspaper business is, how has gender influenced your career, either positively or negatively? There is this image, particularly in the 1970s and 1980s, that the newspaper business in Florida was an old boy's network.

A: Definitely. Well, I will tell you, I was blessed with great timing. I was born just at the right time because, literally, it was a detriment to me, I believe, until I became city editor. That is about the time that things really started to change. Then when the New York Times Company bought this paper, things really changed here at the *Herald-Tribune*. As city editor, you know, women have a tendency to be more nurturing, if you will, a little more tuned in to the employees as individuals. I had a little bit different style as city editor. I had the hard news bent, but I was also very cognizant of whether the employees were enjoying themselves and what they wanted in the way of personal development. So I think that tendency . . . was something that I think propelled me in my career.

I really believe that if the New York Times Company had not come in and bought this paper, I probably would not have risen above city editor, but because there was a more progressive company and a more progressive owner coming in, I was getting advanced pretty rapidly during that period of time.

Q: This is off the subject, but while we are on women in the newspaper business, I would like to get your comments on the recently deceased Katharine Graham.

A: Katharine Graham was somebody I admired very much . . . probably predominately for her courage, but also because she demonstrated to the world that a woman could run a large media company and do it very successfully, that she could champion and advance the journalistic mission, while at the same time strengthening the financial condition of that company. The Washington Post Company was floundering when she was put in charge. It is a double whammy, if you will. The decisions she made regarding the Pentagon Papers and Watergate really put that paper on the map journalistically, and then she was also building a great company that somebody like Warren Buffett would consider to be a great investment.

I had the privilege of meeting her several times, and on a personal level, she was so gracious and so interested in other people's careers—not just women, men too—and real unassuming and self-effacing. Of course, you can see that in her book.

Q: What other women have been important to journalism, mainly in the state of Florida?

A: There are a lot of women, I think. I really could just tick off a lot of names of women who are doing great things in this industry, really great things, and whom I admire and enjoy, and I am happy to say some of them are my friends. They are at all levels. You mentioned Lucy Morgan earlier. Lucy is one of the best investigative reporters in the country and has done a lot for Florida's stature in terms of journalism. I have been on three Pulitzer juries, and I have been so struck by the number of women whose bylines have been on the stories that have been finalists for the Pulitzer. . . .

Q: I noticed that three of the four top positions in this newspaper are occupied by women.

A: That is right. In fact, the *American Journalism Review* just wrote about that. I wasn't real thrilled that we were given that distinction, quite frankly, because it makes it appear as if that is some sort of objective here, and it is truly not. It is about hiring the best people, and if they happen to be women, great. But we are the largest paper in the country to have a woman publisher as well as a woman editor and managing editor.

Q: You left Sarasota to go to Gainesville to be executive editor. Why did you decide to take that job?

A: It was an opportunity to have my own newsroom, . . . to be the top editor in a newsroom. It was a newsroom ready to move to the next level and eager and hungry to do that. [There was] a lot of talent in that newsroom. It was small enough that I could really get my arms around it, and I could still be out in the newsroom editing stories and not tied to my desk.

Q: What influence does the *New York Times* have on the newspapers it owns?

A: It is interesting. When I speak in Sarasota, that is one of the first questions I get. It is very clear that the strong perception is that I have a red phone on my desk, and Arthur [Ochs "Punch"] Sulzberger, Jr. [publisher of the *New York Times*] . . . is calling me constantly to tell me what to put on page one and what our editorials should say—and, in fact, there is absolutely none of that. All of the *New York Times* papers are autonomous, but they have a deep and abiding interest in the business side. I have to draw up a budget every year in coordination with my bosses at the New York Times Company, and I am expected to meet that budget, or have a good reason for not doing it.

But I think indirectly, you know, the quality and the standards at the New York Times Company are so high that it gives us a much loftier platform to operate from than we would have otherwise with other companies, perhaps, and with some private owners. I think that family ownership is not necessarily the best way to go because very often there is a much tighter rein when you have an owner on the premises than when you have a large corporation with very strong standards of rich tradition of journalistic integrity, and they don't want anything to violate that, to undermine that. That is a very reassuring posture to be in.

Q: One of the issues that has come up over and over again is that corporate profits are excessive. Carl Hiaasen told me that Knight-Ridder was requiring them to get somewhere between twenty-two to twenty-five percent profits, and to get to that figure, he felt they had fired too many people— too many necessary positions were eliminated—and that the paper had gone down in quality. Have you had that problem here?

A: Well, it is really a matter of year over year. [T]his year, I think we will probably make budget. Now, we have had to eliminate some positions here because of the downturn in the economy—advertising is down—but I have not had to do anything draconian here. The problem is, once you become a publicly held company, then you have another constituency that you have to be responsive to, and it is a terrible dilemma. It really is. Now, what are the options? The options are you do not play that game. You say, "To heck with the bottom line. We are just going to continue to invest in the product and so on," and then investors take their money and go somewhere else. Before you know it, you are in dire financial straits.

Another option is to go private, and then you lose an awful lot of money for investments in the product. [O]ur press was . . . old and decrepit when we were privately owned. So as soon as the New York Times Company came in, we got a brand-new production facility, all new presses. This building was expanded and remodeled. We started opening bureaus so we could do a better job of serving the communities in the outlying parts of our market. So it works both ways, and I think the real key is to maintain the business strength of your operation without undermining the editorial integrity. That is a difficult balancing act, but as a publisher, I have to look both to the short term and the long term. While we have been cutting costs this year, I have also had a strategic planning process underway to look out ahead and say, "What do we want to be and what can we do to get there and how can we serve this community better?"

Q: Do you continue to do investigative journalism here?

A: We do. We have had several substantive investigative projects this year, but we are not traveling as much as we did in years past. I had to take a page of news . . . out of the paper; that is an average of a page per day. Our paper gets smaller in the summertime anyway, because of the seasonal flux. We lose about thirty percent of our circulation. Of course, advertising follows that. So the paper gets smaller in the summer anyway, and then with the page taken out, that has made it even tighter, and readers notice. So one of the first things I am going to do as soon as we get our bearings, and the economy starts to come back, is that page is going back in. That is really important.

Q: How do your editions for Bradenton, Venice, and Charlotte County differ from the Sarasota paper?

A: Well, this is one of the most heavily zoned newspapers [editions specifically designed for each community] in the country. It was one of the first papers to produce zoned editions. This goes back to the 1960s, long before I came here. We now make over extensively, meaning we change stories and positions of stories. Our sections are actually different sizes, because we are customizing those editions for those communities. So, for example, a reader in Charlotte County, where we have an edition, their 1A will look different from the rest of the newspaper; their editorial page will be different; their obituary page will be different; their whole B section, in fact, will be quite a bit different from the rest of the paper. . . .

Sports is made over, business occasionally. So we make over up to one hundred pages every night to customize those editions so that they are actually produced as if they were being published in that community. . . .

Q: Is this an unusual process?

A: It is, but one that more newspapers are adopting, because every readership survey tells you that local news is what the readers want from you first and foremost, and that has got to be your highest priority, and we think that the best way to deliver a local news package is to actually edit that paper with that community's local news in the forefront.

Q: Do you have separate editors for each of these editions?

A: We do. We have editors on-site. Our Charlotte bureau, for example, has a bureau chief, a bureau city editor, and a separate staff down there. We have about eighteen journalists in Charlotte County just for that one edition.

Q: Talk a little bit more about your three years in Gainesville. What was your major achievement as you look back at your time at that paper?

A: I think my major achievement was rebuilding the newsroom. I was able to rejuvenate and expand that newsroom. The *Times* was just wonderful, very supportive, allowed me to add about a dozen positions and add pages to the paper. In terms of coverage, I think the achievement I am proudest of is the coverage we did of the athletic department and what was happening with Coach [Norm] Sloan [UF basketball coach from 1961 to 1966 and 1981 until fired in 1989] and Coach [Galen] Hall [football coach at UF from 1984 until fired in 1989] and some of the shenanigans there. And I was, I think, proudest of our courage, the fact that we were willing to do something highly unpopular, with the knowledge that in the long term it was going to make that program stronger and, of course, higher integrity.

Q: Did you feel undue pressure about sports in Gainesville?

A: Yes, I did. I felt a lot of pressure about sports. I felt even more pressure, perhaps, about growth, that conflict between the staunchly no-growth camp on one side, the extreme pro-growth camp on the other side, and what I thought was the responsible middle ground, which was growth is inevitable, but how can we do it well, and what does Gainesville want to be when it grows up? We are dealing with the very same issue here in Sarasota.

I think newspapers' role in that debate is so critical, and what we have to do is we have to facilitate that debate and inform people to participate in that debate without putting our thumb on the scale too heavily. [O]ur editorial board is a great microcosm because on the board we have the folks who basically wanted to shut the gates—don't let another person in—and the folks who think that for this community to prosper, it has got to encourage growth. What is right for the community is ultimately up to the people who live here, not to this newspaper. But I think the more that we can open the floor to debate and create that forum and weigh-in to a responsible extent, then we are doing the greatest service we can possibly do for this community.

Q: Growth management is a topic that most people know very little about. So it is really up to the newspapers to inform the public.

A: Well, the public, unfortunately, deals with it on a visceral level. You know, we write a lot about growth and the mechanisms of growth, and most people don't want to spend time with that. They only get involved and care when it means there is going to be more traffic on their route to work or that there is going to be an apartment complex going up on the next street. So it is very, very hard to really educate a community when they aren't dealing with it on an intellectual level. That is a real trick for newspapers, how you get the community engaged and how do you get them away from emotionalism and get them to really think of it in terms of quality of life and guiding principles and what do we want this community to be like ten, twenty, thirty, fifty years from now. It is a real challenge.

Q: In 1990 you decided to return to Sarasota as executive editor. Why did you make that decision?

A: It was difficult to make it, but primarily because I already had a lot invested in this community. It was an opportunity to stay in the New York Times Company, but go to a paper twice the size of Gainesville as editor. So it was a great career opportunity, and personally it was attractive.

Q: How was your job as executive editor at the Sarasota paper different from the Gainesville paper?

A: I think the biggest difference was I had to step a little farther away from the hands-on journalism, so that was a tough adjustment. That was my first, sort of, executive position, if you will, because in Gainesville I was able to manage the executive part of it without quite as much time spent in meetings and with reports. This is just a much more complex operation. We now have six editions. The competitive pressures are much greater here. The market is much more complex and diverse. I came back in 1990, and we redesigned the newspaper very soon after I got back. Of course, I have a penchant for redesigns, but we did that. Then we started SNN [Sarasota News Network], our twenty-four-hour cable channel.

Q: Apparently, the buzzword now in journalism is convergence. I noticed earlier you have been interested in technology, because you set up the first computer system. How did this interest lead to the development of SNN?

A: The first computer system, that was kind of interesting. That was not out of interest. That was sort of out of challenge, because I had never had any exposure to computers and knew nothing about them. I got my pilot's license for the same reason. It was something that I didn't know anything about. Of course, it turned out giving me immense power because I was the only one in the building who knew anything about this system, and everybody, including the publisher, was coming to me to ask, "What do you do here?" and "How do you do this?" [Laughter.] So, really, in any organization now, the people who have the power are the ones who know how to operate the computer system.

But . . . [with] SNN, what happened [was] . . . Walter Matson [president of the New York Times Company] . . . suggested that we visit with one of the New York Times' affiliate stations in Wilkes-Barre, Pennsylvania. So we flew up there in January and . . . we talked about TV and newspapers and how they could get along and what they could do for each other. It was another epiphany. It was an eye-opening experience to really see that . . . we serve the news consumer in very different ways, and they are very complementary.

So we were able to work ourselves through that prejudice — and it was deep-seated — and we approached Channel 40 [ABC affiliate in Sarasota]. They had enlightened management, if you will, and so we forged a partnership long before anybody else was doing this. Again, it was Walter Matson's brainstorm — it was not ours — and we shared news with them. We would give them stories, and they would read the first draft or two of the story and then say, "For more information on this story, see tomorrow's

Herald-Tribune." We got the exposure and the promotion, and more readers were coming to the *Herald-Tribune*, and they got more content, so it really was a win/win. Well, new management came in at Channel 40 . . . and . . . that partnership dissolved, fell apart [1993].

We thought . . . this TV thing makes a lot of sense because it really is expanding our reach. We are extending into markets; we are reaching people, predominately young people, poorer people, who are not reading newspapers to the extent they did years ago. So we wanted to do more. About that time, a new executive for Comcast Cable [one of the country's largest providers of cable, Internet, and digital service] comes in. We start up conversations with him, and before you know it, we are talking about doing a twenty-four-hour cable news channel patterned after CNN Headline News. This is . . . a situation of the planets being aligned, because the president of the New York Times Company at that time wanted to do some experimentation in the electronic realm. There was money there to be had, and we put together a proposal, and it was approved.

We invested $2,500,000 into digital equipment, and six months after we got the approval, we launched the first all-digital TV operation in the country, the first twenty-four-hour cable news channel in Florida, and the first cable channel to be produced out of a print newsroom—in other words a newspaper producing this channel out of their newsroom. What we did here is, we put SNN in our newsroom. I was in charge; the advertising director was in charge of the advertising; and we did it as an inherent part of our operation. That was truly a converged newsroom, although I have a little bit of a problem with the word convergence because I think it is really about multimedia. Convergence will come when the TV set and the PC converge. But our newsroom was, in fact, a blended newsroom.

We determined very early on that . . . what we want[ed] to do is ask print reporters to share information with the broadcast journalists, to write voice-overs for anchors, and to sometimes even do reporting in front of the camera, but generally when they do that, they are being interviewed, they are being asked about the story.

Q: This concept points out what Dan Rather [CBS news anchor] was talking about the other night when he said that you can't find out enough information about stem cells on television; you have to read the newspapers.

A: That was such a progressive statement because what he was saying was, "You know, we can work together, and only together can we fully serve you, the reader, the viewer. You aren't going to get it all from me, and you may not be satisfied with just the newspaper." You hear about it first from TV, more than likely. Your notification comes from television. If you are busy, if you are trying to get the children off to school and you are over-whelmed—you don't have time to sit down and read the newspaper thor-oughly—you can watch TV, and you can hear what is going on. You can go, "Gosh, they are talking about growth east of I-75. That is a subject I really want more information about, so I'm going to go to my newspaper, and I'm going to read about that in more detail."

Then, of course, you [have] the web site. When we launched our web site, then we had a three-way convergence, and that introduced a lot of other possibilities. The example that I love to use is the local police S.W.A.T. team broke into a man's house. They thought he was suicidal. He had a gun; he raised the gun; they thought he was going to kill them; they shot the man to death; and a task force was sent in to determine what happened. When that report was published, we had the story in the paper that really told you everything you needed to know about that story. But on SNN, the reporter walked the viewers through the house, showed them the bullet holes, gave them the sort of dramatic side of the story, and then we sent everybody to the web site to read the full task force report, with pictures and everything. It is a classic example of why multimedia makes so much sense for news organizations and why multimedia really is the key to our future, because if we limit ourselves to one means of distribut-ing information, of telling the story, then we run the risk of some people saying, "Sorry, I can get it just by going here."

Q: My figures are that you reach 160,000 households with SNN. Is that about right?

A: A little low, now. I think it is more like 175,000.

Q: Has that improved circulation numbers for the newspaper?

A: We think so, because our research indicates that. We just did a thorough . . . readership survey, [and] about twenty-five percent of the people sur-veyed said that they went to SNN because of something they read in the newspaper, and a similar number said they went to the newspaper be-cause of something they heard on SNN. The figures for newscoast.com, our web site, were quite a bit lower, but there was still that crossover. To me, that demonstrates that it has improved our readership.

Q: Why is circulation always higher on Sunday?

A: Time. I think people are so time-stressed now, and that has affected news-paper readership more than any one factor . . . my opinion is that we are multitasking, all of us, all the time, and something has to give. Increasingly, the newspaper during the week is what is being sacrificed. But on Sunday they have time to spend with the newspaper and absorb it.

Q: What is the future of the physical newspaper as we now know it? Is it going to disappear?

A: It is not going to disappear as long as I am in the newspaper business. But I do believe that within the next five years that people will be able to get their newspaper by another means, and that might be a CD; it might be electronic ink; it might be some sort of download system with a special printer. I think what will happen . . . is that people will be publishing their own newspaper. But I really believe that for a long time people are going to want something that they can carry around, something that is packaged for them. It is hard to access information in an orderly way on the web site. What you can do is you can drill down so effectively, so if you have a deep interest in a particular subject, then nothing beats the Internet—as long as you know the sources you are using and how reliable they are.

Q: In effect, you package the information for them.

A: Exactly, yes. We have made judgments for them. I love the serendipity of newspapers. I love to just open a newspaper. I am presented with options, and I can get through those options much more quickly than I can create them for myself on the web. The thing about a newspaper is you can just pick it up, and you can start leafing through, and you can pick and choose what you want to read, and you can take it with you and read it wherever you want to read it. [W]hen it comes to in-depth information and the most comprehensive source of local news, newspapers are going to remain pre-eminent for many years.

Q: What is your greatest competition? Is it television, or is it the *Tampa Tribune* or the *St. Pete Times*?

A: Time. I really believe it is time, but when you talk about other media organizations, at this point, it is other newspapers, and it depends on the geographic area. We have no direct competitor in Sarasota, and for the three-county area, we are the largest newspaper. But if you talk about Bradenton, it is the *Bradenton Herald*; in Port Charlotte, it is the *Charlotte Sun Herald*. Tampa and St. Pete come in to a very minimal extent. . . . TV: SNN faces competition from the other TV stations, but not significant competition because our niche is different. We are all about convenience and all about getting news when you want it, not having to make an appointment at 6:00 P.M. to get the news.

Q: You were named publisher in 1999, I believe. How did you happen to get that job, and who made the decision?

A: I went kicking and screaming. I had been approached twice before about going into a publisher training program, and I rejected it. This was just really a convergence of several different things. . . . I thought, "Well, it is either me or somebody else, and I would rather it be me to lead this newspaper because I love this community; I have a lot invested in this newspaper; this has really been my family; and I want to stay with the New York Times Company, ideally." So I really lost a lot of sleep over the decision because I didn't think there was life after a newsroom. I just didn't think that I would be as rewarded as I had been in the newsroom, but I finally came to the conclusion that I would still be advancing great journalism. I would be doing it from a different vantage point and at a different level, and . . . there would be an opportunity to interact with the community in a way that I had not been able to do as a detached, impartial editor, and that had a lot of appeal for me. I was ready to sort of spread my wings and learn more about the business holistically.

Q: Is publisher your most challenging job?

A: Yes, by all means it is the most challenging job.

Q: Why?

A: More constituencies to be aware of and concerned about. Learning parts of the business that I really had very little knowledge and understanding of before, [the] business side predominately, but also the production side. I was sort of one of those arrogant editors who said, "Here, here are the pages; now you worry about how it gets produced into a newspaper." I am touched more by the politics in the issues. As an editor, you can simply say, "Here are the facts; you deal with the truth, or you deal with the interpretation of the truth and what you think is good or bad about this."

Q: What overall goals did you have when you took over?

A: I had several goals. One was a personal goal. I wanted to prove that I had business mettle as well as journalistic mettle. I wanted to prove that good journalism makes good business. I wanted to demonstrate to the community that we were not a monolithic, detached organization but that we were a very caring, concerned organization that had the best interests of the community at heart and that we wanted to be an integral part of the community, that we were open, that we wanted to hear from the public.

Right before I became publisher, I started something in the newsroom called the Reader Advocate Program, where we have somebody at a phone every day to hear from readers. We invite them to call us, tell us if we got something wrong, what we are missing—and it has turned into just a wonderful exercise from both the standpoint of being more open to our readers but also understanding them better and understanding ourselves better. When people challenge you about everything, whether it is the wet paper in their yard or your editorial or how you play the Israeli-Palestinian story that day, you really start to understand yourself better. I wanted to extend that attitude throughout the company and put a greater emphasis on [it]. It is called customer service, but it is really good journalism, too, and it is good business.

One of the first things I did was for the *Herald-Tribune* to start a fund called Season of Sharing. It is targeted toward homeless kids. We have a serious problem here in all three counties [with] homeless families. It is an issue that, really, the root causes [of] are very deep. It is the fact that our income level for service workers is so low here, and we don't have enough affordable housing. But the purpose of this fund is while we deal with these deeper and broader issues, we need emergency money, and we need money that the agencies don't have to justify spending, that they don't have to go through all the bureaucracy and the paperwork. They just have this money, and a family needs this month's rent, or they need an electrical deposit. Then Resurrection House can give it to them.

Q: So, obviously, part of your responsibility as publisher is to work with a lot of community groups.

A: I think that the publisher's responsibility to do that is . . . because there is a lot of symbolism attached to the title. So often I am asked to do things, and they could care less [about] Diane McFarlin, but they want the publisher of the *Herald-Tribune*. I try not to turn down meaningful requests, whether it is to sponsor a table or give a speech or if you are on a panel or just show up. I try to do that.

Q: What new practices have you put in place since you have been in your current position?

A: I think what I feel best about is that I have really tried to facilitate a culture change here, one that is not autocratic, that is not so top-down, but giving the folks on the front lines a greater sense that they have some say, in terms of how we operate and how we deal with readers, with viewers, with advertisers, with subscribers, business customers. I would love to think that everybody who comes to work here looks forward to it, that they feel like they are doing something important for the community and for the industry and that they are appreciated—their efforts are appreciated—but if they are not performing up to par, they should move on, because this organization really won't support that.

In fact, [at] the Readership Institute at Northwestern, we are one of the one hundred newspapers they are studying for that readership initiative, and one of the projects revolved around . . . [workplace] culture. One of the conclusions that they have reached is that a reason for the newspaper industry's decline, if you will, or the loss of readership, is that our organizations operate very much like the military and hospitals, that we are not as responsive as we need to be to our communities, that we are very top-down organizations, and we have rules, lots of rules, and most of them do not make sense anymore, and that the most successful companies in this day and age are ones that have constructive cultures. Out of those one hundred newspapers, I believe it was thirteen that had constructive cultures. [W]e were one of the thirteen constructive cultures, and I am really proud of that.

Q: What are the most important functions of a newspaper?

A: The most important function of the newspaper is the journalistic function, and that is to inform the community in a fair and balanced way, to be as thorough and complete as you possibly can—in other words, [to practice] ethical journalism with the highest standards. The other is to support that mission through a profitable business operation, and the best way to do that is to create an effective marketplace for local business, so that you kind of complete that circle. You create the market by providing credible journalism, because credible journalism sells better than anything in the media world. So you create that marketplace, and then advertisers are willing to pay good money to reach those readers, and that money supports that journalism, so you have got that wonderful circle going.

I think a third role of a newspaper is to set the example for corporate citizenship. I think that newspapers . . . are generally one of the oldest organizations in any community. We are certainly one of the most visible organizations in any community, so we are . . . well positioned to set that example and to sort of set a standard, too, to say to a community, "This is what local businesses and even nonprofit organizations ought to be doing for this community." I hate this term of *setting* the agenda. I don't think this is what we do. I think we support the agenda, and we help the community set the agenda by giving them the information they need, by identifying critical issues.

Q: Do you think readers trust newspapers and believe that they are accurate?

A: No. I think that in Sarasota we probably have a higher measure of trust, not because we are so wonderful, but because of our market. The folks who live in Sarasota predominately are retirees. They grew up on newspapers, and they grew up trusting newspapers, so there is a higher measure of trust here than in most communities, but through nothing that we have done. . . .

I chaired the ASNE [American Society of Newspaper Editors] Ethics Committee three years ago, when ASNE started the National Credibility Project, [and] the first thing we did was hire Chris Irben to do research. It was exhaustive research. It was a good sample of the American public, and what we discovered is that there was not a high level of trust of American newspapers. A shocking number of people, just to give you an example, thought that advertisers influenced what we publish. If they only knew the extent to which most credible newspapers go to prevent that from happening.

What really was painful to me was the very year that research came out was the year that we did two series in this community that cost us hundreds of thousands of dollars, literally five hundred thousand dollars, because it dealt with two very large local businesses, and the series exposed unethical business practices. One CEO went to federal prison because of this series that we did. Both large companies pulled all their advertising, and they were big clients. I was editor at the time; Lynn Matthews was publisher; and he never once said anything to me except, "I know you are certain that this is right."

I said, "I am."

The CEO threatened to sue us . . . but never once did he [Matthews] say anything to me about the loss of advertising. I think most good newspapers function that way, and it is painful to think that the American public doesn't buy it.

Q: How has your readership changed since the time you first came to the Sarasota paper?

A: It is a lot younger and a lot more diverse, and that has been a real challenge for us because when I first came to Sarasota, the *Herald-Tribune* had the highest penetration rate in the country on Sunday. . . . Amazing reach, and that was because it was one of the oldest communities and also one of the most well-to-do communities. So we had older people, lots of time, lots of money, highly educated, widely traveled, just generally very sophisticated people, and they were newspaper readers. Then as time has gone by—in fact, the 1990 census said the fastest-growing segment of our population was the young adult segment. I mean, in terms of community, it is a wonderful thing because the more diversity, the better. In terms of newspaper readership, it has undermined our readership, and our penetration now is in the mid-fifties.

Q: How have reporters changed during that time?

A: Interesting. Definitely more diverse culturally than before. When I came here, it was a lot of white guys in the newsroom. In fact, I was part of the diversity movement—you know, bringing in a woman and then promoting her to city editor was a bit of a shock to the system. So that is probably the biggest difference. I do not know that there is much difference in terms of tenure or longevity, experience level.

Q: How have the letters to the editor changed over the years?

A: This is one of the most rewarding parts of this newspaper, this letters page. The letters are so rich, and the people here are great writers. Unfortunately, even though we devote more space to letters than any other newspaper our size, I would guess, we still can only publish about a third of the letters that we get.

Q: Who chooses your columnists? How do you determine which ones you are going to run and on what days?

A: The editorial page staff does that, and they try to get a nice mix every day of conservative, liberal, middle of the road, men, women, black, Hispanic. We really have a nice mix.

Q: What influence do you have on editorial decisions?

A: Theoretically, I have the final say. In practice, I don't read every editorial before it goes in the paper. There are certain subjects that the editorial page editor knows to come in and discuss with me, and I participate in editorial board meetings. So it is peripheral, but he and I meet on a weekly basis . . . to kind of talk about what is in the news, what is going on out there, and what are we likely to be commenting on in the next week or so and what is our position.

Q: What impact do you think your editorials have on elections?

A: I think the impact is huge. I think it is diminishing, because as this new generation comes up in the world and takes positions of leadership, I do not think that newspapers have quite as much sway as they used to—although it is said in this community that you have to get the *Herald-Tribune*'s endorsement to win an election. But there are exceptions to that, most definitely. Now, naturally, we keep track, we keep score. Our [success] rate, if you will, is generally in the eighties and nineties. Now part of that is because we are listening to the community, and we have a good feel for the community's position already. . . . But there have been times when we have sort of gone against the grain, and we have had good reasons, and that candidate has ended up prevailing. Those are the ones we feel best about.

Q: Is your opinion more important for local races? Obviously, most people will know about [Albert W.] Gore and [George W.] Bush, but they may not know much about a local candidate for judge.

A: The closer it gets to the local level and the more important the office, the more time we will spend researching that candidate and actually interviewing them.

Q: Where would you put yourself on the political spectrum?

A: Definitely more toward the liberal end. I have to confess that whenever I am speaking, because that is always the lament, you know: "You are so liberal." The truth of the matter is we are not nearly as liberal as people make us out to be. In fact, really, I think we are more middle-of-the-road.

Q: People assume that since you are a *New York Times* paper, you would be more liberal.

A: Exactly. Well, they are upset now because they think we are being overly critical of Bush, but what they have forgotten is that we were critical of Clinton when he was in office.

Q: You mentioned that you had served three times on the Pulitzer committee. How do you judge the entries best qualified for that award?

A: That is a tough question, and it comes back to that instinct thing: you know it when you see it. I think the biggest dilemma that we have on these juries . . . is you tend to be swayed by the amount of effort that went into something. That, of course, is generally represented by the length, by the amount of travel that went into it, by the difficulty of the assignment. . . . That, of course, is one consideration, but another is, did this take a unique ability of some sort, or did this demonstrate unusual persistence? Was this idea an amazing idea, or did this break ground that has never been broken before? So there are all sorts of considerations.

Q: How do you get young people to read instead of watching MTV?

A: I don't know. That answer seemed so much more obvious to me several years ago, but increasingly I'm becoming convinced that [with] this generation, it is inbred, if you will. They're geared to electronics; they are used to an awful lot of stimulation; and I think that the younger generation coming up now will read and write, but it will be on computers. What that portends for newspapers, I'm not sure. But I think that as with anything connected to the media, it is all about relevance. It is all about what is relevant to their lives and what they are interested in and what helps them accomplish whatever it is they want to accomplish, whether it is to get better at a video game or to make better grades or to get a good job or to make conversation. You have to really understand what it is they are going for.

Q: I wanted to get your sense of how different European papers are from American papers.

A: You have to kind of divide those into two classes. There are the European papers of Western Europe and the democratized part of Europe, which in many ways are more advanced than American newspapers—not so much in the free-press realm of things, because nobody is better at that than we are—but design, presentation. Newspaper designers look to newspapers in Spain, for example, for ideas and examples, not to American newspapers. So they are more progressive in many ways.

When I went to Prague and Bucharest, that was an incredible experience for me because they are complete babes in the woods about a free press and, in fact, don't really have one. But, you know, it is a semblance of one, and what they are trying to do is figure out how they can press for more freedom and how they can convince their public that freedom is a good thing. They will have to wait, I think, for a couple of generations to pass, because the older Eastern Europeans really want to be told what to do. They don't know what freedom of choice is like; they didn't grow up with it, and they are actually afraid of it, and they aren't willing to fight for it.

Q: What impact did Nelson Poynter [former publisher of the St. Petersburg Times] have on newspapers in Florida.

A: I don't know that there is anybody in Florida journalism who made as significant a mark on the importance of high-quality journalism as Nelson Poynter. I think Nelson Poynter was the man who demonstrated to probably the most memorable extent that great journalism makes a great business. Of course, out of that grew the Poynter Institute and the means to create this wonderful training institution that is now in support of journalism worldwide. They bring journalists in from Norway and Russia and South Africa. They send instructors to those places. So Nelson Poynter's attitude about quality journalism really started all that. His standards were immensely high, and he structured his organization to support those high standards.

[The *St. Petersburg Times*] . . . was a training ground for a lot of people who went on and led other organizations, the *Washington Post* and many others. Rick Bragg, of course, spent time there. So, yes, they have historically paid people well, trained people well, supported people in the highest level of news gathering and editing and photography and design. They really set a standard that is world class.

Q: What is your view of USA *Today*?

A: I don't think USA *Today* deserves a lot of the condescension it has gotten over the years. I think it was frightening in the beginning because it represented change, and change is always frightening to human beings, but especially human beings in the newspaper business. We didn't want anything to change because we were having a good ride there. But they certainly demonstrated that the public was ready for a little assistance, if you will, through visuals and shorter stories and accessing information. It is interesting to me that they have now sort of come full circle themselves, and they are now going back to the long story form for many of their key stories on any given day. . . . They are doing longer pieces inside their A section. So we have sort of met somewhere in the middle. But it is also about niche, and those of us in the community journalism business should have never scoffed at USA *Today*, because USA *Today* was going for a whole different audience. They were going for the traveler.

We were able to get some pointers from them in terms of use of color. They really did a great job at . . . making newspapers more compelling visually and making them easier to navigate. USA *Today* laid a lot of groundwork, but we never needed fear that we were going to have to follow their lead, because we are doing something very different.

Q: What was your reaction in 1999 to receiving the University of Florida's Distinguished Alumnus Award?

A: Surprise.

Q: Quite an honor at a very young age.

A: I will tell you something. We all have certain events in our life that we would cite as being among the most memorable, and that was one of mine. The thing that I think touched me the most about that was when they introduced me and gave me the award—and the College of Journalism, they were on their feet—and then Terry Hynes [dean, College of Journalism, UF] said, "Would you like to shake their hands with me?" So then I got to stand there and shake every one of those graduates' hands. I thought, "This is pretty cool because this makes me a role model, and that is kind of nice." Again, it is a circular thing. I was thinking about when I was out in that audience and the aspirations I had.

chapter 6   **Jesse Earle Bowden**

Jesse Earle Bowden, a small-town boy from Altha, Florida, parlayed his career as editor of the *Pensacola News Journal* into a wide-ranging life as an artist, writer, and civic leader. Since 1965 Bowden has supplemented the editorial page with his cartoons and caricatures. His artwork also illustrates the nine books he has written, including a novel, *Look and Tremble: A Novel of West Florida*; a memoir, *Always the Rivers Flow*; a textbook for high-school journalism teachers; and a number of books about Pensacola history. As an editor and community leader, Bowden played a pivotal role in the establishment of the University of West Florida, the Pensacola Historical Society, and Gulf Islands National Seashore. He has won scores of awards for his writing, art, and contributions to the community.

In this interview Bowden talks about his early interest in journalism and his progression through the ranks of newspaper jobs. He reflects at length on the lessons learned during his career by blending cartooning and writing. He also shares his perspective on being bought out by Gannett Newspaper Corporation and on how *USA Today* and the decline of the independently owned newspaper depict broad trends in the newspaper profession. He speaks plainly on the challenges and goals he faced upon becoming editor in Pensacola, commenting specifically on his editorial stances on the civil rights initiatives of the 1950s and 1960s. He also muses on how both reporters and newspaper audiences have evolved over his long career. Bowden concludes his interview by discussing his involvement as a civic leader and how that is important both philosophically and personally to him.

Julian Pleasants interviewed Jesse Earle Bowden on May 20, 2000, in Pensacola, Florida.

Q: Talk a little bit about the early interest you had in journalism and newspapers. When did you first realize you wanted to be in the newspaper business?

A: When I was a youngster, twelve, thirteen, fourteen years old, I began to try to write stories in my notebooks. My family did not really have any background toward writing journalism, although my mother was encouraging. She read a lot of gothic novels, and she always wanted to write, she said. I was imbued with a lot of imagination, taken from movies and stories I read, and I began to try to write. I also wanted to be an artist at the same time. So I had all these interests of wanting to write and illustrate all through my childhood.

Then, when I reached early high school, we developed a school newspaper, the first one in the history of Altha High School. It was a little mimeographed sheet that I created. I wrote it on my old upright Underwood typewriter that my dad had. I began to work for the county weekly in Blountstown; I would see my stories in print. I just slowly went into that, wanting to write, enjoyed writing. Really, my ambition was to write books, even at that early age, but I found the smell of the ink on the newsprint at an early age and was able to be the editor of a small weekly newspaper called *Altha Times* in the late 1940s. I was seventeen years old.

So I went from there. I began to be a correspondent for the *Florida Times-Union* in Jacksonville. He [the sports editor] paid me fifty dollars a month to phone in or mail in the sports events in the Panhandle. I did the same thing for the *Panama City News Herald* at that time. So I had a little business going by the time I started to go off to college that really whetted my interest in writing. I enrolled in Tallahassee at the campus of the University of Florida at Florida State College for Women, at that time [1947]. After the war, they sent five hundred male students to Tallahassee because of the overflow in Gainesville, [and] I decided to study art and journalism.

I wanted to write, so I drifted over into journalism, made that my major, became sports editor of the *Florida Flambeau*, the student newspaper. I found out that I could draw my own cartoons and write, too, so I began to draw a sports cartoon and write a column in the *Flambeau*. I have been doing that sort of thing throughout my career.

Q: Let me ask about the journalism program. What did they emphasize? What kind of training did you get at FSU?

A: It was a small department, and one of my favorite professors was a gentleman named Earl Vance. He . . . was a wonderful teacher; he encouraged us to get a liberal arts education, which is a noble argument, the technical versus the liberal arts. He said, "Get yourself a good education. Study history and economics and language, and let the technical aspect of journalism fall into its place." So I took that as a guide in those early years. . . . It taught me that, really, I needed a strong education. It is a philosophy I have used throughout my career. I teach writing at the University of West Florida, and I tell these [students] in communication arts now, "Get yourself a good, strong liberal arts education. Take the writing courses; learn to write, but all the other technical aspects of journalism can be learned on the job, because on-the-job training is really what you need."

Q: Is it better to learn on the job?

A: I think it probably is, because [of] what I have found in journalism in my experience at Florida State. We had a course in the history of journalism, which was okay, but it was a textbook course. We had courses in headline writing and copyediting, which is kind of a routine thing you learn on the job, because each newspaper is different. I could have spent more time in other areas of political science, learning American government, economics, maybe some advanced English courses to strengthen myself in the language, where I was learning little technical things.

You have to know how to use the language, how to write a good, sharp, clear story. That is the most important thing that you can learn. But you really ought to have history, economics, language, because, as a newspaper person, you are going to have to deal with everything, from the high-and-mighty and the celebrity to the technical, the scientist, the police beat, the courthouse, and city hall. If you do not know the framework of government, if you do not know how American business operates, if you do not know how education works, then you are going to be lost. So it begins with that liberal arts base.

Q: How about the *Flambeau*? What was it like during this period of time? Was it controlled to a large degree by the administration?

A: They operated semi-independent of the administration, up to a point, because at that particular time, we did not have any really controversial issues that had caused the student rebellion [in the 1960s]. I will share with you an experience we had in regard to that. Earl Dobert . . . was the editor, and he was an aggressive young idealist. He ran into difficulty with President Doak Campbell over an issue that would sound awfully simple today. One of our associate editors discovered that, in the late 1940s, some faculty [members were] teaching black children on Saturday mornings in the black area of Tallahassee, French Town; we thought it made a good story. These people were volunteering their time to help these black children. So we ran a story on page one, kind of a feature story of people doing good service.

The Florida legislature was in session, and Doak Campbell, being a university president who, like all university presidents, was sensitive to what the legislature was saying in those days, called Dobert in, and he told him, "You are going to have to step down as editor of the *Flambeau*, or I am going to have you kicked out of school." Dobert, being one who wanted to finish his degree, resigned, and I became the editor that last semester before I graduated.

Q: What was the issue? Why was he upset?

A: The issue was the black issue, because they did not want the radical faculty out in the early days of the civil rights movement. . . . [T]he Florida legislature at that time was controlled by what we call "the Pork Chop Gang," a term created by Jim Clendinen, the editor of the *Tampa Tribune*. He called them the Pork Chop Gang, and that comes from the fact that they were mostly North Florida rural legislators, before the days of reapportionment, who really controlled the legislature. In those days, [the more urban] South Florida did not have much clout in the legislature. So all across the tier of North Florida, the rural [lawmakers], who were avowed segregationists, [were] in control. So you can imagine the attitude of Campbell—and he probably was overreacting to that—but you can imagine, you got your faculty out teaching black children and, you know, [funding might be in jeopardy].

Q: When you started out with the *Altha Times*, what kind of journalistic activity were you involved in? Were you doing stories, reporting?

A: I was writing all kinds of stories for the paper, whatever came in. Sometimes there were even social items, death notices, a little police and sheriff's department, just anything that came. Mostly, when I worked on the weekly, I learned how to set type by hand. . . .

Now the other paper I worked on was called the *County Record*, in Blountstown. . . . So when I was a student at Florida State, in the summers I would work for him [Wallace Finley, editor]. I would do everything, clean the rollers on the press, try to learn to use the Linotype machine— he had a Linotype—and then I would write stories. I would even go down to the grocery store and pick up their ads and bring them back. There was a lot of fun and excitement in that, so that helped whet my interest in it. The world of the weekly newspaper, as you know, has changed . . . but in those days you had to put it together mechanically by hand. You could see the whole paper come together. So I got experience on how to write headlines, how to compose type, and how to make things fit.

Q: Did you ever have any formal training as a cartoonist?

A: No. The only training I had was two or three courses at Florida State. One was design, and one was oil painting. . . . I wanted to cartoon. I wanted to illustrate. That is when I just started doing it myself. I studied all the cartoonists. So I was just searching when I started doing these sports cartoons, and then, actually here [*Pensacola News Journal*], I drifted into editorial cartoons.

Q: Which editorial cartoonists do you admire today?

A: There are several. [The late] Jeff MacNelly [was] great. . . . [One of] my great heroes of all time [was] Herb Block [he signed his cartoons as "Herblock"] . . . at the *Washington Post*. Bill Mauldin was really my idol. I collected all of his books. I have read everything he has ever written, and his great cartoons. Cartoonists today are better than they ever were.

Q: What makes a good editorial cartoonist?

A: It is the irony, the satire, the fact that you can crystallize an idea about an issue into comical form that would cause the reader to react, chuckle, laugh, say, "Oh yeah." It can be a vicious art. Caricature, historically, has always been a terribl[y] powerful weapon, even in the early centuries in France and England. [Many] caricatur[ists] . . . went to jail because they lampooned the king. The editorial [cartoon] is simply a pictorial thirty-second thought that appears on the editorial page that does visually what a written editorial does. I was an editor who believed in local news and local issues, and most of my cartoons through the years have dealt with Pensacola and regional topics. Very local.

Q: But the cartoon has to be recognizable to the reading public, does it not?

A: Right. Occasionally, I do national [topics], but I always thought that cartoons could be powerful in trying to persuade people. It worked, I think, in such issues that I had through the years, as when we were trying to create Gulf Islands National Seashore. I did maybe one hundred cartoons ripping the people who opposed it and trying to put across the idea. So a cartoon has to have punch, irony, satire, humor, ridicule.

Q: Would you use your cartoon to illustrate an editorial you had written?

A: Yes. It [is] always more effective to have the visual, the graphic, [published with the] editorial that you write. Now we do not always do that anymore. . . . Editorial cartoonists today really kind of stand alone. Most of them are kind of independent of the editorial page.

Q: Do you know of anybody else in journalism who writes editorials and also illustrates them?

A: No, and the book I wrote [Drawing from an Editor's Life] has this in it. A gentleman by the name of Judd Hurd is editor and publisher of a national magazine called Cartoonist Profiles. [H]e called me and says, "I understand you do your own editorial cartoons."

I said, "Right."

He said, "I have looked around, and I have never heard of that before; would you write me an article?"

And I did. It was [entitled] "An Editor as His Own Cartoonist," and I am the only one he ever heard of who did that. It is unusual, but cartooning was really kind of my sideline activity as an editor of a newspaper. I did it because I enjoyed it. I thought it was helpful, but I was primarily an editor.

Q: I have talked to several editorial cartoonists, and it is interesting how they work. Some of them, like MacNelly, for example, got an idea and then spent a large portion of time trying to draw what he wanted to say. Is that how you work?

A: Yes. You [strive for] an idea; you use metaphors. . . . Many of these younger ones who I see just do what we call a "gag cartoon." It is funny, dealing with the Internet or dealing with [topical subjects]. It is not really issue-oriented. Sometimes, you do just a really make-fun thing of local people . . . , and you are really making fun of them, but you are trying to make a point. It is strange. These guys who I have ridiculed and lampooned through the years all want copies of them to hang on their wall. So, yes, that is what you do. That has really been a very pleasing part of my career, drawing.

The only vehicle I could get into was newspaper work. I love the daily business of a newspaper. No two days are alike. Everything is different. You start over every day. It is the only industry where you create a product every day, and it is always different.

Q: A lot of people who are editors and publishers started in sports. Why do you think that is?

A: I could not think of a better place for a young man to begin, because what you deal with in sports is a human drama. It is almost like you are describing a stage play. Sport is competition. . . . It has all the elements of a good story, winning and losing. It gives you an opportunity to write freely because sportswriters, even though many of them [sportswriters] use too many adjectives and overwrite, it is a great place to start. And I recommend it.

The only problem is that sports, to me, was such a limited field. It is a world in itself, and when you have other interests, pretty soon you say, "Well, I have to get out of this." Now a lot of people never lose it, and they want to stay and make a career of it. The great Red Smith, when you read his columns, they were universal. They had a theme to them. He was not just covering the Yankees and the Dodgers. He was writing about the human condition more than anything else. So they were writers more than they were sportswriters. I reached a point where I was interested in other things. I was interested in editorial writing, and I was sort of interested in political science. That is when I backed out of sports, about 1958, and I went on the afternoon *Pensacola News* [as] news editor.

Q: Let me get a definition of your job as a news editor. Exactly what did you do?

A: I worked the wires [wire services Associated Press and United Press International]; I laid out the front page; I laid out all the pages of the entire newspaper. . . . That was a tremendous challenge and quite a contrast to sports; you deal with hard news and you ha[ve] to be fast with it. I was not writing as much, although we had reporters at the courthouse or the police station; they would phone in stories or phone in facts on deadline, and I would take them and write the story.

I found myself suddenly being able to tighten up these stories. Unlike sports, where you had the liberty to flow, you had to write it tight. That was a good school for me, to go from sports, where you kind of have a wild, loose, featured approach to things, more so than hard news, where you have to tighten it up and get it on the page.

Q: Would you get a lot of late-breaking night news for the afternoon paper?

A: Right. Afternoon experience is, to me, better than the morning experience, because what you have to do—the morning paper has come out, and it has all the news in it—you have to come back by ten or eleven o'clock in the morning, and you have to get a fresh angle to everything. Most news would be considered old. You have to go through the morning paper and look at this lead on the county commission and [find] an angle that this morning's paper did not cover. . . . Otherwise, you are repeating what was in the morning paper.

Q: Plus, there had to be some new information. If there were a fire, you might now have the names of the victims, which you did not have before.

A: Right, and it is evolving. Fortunately, you get breaking news early in the morning, crime or fire, and then you run with that as your lead story, because that is what you have. In those days, we had pretty large street sales. This is also passé. Street sales were important to our afternoon paper because you would bring that paper out around noon, when people were going to lunch, and [if] you have a big headline on a breaking story, people are going to buy it. That has all changed.

Q: What was the circulation of the Pensacola papers around 1964?

A: The *Journal*, the morning paper, was about sixty-five thousand daily, eighty thousand on Sunday [*News Journal*]. The afternoon paper [*News*] was thirty to forty thousand. Now at an earlier period, back in the 1950s, the morning paper and the evening paper had about the same amount of circulation. It was a different time. We did not have television, none of that. Then you began to see the decline of the afternoon numbers. Advertisers preferred the morning paper because they had more circulation. I fought for years to keep the afternoon paper alive, tried everything I could to salvage it after I became editor. Now by 1985, when we were forced to close out the afternoon [edition], the circulation [had] dropped to about twelve or fourteen thousand. It was not viable anymore.

Q: That was true everywhere in the country, was it not?

A: Yes, it affected everybody. Afternoon papers just no longer had a purpose. Everybody tried everything they could. What I did with the *Pensacola News* [was to] turn it into a total local newspaper. . . . The entire paper was local news, except on the back page [for] national [news], in total contrast with the morning *Journal*, so I said we are going to do that here. We tried, but people's time and recreation had changed. Neighborhoods had changed. Television began to dominate. One of the saddest days of my life was when I read that television is now the dominant source for news.

Q: From 1964 to 1966, you were the editorial page editor for both papers. What were your primary duties in this position?

A: I [wrote] the editorials and design[ed] the editorial page. . . . That was quite a chore. I had to do morning editorials and afternoon editorials.

Q: You wrote all the editorials?

A: Yes. The *Journal* had a stack of, I think, three editorials. [For] the *News*, I redesigned the page so I did not have to write quite so much. I wrote one long one and one short one for the *News*. I did that for eight months, both newspapers. You still had all the editing chores in the old hot-type [process]. You had to pick [the] cartoon and select your syndicated columns and lay them out and edit them—make them fit—and then write the editorials, and I [was] still doing the cartoon, but I was a lot younger then and having a lot of fun with it. I found that editorial ideas come to you, play[ing] off the news.

I did not use much canned stuff. A lot of papers would look to editorial services, which are frowned on totally. I looked at some of those, but I said, "Good Lord, that has nothing to do with Pensacola and Florida; we do not need that in our paper." So I tried to write them, and I tried to keep them as local as possible.

Q: What is the hardest thing about writing an editorial?

A: Getting the idea. Writing it is, to me, fairly simple. When you have a problem, what is the problem, what is the solution, what is the recommendation? But finding ideas—and you have to go through [the] newspaper every day and pick up ideas coming out of the county commission, city council, environmental issues, even plain neighborhood issues, clean water, and find a new angle to that and develop your policy. You [must] have a policy, principles that you believe in. . . . If you can be persuasive toward your own hometown, then that is the value of a newspaper editorial.

You cannot ignore certain bigger issues that [affect public affairs]. You also write about Social Security; you write about the military, because that affects everyone, even local[ly]. You look for military topics because we have a tremendous military establishment here on the Gulf Coast in Pensacola and Fort Walton Beach.

Q: Did you consider yourself, at this time, conservative or liberal?

A: I sometimes call myself a Jeffersonian. I believe in absolute individual freedom. I believe in small government. I am pretty frugal and conservative when it comes to spending the taxpayer's dollar. I am very liberal on human rights and civil rights. I used to be more conservative in the sense of the Goldwater/Reagan-era conservative. I was more into that at a certain time, but I am [also] a strong environmentalist. . . . I believe in family values. I believe in the American system. I believe in free enterprise. I think the perception was when I ran the editorial pages . . . that I was probably more conservative than I really was. I always stood up for black American rights, even in the early days. In the 1960s the paper was pretty progressive in that. But we believed in free enterprise, respected it. You do have to be sensitive that business is important to a community, but so [are] the people's rights, so is the environment, so are governmental controls that prevent overbuilding and [serve] people's interests. So you have to do a balancing act.

Q: Let me ask you about some specific issues and get your response. What was your reaction to both the Civil Rights Act of 1964 and the Voting Rights Act of 1965?

A: I thought both of them were needed, had to be.

Q: Did you get much criticism for taking those stands in the Panhandle?

A: Well, yes, a little. In this area, as conservative as it is, we did not have that kind of turmoil that you had in Mississippi or South Alabama. Even before *Brown v. Board of Education* [1954 desegregation case], my predecessor, Marion Gaines, was advocating desegregation, and we carried that on. No question, we criticized Dr. [Martin Luther] King. We thought he might be going too far, but we were not alone in that. Everybody was saying that. You look back on it now and say the man really did a tremendous [service] for this nation, but at that time the idea of people protesting and walking in the streets was a little bit foreign to us. Our paper thought protest and that sort of thing just was not the way to go. We preferred more sitting down and working out [dialogue], which was not going to happen. You need that kind of agitation from time to time to make things happen, but I think generally, overall, we were pretty supportive of that.

The violence that occurred in Birmingham, yes, we hit that hard. Of course, anytime children are killed at church [a Birmingham church bombing killed four African American girls], you have to [object]. We did not get much criticism on that. We had some local marches here led by a civil rights leader, and we met repeatedly with that group, trying to work it out. The paper was trying to be a mediator, and we never had any real violence. . . . What I am saying is that we were trying to find a middle ground to bring the blacks and whites together. The perception of equality was still grounded in the Old South idea that we ought to have a separation of races. Then a later generation comes along and realizes that we have to have a melting pot, that we have to come together, that we need a colorless society. I wrote an editorial about what King said about a colorblind society. We need that.

So I guess my editorial thrust was moderate to liberal at times and [at times] somewhat conservative. Al Neuharth [founder, *USA Today*], the president of our company, used to say the editorial page should never be predictable. If they know you are a right-wing newspaper and what you are going to say every day, you are playing to the choir. You have to be unpredictable and be loose. Think about the issue. Let the issue determine what you are going to say about it, as long as you keep a common thread to [basic editorial principles].

Q: Did the paper always make recommendations in political races?

A: Yes, they did during my time. As a matter of fact, they started it, really, back in the 1950s. I always advocated that very strongly. . . . [I]f you, as a newspaper, have a voice, have a page devoted to opinion, and you take a position on whether to build that parking lot over there or whether we ought to have a park over here or whether we ought to save the bayfront or whether the sheriff is getting out of line and is a little bit too loose with shooting criminals—if you take those positions daily, when it comes . . . the time for your people living in your local precinct or local governmental unit, state or national or whatever, they have to make a decision to pick their leader. The newspaper ought to have the backbone to come out and say what it thinks about these candidates and make a recommendation, not an endorsement: "Today, we say *x* ought to be president, or we recommend him." Tell the reader why, and move on.

The next day, if he does something after he is elected [that] we disagree with, we take him on. That relieves you of this burden of having the allegiance connection to the political candidate. All you are doing is making a recommendation. Now readers perceive that wrongly. They think you are in bed with the candidate you are endorsing, and you do all kinds of ways of trying to prove you are not, by offering the opposition space on the editorial page to sound off. We always did that. If it was a two-candidate race, we recommended [one] person, and [the other was given] equal space, four hundred words, and we [printed the response]. That helps. Then we opened up our letters-to-the-editor page to let people talk about candidates.

Q: Do you think your recommendations had much impact?

A: On certain races they had a lot of impact. For instance, judicial races, which are often nonpolitical. People would run for judge in Florida, and about all they would tell you was where they went to school and who their wife is and their basic biographical [information]. In the large election in

November, usually, you had a pretty large selection of circuit judges running for county judge. We found that our recommendations were [effective] a lot of times, because people do not perceive those races as being partisan or political, and they look to the newspaper, [knowing we had] researched them, and [they will want to consider our] recommendation.

Now if you get a hot sheriff's race in this county, the newspaper might not be as influential as that, because that gets awfully partisan and bitterly brutal sometimes, and other factors carry it. That should not deter you from taking a position, a logical, sober analysis of what the person can offer in the office.

Q: From 1966 to 1969, you were editor-in-chief. How did you get that position, and why did you take the job?

A: I got that job because . . . Marion Gaines retired after a twenty-[six]-year career. So one day Mr. Ball [Braden Ball, the publisher] called me into his office and says, "Can you run that department over there?"

I said, "Sir, I can try."

He said, "You are the new editor. You go back over there and call them into the conference room, and you tell them that you are taking over as editor." I was thirty-four.

I went back, and I got them all in the newsroom conference room, and I told them, "Braden Ball just named me editor-in-chief of this newspaper."

All these guys I had worked with—some of them had been there longer, and they thought they might have a shot at that job one day, and there was a little coldness there for a few hours, but it [subsided], and I took over as editor. That is how I got the job, because he was so pleased with the work I had done, first on the news, winning some awards, and then writing editorials.

Q: At this point, who owned the paper?

A: Gannett bought us in 1969, but when I became editor, John H. Perry. Perry's father bought these papers, including the whole newspaper here, in the 1920s and put them together in the News Journal Company in 1924.

Q: What influence did John H. Perry, Jr., have on the paper?

A: Very little. Now the older Perry, John H. Perry, Sr., was a Kentucky libel lawyer. It was almost Scripps-Perry [instead of Scripps-Howard]. He [considered joining] Scripps, [but] Perry went out independently and began to buy newspapers. [He] saw a frontier in Florida and came here and began to buy [other] smaller papers that did not have any money, a lot of them

[with] Ed Ball's [financial support]. [Perry and Ball] were close. He died in 1953. I came here in 1952, so I never knew the [senior Perry]. . . . But John [Jr.] lost interest, or had no interest, in the newspaper business. By 1969 he started selling off his newspapers. [Perry owned twenty-seven newspapers in Florida.] Ours was the first to go, to Gannett Company for $15,500,000, which sounds like very little money today, and then all the others began to split up. Palm Beach went to Cox, and Freedom Newspapers bought Panama City and Fort Walton Beach, and Ocala [went to] the *New York Times*.

Q: How did things change under Gannett, and what influence did they have on you?

A: They had a lot of influence, of course, but they did not change much, other than they instituted a better financial reporting system to the new corporation. . . . Gannett was becoming a public company, and they owned a lot of newspapers and were buying [in] Florida. They put in new rules in that regard.

I anticipated what they might do here, and I redesigned the paper, based on the paper *Today at Cocoa Beach* [sic] as it was called then, later renamed *Florida Today*. They had opened the four front sections to all news, sports, local, living. So with angle bars on the press, we were able to get the four-section newspaper, in both the morning and afternoon, by the time Gannett got here to talk to us, and they were impressed with that. I had read everything about Gannett and some of the things they were doing, and I was making sure we were on the ball team. They were very good to me. They were good for [our] company, a large corporation provid[ing] resources for a medium-sized newspaper. They built a new pressroom, expanded the building, began to put in [computers to replace] the hot-type operation in the 1970s [with] all new equipment.

Q: I am interested in what you think of *USA Today*.

A: I think that *USA Today*, now, is a solid, good-reading newspaper. I take it in my home and read it every morning. At first, I thought it was a bit flamboyant and [had] flashy content, not much worth beyond the headlines. For a commuter newspaper sold in airports, it might have been fine. But it has settled into being a real strong newspaper, as its circulation indicates. The concept of a national newspaper has merit, [but its] problem is [a lack of] base. It has no home, other than the nation. That, to me, lends itself to having lost something. . . .

A lot of that was Neuharth's influence; he was trying to be totally different from what his good friends on the *Washington Post* and the *Wall Street Journal* were doing. He had an idea which first manifested in Cocoa with *Today*, and he just took that [concept] and, with the help of a lot of people, brainstormed an idea that they could launch a newspaper that could be sold all over America. The technology was there with the satellite to feed out of the Washington area [to printing sites around the country], and it worked. Now others have refined what he started and turned it into a household word, as far as newspapers are concerned.

Q: How important were innovations like graphics, the colored weather map? Did that help circulation?

A: Those were very helpful in the beginning, and the pioneer was the *St. Petersburg Times*. Back in the early years when television was coming on in very vivid color, newspapers had to find ways to be more attractive. The *St. Petersburg Times* really was a pioneer of the early graphics in America. . . . [*USA Today*] did have a [large] splashy weather map; then suddenly every newspaper in America was emulating [that map]. But I notice [most] have gone back to smaller maps. All of that was not necessary, but it was an effort to create a newspaper like it was a television screen, in print. I cannot fault it. I do not totally agree with its design. As a [student] of newspaper design, there are a lot of things I would not do, [but] they seemed to enjoy [experimentation]. But in the graphics age with computer[s], you can [create effective images], column rules and borders and everything.

But *USA Today*, to answer your question, is, I think, a very valid and important element to American journalism in its time. They have colorful writing. They have some good writers. They have helped enterprise a lot of [practices] that other newspapers now follow, [like] writing tight, short stories. I do not always like that; sometimes you get too cryptic [and] miss [elements of the story]. You read a good strong story in the *Miami Herald* and the *Washington Post* about an issue, and you have a full understanding of it. You read *USA Today*, and you get the cream off the top of the milk, so to speak.

Q: One of the criticisms is that it is now "McNews." People do not read newspapers very much, and this is really a lesser form of what we might consider a regular newspaper. So a lot of critics do not like *USA Today* because it is too short and too lacking in information.

A: And that was its design, a quick read—you know, the McPaper. . . . But it put Al Neuharth and Gannett on the map. Gannett had some image problems. They ran small-town newspapers, and [*USA Today*] gave them [stature]. So *USA Today* is a new dimension to the printed word at a time when some of us in the back of our minds have fear that the day is coming when the printed page is going away, and it is all going to be electronic.

Q: Will there be a day when you will get your newspaper on the computer, and you will not actually have a physical newspaper to handle?

A: I do not anticipate that until, maybe, another generation. I think the printed word is going to be around a long time. We are so attuned to that, picking up books and newspapers. . . . Newspapers are different today. They are going to have to be different. Public journalism is coming [in vogue], getting back to your community, getting involved with your community. Get close to the readers, and ask them what they think. I always talked about [how] we have to improve writing. Well, we should have improved writing all along, but we were improving writing because we wanted people to read these stories, because they had television, and everything was instant news, radio. You have to write your story so that they are so compelling people have to have them.

Q: Because of your physical location, you are not in competition with the *St. Petersburg Times* or the *Orlando Sentinel*.

A: No, we did not have those papers coming into our market. It was not feasible for them to haul a newspaper that far. We cannot even do well in Tallahassee. It is so far away, and it is costly to get the papers there. We must look at our immediate readership, because the advertiser knows that these are the people buy[ing] his products, and he buys ad space from us. So we have to serve him more than to go out and try to get these large numbers of circulation, which are not profitable from a standpoint of the newspaper. You just settle into your region.

Q: When you took over as editor, what specific goals did you have?

A: My goal, number one, was to be the dominant newspaper of the Panhandle. We were the only morning daily in the Panhandle at that time. But to try to be the dominant and best-read and the most influential newspaper in West Florida, because we were the largest.

Q: When you took over, were there some specific problems, either financial or in terms of circulation or the editorial policy, that you had to deal with?

A: I began to try to recruit a better-educated reporter. The problem I had with that was, again, economics. I could not pay them as much as the *Miami Herald*. I used to hire people out of, like, LSU [Louisiana State University]; they always loved to come to Pensacola because of the beaches. They would come to work for us, and in six months they were working at the *Miami Herald*, because the *Herald* in those days was always looking for good people, and they could hire them from us [with higher salaries]. That is no longer as much of a factor with the paper here. It is [under] Gannett, and we got the salaries up to be competitive.

I began to expand the sports staff. It was small. I put in a photo department that the newsroom had never really had. This sounds really old-fashioned, but we had one photographer and an assistant, so we began to expand that. We did not have an art department or a graphics department, and I brought in a graphic artist directly from Cocoa, who had helped develop *Today*.

I made a lot of revolutionary changes on this newspaper when I took over. First of all, one of the things [was], we were identifying people with race. You know, "John Jones, Negro, arrested last night." I stopped that. I changed the Society pages to what I called at that time, "Living." I call it "Life" now. We began to [respect] the civil rights movement, the concern for blacks. We had a debutante cotillion here that was kind of a social [event], and they always got a big spread with their daughters coming out, and it was all white. By that time the blacks decided they would have one too, and they could not get in the paper. I gave them the [same] space as the whites. That caused me a little grief among the social gentry here, but that was the right thing to do. We broke those barriers in covering things that the paper really had never done before.

Q: How did the role of women change, during the thirty years or so you were editor?

A: Tremendously. Anyway, [when I became editor], we did not have many women in the newsroom. They had mostly just women [working on] the social pages. There were not any over on the other side. So we began to change that, and I hired several people to come in and be reporters and cover city hall. So that began to change. Now we have about as many women as men in the newsroom.

Q: What about hiring of minorities?

A: I hired, I guess, the first black reporter, a woman. I forget the year. The problem we had and still have is you cannot keep them. There are not enough. They come here and stay a short time, and the *Tallahassee Democrat* or a Knight-Ridder will grab them, or some of the other larger papers. The *News Journal* now has [several] minorities. The assistant editorial page editor is black. He is from South Carolina and is a very good man. That is no longer a factor, but it was tough to find [qualified minorities]. . . . Hiring minorities is still a concern in the newspaper business. That is the reason all the newspaper companies pump so much money into Florida A&M's journalism school. They are trying to groom young blacks for our business, because we have to realize that there is a black community which should be covered just like the other.

Q: How have reporters changed over the same period of time?

A: Reporters have changed tremendously. I used to have some old-timers. . . . I had a guy who came to work on that afternoon paper, and he would write you a feature story that would stand up for the edition. By noon, he would have it ready. He would go down to the Coffee Cup, a favorite restaurant, find some character, develop it into something, tie it to the day's news, and he would have a nice feature. Then he would come to the paper and get on the phone, and he would take police stories and write them up. He would write ten, twelve stories during one news cycle. Today, you are lucky if a reporter writes two stories a week. You give them an assignment, and they have three weeks to enterprise. In the old days I had reporters who could turn out those stories in hours, and that is still a frustration to me, why we cannot do that. Newspapers are not as immediate as they used to be.

Q: Are the stories written any better?

A: No, not really. Well, yes. Say you are doing an environmental story or a story that is a little bit investigative. I am not talking about that. I am talking about just grabbing a story for morning edition that would be soft, reflective of something tied to the news. I do not see much of that anymore. I think the system has just lent itself to giving them more time to think it out better and make sure it is right. That is good if you have the numbers of people to do it.

Q: Part of it has to do with lawsuits. Newspapers have to be accurate.

A: Yes, you have to double-check it. You have to check with lawyers, and you make sure. You have to go through a series of editors if it is a sensitive story, but I am talking about just routine stuff. A police story that might be just kind of interesting with the angle it takes. He [the old reporter] could do that in a few minutes. I do not sense we have that anymore. I have always made a point of not criticizing the younger generation, because I think some of them are much better than anything of my time. Better educated. More interested, I think. So many times in the old days, we had a lot of cynicism, and people did not have the background, [but] they were good writers. . . . [M]ost of these kids today are college graduates. Unfortunately, so many of them are discovering that the newspaper way of life is not what I want. I want to go out and do something that I can make more money out of. It is one of the real problems of the profession today.

Q: How has the newspaper audience changed during your career?

A: They are more demanding. . . . The sophistication of the reading audience is much higher. I think what I am saying is that, in an earlier period before television, people who relied almost entirely on the local newspaper for their news were forced to take what they got. Today, they have so many choices that they can quickly tell whether they want to have that newspaper or whether it is satisfying their needs. . . .

Newspapers, I guess, are the last mass medium, and that is our only hope for them, in that television is so fractured with cable, and radio is all talk and music. I always tell students, "You know, radio came along and scared the devil out of the newspaper business. Here suddenly, you can hear the news instantaneously." I mean, radio went on and had its heyday, and the newspaper is still going. Along comes television, and suddenly they say, "Well, we are not only going to hear the news, but you can see it instantaneously, and that is going to cut [us out]." Well, the radio panicked, and radio had to adapt. It did. It went to talk. It went to music. . . . But the newspapers have been steady. . . . You still read the crossword puzzle, the comics, the death notices, about what your local government is doing, read a little bit of the social news pertaining to your neighborhood. You have all that in one package.

Unfortunately, it is printed on paper. I remember reading that Ted Turner said. . . , "The newspaper business is the only business I know where you have to cut down a tree that we need to keep us warm, to print the news that is old on the day it is printed." That is true. It is cumbersome, all the way from a tree in Canada or a forest in Canada to a mill to the *News Journal*'s off-set press, and we are grinding it out and delivering it on your lawn. Here, you have an electronic medium that can pop [a] column [and news report] onto the Internet right into your home and probably down the road onto your television set.

So I do not know what is going to happen there, but I do not think anything has changed as far as journalism is concerned. Our role is to keep the public informed and, in a sense, to guard democracy; . . . we are the watchdogs. I do not think that is going to change. I have seen television do more and more entertainment. It was not news. . . . There is nothing better than when you have a tragedy in America [and] TV . . . can do a marvelous job of covering those . . . events. . . . You cannot get better than that, but not the day-in-day-out information that people need to guide their lives and pay their taxes.

Q: How would you rate your paper compared to papers of comparable circulation, as well as the larger newspapers in the state?

A: I do not see any weak papers in Florida anymore. I think Florida is really blessed with some great newspapers. You know, the [Miami] Herald, of course, and the St. Pete Times. You look at all the others, the old Fort Lauderdale News and the Sun-Sentinel. Really great newspapers. The Tampa Tribune. Then you get into what I call the medium-size newspapers: Tallahassee, Gainesville, maybe Ocala, all of that level. They are all attractive newspapers.

Q: How have the letters to the editor changed over this period of time?

A: Much more literate, less vitriolic, although . . . you still get them from all kinds of people, and you do not publish those kind.

Q: Do you edit them, or do you print them in full?

A: We have a word limit, like three or four hundred words, and if it is a few words over, we still go ahead and run them. If it is too long, we send it back and say, "You have to cut it down." If you ran half of it, the guy would complain . . . , "You cut my stuff, and my main message was in the second page." If it is just a few words over, they go ahead with it.

We have another vehicle at the newspaper I developed years ago, called Viewpoint, on the op-ed page. If you write a column about an issue, say five to seven hundred words, and you run it with your picture on it, we offer that to people who head organizations, voluntary or even politicians . . . , [anyone] who might disagree with our editorial position. My view of the editorial page is that it is a melting pot of ideas, our voice is on the left-hand column, but everything else on those pages is somebody else's view, either syndicated columns, cartoons, letters to the editor, or Viewpoint articles. I figured it up one time, and we run far more words from other people, the local voices, than our words.

Q: Who chooses the letters?

A: The editorial page editor.

Q: Based on what criteria?

A: Based on first-come, first-serve. At a paper our size, we try to be fair to everybody. If you write a letter and it is reasonable and it conforms with the rules we have laid out—we do not tell you what to write—you will get in the paper. If you have a letter that libels somebody . . . , the newspaper is responsible too. You have to be careful in that regard, and you have to be sensitive to other issues. And make sure it makes a point.

Q: How often did you use syndicated columnists, and how did you choose which ones you would use?

A: We use them daily. Most syndicated columnists [write] three a week, and you pick and choose from those and run them on regular days. You always try to get the ones that were popular and representative of a variety of viewpoints, whether liberal or conservative. You try to get a balance. . . . They recently added Molly Ivins, who writes a humorous column out of Texas, and they added Walter Williams, a black conservative. He writes an interesting piece, and that gives variety. I always add James Jackson Kilpatrick, a beautiful writer. He was a true conservative, but just a good writer, a constitutionalist. We always had [William F.] Buckley and Ellen Goodman and various others. Dave Broder, the best political reporter out of Washington.

Q: But you chose them, and not Gannett?

A: Oh, yes. Gannett used to have a slogan: "We make a business of not running newspapers." Even though they inherited me in 1969, never one time did Gannett ever tell me what to write, not in my entire career. I was fortunate in that regard. Editors really have to be sensitive to what the company is, but as far as the editorial position that the *News Journal* took during my career, that was under my direction. In the latter years, after we had developed an editorial board . . . composed of the publisher, who frequently sat in or sometimes chose not to, the editorial page staff, perhaps the managing editor—a lot of minds came to work on developing . . . what we would say about issues. We would meet a couple of times a week.

Q: Did you have any problems with advertiser discontent with your editorials, and would that affect what editorials you ran, or advertisements?

A: Yes, not because of anything we did editorially, but it was some stories that we were running. . . . [W]e ran a story that was developed locally about one of these companies that will sell you a car almost by mail, and you can get it much cheaper doing that. Here was a big spread [the newspaper] ran one day on the business page, and the publisher at that time tried to encourage them not to run that story, to hold it for a day or two, and he was absolutely right. They ran that story and did not worry about it. In a story like that, you got, "I can buy a car cheaper by this process than I can going out to one of the lots in Car City." It stands to reason, in my view, let us get Car City's view of this. You know, if I can buy a car cheaper than you can sell it, what do you think about that? They did not get both sides. And when it came out, they [the car dealers] got real upset, and one of them led a little boycott. It did not last long because they needed the advertising.

I think most people who understand how newspapers operate understand that the opinion page is opinion. They say, "Well, I did not agree with it, but you have a right to say it." The reason I think we did not have any problem is that we were always very careful in an editorial not to make the grievous error of misinformation or casting people in a bad light unnecessarily. Cast the issue in a bad light, maybe, if you need to, but not the individual or the commercial concern or whatever.

Now we did have a lot of opposition for some of the things we stood for in this county, like consolidating government. We tried to consolidate city and county, [and] we just lost like crazy because people did not want to change their form of government. I think three times during my era as editor, we tried to [establish a] charter government, which failed each time. And, at least three times, we advocated an appointed school superintendent, which failed each time.

But I have not had that pressure from advertisers. The only ones I have had is when some reporter would goof up a story so badly that it affected an advertiser. I had a guy writing us a consumer column one time. He went out to get his car fixed, and they messed it up. He got into a real argument with them [and returns] to the News Journal and [criticizes] people who repair cars and just brutalizes them in a column, in kind of an oblique way. The guy called up, and he was really upset. It turned out that the reporter would not pay his bill, and we had to fire him. So when you take an issue like that and make it personal in the newspaper, you can get yourself into real trouble.

Q: Did you cover the legislature very closely?

A: In the early years of my career as editor-in-chief, I was fortunate to have the dean of political writers in Florida, named Maurice "Moose" Harling, who will be remembered as Reubin Askew's mentor and also his press secretary for the eight years he [Askew] was governor. Moose had a knowledge of the legislature and covered it thoroughly for us, and he was the only newsman I ever knew who was honored by both houses of the legislature for his long service [in] covering the legislature. We covered it that way.

[N]ow we depend on a bureau with two or three people there, representing Fort Myers and *Florida Today*. They cover all these delegations, and they do not get too close to either one of them. I think we are doing a disservice in that regard. We have gotten away from covering the major [action] that affects people the most, laws affecting your taxes. We have gone more to what we call people news, and what are people doing? That is good. I do not disagree with that, but we do not have that solid political coverage that I thought was important in my time.

Q: Describe your relationship with Reubin Askew.

A: Well, very close. He and I were at Florida State together. He was president of the student government when I was on the *Florida Flambeau*, and we got to know each other then. . . . [I]n those early years at Florida State—he denies it today—but he used to sit around, and we all knew that he was going to try to be governor of Florida one of these days. The *News Journal* did not endorse him when he made his first run.

Q: For governor?

A: Yes. Then Reubin made such a strong run in that first primary. Al Neuharth, the president of Gannett, called up the publisher and really shamed him, said, "Good Lord, Braden, you did not even support the local boy for governor." Well, we came back in that second primary, and I wrote a glowing editorial about how we had to have Reubin as governor. He grew up kind of poor. He had to work hard. . . . I always said a person from Pensacola probably cannot ever be governor because he is going to be perceived as being too local, too provincial. Reubin, from the very beginning of his political career, had a total Florida concept to everything he did. He was concerned with all areas of Florida. He was not an old West Florida "Pork Chopper."

Q: How would you assess his two terms as governor?

A: I think he did some great things, . . . and I think he was a popular governor. I also have great respect for Bob Graham, who followed him and who, I think, just did a marvelous job as governor. LeRoy Collins, Reubin Askew, and Graham, to me, represent what I would consider the modern era of transition in Florida.

Q: I am certain that you believe that editors need to be not only community leaders but involved in community affairs, and I wanted to discuss two or three areas where you were heavily involved. One would be the development of the University of West Florida. Explain the importance of having a university in Pensacola.

A: That was 1967 when the university finally began. I thought it was a real breakthrough of ideas that was going to help this region more than any I could think of. . . . We did not have a research library in this region. Here was an opportunity to provide higher education for this part of the Panhandle. . . . Here we were going to have our own university. . . . So I editorialized [and drew lots] of [supportive] cartoons. Yes, it is one of the big breakthroughs of my time. It changed the character of this area. Unfortunately, the University of West Florida has not grown like we thought it would in the projections. I attribute a lot of things that have happened here in this town to the coming of that university. So it changed us, and I was proud to be a part of the campaign that brought it here.

Q: Discuss your role as a leader in the development of Pensacola's historic preservation and how that has impacted the city.

A: I began to write about it [historic preservation] and how we were missing out on what could be perceived as tourism because we were not preserving what we had here, an old four-hundred-year-old city that had some Spanish and early American landmarks that really needed [preservation]. [F]inally, the city council decided that they wanted to do something about this. We had discovered that the old Seville Square was Spanish and that we ought to try to save that neighborhood. They appointed a historical advisory committee, and . . . I was chairman of it. We started with that, and . . . it led to the creation of the Historic Pensacola Preservation Board through the legislature.

In 1982 Bob Graham appointed me back to the [preservation] board . . . and I have been chairman ever since. I served as president of the Historical Society for eight years. I . . . led the campaign to raise over five hundred thousand dollars, to endow the Historical Society so they could survive. They were depending on a little stipend from the city and county, and they did not have any money. They were just struggling. Now they have their own museum and their own building. I did not overuse the editorial voice of the paper for the history, but every time I had the opportunity to write something about the importance of history to this area, I did it, not because I would get any monetary gain out of it, but because it is important to the character of this city.

[T]he thing that I am really the proudest of, my crowning achievement as an editor, was Gulf Islands National Seashore. Now that was really a fight. Even the chamber of commerce came out against us. I stayed right with it. We covered it thoroughly. I said, "You will give the opposition their say in the paper," and we finally won with the help of many good people in this community—environmental groups, garden clubs, university faculty, average people who thought we ought to have a national park rather than just destroying our beaches with overbuilding. That was my proud editorial campaign because it really was a campaign. I made speeches, and . . . I drew [150] cartoons. But we finally brought the people to our side and won, and Sikes [Florida congressman Bob Sikes] got the bill passed. It was signed by Nixon in 1971.

Q: What are the benefits and the negative aspects to the relationship between the community and the military, particularly the naval air station?

A: The benefit is that the navy is a strong economic component to our community, as well as cultural. They have been here a long time, as you know. The old Navy Yard, since 1825, and the flying aspect in 1913, [continuing] today. The navy is steady. It is a government payroll that provided jobs all through the depression. . . . Pilots marry girls from here . . . and we are known as the mother-in-law of the U.S. navy. So the relationship is almost a love-in between the business or community and the navy.

What has happened is that the negative—if it could be perceived as the negative—is that we have spent all our talent and energy and resources trying to protect the navy [rather] than the other aspects of legitimate organic growth of the community, whether it be business and industry or culturally or educationally with the university. We let that suffer, trying to protect the navy. So we have that love relationship with the navy, and it very well may have diminished our ability to diversify our community through new enterprises.

Q: Let me finish with one major question. What did you want most to accomplish in your journalistic career when you began, and do you feel like you did so?

A: I indicated to you earlier that I wanted to put out the best newspaper in the region of my birth, where I had grown up and loved. That was it, a real quality newspaper. In a sense, during that period of thirty-one years as editor-in-chief of the *News Journal*, I became, kind of, two people. I was an editor, and I was out in the community. My publisher said . . . , "Get out and lead this community; you can do it." I took him at his word, not to go out and lead it, but to set forth principles and projects that I thought were important to this region, to help put us on the map and help us grow: the seashore, historical program, university, downtown redevelopment, bayfront redevelopment, modernizing the local government. All of those things I thought were important. I not only wrote about them, but I participated in them, not in a political way. I never participated in any political operation at all, never gave a dollar to any political campaign or anything like that. . . . I was an active, hands-on, community-minded editor.

I hesitate to say what happens today, but I do not think you are going to find many editors who do those kinds of things. They do not serve on committees or chair boards, but I always thought that was important because it gave me a profile in the community; it helped me understand the community; it gave me ideas to work for as an editor.

Your service is for the community, not for your own personal gain. I like to think that I achieved both to a certain extent. Also, I think some of the things I have done really have improved the community, and I am very proud of all of that. I did modernize the *Pensacola News Journal*, changed the whole design of it, and added to the staff. At the same time, I was able to get out into the community and do things that actually became reality with the help of a lot of good people.

Weekly Newspapers

chapter 7 **Tommy Greene**

Tommy Greene was born in Madison County, Florida, on October 28, 1938, the son of a timber merchant who claimed to be the largest distributor of railroad cross ties in the southeastern United States. Greene grew up poor and spent his youth in the swamp, extracting turpentine or logging lumber. He later told friends, "I may not have been born in a log cabin, but as soon as we could afford one, we moved." In 1957 he graduated from Madison High School only because, as he explained, his dad "had something pretty heavy on the superintendent," and "with my wife slipping me notes, I got out of high school."

Greene attended North Florida Junior College, Jacksonville University, and Mercer University and then served in the army until his honorable discharge in 1962. After giving up on the farming and turpentine business, Greene decided, although he had no experience whatsoever, to begin a local newspaper. He founded his first paper, the *Madison County Carrier*, on August 5, 1964. He then began buying other newspapers across the Panhandle of Florida, including his competitor, the *Madison Enterprise Recorder*.

Over the years Greene has established himself as one of the state's most colorful characters. He always wears green, down to his underwear and socks. His office, his truck, and his pen are green. One daughter is named Emerald, and one son is John Deere. He lives in a green house, eats green grits, and declares: "If it ain't green, it ain't mine." He explained his choice of a monochromatic life: "I don't have what it takes to compete with the average person out there. If I hadn't been different, I would have been a flop."

Greene believes in a conservative philosophy and resents government intrusion in the private lives of citizens. He sends back all the money he receives from the government, including checks for jury duty and military disability. He also plans to refuse Social Security: "That way I can write an editorial about welfare, and I'm not a preacher who sobered up Sunday morning so he can preach about drunks." He vehemently attacks welfare: "It lets you earn more with a houseful of bastards than with a pen full of hogs." Greene also favors capital punishment: "The last public hanging was right here in Madison County. If I was the supreme ruler, I would bring 'em back. I would execute all criminals—shoplifters, you name it—and all their lawyers, and then we would rid the country of thieves, and we could sleep with our windows open."

Over time Greene has branched out into billboards, real estate development, cattle, a retail store, nursery, self-storage warehouses, farming, and a hunting and fishing lodge. He set up Madison County's community-access television station, the first such station in Florida. When asked about the details of his business ventures, he declined comment: "You're waking up dogs that people don't even know is asleep."

Throughout his career Greene has made it a habit to stick up for underdogs and "to do good for the community." He was the youngest president of the Florida Press Association and over the years has been very active in community affairs: chairman of the greater Madison County chamber of commerce, president of the Madison County Development Authority, co-founder of a charter school, a Boy Scout and Explorer troop leader, founder and president of the Madison Museum, and many others too numerous to mention. He has won many journalistic awards and, in 1994, was Madison County's citizen of the year. He is currently drawing and painting, working on a history of Madison County, and recording his memoirs: *The Belly Side of Me and My Trashy Friends*.

In this interview Greene discusses his early life in the turpentine industry and why he left it, as well as how he decided upon the newspaper business for his next venture. He explains how he managed to set his newspaper apart from its competition and subsequently to build a network of local papers throughout northern Florida. His involvement in the Florida Press Association is described at length, as well as his love for, and commitment to, Madison County. Throughout the interview, his patriotism, conservatism, instinctive business sense, and off-beat, colorful personality shine to full effect.

Thomas H. Greene, Jr., was interviewed by Julian M. Pleasants on June 27, 2000, in Madison, Florida.

Q: Describe for me your early life. What was it like?

A: I grew up in the shadow of my daddy's sawmill, so I grew up in the cross-tie swamps and the turpentine woods. As I got older, then we got to poling, or logging the big timbers for the big poles like went around the football fields and these big utility poles.

Q: Was working with those logs pretty dangerous work?

A: Yes, sir. In fact, it's one of the most hazardous businesses in America, as I understand.

Q: And you had one bad incident where you got trapped under some logs. Would you tell me about that?

A: Yes, sir. After I got out of the military, I came back and married my childhood sweetheart. We went all through school together. I was logging by day and farming by night, and we were top-loading. . . . [Y]ou take a tractor . . . and . . . pull the logs up on top of the load of logs that you were going to haul out of there on the truck. The load shifted on me and pinned me under it, and I thought I was dead, but the good Lord saved me. I promised God I'd never go back to logging if he'd get me out of those woods alive. He did, and I've kept my promise.

Q: Who did you hire to help with the turpentine business?

A: You hire only turpentine folks. There's a certain—you can call it a breed, or certain kind of people, that just do that. That's what they want to do, carrying those one-sided buckets. You go through and make your rounds . . . all the way through these woods, and a lot of it is down at the edge of the swamps. But you cut your trail. It looks like animal trails, but it is big enough for a man to walk through. You try to make your rounds so that when you get back to the wagon, you've got a full bucket. . . .

It took strong men to do this because it's hot down there. You're working them in the summertime. You're constantly pulling and chipping, and then when you're dipping, you're carrying that heavy bucket. You're down in that heavy overbrush. There is zero wind blowing, no wind. You got the sun bearing down from the top, and it's like cooking in an oven down there. So people that turpentined were an unusual breed.

One problem we would have is stealing families, where the other turpentine woodsmen would come in and steal your help through the middle of the night—just load them up—because all of these people that were turpentiners would wind up getting heavy in debt. They were kind of a hand-to-mouth people. So you would go to pick them up the next morning, and the house would be empty.

I [once] thought we was going to stake out one of our houses where we had found out somebody was coming [to steal one of his families], . . . and we were going to wait on those people, which we did, and we caught them. It wasn't unusual when they backed the truck up to unload one of our houses; we'd just walk up there and shoot the tires out from the truck and send them walking. Then they would have to come get the truck the next morning, and that's when we'd have the law waiting on them to explain our law.

Q: Talk about your early education.

A: As hard and conservative as I am today, which came, I am sure, out from my daddy's shadow, I got what some would consider an extremely liberal education extremely young in life. That made me a better man to get into the newspaper business, of which I knew absolutely nothing about, because I knew that failure was not an option in anything I went after.

I started off at Madison Elementary . . . and went all the way through. I failed one grade. I never was much [of] a student. Reading and spelling, to this day, I don't do well. Nothing leaves my desk that my wife doesn't proof. She majored in English—they say that's the reason I married her. I mean, I do not spell. I write. . . . I've got some movies that I'm working on now and some short stories and a novel. But spelling is out of the question.

Q: You studied criminal justice at one point. How did you get into that and why?

A: After I got into the newspaper business, I wound up doing all the photography work for all the various branches of law enforcement here and gave them the pictures. So I wound up being able to work crime scenes, in the beginning, just from what they told me to do. Then I studied it, and we knew what to look for. . . . Well, during that time, and this was back in the 1970s, they had a big cattle ring going on in the state of Florida. They were stealing cattle, which was big business, and it was big crime. And I've made front-page notes of this a number of times, and there's not a judge in this country that can get confidentiality out of me. When I tell somebody what they tell me is confidential, I would look forward to rotting in jail before I'd tell a grand jury or anybody else. Now I'm locked in on that solid. My word is absolutely my bond when it comes to somebody telling me something that's private, which has helped me.

ǫ: What did you do when you returned to Madison after military service?

ᴀ: The only thing I knew was the woods. I was turpentining and logging and pulpwooding in the daytime. Then I had lights on all my farm equipment, and I'd farm at night and then reserve Sunday morning for church and Sunday afternoon with getting all my equipment ready so I could get everything back in shape for Monday morning.

On the first of June, I was in the middle of a field, and my wife was there. I'm out there, hot and sweaty and dirty and grungy and all that, working on an old harrow that should have been in a junk pile. I stood up, and I looked over at my wife, and she was trying—you know, she doesn't know anything about mechanics, but she would hand me that wrench when I'd finally show her the one I needed. But she was trying to help, and I just stood up and threw that wrench as far as I could throw it, and I said, "There's got to be a better life somewhere." So I walked out of the field, left the harrow and the wrench. I didn't even go back and look for the wrench.

But a few days later, about three-thirty one morning, I was sitting up in there as miserable as I've ever been in my life. No job, no work, no nothing but a wife and a brand-new baby. [And] I'd already exhausted all of my efforts of trying to find a job. One place up here making hubcaps, a man told me he was laying off, not hiring. I said, "Mr. Musser, I need some work, and I was wondering if you'd hire me—you know, if you have an opening for me."

And he said, "No, we're laying off right now, but if we had an opening, if I was looking for somebody, I wouldn't hire you."

I was quick-tempered back then, but I stood up, and I said, "Mr. Musser, I thought we were friends."

And he said, "Tommy Greene, we are friends, but you have too much talent to be stamping out hubcaps the rest of your life, and if you get on that assembly line back there, you're going to wind up getting in a rut, and you may never leave this place, and I'm not going to do you that injustice. Now you get out there, and you can find something you can do." He said, "But right now, we're not hiring anyway."

When I left there, I didn't know if I was mad. But he was right. You know, the difference between a grave and a rut is that a grave has got both ends closed on you, and the longer you stay in a rut, the closer those ends come.

So I tore open a paper grocery sack one night and made a list of a couple of dozen things I wanted to get into, and I can assure you logging and farming were not two of them. . . . I listed a bunch of them, and then to the right, I listed all the items I needed for each one of them. I found office supplies and advertising in every one of the businesses that I wanted to get into. So I sat there for a few moments and I said, "You know, let's see if I can pick out some trees in this forest." I said, "You know, if I got into the office supply business and the newspaper business, I could buy my office supplies for the newspaper wholesale, and I could take the newspaper and advertise my office supply store, and this, to me, is about as close to perpetual motion as I'm going to get."

There was a hundred-year-old newspaper in our town, a father-son operation. The son, to me at that time, was an old man. I was twenty-five years old, and he was probably fifty, and his daddy was probably seventy-five. He had a degree from the law school at Harvard. They were wise old men, and I was so full of ignorance and energy, I didn't have sense enough to know that I couldn't make it [purchase and run the paper]. Failure never crossed my mind as an option.

Q: What was the name of that paper?

A: The *Madison Enterprise Recorder*, founded in 1865. Anyway, first thing [my wife] told me, she said, "Tommy Greene, you can't spell; you don't read; how do you expect to run a newspaper?"

I said, "Well, if you'll do the spelling and the writing, I'll do the drawing and the figuring." I said, "I can figure out a way to make this thing work if you'll do the spelling and the writing for me."

They [the newspaper owners] were real friendly and nice to me, but they'd just tell me right quick that new newspapers don't last. . . . The only person [to encourage me was] Carr Settle in Monticello that had the *Monticello News*. I went in and introduced myself to him, and he said, "I can tell you right now, it's going to be the toughest thing you ever tried, but you're not going to be happy till you can look back and say, 'At least I tried it,' so why don't you go on and . . . get it out of your system. . . ." The more they told me I couldn't do it, there was just something—I don't know, it was like cross wiring a battery, I guess.

Then we went up to Jim Thompson up in Callahan, Florida, and told Mr. Thompson up there that we wanted to put out a newspaper and we understand he had a printing press, but we didn't want anybody to know about it.

He says, "Well, have you decided if you're going offset or letterpress?"

I said, "Well, Mr. Thompson, really, we haven't made our mind up."

He looked at me and he said, "You don't know the difference, do you?" And I said, "No, sir."

He said, "You two kids are just out for a good time." He said, "Yeah, we can print you, and the [printing] world [prefers] offset, so let me tell you what you're going to need." So he took us to a restaurant, and he made out a list there on the napkin of things I needed to get, to get into the newspaper business.

Q: Where did you get the capital to get this business started?

A: All my life, from day one and I haven't stopped, I pinched pennies and saved my money. When I would go to the theater, my mother and daddy would give me a quarter, and my brother, and we would walk across to the theater. . . . Well, a quarter—it took us fourteen cents to get in the show. We called it the picture show. Then you could get a cold drink, a Coca-Cola, and a bag of popcorn for a nickel each and bubble gum for a penny. So that took up the quarter. Well, I'd spend the fourteen cents to get in the movie, but I'd put that eleven cents in my pocket. I never bought a single piece of gum or a single Coca-Cola or a single bag of popcorn. I'd bring that eleven cents home every Saturday.

Plus, my daddy gave us ways that we could make money. I was selling slabs coming off the sawmill for firewood. So I had a way. The one that my mother never approved of, but my daddy told me that I could do it as long as I was there on the farm, but for me to never do it any other place—and I stuck to that—I always kept cornbuck. Daddy had a big sugarcane mill and a big evaporator . . . , so he was selling sugarcane syrup. Cornbuck, basically, is kind of like beer made with corn, where you shell out your corn and, if you are making good [moon]shine, if you had fifty pounds of corn, you'd put in fifty pounds of sugar. [W]hen you drain that buck off, you can drink it as beer.

Q: So you had saved enough money over the years to start your business.

A: Every time I'd get a jar of money, I'd bury it, and I had money buried. I was going back, digging up jars of money I had buried.

Q: Your first edition is August 5, 1964. What was your first paper like?

A: It was an eight-page tabloid. We laid the first paper out on the wrong side of the layout page and didn't know it till we got over there and Mr. Thompson like to have come into a back-flipping fit. It was all black grid, and we were supposed to put it together on a layout table, a light table, with the black grids on the bottom side, and we had them up on the top side. We put an index in it because the other paper didn't have an index, but we forgot to put any page numbers in it. We had a complete page just left vacant, so I took a black magic marker and announced our grand opening—"Come by for some free drinks and hot dogs"—[but] there was no address or nothing, so nobody knew where we were open. Nobody knew anything. It was a—well, we look back now, and that first paper was quite a joke.

So I started off with one employee, and I was selling advertising through the daytime. When my wife would come in after school, she'd come straight back, and she'd proof the ads that I'd brought in. . . . Then the stories I'd bring in, she'd do the same.

Q: You were the reporter and the boss, and you two did everything. How did it go initially? Did you get ads right away?

A: The first edition, we got a good many because, you know, I worked at it. Sleep is something, to this day, I've never been fond of. . . . I resent lying down to go to sleep. It's a total waste of life, in my opinion. The only difference between sleep and death is a heartbeat, and that's always been too close for me.

The first thing, in 1957, when I was going off to school, my mother and daddy gave me . . . a little old dictionary, and I still got it, carried [it] all through [my] service. It's a little old pocket dictionary, and the first thing I did was mark out those four words: *impossible, can't, if,* and *but.*

My mother says, "What are you doing marking up a brand-new dictionary?"

And I said, "I don't want those four words in my book."

Q: How long did it take you to become established as a newspaper? I know in the beginning you gave away the papers. Did that help?

A: Yes, sir. I mailed them out to every box holder in the county for a year and a half.

Q: Were you able to get enough advertising to carry the paper?

A: I still got my first deposit books and records. . . . You can see half of those checks is stamped "Insufficient funds." So the bank president would call me up and tell me how much I was overdrawn, and I'd just laugh about it.

I said, "Well, you must know that I'm not going to leave, because if I'm overdrawn, then apparently I don't have enough money to leave town."

The banks worked with me real well because, of course, I grew up here, and they knew my folks.

Q: How about the supply-store business—was that successful?

A: I bought $240 worth of discounted office supplies out of the back of a man's truck. So we started from there, and the office-supply store went real well in the beginning. We kept it for thirty years.

Q: What was the name of your paper when you first started?

A: The *Madison County Carrier*, and people told me, as bad as I spelled, I probably meant to say *Courier* and did not know how to spell it. I put a back slant on it also, a left-handed slant. I'm left-handed, and I just wanted something different. I named it that because we were going to be carrying the news and the advertising and the information for the people of the county. I didn't realize that the word *carrier* also meant some other bad things. You know, I was a country boy come to town. I was just short of being web-footed when I got up here.

Q: Is there a point where your circulation matched the circulation of the established *Madison Enterprise Recorder*?

A: It started off greater because I was mailing free to everybody.

Q: But once you were charging for the paper?

A: We still continued to print more papers, because I was working stuff as I studied his newspaper. He [*Madison Enterprise Recorder*] was a social-type newspaper. He had a more liberal slant that a lot of country Crackers of Madison County liked, which wouldn't be considered liberal under today's standards, but, back then, it was. Almost no pictures because they were hot metal. . . . But he made money.

Q: Because he was the established paper?

A: Well, he was the only paper, but after I opened up, and I was struggling, I bought nothing that I could make or build myself. When I bought equipment, I saved the packaging—most of it was wooden packaging back then—and I'd build tables, light tables, drying tables, whatever I needed to do. I didn't throw anything away. I even saved the nails that came out of those packages. We never threw away a piece of paper that was white on one side and had been typed on the other. Everything was used to the max. I guess one reason I stayed in business is that I kept my expenses to the absolute minimum.

I worked as close to twenty-four hours a day as I could work. Our office had an old hard concrete floor out there, and I'd take a stack of newspapers and lie down on that floor and put those papers under my head for a pillow and set my clock for fifteen minutes or ninety minutes later. That seemed to have been the two times that I could wake up feeling good.

Q: Did the competition make him any better?

A: I think so. That was a fine old gentleman [T. C. Merchant, Sr., the owner and publisher] that had his own niche, and it worked. It really did. So what I had to do was something different, so I wound up putting blood-and-gut pictures on the front page: car wrecks, murders, bodies, hard-hitting editorials about this government that was caving in on us. . . . I wrote all my own editorials. I'd write them usually late at night, and when I'd go home to wake my wife up to get her ready for school, she would proof them for me.

[One time], we didn't get called [by the police to cover] the bust-up [of] a liquor still. I got a call at three o'clock that morning, and someone told me, "Did you know there was a liquor still busted yesterday afternoon?"

And I said, "We didn't know anything about it." Because I encouraged people to call, my motto was, Put Tommy Greene on the scene, twenty-four hours a day. My motto was, "If it happened in Madison County, I wanted to be there." I didn't care what time it was.

Q: Would the police usually call you?

A: Yes. I worked with them hand in glove, rode with them, backed them up when it came to fights. I always worked hand in hand with law enforcement and still do.

So when I found out that the sheriff had gone out there and busted a liquor still—we were getting ready to go to press the next morning—I just wrote a front-page notice that I knew nothing about this liquor still: "[And] did the sheriff own part of it? You'd have to ask him." I asked a whole bunch of really intimidating questions: "Had the sheriff been involved with other liquor operations in the county? Don't know, have to ask him," and all the way through. All of these things . . . , I didn't say that he did any of it, but I asked those questions, and every time I'd put his night number and his office number and told them that both phones were twenty-four-hour-a-day phones. Of course, when the paper hit the street, he pitched a fit. I told him, "Next time, you call me." That got his attention, and we were called from then on.

Q: What day did you publish?

A: I hit the street Wednesday night; Thursday morning was the paper date. We was primarily a Madison County deal, and my theory was that if the moon fell, we didn't care unless it messed up fishing in Madison County,

Florida, or somebody from Madison was on that moon. Our target was Madison County, Florida, and its people.

Q: And was that enough?

A: [We] survived . . . because, to this day, if the United States bombed Canada, we'd probably have something to say about it, but that's not of interest to us. It's of interest to me as an individual, but as far as that newspaper, if somebody wants to know about Madison County, Florida, then we've got the only thing in town.

Q: And what happened to the *Madison Enterprise Recorder*?

A: The other newspaper thrived and continued on, and nobody could understand why, because no town is big enough for two newspapers. But, again, he was so unique and unusual, and, I guess, as I look back, I was also. Mine was in the extreme opposite direction. The bigger somebody was, the quicker I wanted to take them on, and the people out there, by nature — they may tell you they don't want to see blood, guts, and fights, but you let one break out in a grandstand and see if they continue to watch the football game, or if they look at that fight. You know? I mean, it's just human nature. And I guess it was the competitiveness in me, . . . my daddy's raising, that, you know, we didn't come out of those swamps 'till we got what we went in there after.

Q: But they finally closed down?

A: He sold out to a [con]glomerate, and then that [con]glomerate sold out in 1983.

Q: When did you start buying other newspapers, and which ones did you purchase?

A: The first one that I bought was one that we were printing here, the *Mayo Free Press* [purchased August 5, 1976], which was also an extremely old paper.

Q: What was your second paper?

A: My second paper was the following January tenth. I bought the *Branford News*. . . . I went to Lake City and bought it from Tom Haygood. We put the deal together pretty fast.

He said, "Yeah, I'll sell it."

And I said, "Okay." I said, "Here, let me give you some money down on it."

And he said, "No, I don't need it."

And I put a hundred-dollar bill, and I said, "Let me give you one hundred right now; just write me a receipt out as a down payment and the balance due, and I'll get you this money back—how about in the morning?"

He said, "Well, fine."

I don't know what was in me that day, but on the way back to Madison . . . I saw a city block there that was vacant. So I . . . bought that city block. I came home and told my wife that we had bought the Branford paper and the city block uptown, and that was another one of those fine times when I thought she was going to leave me.

[The next paper was when] . . . I drove over to White Springs and got me a post office box and telephone number and . . . went over there and parked my motor home in a trailer park over there . . . and spent a week over there, and I opened up the *White Springs Leader.*

Q: Was there a paper there at all?

A: No, sir. I eventually put it [*White Springs Leader*] up for sale and . . . just closed it, pulled out of there. That's during that time when Judge Smith in Lake City, the circuit judge, was accused of the big dope dealings and served some time for it, and all this big drug trafficking was going on. We didn't know it, but the old hotel that was there was the main headquarters. My newspaper staff and I were not aware of this, until they all of a sudden just quit. Everyone just quit on me. I found out later the little girl [his reporter] . . . had been given threatening [warnings]. Our phones were tapped [because] she was doing an investigation on this Judge Smith and all these other people and was writing all these heavy, hard-hitting stories. I told them, I said, "You know, if it doesn't rattle some cages, it's not worth writing. I want some cages rattled."

So we just got threatened out of business, and I didn't realize it till after the fact, or I think I would've moved over there and probably wound up getting waylaid one night. It got real serious because that was during the time that a Mr. Gate went missing, the road guard . . . and they found him tied to a tree and executed, a bullet in the back of his head. She was doing a story on that, and we had run the pictures down in those woods. There was three or four different people who'd gotten killed during that time, so, yes, it was serious business.

My advertising lady, who lives here in Madison now, . . . she was the heartbeat of the profits. She could sell snow to an Eskimo.

Q: What finally happened to the *Madison Enterprise Recorder*?

A: [Greene discusses his competition with that paper]. The [con]glomerate had moved in a girl in here [as publisher] that . . . must have been raised on blood, because she went after mine. So that's why I brought my people in, and I said, "We're getting ready to go twice a week, and we're going to start today." This was a Monday morning. I said, "Friday, we will have a second paper on the street." That's what I've always done. We've always moved. Let's do it now! Don't plan to do it, because if you plan to do it, then the word gets out and this, that, and the other. So we just do it.

One of the people up there said, "What's going to happen if this thing doesn't work out twice a week?"

I said, "Then we'll go three times a week, four times a week, five times a week. We'll put [it] out twice daily. That other paper is not going to whip us." They had the finances to do it with, or do it under normal conditions. So we were sitting here, and I was losing money.

We fought for two years. The last year, we'd lost $35,000. They'd lost $140,000, according to their own spokesman. So Mr. Ricketson called me, [and] we went over . . . and had three different meetings. In those meetings I sold him the *Mayo Free Press*. And I bought the *Enterprise Recorder*.

Q: Why didn't you merge the two Madison papers?

A: My thought was two things. Number one, I didn't want to give up my baby because it was so well established, the *Madison County Carrier*. I did not want to close down a legend. The *Madison Enterprise Recorder* had been here since 1865.

Q: But they were losing money.

A: They were, under separate ownership. That's when I called my daughter in. My daughter is good with figures. . . . She became our bookkeeper and our general manager. I stopped publishing the *Carrier* on Fridays and came back to once a week with the *Madison County Carrier* and moved the *Madison Enterprise Recorder*, also a Wednesday publication, because we were butting heads, Wednesday-Wednesday, to a Friday publication. So rather than putting out two *Madison County Carriers*, one on Wednesday and one on Friday, we're now putting one *Madison County Carrier* out every Wednesday and a *Madison Enterprise Recorder* out every Friday.

The *Madison Enterprise Recorder* carries certain columns every week, that these people that like those columns can look forward to, and weekend-type news. We also carry hard front-page news, the same as the *Madison County Carrier* does. And we got certain columns that run in the *Madison County Carrier* every week that do not run in the *Enterprise Recorder*. So there are two separate banners in one respect, but they are still owned by us.

Q: When you started out, what were your ultimate goals for that paper?

A: I wanted to let the folks of Madison County know that if it happened in Madison County, Florida, they could read about it in the *Madison County Carrier*, period. I didn't want anything missed, and we worked desperately to cover the county.

Q: What do you consider the most important functions of a newspaper?

A: Truth. There's no truth on this planet that I'm afraid of, period, and when I find, especially a government official—elected, hired, appointed, any way, shape, fashion, or form—that is not totally leveling with me, I instantly smell a skeleton in his closet, and we don't quit digging till we destroy that closet or find that skeleton. I think the editorial pages, the letters to the editor, are first and foremost. We need pages there that the public can sound off in. We need to be an alarm clock, not to alarm people but to awaken people. Basically, we need to be, kind of, a half-breed dog, between a bloodhound that can sniff out wrongdoings in government, and then a bulldog, with an attitude that would be just about like a brain-dead bulldog with lockjaw. We hang in there until we get that story, and we expose what's out there.

Q: Did you try to balance your editorials with the letters to the editor, so if you took one position, you would print letters representing the other view?

A: Yes, sir. I never answered but one letter to the editor in the same edition, and that came from a feller in Madison who was going to the University of Florida down there and wrote me a letter to the editor and says, "I guess you must be an FSU [Florida State University] fan, being that you live so close to FSU." I says . . . , "I'm going to take exception to my policy, and I'm going to answer this letter in the same edition, and that is that when FSU and Florida play one another, I hope they both get beat, because neither school let me in."

That's the only letter I've ever answered in the same edition. I'd answer in the following [edition], and that does two things. That gives the writer, the author of that letter, the one that's ticked off or whatever the case may be, that sees a different view than I do, gives him an opportunity to express himself without a rebuttal. It gives me an opportunity to come back, and when you get in this type [of] tennis match, then you build readership. You know, what are they going to say next?

Q: So with two papers you now have a much larger staff in terms of reporters and columnists?

A: [Actually] we have a third newspaper, *Madison County News*, . . . [which] has been established . . . for about five years. We have a total circulation of nine. The *Madison County News* that we started about five or six years ago is really a scavenger paper. It's a one sheet, eight and a half by eleven. We run off ten or twelve copies of it. We pick up just stuff that we've run in either the Madison paper or the other paper that's already set up. It takes us about ten or fifteen minutes a week to do it. We've met all the criteria of the post office. It's as legal a newspaper as the *Madison County Carrier* or the *Enterprise Recorder*, so we got three legal newspapers.

A number of years ago, a paper started in here, just one that was coming off of a copy machine, and that came out on an eleven-seventeen folded and was running off three hundred copies. So when they hit the street one week, the following day, we came out with the *Madison County News*. I said, "Madison won't have three newspapers unless all three of them's mine." So, right now, we've got the three legal newspapers.

The *Madison County News* . . . sells for nine cents apiece in one location, which is our uptown newspaper office. Nobody buys it. The subscriptions are one hundred dollars a year. We have no subscribers. But it's sitting there, and if we ever need to bring it to life for any reason, it's sitting there idling on the runway.

Q: Let's talk about your association with the Florida Press Association [FPA]. You eventually became the youngest president of the Florida Press Association. How did that transpire?

A: Well, our first Press Association [meeting] that we ever went to was in 1965. . . . My wife and I were both twenty-five years old, and it looked like everybody in that bunch down there was a hundred. I realize now that they weren't. I just, from the beginning, knew that if we stayed in the newspaper business, we needed to find out something about the newspaper business and that nobody should know better than the people associated with the Florida Press Association. I didn't even know that there was a Florida Press Association when we opened up the newspaper business.

Again, I stayed in the newspaper business out of sheer energy and ignorance, and that is the absolute truth. I didn't know what we couldn't do, so we did it. Then I became just heavily involved with the association and wound up on the board right quick-like. . . . One of the things that I wanted to do was to get our Florida Press Association on good financial ground, which, during my years on the board in the beginning, it was not, and we were all very concerned about it. Then, the Florida Press Association membership was extremely low, and, again, I have more energy than control. That's always been a major problem of mine, I think. But I told them, "If I become president, I will visit every single newspaper in this state." So I wound up as vice president, and then I became president.

Q: What year was this?

A: 1974–75. I bought a thirty-six-foot Pace Arrow motor home. . . . So . . . we toured the state of Florida in that motor home. We went to every single solitary newspaper in this state. We didn't miss a one. So we put on a campaign and . . . we found out that people were wanting to join. A lot of them didn't even know about the Florida Press Association . . . and we worked really hard and heavy on trying to get the profitability of it turned around and get a positive image, and it worked. We brought in a bunch of members.

Q: When you talk about lobbying, give me an example of what the FPA would do for the members of the association.

A: At any given session—and the fate of no man is safe as long as the legislature's in session, and especially the fate of the newspaper because somewhere in this great state of Florida, some newspaperman has ticked off some legislator. So they go to Tallahassee with a spur under their blanket, and they're going to get that newspaper. [One legislator] was determined to eliminate the three times that you run the delinquent tax rolls and bring it down to one time [which would have reduced the paper's revenue by two-thirds]. . . . Dick Shelton [executive director of the Florida Press Association] kept us aware of what was going on, all the newspapers across the state. Consequently, that bill never got out of committee. Now had we had somebody over there that was not as sharp enough on it as Dick Shelton or a Reg Ivory—if we'd had someone else that was coming in drunk and not showing up at these meetings—that thing could've eased on through.

Q: Let's discuss some broader issues. How is your audience different today than it was in 1964?

A: Well, we have a lot of newcomers who have come into this county, but we have still stuck, I guess, to our original deal, that if they want to read about something else somewhere else in the world, then they need to get a daily paper or USA Today or something else.

Q: How has the county changed in thirty-five years?

A: In some areas, it's made major changes. We have people moving in here—we call them "South Florida Yankees." They come from the North and they go south, and then they get fed up with that down there and they . . . move up here. We're the ham between the two pieces of bread. Every time somebody tells us, "Well, this isn't how we do it up North," we tell them to take I-95 or I-75 north and do it now."

The worst thing that happened to the state of Florida is when Bob Graham promoted this $25,000-a-year homestead exemption. It threw the burden of property taxes now all on the businesses, and the one that's hit the hardest is agriculture. Our problem now is we're getting so many people moving into North Florida who want an acre of land and a two-thousand-dollar mobile home, and, consequently, they're not paying any taxes. They come up here either retired and not producing any goods or services, or they come up here with a trailer full of young'uns that we've got to school. We've got to protect them with an ambulance and law enforcement and fire protection and all this other stuff, and they're not paying any taxes. That's really bringing a hard crunch in on the locals that's been here over the years, who have bought land and has to live off the land.

Q: This is still a pretty conservative county, is it not?

A: George Wallace was somewhat liberal, in our opinion.

Q: Do most people here vote Republican or Democrat?

A: The Republican Party has really flourished out. We got ten thousand voters in Madison County, Florida, and we're looking now at right about two thousand of them are Republicans, and they are coming on hard and heavy.

Q: With the state legislature and the governor controlled by the Republicans for the first time in the history of the state, that shows the whole state has changed.

A: This pendulum—and the swingin' pendulum is what keeps the clock ticking—has swung so far to the left until it's bringing on so much resentment towards government. I've got a lot of resentment towards our government, not towards this country because, like I say, I'm still standing [when] the flag comes by. . . . I've never accepted a penny to build a bluebird nest or build a fishpond, and they're doing it right here in this county. You can get money today to build bluebird nests.

Q: When you first started the newspaper business, was there much competition from radio? And how did you deal with that?

A: When somebody would say, "Well, I'm spending this much money with the radio station," I'd say, "Well, good, but I can show you this: when it's published, it's permanent." I think we had a big advantage over the radio station in several respects. We had something they could hold [a newspaper] in their hand, and they knew that it was something you could clip coupons out of.

Q: Do you think that's going to change, that everything is going to be on the Internet?

A: We're looking into that. In fact, we're already on the Internet. I don't know how, but we've hired somebody to help us learn. I told my children all these years, "You know, if you're not living on the edge, you're dying in too much space."

Q: Have you ever had any pressure from an advertiser because of something you either had written in an editorial or printed in an article?

A: The best way for somebody to get something on [the] front page is to tell me what they're going to do if I print it. God be my witness, it goes on front page. It may have been an inside story to start with, but it'll go on front page with an editor's note that we don't take threats and they can take their money and walk with it, because the newspaper business never kept me in the newspaper business anyway. It was my other doings that did.

Q: Would you discuss how you have adapted new technology over the years?

A: When something new was on that drawing board, we wanted to be the first to get it. In 1982 I got to hearing about this LP TV, and I didn't even know what it stood for [low-power television]. They had to retrain me to operate one of these remote controls. So I'm not technically knowledgeable. But the first thing I did was applied for the TV license, for a television station. So in 1983 we put our television . . . on there. That works hand in hand with our newspaper because we were already in the news-gathering business. So we became the second in the nation and the first in the state of Florida to have a TV station here, and we still operate it.

Q: What content do you have on the station, and how many hours do you operate it?

A: We operate twenty-four-seven, 168 hours a week, around the clock. We've got several things right now that's never been tried anywhere else in the country that we think will work, and we're getting ready to [implement] that. . . . Any time of the day or night, you can turn on and we've got these ads up there where you can buy and sell and trade and swap. We go on six- and twelve-hour tapes. We promote Boy Scouts. We promote the National

Rifle Association. We support Americanism and all, at all levels. We promote the Church of Jesus Christ of Latter Day Saints, the Mormons, real heavy, and any other church that'll bring us in tapes.

Q: You obviously are very involved in community activities. I notice that you're a member of probably every club that exists in Madison. Why do you think it is important for a newspaper publisher to be civic minded?

A: If you're not totally committed to a community—and I loved it so much, my second son was named William Madison Greene—totally dedicated to this type work and have, I guess, a certain degree of insanity about you, it's not the right job for you. I wanted my community to be the very best community on this planet, second to none. One of the sayings that we've got: The problem about being second is that you're the first one to see the winner and the first one to see the loser.

Q: Were you heavily involved in politics?

A: I've always been involved in politics. I like the behind-the-closed-door-type stuff, one on one.

Q: But you've never held political office?

A: No, sir.

Q: But isn't your opinion fairly influential in this county?

A: I don't know about that. I'm just a country boy that stuck it out. I put on a lot of socials. My motto: If you don't wake up to a party, start one. Consequently, I try to stay in very good with all the local and area state politicians, and I wound up getting on as a state witness to that execution [John Spenkelink]. I've always believed in capital punishment. Swift and severe justice, I think that's an absolute key. In fact, I've run in the paper several times in my editorials, if we want to stop crime, we need to execute all criminals and their lawyers. I was asked then if I believed in the electric chair, and I said, "No, I'd prefer electric bleachers."

Q: You started a newspaper without any journalistic training and learned on the job. Do you think that people in the newspaper business need a journalism degree?

A: Not to knock our J[ournalism] schools, because they may be changed from sometime back, but the first thing we tried to do was deprogram them [new employees]. We were having students, J-school graduates, come to us that had not taken a photographic course. Now last St. Patrick's Day—because of my all-green doings, I'm always interviewed around those days—they sent two people to cover one story. They sent a photographer, and they sent a newswriter. That would've never happened [here] and does not happen in our business because the same person who's going to write that story is going to take that picture. We're not going to have two people on the payroll doing the same job.

Q: What's the future of independently owned weekly newspapers?

A: We could sell out today to a [con]glomerate. I think it's getting slimmer and slimmer that you're going to find independently owned newspapers, of any kind. . . . Right now . . . Monticello and Madison . . . [are] the only two independents that I know of in North Florida.

Q: What is the major source of income for a weekly newspaper? Is it still advertising?

A: Yes. Advertising, advertising, advertising.

Q: Do you think that the larger chains can buy up these independent newspapers and operate them more efficiently than an individual owner?

A: What they do, they come in—like, for instance, if they bought up Greene Publishing, they would come in, and they would trim it down to the bone. Madison people would not be getting the same newspapers that they're getting today. They'd have this thing cut down to a survival-type publication. It's going to be extremely difficult for a new paper to come in against a [con]glomerate. A lot of people, just like me, gets into the newspaper business not knowing what's in front of them, and most of them's smart enough to get out.

Q: When you look at the time you've been in business with this paper, what has been the paper's greatest contribution to the community?

A: Whew. Well, we have promoted industry as hard and heavy as we can promote because without that, we don't have a tax base. Industry includes agriculture. . . . We promoted law enforcement, and a lot of times we'd sit on a story . . . so that we wouldn't break something before they got their case put together. I'd say our biggest contribution right now is trying to keep as much government control out of our lives as anything. Right now, I just found out yesterday that now you've got to go get a permit for a man to slip an air conditioner in your window, even if he plugs it into a one-ten outlet, and they [are] getting ready to go from a twenty-dollar permit to a forty-dollar permit.

Q: When you look at your career in journalism, and I know you have other interests, are you satisfied with what you've accomplished, given where you started?

A: Well, I've never been content in my life, so I don't really know how to answer that. I'm happy that I've reached the thirty-five-year mark and I've got a daughter that can take this paper and go with it. I was extremely blessed that my wife has got the sales ability and the love to sell. She stays in on that telephone all day. She'd sell toe tags in a hospital waiting room. So we've lived one endless party, and we made a party out of this newspaper business. When it gets too rough, she and I will maybe take off one night and go somewhere, but we're back the next morning.

chapter 8   **S. L. Frisbie IV**

S. L. Frisbie was born in Bartow, Florida, and graduated from Florida State University in 1962. He then joined the U.S. army as a second lieutenant and spent the next two years working in the Army Intelligence Corps in Washington, D.C. Upon discharge from the army in 1964, he joined Frisbie Publishing Company to work on the *Polk County Democrat*, a twice-weekly community newspaper begun by his great-grandfather and grandfather. The *Polk County Democrat*, which has been operated by four generations of the Frisbie family, currently publishes four newspapers. Frisbie is a past president of the Florida Press Association.

In this interview Frisbie gives a brief history of the paper begun by his family and describes the growth of that newspaper and the purchase of papers in surrounding areas. He discusses his grandmother's and mother's involvement with the family business. He talks about the changing technology in newspaper printing and the formation and publication of the *Polk County Times*, which covers local government. He considers the role filled by local, weekly newspapers in the community and the impact of the paper's editorial endorsements on local politics. He discusses the changes in the paper's audience and circulation, while reflecting on the challenges of running a weekly newspaper, including staff relations and hiring practices. He assesses the importance of independent newspapers and the future of his paper. He concludes with comments on the future of newspaper publishing in general.

S. L. Frisbie IV was interviewed by Julian M. Pleasants on October 23, 2001, in Bartow, Florida.

Q: Talk a little bit about the history of this newspaper. I know it goes all the way back to Mr. Sayer L. Frisbie, who got interested in the newspaper business in Iowa. Explain the history of the paper from the time the family came to Florida.

A: This newspaper was established on August 28, 1931, as a weekly newspaper, once-a-week newspaper, by my great-grandfather, Sayer Loyal Frisbie, and his son, Sayer Lloyd Frisbie. They had been in the newspaper business off and on together for quite a number of years beginning, as you say, with Great-Granddad's employment at, I believe, the age of eighteen in Iowa. . . . Great-Granddad moved to Bartow to start a printing company, and my granddad, Sayer Lloyd Frisbie, was working in Tampa, originally at the *Tampa Tribune*; then [he] went with a boomtown daily that started up. When that paper closed, he went back to the *Tribune*.

In 1931 he got the itch to start another newspaper, to own his own newspaper again with my great-granddad, so he moved to Bartow, [and] published originally, I believe, on Fridays, printing in the printing plant of Bartow Printing Company. They started up against an established five-day daily in the depth of the Great Depression, which I have said many times is probably one of the more dubious business decisions in Florida newspaper publishing history. They continued as a weekly; then, in 1946, bought the competition, which was the *Polk County Record*.

Q: Let me go back to 1931; why did they make that dubious business decision?

A: I have never asked Granddad why he got the itch to start his own newspaper over here. He had, obviously, the production facilities through Bartow Printing Company. Why in the world he left the *Tampa Morning Tribune*, as it was then called, to come and become a struggling weekly newspaper publisher is a question I do not know the answer to.

Q: There were two problems: one, there was already an established newspaper. It would not seem that there would be enough room for two papers. And then it was during the Depression. How did they manage to survive?

A: I have been told . . . they would do what was called "kiting" checks. They would write a check from one company to another company, [and] put it in the mail to Tampa—what today would be called "float." The checks would clear because [of] the money they were sending back and forth and the delay that it would take for the checks to clear the bank. I do know that on the bank holiday, when of course all the banks [were] closed [by President Roosevelt], . . . some customer had paid his advertising bill, I believe the story is, with three dollars' worth of dimes. Granddad assembled the staff and divided out the dimes equally among the number of people who were there, maybe half a dozen people.

Q: It started out as a free circulation, tabloid-type newspaper?

A: That is correct; it was free circulation, and Dad has told me a number of times that the format tended to change . . . , based on the size of newsprint they were able to get their hands on. Particularly during the war years, but also in the early years when it was being done at a job shop, the format tended to change according to the availability of stock.

Q: An interesting point in the development of the paper was 1942. For the first time, you got the right to print the Polk County delinquent-tax list. Why was that so important?

A: The delinquent-tax list, at that time and for many, many years after that, was a bonanza in Polk County. The price was fixed by agreement between all the publishers in the county and the county tax collector. It was rotated among the newspapers . . . , but it was a bonanza. It was worth its weight in gold to get the delinquent-tax list.

Q: In the 1940s there were eleven newspapers in Polk County?

A: That is my recollection; [I am] talking about paid-circulation newspapers now. I can count them up for you. The dailies were the *Lakeland Ledger*, *Winter Haven News Chief*, and *Lake Wales Daily Highlander*; the week-lies were Lake Wales, Frostproof, Fort Meade, Bartow, Auburndale, Mulberry, *Winter Haven Herald*—Haines City, I believe was the other one.

  Polk County has the dubious distinction—dubious to those of us in the business—of being one of the most competitive newspaper markets in the country. Not all of those papers are still published, incidentally, but two of the three dailies are still around. One of the dailies, the *Daily Highlander* in Lake Wales, has folded, and several of the weeklies have folded. I do not believe there are any more new paid-circulation papers in the county.

Q: Some time ago Loyal Frisbie [S. L. Frisbie III] began writing a personal column, and I guess he is still writing that column, which is called "Off My Chest."

A: That is correct. His very first one, fresh out of college, was entitled something like "Picture of a Young Man Talking to Himself." He writes generally about whatever interests him at the moment. Growing up as the son of an editor, I sometimes found our family squabbles made it into the paper. He wrote extensively about his travels, as did Mother. Sometimes it is [about] local issues. I think the title "Off My Chest" says it well. [He writes about] politics, international situations, local situations, talks about his dog Queenie, who has been called the most famous dog in Bartow.

Q: So this is more commentary than editorial.

A: Yes, it is very much a personal column. At one time his column probably represented the editorial policy of the paper, back before we had regular editorials. We now have conventional editorials which express the editorial position of the newspaper. He and I each write personal columns, which tend to be purely personal observations. During World War II he was drafted in World War II and served as an infantryman. His column was called "Private Opinion." His columns during World War II were written in the form of letters home; otherwise they would have had to go through extensive censorship. Obviously he was circumspect in what he wrote about in terms of anything that would have been helpful to the enemy. Again, [they were] personal observations.

I remember, particularly, he had his feet frozen at the Battle of the Bulge and spent a lot of time in hospitals. The exposure for the first time to integrated facilities in the army—the hospitals, of course, were integrated by a matter of practicality and exigencies of the service, as they say, even before the total armed forces were integrated.

Q: This newspaper has an unusual history. I understand that this is the only paper in the state that has been run by four generations of one family. So in the early years, Lloyd was the publisher, Loyal was the editor, and Richard was involved as business manager. Is that correct?

A: At the time that my dad and his brother Richard and Granddad and Great-Granddad were here, I believe that Great-Granddad carried the title of president of the company; Granddad was publisher; Dad was editor or managing editor—I am not sure which term he used. On a small paper, it does not make a whole heck of a lot of difference. Richard, his brother, was business manager—also sports editor, but principally business manager.

Q: I also understand that their wives worked at the newspaper as well.

A: Absolutely. Great-Granddad's wife did not work at the newspaper; she was an educator. Granddad's wife, Cricket . . . came in. It was the classic story; weekly publishers have been using this scam for years: "Well, somebody is on vacation for a couple of weeks; honey, would you come in and fill in?" That two weeks stretched into a career as a society editor.

My mother, Louise Frisbie, came into the business on a regular basis when Dad was drafted, to help out during World War II. She not only was, in effect, managing editor of the paper, basically she was the news staff of the paper, but I believe she was also stringing, probably for the *Tampa Tribune* and possibly for the *Lakeland Ledger* at that time. I do not know if that was represented to her as a temporary arrangement, but I do not doubt that it was, because that was the way we usually pull these scams.

My wife came into the business back when I was in the National Guard and was drilling Wednesday nights. She came in to just proofread on Wednesday nights to help us out a little bit. She is now our head book-keeper, corporate treasurer, and number-two person in the business for what is now four newspapers that we own.

Q: Talk a little bit about your mother, Louise Frisbie, because she is not only well known as a correspondent; she wrote several books, the most significant, I think, is *Peace River Pioneers*.

A: Probably that would be the best known. Yes, Mother started a second career . . . as an avocation in the sense that she never got rich at it. It remains a very active role for her. In 1969 the *Polk County Democrat* started a Fort Meade edition. . . . So Mother began writing a series of historical articles on the town of Fort Meade and discovered that she had a real love of history, even greater than she realized. So from that she wrote a book called *Peace River Pioneers*, which is about the history of the four counties which abut the Peace River: Polk, Highlands, Hardee, and DeSoto.

Q: In 1962 you finished at Florida State University and came on board as managing editor. At that point, what other family members were still working with the newspaper?

A: [I] did my two years of active army duty, came back in 1964, and joined the staff as managing editor. That was just a few months after my grandfather had died. Great-Granddad died when I was in high school, so Dad was editor; his brother Richard was a business manager. My grandmother had [retired] by then, so it would have been the two of them, just the two brothers, Loyal and Richard.

Q: Did you ever think about any other career?

A: I never seriously considered it. I grew up in the newspaper business. My parents did everything they could to dissuade me from going into it, because they did not want me to feel like I had some sort of family obligation to carry on—then later told me when I made that decision, they were delighted. They also had a clear conscience because at every turn they said, "You do not have to go into the newspaper business; consider other fields."

Q: In 1969 you purchased the Fort Meade paper. Why did you decide to do that, and how has that paper done?

A: It has been excellent as a part of the total operation. We would be hard put to publish a freestanding twice-a-week broadsheet newspaper in a town of five thousand people with a very small merchant district. But as a part of the entire operation—extending the advertising reach of the *Polk County Democrat* and giving us the ability to cover, for instance, county-seat news—it allows us to give something to the community that the community would not be able to support with the volume of advertising that is down there.

Q: In 1971 you got an offset press. How did that affect how you put out the paper?

A: Dramatically. The letterpress, or commonly called "hot-type," was basically a technology not terribly unlike [what produced] the old Gutenberg Bibles. The majority of type was no longer set by hand, although we still set a lot of headlines and a lot of grocery ads in hand-set type. At that time, a typesetter or a Linotype operator, a person who operated a Linotype machine—that was an apprenticeable trade. The apprenticeship period was five years. [When we began setting type on] computers, the training period for typesetter dropped from five years to about two weeks.

The materials that we used when we were hot-type, everything was cast in lead slugs. In order to pick up that stuff, basically you had to have the upper-body strength of a man. Printers, almost one hundred percent at that time, were male. We went from a totally male production force to one which became largely female because no longer was [heavy] lifting a responsibility. It was also considerably safer. When I was working as a teenager down at our old plant, [I] became, among other things, a stereotypist. This is [a] person who casts printing plates in lead. You did this by scooping melted lead out [of an iron pot] and pouring it into a machine. I remember the guy who trained me said, "You learn to spit real fast and real accurate." It was just an occupational hazard that little droplets of hot lead, melted lead, would land on your hands and arms. We were lucky we never had anybody seriously injured, but there was that degree of danger involved.

Q: In 1997 you began to publish the *Polk County Times*. Tell me what that is, and why you started publishing it.

A: *Polk County Times* is my wild idea that only I thought would succeed. I was driving home . . . , and I said, "Mary, I am going to start a new newspaper; it is going to be modeled after *Army Times* and *Air Force Times* and *Navy Times* and *Federal Times*. It is going to be called *Polk County Times*." She looked at me like I was crazy. I said, "It is going to be a niche publication for county government. . . ." Polk County is a county of almost five hundred thousand people. So even though we are the third largest—and a rather distant third largest—town in Polk County, we are the county seat. Somebody was saying at this economic-development committee meeting, "I wish my business could reach those thousands of people who work here in the daytime and go home at night." The little lightbulb lit over my head said, "Well, Bozo, is that not the business you are supposed to be in? Putting merchants in touch with their customers and potential customers?"

I announced it to the staff. They thought I was crazy; only a few of them actually told me so, but it was clear from the expressions on the faces of the others. The beauty of *Polk County Times* is that we do a great deal of county-seat, county-government coverage: both county commission and school board, the sheriff's office, other county agencies. So basically the reporting was already done. The merchant community was very interested in reaching these county employees. Neither the county commission nor the school board had a viable house organ or employee newsletter.

It was a relatively easy sell, to sell them on the idea that we would like to publish this publication; we would like for you to distribute it through your mail rooms, so our circulation costs are minimal, because there are no carriers to be paid and no postal bills to be paid. The school board has been an advertiser in the paper since the first issue. The county commission, or county government, has been an advertiser in it since sometime in the first year. Just in the last two or three issues, [the] Polk County sheriff's office, which was also looking for a way to communicate with their thousand-plus, maybe two-thousand-plus [employees], saw the value in using this as their internal communications [vehicle].

Q: So this goes out monthly, and there is no charge?

A: Once a month. That is correct; it is free circulation.

Q: So how do you make money?

A: We make money by charging about fifty percent more for advertising in this than we do in our paid-circulation papers. That was one of the [reasons] that the ad department looked at me like I was crazy. I said, "I know that you are wondering, 'Are we going to be selling in competition to ourselves?' The answer is yes, of course we are, because there are [only] so many advertising dollars out there, but we are not going to do it on the basis of price." We charged a premium rate of approximately ten dollars a column inch. We have contracts and stuff, but it washes out about ten dollars a column inch for *Polk County Times*. At that time, that was a good fifty percent higher than the rates for our paid-circulation newspaper.

Q: So you were not crazy?

A: Yes, I was crazy, but we were successful nonetheless.

Q: In 1998 you purchased the Lake Wales paper. Why did you purchase that paper, and how has that worked out?

A: The *Lake Wales News* is five years older than the *Polk County Democrat*. The *Lake Wales News* was founded in 1926 and had been under the management of father and son of the same family, just two generations, for that many years, from 1926 until 1998. The Brice family at *Lake Wales News* and the Frisbie family have been friends for two generations on their side and three or four generations on our side. We had printed the *Lake Wales News* for the better part of twenty years. . . .

Owen Brice had a stroke, and his three adult daughters came to me and said, "Would you help us keep the newspaper alive until we can decide what to do with it?"

I said, "Yes, I will be glad to do that."

They said, "We will have to pay you."

I said, "Oh no, this is a labor of love for Owen; he would have done the same thing for us. Incidentally, when you decide what you are going to do with it, I hope you will give us first option."

There were basically two possibilities, sell it or close it. They came to me because they did not want to close it. This was on a Friday. They said, "Would you come over Monday morning and let the staff know that you are going to be helping us run [the paper]?"

I said, "No, the staff needs to know this now. It has been three weeks, and I know that they are wondering from day to day what is going on."

So I walked in and said, "Hi, I am S. L. Frisbie; I have not met you folks yet; I have no authority; I cannot sign checks; I cannot hire and fire; but I am going to help you keep the *Lake Wales News* going. Anything is open to negotiation, except we will not cease publication."

Within a very few weeks, the daughters had convinced Owen's wife, Laverne, who was his partner in the business, that the smart thing to do was to sell. Finally, we did negotiate a purchase as of close of business,

March 31, or, as I sometimes said, [on] April Fool's Day of 1998, I became owner of the *Lake Wales News*.

I said, "I am not interested in buying a shell; I want to buy an operating newspaper," so all the members of the staff did stay on.

Q: How is the Lake Wales paper different in content from the *Polk County Democrat*?

A: [Our] Lake Wales [paper], even more so than [our] Bartow [paper], is oriented one hundred percent to community news. [In] Bartow, not only do we have the community of Bartow, but being a county-seat newspaper, county government is the biggest business in town. We have a great deal of coverage of county government. In Lake Wales, we run a few county-government stories, generally, though, only those which have specific applicability to Lake Wales. Also in Bartow, having [a] substantially [greater] number of pages per week, we run a lot of features.

Q: If you look at all four of the papers, what is your main source of advertising? Do you get a lot of local restaurants and car dealers? You said you do not get grocery advertising anymore.

A: Right, in Bartow the only grocery advertising that we have is Publix inserts, [and] we get retailers, auto dealers, [and] some amount of chain-store advertising. The nature of our business is that weeklies rely to a great degree on locally owned independent businesses, where the local manager is, in all likelihood, the local owner and makes his own decisions. The chain stores to a large degree believe in daily newspapers, no matter where the daily newspaper is. They just simply do not believe in weekly newspapers, in many, many cases.

Q: I would assume most people in the county read the *Tampa Tribune* or the *St. Pete Times* or the *Lakeland Ledger* as a daily newspaper. They also get news on television. Why is a weekly newspaper important?

A: To me, the role of the weekly newspaper—and I have said this many times to readers and anybody else who cares—[is] that we do not try to be a little *Tampa Tribune*. We cannot begin to compete with the *Tampa Tribune* or the *Lakeland Ledger* on the scale that they can in covering statewide, national, and international news, or, for that matter, news of the total county.

What we can do, and what the nearest large daily newspaper cannot do, is to cover, if not everything that happens in our communities, a whole lot more than anybody else can cover. We can and do cover civic-club meetings and chamber of commerce luncheons and print substantially more detail in weddings and engagements and social activities, large volumes of school news in all three of our community publications. We have a great deal of church news, local features, much more in-depth coverage of [the] city commission in each of our three communities than the dailies can devote space to. What I tell people is that everybody ought to read a daily newspaper. I read two. But you also, to really have a thorough understanding of what is going on in your community and to read about what your friends and neighbors are doing, [ought to read] the community newspaper. The . . . weekly newspaper is the only place you are going to get that degree of local coverage.

Q: How do you go about deciding which candidate to endorse for political office, and what impact do you think that endorsement has on the voter?

A: We decide. That is a classic editorial "we"; the editorial board is me, and if we have any other member of the staff who wants to sit [in] on the interview, they are welcome to do so. I almost never get any takers on that. Occasionally the school-board reporter will sit in with the school-board candidates. Occasionally, Dad will sit in, but not often. We make the decision, at the risk of sounding over simplistic, based on who we think will do the best job.

The name of the paper is the *Polk County Democrat*, . . . [but] we have endorsed every Republican candidate [for president] since . . . [1964], both when Dad was making the decisions and when I made the decisions — some years with more enthusiasm, and some years with less enthusiasm. Dad and I are both conservative in our political positions, [and believe] that government is best which governs least. A little bit of an oversimplistic comment, but we believe generally that it is better for people to make their own decisions than for government to make decisions for them.

In local races the [party affiliation] is barely even a consideration because, especially when you get closer [to] home than the state offices and senatorial candidacies, the party labels are really a matter of convenience. Right now, Polk County is voting about 55/45 [percent] Republican for everything, so the politicians [who] can hear thunder and see lightning are registering Republican.

We try to interview every candidate. We send out an invitation to every candidate to come in for an interview. Those who do not come in, we consider them even so. I generally spend one to two hours with each candidate. I have said many times that we endorse not because we are any smarter than anybody else, but because in a county of a half a million people, there are not many people who have the opportunity to sit down one-on-one with the candidate for an hour or two hours at a time. We do. That is the value we see in our endorsement to the readers.

Q: In local races the endorsement is probably important, because I doubt very much that the average voter knows anything about judges. They probably know the candidates for governor and president, but they would not know much about some of those offices, would they?

A: That is correct. As far as the importance, I asked a veteran campaign manager that one time—exactly what you asked me: "Just how important are our endorsements?"

His or her response was, "Considerably less important than the candidates think they are, but they want them anyway. . . ."

I have had people tell me, the people that absolutely know nothing about the candidates will tend to just accept our endorsements for the reason they do not know anything else. I have often said, "The bumper sticker on your next-door neighbor's car or the yard sign across the street from your house is also an endorsement. If you know and trust the judgment of the person driving the car or the person who lives in that house, that is a bona fide endorsement."

Billboards to me are meaningless in terms of anything other than just name recognition. I think [our endorsements probably have] some impact. I think it is probably less than most of us in the business would like to think. In the presidential and probably even gubernatorial races, I doubt that we sway one vote in a hundred. People know who they want for president; they know who they want for governor; but we have still got to go out and give it our best shot.

Q: What would you consider to be the most important functions of this newspaper?

A: From an editorial-leadership position, I think that it is important for us to speak out, to take editorial positions on important issues, even if and perhaps even especially, if it is not a particularly popular position to take. Which is not to say we do so every week.

Q: I noticed that in today's paper, there is an issue that is rather controversial. I understand the county government wants to post the Ten Commandments.

A: The county commission was planning to post the Ten Commandments as an historical document, thereby attempting to get away from first-amendment issues. I said . . . that the moral precepts expressed in the Ten Commandments . . . can stand on their own merits, . . . , about half of which are part of the legal codes of every civilized country: thou shall not kill, thou shall not steal, thou shall not commit adultery, bearing false witness, perjury. I think it is a shame that in order to post these fundamental moral values that we have to pretend that it is not a religious document, that it is an historical document. I will tell you that although I feel that is the case, that is not a big issue with me. That is not something I would go to the mat with somebody over. [The] *Lakeland Ledger*, incidentally, said just the opposite, [said the county is] heading for a legal hassle for no particular purpose.

Q: What is the hardest thing about running a weekly newspaper?

A: Oh, let me count the ways. Probably the biggest challenge, particularly [as] an independent weekly newspaper (we are not part of a group unless you consider that our four papers are a group), . . . is recruiting and training people. We do not have a farm-team system. If you are a *New York Times*, or a Gannett, or a Knight-Ridder, you have got the small papers out there where you not only are training the editors and publishers of your big papers, but you are training pressmen. [The] hardest job I have to fill is pressman. . . . [W]e are not hiring people away from the *New York Times* chain on the basis of the money we pay. To a lesser extent, [that is also a problem] with the reporters. Almost everyone who starts with us starts as entry-level, and we train them. I enjoy training young people and new people in the business.

It would certainly be nice sometimes to be able to hire someone who has five years of experience as an advertising salesman or five years of experience running a press or three years of experience as a reporter. But the financial realities are that the weekly field is an entry level into newspaper journalism. The hard realities are that the income levels of weekly newspapers, with relatively few exceptions, are not nearly those of the daily newspapers.

What we can and do attempt to offer is a very family-friendly operation. If the kids are sick, we understand that there are more important things than coming to work some days. We try to offer a sense of participation for employees. The reporter [who would] have to write obits for five years on a daily newspaper will be writing front-page stories [for us] in his or her second week on the job here. We genuinely involve the staff in making decisions.

Q: Since you have been involved with the newspaper, 1964 to the present, how has your audience changed?

A: [O]ur core readership historically has been the folks [who] grew up here, went to school here, raised their kids here, and would not miss reading an issue of the *Polk County Democrat*. They come in [after] they have been on vacation [to pick up back issues], or they have it sent up to the mountains in the summer because they just would not miss an issue. As we become a more transient society, and that certainly is the case with our markets, the change in our readership is that those core readers are dying off, and the new readers are here one year, and next year they are off somewhere else. My perception, at least, is that is our biggest challenge in maintaining readership is trying to appeal to the person who is really only interested in what is the latest thing going on in Afghanistan and really does not care [about] . . . the big issue in Bartow.

Q: What is your circulation now?

A: Combined circulation of the *Polk County Democrat* and the *Fort Meade Leader* is in the neighborhood of six thousand. [W]e are probably down about ten percent from our all-time high.

Q: How has Bartow changed since 1964? I am not just talking about the transients, but the town itself.

A: Within the merchant community the biggest change is that there are fewer and fewer locally owned sole proprietorships, more and more chain and franchise operations. The growth of both city government and county government has been geometrical in relation to the growth of the community. One of the biggest changes, and it certainly is not limited to Bartow, but in my opinion the biggest change in Bartow in the years that I have been covering here is the coming of the integration of the school system. With the integration of the school system has come, in a large part, the integration of society. Integration not only in the numerical mixing of races, but in a genuine sense of camaraderie, friendship, and understanding which has come about because of the forced integration at the school system. We have become much more empathetic and understanding of each other.

Q: There are not many independent newspapers in the state of Florida. How have you managed to avoid being taken over by Knight-Ridder or the *New York Times* or a larger conglomerate?

A: Just say no. . . . [T]en or twenty years ago, when there was a frenzy to buy up newspapers, we would get a serious inquiry every few months. It was terribly tempting to take the money and run, but to some extent I think the nature of community journalism, certainly the nature of the Frisbie family, is that we have always wanted to be independent. We were more interested in working for ourselves and making our [own] decisions than we were in getting rich.

Q: Also, from what I understand from talking with other newspaper publishers, if you are part of, let us say, Knight-Ridder, they are going to make certain demands on what profit level you achieve. They may not interfere with your editorial policy, but in order to achieve the bottom line, the chain papers do less investigative journalism, they have to fire some of the people who work there, and they, in the view of some critics, do not turn out as good a newspaper because it has now become a bottom-line business as opposed to a newspaper trying to serve the community. Do you think that is a fair assessment?

A: Absolutely. Several years ago I was moderator of a panel at [the] Florida Press Association. I believe it was four publishers who had sold to the chains, and in each case they were community papers; I think all [were] weeklies. Three of the four of them said that they were very disappointed with how it had turned out. Although they had come out very well financially, as I recall three of the four of them had left the papers. . . .

Contrary to the public perception that the *New York Times* buys newspapers so that it can dictate editorial policy and determine who is going to be the next president of the United States, the *New York Times* buys newspapers to make money on them. Yes, there are [financial] pressures. I tell folks that come to work here that you will never make as much money working at the *Polk County Democrat* as you could make working for government or working for the phosphate mines or even working for the daily newspapers. But since 1931, when we were established, we have never ever laid off an employee, and it is my hope to retire with that boast intact. We have fired some people, but it has always been on the basis of job performance or whatever. We have never had to say, "Joe, you have done a great job for the last five years, but business is down, so this will be your last paycheck."

Q: When you retire from the paper, is there going to be another Frisbie to come along and run the business?

A: My children are all aware of that opportunity, [but] thus far, none of them [has] availed themselves of that opportunity. One daughter and son-in-law have said, "Keep asking us before you make any irrevocable decisions." I have told our supervisors this, [that] my first choice would be that my family would take over the paper. My second choice would be that somehow the employees could get together through an ESOP [employee stock ownership/option plan] or whatever, form a corporation, buy the paper. Our third choice would be that someone in the community with a continuing interest in the community and in the newspaper would buy the paper. My fourth and final choice would be to sell out to a chain. You can sell out to a chain any time. That is the easy way out and probably the more profitable way out.

Q: What is your view of USA Today, and do you see that kind of newspaper, that format, as the future of publishing in America?

A: I think there has been a lot of imitation of USA Today, most notably the weather maps. But I recall hearing either John Quinn [senior vice president and chief news executive, Gannett Co.] or Al Neuharth [founder, USA Today] [speak] to the Florida Press Association one time. He said, "They call us McNewspaper; I wish they would quit stealing our McNuggets." A great deal of the format, particularly in the daily newspapers and to a much lesser extent in the weekly newspapers, is taken straight from USA Today. The use of graphics, pie charts, big color weather maps, the shadow-box format that they use to set [highlight] their stories, the idea of a dominant front-page story as opposed to the major story of the day—it is the issue du jour, if you please. I see that more and more in a lot of the dailies.

USA Today believes in a high story count of short stories. One of my approaches, and part of my theory on what we can do differently in our community, is we can devote thirty or forty column inches to a story of local importance in almost every issue. . . . In that sense we are different from the USA Today approach, which is lots of short stories, to the point. I am not sure we are right. Certainly I am not one to lecture Al Neuharth on how to be a success in newspaper publishing.

Q: What is the future of the newspaper as we know it today? Are we going to eventually go to electronic newspapers?

A: I do not believe so, and partly because I hope we will not and partly because I remember my dad saying that when AM radio came along, that was going to be the death of newspapers, and when FM radio came along, that was going to be the death of AM radios and newspapers; when TV came along, that was going to be the death of AM and FM radio and newspapers; when the news crawlers across the bottom of your cable channel came along, that was going to be the death of newspapers. I think that the printed word is going to be around for a long, long time to come. I know that we are going to be scrambling harder and harder to hold our share of the market, or even to hold a sufficient share to remain profitable.

Q: What have you done in hiring minorities for the paper?

A: Not much, quite honestly. We have interviewed; I really want to say that we made a conscious effort to hire minorities when we have [had] the opportunity to do so. We do not get that many minority applicants, and the hard truth of the matter is, particularly at the professional level, the journalist level—that is to say, someone with a four-year degree—the dailies are going to grab up talented minorities just as fast as they can, and they are going to pay them fifty percent more than we would. I have made, as I say, a conscious effort to try to get more, to be more reflective of the community, and have not had a whole lot of success.

Q: What do you want to accomplish in the remaining part of your journalistic career?

A: To a certain extent, continuing to do those things which I feel like we do reasonably well. I talked about the importance of strong editorial leadership where it is needed and thorough coverage of the news, as opposed to a once-over lightly, which the nearest metro daily can do in any small town. From my personal standpoint, doing everything I can to ensure a smooth transition to new management, whether it be one or more of my children or some new owner.

To some extent, to maintain the quality and the standards that we have maintained. With my father not in the greatest of health and being eighty-six years old and wanting to slow down a little bit, we currently have only one generation of the family actively involved in the newspaper management, which I guess is probably the first time that has happened since the paper was established.

African American Press

chapter 9 **Garth Reeves**

Garth Reeves inherited the *Miami Times* from his father and was publisher from 1940 to 1993 except when he served in the U.S. Army, from February 19, 1942, to December 18, 1945. Born February 12, 1919, in the Bahamas, Reeves grew up in a segregated Miami and was profoundly affected by his military experience in World War II. Initially displeased with the hypocrisy of the United States, which employed him as a soldier in World War II but denied him basic rights because of segregation, he thought about leaving the country for good. Instead, after a talk with his mother, he threw his energies into using the newspaper to advocate social change.

He established himself as an important figure in the Miami community during the civil rights movement by taking a direct role in desegregating Miami beaches and golf courses. His mother, a student of Ghandi, told him, "Don't run from what you don't like. If you don't like it, change it." He also maintained a voice in the governing of local boards and charities, using his clout to prick the conscience of other Miamians in order to bring about social justice. His service to his community is honored by countless awards from the Boy Scouts of America, the National Business League, the Urban League, Florida A&M University, YMCA, and the National Newspapers Publishers' Association.

Reeves reflects on growing up in the vibrant community of Overtown and how Interstate 95 disrupted that neighborhood. He discusses how his service in World War II shaped perspectives that influenced his management of the *Miami Times*. Of particular note in this interview is his lengthy discussion of his involvement in the civil rights movement and beyond, and how the

Times strove to provide an important and otherwise ignored perspective to the white Miami newspapers. He also comments on issues important to Miami today, including the controversy over religious leader Henry Lyons and how the rapid infusion of ethnic minorities in Miami has affected blacks. This discussion of specific events lends a particular energy to his concluding remarks on the role of journalism in society.

Garth C. Reeves, Jr., was interviewed by Julian M. Pleasants on August 19, 1999, in Miami, Florida.

Q: When and where were you born, Mr. Reeves?

A: In Nassau, Bahamas, on February 12, 1919.

Q: When did your parents come to Miami?

A: May 11, of the same year.

Q: Why did they come to Miami?

A: My father was on his way to New York to buy printing equipment to start his own business. He had a small printing business on the side in Nassau that he operated out of his home. He worked for the *Nassau Guardian* newspaper. He had a brother, Fred, who lived in New York, and he was going up there to buy equipment and come back and open his own business. He never got to New York because he stopped here in Miami, and he met some friends whom he had known before from the Bahamas. They said, "This is the place you should drop your anchor; this place has a lot of potential." Now I do not know how they could see potential in Miami back in 1919. Really, I do not think there were thirty thousand people in Miami at that time, and [there were] strict segregation laws and things like that. I guess those old people had vision. They said, "We think that something is going to happen here."

Instead of going to New York, he stayed in Miami and opened a business. He never went to work for anybody else in this country. He bought printing equipment, and his two friends went in with him. I think they formed a company, the Magic Printing Company. Like all new business, it did not flourish right away. It took a little time . . . ; [eventually] my father bought them out for a grand total of $375, which was a lot of money in those days, and he kept the business going for himself.

Q: The *Miami Sun* was the first paper?

A: Yes. That was, I think, in 1920, and it only lasted eight months because World War I was going on, and there were people shortages and other problems. He was a master printer. He was very good at his craft, and he did well with his job printing. [On] September 1, 1923, he started the *Miami Times*. It was a struggle, but he was proud of his reputation of having gotten out a paper every single week . . . in spite of hurricanes, mechanical failures, [and] labor problems. We will have completed seventy-six years on September 1, [1999], and we have never missed an issue in those seventy-six years. I feel very proud of that, too, having taken over for my dad. But it has been a struggle.

I remember we had paper shortages during World War II. In fact, the *Miami Daily News* was the dominant paper here then, instead of the *Herald*, and we used to buy paper from them, the end of their rolls that they would usually throw away. They would cut it up in flat sheets and sell it to us, and it kept our paper going. I never forgot that.

Q: It must have been difficult during the 1926 hurricane. It is amazing you could get a paper out under those conditions.

A: I remember the electricity in our part of town stayed off more than a week. That was the only way we could get the paper out, by turning the wheel by hand, and I remember seeing those men do that.

Q: When did you start working for the paper, and what did you do?

A: I have never had another job in my life other than the four years I spent in the army, serving Uncle Sam. But I started off as a printer's devil around the print shop, sorting pie. . . . Sorting pie is the type, when individual characters get mixed up, and you put them all in a pie box. My job was to sort them [and] clean up the place. Then I got a paper route; I guess I must have been ten when I started. . . . That was a good experience because I remember my dad used to print the paper one page at a time. First, he would fold the page in half and print that. Then, he would print the other side. Then, he would have to reverse that page, and then he would print the other two pages [a total of eight pages]. The press we were working on was no more than a twelve-by-eighteen press. Boy, it was a real project getting out newspapers in the old days, but that is what you had to do.

Q: What was your readership, in numbers?

A: We printed about five or six hundred papers a week when we started.

Q: Is this where you got your love of journalism?

A: No, really, I was not really [in] love [with] journalism. . . . I was not obsessed with journalism because my dad never made a lot of money out of that newspaper, but his commercial job printing subsidized the newspaper in those lean years. I would always wonder why he spent so much time on that newspaper instead of on his job printing, where we were making a good deal of money. I remember him saying to me, "One day, this newspaper will be more important than the job printing." I could not see that in those days, but he was right. There came a day in the 1960s, maybe the 1950s, after the war, [when] we continued to have the job printing and the newspaper, but the newspaper began to catch fire. Job printing began to get in the way of the newspaper because the newspaper began to grow.

Then, having come out of the army and having been treated like I was, made me take a different look at the newspaper part of [journalism], the power of the press. I knew that segregation was terrible. I suffered in the army because I had to accept that. They sent me away from here, saying, "You are going out to make the world free for democracy, and we have to defeat men like Hitler and Mussolini." They were waving that flag at me, but they treated me like a damn dog, because I am black. It was a terrible thing to accept: you are laying your life on the line; you are overseas; and you see them treating the German prisoners better than they treat you. It just does something to you. It takes your manhood away.

I never could deal with that. That bothered me. It bothers me today. . . . I have a twenty-five-foot flagpole in my yard, on the water where I live, and I have never hoisted the American flag on that pole. I just cannot do it for some reason. . . . But I will never forget the way my country waved that flag at me and then treated me, under the false pretenses that I was really there to help save this world for democracy.

Q: Did you volunteer, or were you drafted?

A: No, I was drafted. In fact, I went in the first black contingent to leave Miami. Everything was segregated.

Q: What unit was this?

A: I went overseas to Europe with the 383rd Engineer Battalion. I was assigned to coast artillery . . . and was fascinated by the ninety-millimeter guns, and I put in for officers' school. I was accepted, and they cut my orders and sent me to Fort Belvoir, Virginia. A black sergeant picked me up at the station. He looked at me strangely, and he said, "Are you Sergeant Garth Reeves?"

I said, "Yes, I am."

He said, "Well, I am supposed to take you to the fort, to officers' training school, right?" He said, "Are you sure they did not make a mistake?"

I said, "Here are my orders."

So we are riding back to the post. This was a black guy, and he said,

"Sergeant, I have been on this post for twenty-two years, and I have never seen a black guy come . . . into this coast artillery school."

I said, "Well, you see one now." I said, "They did not make a mistake." He said, "Well, I'll be damned."

And I went to the post. I got there at night, around eight o'clock. He took me in to this captain who was on duty, and the captain looked at me strangely. He told the sergeant, "Put him in the room down there."

The sergeant took me down there, so I slept that night. I got up the next morning, and they had cut orders for me . . . and moved me right out of there. They just overran the orders from the headquarters in Europe.

Q: Were you in the Pacific theater?

A: I was in Hawaii. We went back at the time when we were getting ready to invade Japan, because the war in Europe ended while we were still at sea on the boat going over [to Japan]. Boy, we were all happy about that. We wanted the ship to turn around. They said, "No, we still have another enemy over there; Japan is still there." So they were building up the forces in the Pacific to invade Japan. God, I saw the intelligence reports, that we were really expecting two million casualties in the invasion of Japan. None of us felt very good about that. We figured we could win the war, but, God, it was going to be very costly. But, sure enough, they dropped the big one on Hiroshima, and the Japanese changed their minds. I was very happy about that. The war ended, and we were still there in training in Hawaii.

Q: Did you have white officers in those segregated units?

A: Yes. The first unit I went into [had] all white officers. They had one colored [man]. He was the chaplain, the minister. The NCOs were all black. Only the officers were white.

Q: While you were in this unit, were you discriminated against by these white officers?

A: No, not the officers themselves. I believe they realized that they were taking men into combat. You arm them, and you know you [have] to treat them like men, or you are not safe. I think they were smart enough to realize that. It was not the discrimination. It was just the policy and the practices of the army.

Q: You attended Booker T. Washington High School in Miami, which obviously was a segregated school. Give me some idea of what kind of school it was and what kind of education you received.

A: Booker T. Washington had a great building. I thought it was the most beautiful thing I had seen when I went to that school [1931]. [But] . . . in the classroom, the Bunsen burners were broken in the science labs, and I noticed that our science teacher, when he did an experiment, he did it, and we just watched. I wondered why we did not do our own experiments. He said, "Well, this equipment is broken, and they have not repaired it." I remember, the whole year, they never did repair it. Another thing was the books: we got the secondhand books from the white schools, hand-me-downs and things like that. We never got new books. Even the athletic equipment. The black schools did not have any athletic budget to buy jerseys and football togs. So Miami High and Miami Edison used to give us their old togs from the last year, and we used it in practice. We would have to buy jerseys to have for the games. That was the way things were.

I remember when I was going away to [my military] service, I confided to my mother. I said, "My heart is not in this; I am going against my will."

She said, "Well, I want you to be a survivor; I want you to come back home. You do not have to win this war by yourself." She said, "You try to make it back home because I say things have to get better one day, but it is not going to happen overnight."

I thought about that a lot of times because I had some situations in the service that were very disgusting. I remember once when I, heading to the Pacific coast to go overseas, over to the Pacific, I got on a train in New Orleans. The conductor came by. I got my ticket, and I said, "When are we eating? I am hungry."

He said, "Just sit down over there; I will be back."

An hour later, he had not come back. When he came back about an hour and a half later, . . . I said, "I am hungry, and I am ready to go to bed now; I wish you would show me where my bunk is."

He said, "I am busy right now; you sit down over there, and I will be right back."

Three hours went by, and the guy never came. I never ate. So I confronted him. I said, "Look, you have my ticket there." I said, "I have meal coupons to eat; I am tired, and I want to go to bed."

He said, "You sit down; you sit down right in that coach right there."

I said, "No, no, no." I said, "Something has got to be wrong here." They had military police riding on the train, so I went to the military police and I said, "I want you to come with me and talk to this conductor. . . . I am ready to go to bed, and I have not had anything to eat."

So the conductor looked at him, and the military police[man] told me,

"You do what that white [man] told you to do, or I will have to lock you up on this train."

So I rode across the country sitting up in a coach, and I had to buy my food because I could not go into the dining car. Something like that, it is kind of hard to get out of your craw.

Q: What was Overtown like in the 1930s? I understand it was sort of a Harlem of the South.

A: It was great. Neighborhoods were really neighborhoods. Any mother in that neighborhood could discipline anybody's child. It is quite different today. If Mrs. Johnson next door saw me getting out of line, she would straighten me out, even to the point of punishing me, spank[ing] me. Then, when my parents came home, she would tell them what happened. Well, then I would get another whipping. But everything was so different during that time. Booker T. was a closely knit school. We had a lot of pride in that school. [There was] no graffiti on the walls or anything like that. Nobody was tearing up anything. I had gotten so that back in those days, I guess, the segregation did not bother me that much because I had not seen anything of the outside world, and I seemed to have had everything in my neighborhood that I thought I needed or wanted.

Q: What is your view of the impact of Interstate 95 when it was routed through Overtown?

A: It really destroyed the black community, because up until that time, we were all right there together, and we had our own real community. But when I-95 came through, it came right through the heart of the city, right down 6th Avenue. . . . The people started moving out. The thing is, there was no place to go, because when you moved out, really, from Overtown, the nearest place was Liberty City. . . . So where we are now was all white [back then]. From 62nd Street on back, it was all white. The real estate agents got into it, too. They saw a good way to make some money. They started selling homes to blacks in these fringe areas. Well, the whites started to move once one black moved into the block. It was like everybody had to go then; they had to leave. That is how Liberty City opened up.

Then a lot of people were stubborn about leaving, and we had some terrible incidents about integrating some of these neighborhoods. They had a bombing. . . . Blacks just started moving in, and the whites did not like it. They set off a dynamite charge in one of the vacant apartments. I guess I reacted just like everybody. I got my gun and put it in my pocket, and I [went] out to see what in the hell was going on. The police came, and nobody was hurt or anything, but the hostility was in the air. It was like they were bringing a war to our community, and the black people were very upset. But we managed to get over that.

Q: You started as a reporter. What did you cover?

A: Everything. In a black newspaper, you had to be versatile. You had to write an obituary today and a wedding story tomorrow. That is why I think a black journalist had an advantage over a white journalist because when a white journalist went to a newspaper, they gave him a certain spot, a niche, and that was all he did. We had to do everything.

Q: Did you have any journalism courses at Florida A&M?

A: When I went to A&M, the only school of journalism was at the University of Florida. I told my English teacher, and he said, "Do not worry about that." He said, "Just take all the English courses you can, and you will end up being a good journalist." So we took all the English courses, literature and all that. It is really enough. I worked on the school newspaper.

I got the bug for the newspaper, the journalism bug, when I came back from the war. . . . I told my mother when I came back, I [was] not going to stay because during my four years in the service, I had been to a lot of different countries, and I had been to a lot of states. So I told my mother, "I am going to try someplace else."

She said, "Well, your dad is kind of depending on you; you are the only boy, and he was hoping you would take over the business."

I said, "Really, I would like to help him, but if I stayed around here, Mama, I will get in trouble." I said, "I think I have made a sacrifice for my country, and they do not respect me for that."

She said, "You do not solve problems by running away from them."

It kind of caught my attention there, my mom talking down to me. I said, "Well, this problem is a little too big for me, and I don't think I can solve it."

She said, "You haven't tried. Anyhow, you think about it."

When men have done their best, angels can do no more—my mother always told me that. She said, "But make sure you have done your best before you give up. . . ."

So I thought about it, and I said, "I will tell you what: I will give you a year [to] see if we can do something."

Then the newspaper became my primary objective. You have got to have a propaganda arm in order to get anything done. I had not been active in the NAACP [National Association for the Advancement of Colored People], but I became an active member. I got the newspaper in the fight, publishing the protests and . . . writing articles about the evils of segregation. We had a very good president of the NAACP, Reverend Theodore Gibson. He was a fiery leader of the NAACP. I remember Father Gibson used to stop by the office sometimes and say, "Garth, what problem will we attack next?"

I remember one day I told him, "You know, we really ought to go after the golf courses." I said, "You know, I like to play golf, but they only let us play on Monday." Monday was the day they maintained the courses. They were watering the lawns and cutting the grass, and you are out there trying to putt.

He said, "Well, hell, let us do something about it."

Sure enough, we organized a group called the Cosmopolitan Golf Association, which was a group of black golfers. We started planning our fight with the municipal golf course. We had two good NAACP lawyers there. We did not have any money to pay them, but these guys were committed. If we got the $380 — I think that is what it cost in those days to file a suit — they would file it for us. So we decided to file the suit. We did this back in the 1940s, but the suit lasted seven years, I think. It went all the way to the Supreme Court, and it became a landmark case [*Rice v. City of Miami*; Joseph Rice was a regular member of the Cosmopolitan Golf Club]. The Supreme Court ruled that you cannot take tax money, build a golf course, and restrict any of the residents. Simple as that.

Q: Was the black community in Miami aware of the tremendous significance of Jackie Robinson breaking the color line in major-league baseball, then the number one pastime in America?

A: Oh, definitely, because, boy, everybody loved baseball. We had our black league; the thing was to really get it opened up. We knew it would happen one day. Believe it or not, I was one of those lucky guys. . . . When the season opened in Brooklyn that Monday — the Dodgers and the Giants in Brooklyn — I was in the stands when Jackie Robinson took the field for the first time. I saw it: major-league baseball integrated. To me, that was a great day.

Q: Was the audience integrated?

A: Oh, yes. Because it was Brooklyn.

Q: Do you think people today recognize what an extraordinary hero Jackie Robinson was and what he had to go through, what courage it took?

A: I do not think many people realize it. That was a tremendous thing that he did. Pee Wee Reese [MLB player, 1940–58] died this week, and I remember how Pee Wee was the only guy on the team who stood up for Jackie. I'll never forget that, when they were booing Jackie.

Q: At the *Miami Times* you started as a columnist. Then you went to managing editor, then editor and publisher. How did that transition take place, and what different responsibilities did you have in each job?

A: They were actually overlapping because I always did whatever had to be done in the newspaper and, at the same time, [kept] the commercial job printing going, because that [was] where the real money was. When I became active with the NAACP and we started the civil rights struggle, I had to keep that part of it going. That was my job to write the articles. My dad always wrote the editorials. He never wanted anybody else to write his editorials. If I had a strong position on something, I usually took it to the front page, in a front-page editorial, and he maintained his column.

Q: Did the *Miami Times* write editorials to persuade the community as to how to vote?

A: Yes, we would do that. We always made our endorsements, and we have such a following, a believability in our newspaper. Black people believed in the *Miami Times*. What they saw there was bible to them. We built that up over the years, I imagine, by fighting their fights and not sacrificing integrity in any way.

Q: For example, would you have urged them to vote for John F. Kennedy [35th U.S. president, 1961–63] in 1960?

A: Oh, definitely. We supported Kennedy all the way. He was the only president for whom I left Miami to go to his inauguration. I was really enthralled with that man. I thought, this is a new type of politician here; this country has got to change with a bright, young man like this who, I thought, had his head screwed on correctly.

Q: There were some fairly serious riots in the 1960s in Miami, and there was one in 1988 in Liberty City. What was your position, editorially, on those riots in the black community?

A: Editorially, we did not call them "riots." We called them "protests." Sure, everybody else called them "riots," but, editorially, we were saying that the people were not just rioting to be rioting. They were protesting wrongs that were piled upon them year after year and that it looked like nothing was being done about it. That is when we had some serious problems with police brutality. We were protesting editorially and every way we could, in mass meetings and everything. But we could not get the city officials to really react to this thing, to really do anything about it.

So our editorial strategy was, let us attack the top law-enforcement person in the county, the state's attorney. Someone said, "You are crazy; how are you going to attack Janet [Janet Reno, state attorney for Dade County, 1978–93; U.S. attorney general, 1993–2001]? Janet is our friend. She is the only decent person down there. Why are you going to jump on [her]?" Yes, but we have to get attention to this problem of police brutality. And it worked. We wrote a piece in our paper saying, "Janet Reno is to black people what Hitler was to Jews." That was awful.

Janet asked me, "How could you write that about me?"

I said, "We had to get your attention."

The *Miami Herald* picked it up and said what the black newspaper said: Janet is a racist. People started talking about it, saying, "Police brutality in this town is bad." Then the grand jury got on it and everything.

Later on, I had to apologize to Janet. I said, "Janet, you have to do what you have to do sometimes." I said, "That is what we had to do; we had to use you to get the attention."

So once the state attorney's office was attacked, they had to respond. Well, what could we do?

Things really changed after that. The police were getting away with too much. We had a chief [in Miami] named Walter Headly, [who] was known to have a dossier on every official in the city. . . . Nobody bothered Walter Headly. So the *Miami Times* came out one week with a front page saying, "Headly should be fired. He is a disgrace to this city, and we do not need a man like that running this police department, because brutality is rampant, [and] he is not doing anything [about it]."

Oh, we raved about it, and the *Miami Herald* picked it up the next day and said, "The black newspaper is calling for the dismissal of the chief."

Everybody said, "Aren't you scared writing about him?"

"Hell, no." You have to bring these things to the attention of the public if we feel that we are right, if they are mistreating us, and they are not doing a damn thing about it. Sure enough, Headly was fired a couple of years later. We started the movement.

Q: After that, they began hiring more African American policemen?

A: Right. Well, we had African American police even with Headly there. . . . The [black] police went through a lot, too, to maintain their jobs. You know, they were not policemen fully; they were patrolmen. They could not arrest whites. They were restricted to black areas. Still, it got our foot in the door. That is why in my civic activities around Dade County, I wanted a seat at the table. If you did not have a seat at the table, how could you be heard?

Q: In civil rights, how did you view Martin Luther King's gradual, pacifistic approach as compared to, say, the more aggressive tactics of Malcolm X and the Black Panthers? Where did you stand in that ideological split?

A: I was with King to a certain extent. My mother always said, "You do not pick a fight you cannot win." You cannot win if the other guy has a gun, and you have a slingshot. We did not have any guns. We did not have anything to fight with. I was afraid it was going to be a real serious bloodbath if we did not go with King. If we went with Malcolm, it was going to be really, really rough. Things might have changed faster, but it would have been bloodier. King was making a lot of sense, and history proved him right. I think the real reason King was murdered is because King was beginning to get the poor white people of the South to see that, really, it is not just what [was being done] to black people; [someone with] white skin [was] not much better off with low wages.

Q: How was your paper received by the white community? Obviously, the *Miami Herald* read what you wrote. Did other civic leaders?

A: They always viewed us as a responsible black press. Responsible—I liked that. My dad was far more conservative than I was, and he always used to quote an English philosopher—I think his name was James McKinley— who said, "Never have a group of men resolved a situation more meaningfully than when they sat around a table and talked about it." He thought that if you talked about a problem in a meaningful manner and truthfully, being honest with yourselves, you can do it. You know, that worked [with] integrat[ing] the beaches in Dade County.

I will tell you the story on the beaches in Dade County. We arranged a meeting with the county commissioners at Crandon Park. They agreed to meet with us, the NAACP delegation. They did not know what to expect. They did not know if we were planning a demonstration, because demonstrations were going on at the time. Our strategy was, we would bring all our past tax receipts from the county, and we would appeal to their sense of fair play.

We said, "Gentlemen, we are here today for a redress of a grievance that we have, that you have about twenty-eight public beaches here in Dade

County, and blacks are restricted to only one, Virginia Beach. We feel that is wrong. All of us are residents of Dade County. We are all taxpayers, and none of us have criminal records. We brought along our tax receipts so you could see that we were freeholders . . . and we [had] paid our taxes. Now we notice on this tax pie chart that eleven percent of our taxes goes toward the maintenance of parks, playgrounds, [and] beaches, so we think that you are doing wrong when you restrict us to one beach, and you are taking our tax money and maintaining the total of twenty-eight beaches."

They listened to us, and nobody said a word. They had all the commissioners there.

We said, "We have had our attorneys research the laws of the state and the county, and there is no law on the books that says black people cannot enjoy the public facilities. So we would like an answer from you."

They would not give us an answer. They said not a word. [There was] nothing to say.

So we said, "We are coming back at two o'clock today to use this beach, and if you want to put us in jail or beat us up like some of your police officers have been doing, that is all right. We feel that we need some sort of answer and some sort of resolution to this problem." And we left.

Though we might have had a dozen or fourteen people with us that morning, when we got ready to go back, we had about half that many. But we went back at two o'clock. There were a lot of policemen out there. . . . They did not know what to expect. We did not know what to expect, either. Somebody told us, "Do not go into the bathhouse." We could hear a lot of noise in the bathhouse. They said a bunch of white hoodlums were in there, waiting to beat us up when we come in to change into our swim trunks, and the police were going to conveniently not answer the call. So we did not go there. What we did [was] we slipped on our trunks under our clothes, and we walked down to the beach. The police didn't stop us, and we just walked down to the beach, . . . kicked off our sandals, took off our slacks, and went into the water. Nobody said a word. No police officers came up. Some reporters were out there because they did not know what was going to happen. We stayed in the water maybe a half hour or so, and we came out of there.

From that day, and I think it was November 7, 1957, the beaches of the county became integrated. Blacks slowly began going to different beaches, any one they wanted.

Q: What was the *Miami Herald*'s position on all this civil rights activity?

A: The *Herald* was not editorially positioned as it is today. You see, it was not popular to take the position of blacks during the civil rights struggle. I guess they were looking towards their population. Ninety percent of their readership, I guess, was white. They skirted a lot of issues, and they tap danced around a lot of them.

Q: Didn't the *Miami Times* get bombed one time?

A: Yes, and believe it or not, by a black group. They had an organization called BAMM, the Black African Militant Movement, I think it was. These guys were always attacking us for not being militant enough. They thought we should urge the people to riot. A lot of it did not make sense to us. Editorially, we were not going to do that. We would get these letters to the editor saying we were not militant enough and [that] people should rise up and all that. But one night they threw a bomb, more like a Molotov cocktail, in our front door. It smashed the glass, but it burned just the front. It burned out before it could do serious damage to the building.

Q: Did you ever get any phone calls or threats or letters from the Klan or other racist organizations?

A: Yes, we would get those, but we would just throw them away. We would not even print them.

Q: When a racial incident took place, the white press would give one interpretation, so you had to reinterpret or clarify some of the facts. Was that an essential part of your function?

A: We called it "writing it from a black perspective," because the white perspective was quite different from the black perspective. I have been convinced in my general experiences that objectivity is a myth, because a writer can take that story and turn it any way he wants to. So if the white reporter views a demonstration in the community as a riot, the *Miami Times* might view that as a protest. That is it. . . . You can be as objective as you want to be, I guess.

Q: Another thing that you did—and I presume this is part of your function both as a newspaper editor and a human being—was to be active in not only the black community but in Miami-Dade, in general. Did you feel that was a specific responsibility that you had as editor of the paper?

A: Definitely, because there were so many powerful white organizations that really ran the town, like United Way. They did not have any blacks on the board. And the Boy Scouts. I wanted to get in there because I was going to have my say: "You know, you are not going to like what I am saying, but at least I will have my say, and I am going to say it in such a way [that] I am not angrily accusing you of racism as such."

When I sat on the board of Miami Dade Community College, the legal team would come in, and I would say, . . . "How many minority lawyers do you have on your staff?"

He would say, "Well, we really do not have any; it is not that we have not been looking for them, but none of them have applied to our firm. . . ."

So I said to him, "You know, this community college represents all segments of the community, and, possibly, you should not wait on them to come to you; you might seek them out because we would like a legal staff to represent . . . all segments of the community."

The second time he came, I did the same thing. I think he had one Hispanic the next time.

The third time he came, I shoved it to him. I said, "No, I am protesting right now, and I am asking all my trustees to vote with me against this law firm representing our college, because for six years, I have been asking him to include minorities on the firm. He has not done it, and I think it is time that we make a move. Mr. President [and] Mr. Chairman, I think that we should look for another law firm. . . ." Moved him right out like that.

You see, if you have a seat and you do it in such a way [that] when you are in this dominant white group and you are the only black sitting at the table, whatever you say is not going to mean very much to them because they know they have the votes, but you kind of prick their conscience.

Q: You were the first African American, I believe, to serve on the board of the United Way?

A: Yes.

Q: The same for the Boy Scouts?

A: Right. They did not feel uncomfortable with me, I do not think, because I had paid my dues in the community. I felt I had done a good job, and I was working for the same thing [they] were working for, for a good community, a good wholesome community. So nobody really objected. But then I would always be their conscience. You would be surprised to know the racism that could go on in a meeting if only all whites are in the room. So I am listening carefully to what is said, and I am making my little notes.

Q: Would you do editorials about, say, for example, the law firm that was dismissed?

A: No. Believe it or not, I did not even write it up because I did not want people to think I was using that as a forum for a newspaper. It was not my job to make news for my newspaper. It was to get something done, to help this community become more rounded.

Q: How many readers did you have in the 1950s, and how many do you have today?

A: In the 1950s our circulation was possibly about seven thousand to ten thousand. Today, we are twenty-two thousand.

Q: What is your major source of advertising?

A: Corporate. We get a great deal of corporate advertising. We have Sears, K-Mart, General Motors, Coca-Cola, [and] Pepsi. I remember, five to ten years ago, we were heavy on automobile advertising. Right now, we do not get a lot of automobile advertising. . . . We usually get a lot of grocery advertising. . . . Now the health organizations today are big because everybody has health services. Everybody has some Medicare or Medicaid.

Q: That reminds me of another struggle you had, to integrate Jackson Memorial.

A: That is right. My mother had diabetes, and she was losing a leg. I went out to the hospital to see her. There was no air-conditioning in this west wing where they put all the blacks. It had an electric fan that was doing a poor job. I had to do a sit-in outside the administrator's office. They kept me out there all day. I made some phone calls to some politicians and things like that.

The next day, they moved my mother to a ward in the wooden building. A couple of black nurses came up to me and told me, "That is the first [time] a black person has ever been in that building." She said, "I have been working here twenty-two years."

I said, "Well, things change after a while."

If nobody could test it, you see, nothing would get done. Everybody seemingly would go along with the status quo. My newspaper never protested it . . . , but it hit me right at home that my mother was about to lose her leg and, Jesus, look at the conditions. Segregation is such a terrible thing, and it is senseless.

Q: Let me ask you about another controversial issue. You might recall the controversy over Reverend Henry Lyons [former president of the National Baptist convention].

A: Yes.

Q: Reverend Lyons was charged with several illegal activities. Some of the members of the black community defended him in the beginning because they thought the white authorities were unfairly prosecuting Henry Lyons. What was your reaction?

A: Listen. There is only one way to put it. Henry Lyons was a crook, and I abhor people who would try to smooth that over. If you are a thief, you are a thief. We do not do ourselves any good by protecting a thief. Here is a man, head of one of the largest black religious organizations in the world. He could have done so much good, had he been an honest man. But he was a dishonest man, and he hurt so many people by that.

I do not think we should find excuses for dishonest people. . . . Everybody should be accountable. Newspapers, too. But we have not had that accountability. I do not want to make excuses for politicians who are being tried for bribes and stealing money. Damn it.

A lot [of people] said, "But the white guys are doing it."

Well, it's still not right. I tell a lot of black guys that. I say, "And don't you think, with your black face, you can do everything a white politician can do and get away with it." I say, "The country is not like that."

I saw in the paper recently that people are trying to shorten his [Lyons's prison] term. Why? He has done his harm to the black religious community of this country. Why let him out to do more? No. Let him stay there and pay his debt to society. That is the way I look at it.

Q: What do you think are the most important functions of your newspaper?

A: Number one, to keep the people informed, basically, and to educate. Education goes a long way because there are so many services that are offered by government that people who are not well informed do not even know that they are there. . . . Like health services. There are a lot of free health services that you could get almost everywhere. But if you do not know about them, you are going to be sitting over here with diabetes, dying from it, and not even know you have it, because you have not availed yourself of these health services where you can go down and get examinations. There are a lot of social services, even, that are available to people that people do not know about. There are a lot of people in our community who are really not sophisticated enough to interpret a lot of things to their best advantage. We need to educate them, explain this to them, and make it known to them. I think the black newspapers have to work very closely with the churches, because our people believe in their churches.

Q: When you took over the paper from your father, did you change much?

A: No. I found that the things my dad told me that I thought were not exactly right, or not good for the paper, he had a lot more smarts about him than my young mind thought he had. . . .

Q: Has your audience changed, from 1950 to the present?

A: Not basically. We usually hold onto our readers. I do not know if we have as many young readers today as I would like to have, but we kind of aim ourselves at the middle-aged voting community.

Q: How has Miami changed in the years since you have been with the paper?

A: I thought that the Mariel boat lifts set the black community back twenty years, because once . . . the Cuban refugees came to this country, we sort of changed our attack against beating the drums for black people to [include all] minorities, and that was a mistake. I hate to admit it, but that was a mistake because we included the Hispanic brothers along with the black. Basically, the Hispanic refugees never really joined with the black community in any way, and we included them in our suits when we amended our suits to say "minorities." That was meant to show that we are fighting for all minorities, but we did not get that kind of cooperation from the Cuban refugees. They did not really come in with us.

In fact, I think that the refugees hurt the black community of Dade County more than it did anybody else. . . . Instead of all the black people really sticking together in their fight for equality and human decency, I see some divisions between American blacks, Caribbean blacks, the Haitians over there, the Jamaicans over there. America is a melting pot like that, but I think that black people must understand that they are in a position where they are easily identifiable, and the history of this country has shown that there has been always this kind of innate resentment of blacks. This is where we come from. We have not overcome it yet. Racism is still rampant in the country. I think there is so much more work to be done.

Q: Have you changed your editorial policy, now, back to strictly supporting black causes, as opposed to minority causes?

A: We are slowly doing that. I think it is necessary.

Q: How have the letters to the editors changed over the years?

A: Not a great deal. We do not get as many today as we used to get. I do not know if people are getting complacent and feeling that they have it made or that the problems of this country have been resolved. I do not know. We invite letters to the editor because we like to know what people are thinking. I wish we had more to give us a better insight on people.

Q: How has technology changed the newspaper business?

A: Considerably, from the day we set type one character at a time. . . . My daughter is installing a new technology system now, and it is on order. It is going to be the most up-to-date thing that we have.

Q: One theory is that in a few years, everybody will use the Internet, and people will not have the physical newspaper anymore. Do you see the end of newspapers?

A: I don't think so. I think the newspaper will always be a part of the community. I remember when segregation was supposed to end in the schools and the different public facilities. Everybody was saying that this would be the end of the black press, that there was no need for a black press now with the segregation ending. But that was not true. In fact, that pointed out that the black press was needed more than ever.

Q: How many other African American newspapers are there in the state?

A: We have about fifteen.

Q: Are most of them the same size?

A: We are the largest.

Q: Do you use syndicated columnists, like William Raspberry [Pulitzer Prize–winning nationally syndicated columnist for the *Washington Post*]?

A: Yes. In fact, let me tell you a story about Raspberry. We have been using Raspberry for many years. The *Miami Herald* had the rights to the Raspberry column, but they very seldom used it. When I originally wrote for the rights, they said the *Herald* had that territory. I wrote back and said, "Well, they are not using it." I said, "I read the *Herald* every day, and I might see one Raspberry column every two weeks." So they started sending me the column, and I started using it. Then the *Herald* picked it up. They would not miss a Raspberry now.

Q: Any other columnists you use?

A: Yes. Carl Rowan [African American syndicated columnist] and Jesse Jackson's [African American political leader, clergyman, and civil rights activist; U.S. presidential candidate, 1984, 1988] column.

Q: Do the columnists provide a more national view and expand the parameters of the paper a little?

A: That is right, but I try to stay as black as I can. I try to pick the news that you do not see, that you will not find, in the *Herald* or the *Fort Lauderdale Sun-Sentinel*.

Q: Would you use a white columnist?

A: Sure. In fact, I had a white sports editor way back in the 1960s. He was the only white on my firm. I did like the whites. I put him right up at the front desk.

Q: So everybody could see him.

A: Everybody could see him.

Q: Looking back on the time that you have been with the paper, what would you say is your most important contribution to the community?

A: I believe bringing the people the news of their community every week in an unbiased sort of way, from a black perspective, and trying to steer them. You are not supposed to steer, I guess, but we try to do that. We try to kind of steer them in the right direction, editorially.

Q: What do you consider your most important personal contribution?

A: To this community, I think my most important contribution other than the newspaper was taking a leadership [role] during the civil rights struggle, in things like the golf lawsuit and the beaches. Somebody had to do that. Everybody knew it should be done, but everybody was standing around waiting on somebody else to do it. . . . Somebody had to step forward. If you are writing about it every day, protesting it and saying, "This is wrong, and we should do something," well, when they ask for volunteers, your hand should go up, or else you are not for real.

Hispanic Press

chapter 10   **Horacio Aguirre**

Horacio Aguirre was born in New Orleans, Louisiana, to Nicaraguan parents and holds law and political science degrees from the University of Panama. He began his career in journalism as an editorial writer for *El Panama America* in 1948, then became a founding editor and editorial writer for *Diario las Americas* in 1953. In the course of his career, he has held various leadership positions in the Inter-American Press Association, including a term as president from 1983 to 1984. He has served on the executive committee of the World Press Freedom Committee and is a member of the Association of Cuban Journalists in Exile and the World Association of Newspapers. He is also a member of the American Society of Newspaper Editors and the International Press Institute. Aguirre is active in the community of Miami, serving as the vice president of the board of directors of the Florida Grand Opera and as a member of the board of trustees of the Miami Art Museum. He was also named an honorary president of the Latin chamber of commerce. He has received several honorary degrees and awards, including honorary doctoral degrees from St. Thomas University (1976) and Barry University (1997) in Miami, the Good News Award from the Miami International Press Club (1999), and the Great Floridian Award (2001).

In this interview Aguirre describes the beginnings of *Diario las Americas*, its competition with other Spanish-language newspapers, and its target audience. He discusses various topics covered in editorials, including Fidel Castro, Elian Gonzalez, and the 2000 presidential election. He also gives his impression of the future of newspapers. He talks at length about the Hispanic community in Miami and the Mariel boat lift, analyzes the U.S.

government's position on immigration, and explains the relationship among various Hispanic groups living in Miami, telling why his editorials are printed in both English and Spanish. He describes his paper's endorsement of candidates and the impact endorsements have on voters. He concludes the interview with an assessment of the contributions of *Diario las Americas* to the Hispanic community.

Horacio Aguirre was interviewed by Julian M. Pleasants in Miami, Florida, on August 22, 2002.

Q: Why did you decide to start a newspaper in Miami?

A: Miami, in that time, almost half a century [ago], was a great inter-American city, and now is more than that. We considered that the era of the jet . . . [was] almost coming immediately, and if we print the newspaper in Spanish in Miami, we can use the airlines . . . to [have the newspaper] two hours and a half later in New York, two hours and a half later in Panama, four hours and a half or, at the maximum, five in California, two hours and a half or something like that in Puerto Rico, and in many cities of the United States.

Also, the cities in this hemisphere where they would have interest in a type of paper that is concentrat[ing] on all the news about the world, more especially inter-American news, including news of the United States, local news of the state of Florida and metropolitan area of Miami, and news of all the Latin American countries. It's a paper of general information about the world, not only about Miami or only about the Latin American countries. Our slogan is, since the first day, "For liberty, culture, and hemispheric solidarity." But after the hemispheric solidarity, we can include—and we include always—the human solidarity in all the world.

Q: Is *El Nuevo Herald* your main competitor for circulation or is it a different kind of paper?

A: I consider *El Neuvo Herald* competition because they start[ed] fifteen years ago, and they follow, not the policy, but the idea of *Diario las Americas.* We create[d] *Diario las Americas* because we knew at that time that Miami was not only a city with people who speak Spanish because they come here as tourist[s]. Miami used to have a permanent population [of] about 125,000 to 150,000 persons, but the idea was not only to cover them, [but] to use them as a base to send the paper to other places, and the qualities of those inhabitants who spoke Spanish at that time was a very high quality. That means [they] could speak perfect English . . . but they need[ed] to view more information about the Latin American countries or about the Latin culture. . . .

Q: So this was originally directed to the more educated Spanish speakers in Miami?

A: In certain aspects, yes, but in other aspects, to try to educate people who [have no] education. In other words, in one way we reflect the public opinion that exists, and in other aspects we create public opinion through the quality of our news and our orientation. We used the [educated] people as permanent reader[s] from the beginning, and also we started to educate persons that, for one or another reason, were not well educated, and because [of] the prestige of our paper, they were reading the paper, they were learning through the paper about many things that perhaps they [did] not know before.

Q: When you started *Diario las Americas*, what was your initial newspaper like? How many pages? What was your circulation?

A: We start[ed] with eight pages, trying to concentrate in eight pages on the different aspects of the information that was necessary to offer to our readers. But always we start[ed] with news, first of all, about the countries well represented in the community, because it's logical that they [would] like to know what [is] happening in their own countries, but not only in their own countries, in the other countries neighbor[ing] them.

Q: I noticed that in today's paper you had news items from Panama and Honduras and Nicaragua. I also noticed an article about President Vicente Fox [president of Mexico, 2000–present], who had canceled his visit to the United States because a Mexican citizen had been executed in Texas.

A: Yes. We have to offer this information as news to the people.

Q: Do you put your paper to bed in the early afternoon?

A: No, no, no. Later than that. We finish with the paper about three o'clock. Immediately, we send the paper to the airport to [put it on] the airplanes to [go to] the cities . . . and immediately to the stands and drugstores, and immediately to home delivery. If you are a subscriber, you'll receive the paper in your home always about seven o'clock P.M.

Q: What is your circulation today?

A: Our circulation today is about sixty-five to seventy thousand.

Q: How much of that is in the United states?

A: I can say about ninety percent, because out[side] of the United States, you can buy this paper in the more popular and well-known streets of Buenos Aires, but it's not for everybody—they have good newspapers over there.

But the majority of our readers are in the United States and, naturally, in the south part of Florida.

Q: When you started out, what were the ultimate goals for your newspaper?

A: The normal aspirations. Our purpose was to establish a permanent newspaper in order to inform, to reflect public opinion, and to create public opinion in accordance with our ideas, which are our ideas in the political field—democracy—in the civic field, in the moral field. We have without any doubt the purpose of defend[ing] the morality of our society.

Q: What do you choose to write about in your editorials?

A: Many topics. For instance, the . . . visit of the Pope in Toronto or the visit of the Pope in [Poland], his home country, or it could be about the elections, the civic obligations of the people to read about the candidates, to ask about the candidates in order to be ready to vote for the proper persons. All the things that represent human interests, we cover in the paper.

Q: Did you write an editorial about Pope John Paul's visit to Cuba?

A: I said that he represent[s] a lot for humanity, not only for the Catholic people, for humanity. He is [an] exceptional person. We consider that he could influence, not . . . the government, but . . . the people [of Cuba], to show them the support of the Vatican and also the lessons that they could learn from his speeches, his homilies. We were not against his trip; we did not criticize him for [this]. I criticize[d] Castro when Castro almost insult[ed] him in the first speech.

Q: How many people work at the newspaper?

A: In all the departments? Probably about two hundred, including the circulation department and advertising department, shop, and so on and so forth.

Q: I noticed in the paper today there was a letter extolling Evita Peron [wife and political partner of President Juan Peron, Argentina] as a great woman.

A: Yes. That, I think, was written by somebody who wrote a book about her. And I will tell you something. I was the editorial writer of *El Panama America* at that time, and I was not in favor of the policy of Peron against the democratic concepts and against . . . the freedom of expression. In his administration, with the cooperation or inspiration of his wife, [they] only were publishing things in favor of the government. But that [does] not mean that if this gentleman sent us a letter or [wrote] an article about Mrs. Peron [that] we will not use it. We give the opportunity [to] him and the opportunity to our readers to see the other [side of the issue].

Q: Would you have any negative response if you wrote an editorial that might be critical of the Cubans in Miami?

A: The only thing that I can tell you is this. I will write any editorial that I consider proper in accordance with our ideas and our philosophical concepts of the situation. If we [are not] accepted by all the Cuban readers, that will not be the argument . . . to change our position. In connection with the embargo [U.S. embargo against Fidel Castro], I am in favor of the embargo, and I know that . . . the majority of the Cubans are in favor of the embargo, but [there] could be important [people] that are against the embargo. As a matter of fact, we have, on certain occasions, people who write articles . . . with a high sense of responsibility that [do] not necessarily coincide with the editorial position of the newspaper.

Q: What was your editorial position on Elian Gonzalez?

A: In favor of Elian Gonzalez under the concept that Elian Gonzalez was supposed to be in the United States, where his mother brought [him] from Cuba. I wrote several articles about this because it's a matter of my professional [opinion] — I'm a lawyer. The *patria potestas*, which is a concept of Roman law, is in favor of the boy, of children, not in favor of the father of the children. The government of the United States decide[d] in favor of the father, not in favor of the children, and really was in favor of Castro. That transformed this case in[to] a political case.

Q: Do you see having Elian Gonzalez back in Cuba under a dictator as violating his rights?

A: Yes, Cuba, [is] obligate[d] to educate this boy under the communist doctrine where they do not have any civic rights, civil rights, democratic rights. That is a matter of the constitution. When [the U.S.] put him in the hands of Fidel Castro, [they] are obligating him [Elian] to become a communist.

Q: Since you can now get newspapers on the Internet, do you think there will be a time when we will no longer have a physical newspaper?

A: That is a matter of great discussion. I personally feel that there are many persons that will use the Internet, but will [not] accept the Internet as a monopoly. There are concepts, traditions, including the new generations that will like to read a book and a newspaper. In many aspects, you can possibly feel, at least I consider . . . that the paper, the newsprint . . . has a soul.

Q: You're saying it's tangible; you can touch it; you can hold it; and therefore —

A: You have the impression that [it] has a soul.

Q: There's a connection when you hold it.

A: You remember when radio start[ed]. Many people thought when the radio start[ed] with a program of news, that [meant] that [it] probably [would] reduce or eliminate the newspaper. They offer very, very good information in capsules, but they don't kill the newspaper. They use the newspaper, in many occasions, to include in their program.

Q: I was talking with Tom Fiedler, of the *Miami Herald*, about the 2000 presidential election, and an observer could find out exactly what was happening on CNN, but it took a newspaper to interpret those events and organize the information for the reader. You couldn't get that depth and analysis on television. Do you feel like that's one of the purposes of your paper?

A: I agree with it. In some occasions the television and the radio stations are very good for certain types of information, but, for instance, in television they only have three seconds, five seconds [if] it's something large. In a newspaper you [get] more information.

Q: How has the Hispanic community changed since you've been at the newspaper?

A: There is no [doubt] that the presence of the Cubans in this community have [has] transform[ed] substantially the physical and cultural aspects of this great city of Miami, which was a great city before then, too. At the beginning, half a million Cubans [came] over here under very well organized systems, with the coordination with the [federal] government, Freedom Flights, and so on. They contributed enormously to change . . . the physical and cultural and human activities of this community because Miami did not have [that] in that time. At the beginning, in a few years they have [Cuban refugees] who were working in [jobs like] elevator [attendants].

I remember . . . this case in the Columbus Hotel downtown. . . . I saw somebody opening the door, closing the door, and reading something. I saw what he was reading in Spanish, a great thinker, Ortega y Gasset [Spanish philosopher, author of *Revolt of the Masses*]. Normally, the person who is reading [Gasset] will not be working in [an elevator], will not be reading Emerson too. Could be a nice person, but [he] would not be doing that. These half a million persons that come were the best type of persons in each social level, the best manicurist, the best barber, the best physician, the best lawyer, the best teacher, the best in each aspect of the social organization of the country.

Q: You're talking about the Cuban exiles, 1960 and 1961?

A: The first half a million, but not only them. For instance, in the Mariel [incident], Castro sent some delinquent persons, but [in the] many people that [came] in the Mariel boat lift, you found sopranos, lawyers, very, very good persons, high-quality persons with good manners . . . and they continued their studies over here. Many people think because Castro sent, infiltrated, people that he took from the jail and sent over here in order to discredit the community—despite that, they are very, very nice persons. In my opinion . . . criminals were in the jail, and Castro put [them] out in order to send [them] here with the honest people, but the majority of the people were honest people.

Q: But there were criminals and people who had been in insane asylums, as well, in that group?

A: Very, very small proportion. I am one of the persons that know these exiles. Including because I am not a member of the exile [group], I have more opportunities to identify them. The great majority of them are nice persons . . . and good workers.

Q: That's very interesting, because the general impression has been, even in the history books, that Castro really fooled Jimmy Carter and dumped all of his undesirables on Miami.

A: That happened, but not in [great] proportion. . . . [B]ut the majority, ninety-eight percent, were nice persons. That does not mean that they were the best doctors, but decent persons.

Q: What is your editorial position toward the U.S. government position on immigration into the United States?

A: There are many aspects [to] this problem. The inter-American solidarity, in [a] certain way, obligates the United States to open the door to the good people that are suffering tremendous tyranny or bad situations in their countries. We have to take into consideration that the United States [became] a great country through immigration, through Ellis Island in New York. Naturally, the circumstances change in accordance with the time . . . , but the immigration authorities have to be careful in order to investigate who is coming . . . to the United States. But in general terms, I am in favor [of] the United States, through special [well-thought] methods, permit[ting] people [to come] who will be important for this community.

If we don't have in this country people who like to go to certain places to [harvest] tomato, and you have to send somebody with a master's degree to cut the tomato [off the vine], the tomato will cost fifteen dollars apiece because you don't have people who like to do something like that. Who will be in the tomato area doing this work if they don't bring the people from there to here?

Q: So you would encourage what we would call "guest workers," who come over here and work and return to Mexico or their home country.

A: That has to be studied carefully because [it] could destroy the family solidarity of the people and [involved] the use of the human being like an instrument. . . .

Q: Do you think the federal government gives enough assistance to both the state of Florida and to Dade County to take care of immigrants? Because when they come to Florida there is a need for schools and housing.

A: Absolutely no[t], and I will tell you something. The people come to this area, come to the United States, and the United States has to assume the responsibility [for] them. The responsibility for schools, for medicines, and for everything is [an] American problem. It's not only [a] Miami problem or [a] Miami-Dade County problem. The government of the United States, [on] many occasions, [does] not [give] help in accordance with the best tradition of this country to these people who are living here, organizing a new life without the support of the federal government. At the beginning of the Cuban exile, I will say that the federal government helped, [gave] important help.

Q: Are there any political or economic conflicts between the Cubans, who obviously have both political and economic power in Miami, and other Hispanics?

A: No, in my opinion there is no conflict. If you have many Cubans, the many Cubans are together between them[selves] more than [they are] with the Nicaraguans. I am a Nicaraguan, and in many occasions they consider me [to be] a Cuban because I coincide with them in many things. First of all, the solidarity of the Latin American people exists particularly through the language and the concepts of life. There was a great poet and philosopher of Spain, Miguel de Unamuno, who wrote a poem about the language that says: "The blood of my spirit is my tongue [my language], [and my country] is there [where Spanish is spoken]." He was a Basque from España, but he considered that any country [whose] official language is Spanish and the people speak Spanish [to be] part of his home, part of his family. It's a very, very beautiful poem and something that you can hear in any Latin American country.

In the case of Elian Gonzalez, the . . . great majority of the Cubans considered immediately that they, as Cuban[s], were obligated, so to speak, [to] coincide with the feeling to be in favor of the status of Elian Gonzalez in order to [allow him to] permanent[ly] live in the United States, where his mother brought [him], [with] tremendous sacrifice, from Cuba to here in order to live in a freedom country. They immediately thought, "I am a Cuban; he is a Cuban," and everybody [felt] Cuban, despite . . . the love to the United States and the recognition that they are a citizen of the United States. But in this moment they consider[ed], "I am a Cuban from this aspect, for this purpose."

Q: Why are your editorials in both English and Spanish?

A: Since the beginning, since the first edition, the paper has [had] the editorial[s] in English and in Spanish. The great majority, very great majority, of the readers [of the paper] are using the Spanish text, but we have the English text for the schools in the United States or Americans who [want] to know the point of view of a paper [that] is printed in Spanish under Spanish-speaking direction, and [we] suppose that you like to know the position of [a] certain segment of this community represented in *Diario las Americas*. The translation will permit you to know our philosophical position or logical position about certain problems. Even though you [do] not agree, you like to know the reasons.

Q: In the election of 2000, did you endorse a presidential candidate?

A: Yes.

Q: Who and why?

A: We endorsed Mr. [George W.] Bush [U.S. president, 2001–present]. The other question, why, [is] because we considered that was the person more identified with the ideals and interests in the field of ideas . . . with our community, and his point of view [coincides] with our point of view. We recommend[ed] to our readers to vote for him, but that [does] not mean that we eliminated all the information about the others or [did] not use the space if they [want] to put in advertising or something like that from the other party.

Q: Do you also make recommendations about local elections for mayors, for judges?

A: Yes, in the majority of the cases. When we have doubts about who is the best . . . , maybe in some occasions we only say every citizen has to study carefully the conditions of each candidate and vote in accordance with their opinion, and don't forget the importance of the vote, even though the law [does] not obligate. We consider it a civic, moral obligation to vote. It's not because the law requests this, but not to use the democratic instruments is a tremendous mistake because you have to exercise [them].

Q: What impact or influence does your editorial position have on voters? Do you think that you persuade them?

A: I don't like to be arrogant, but because [of] the trajectory of our newspaper, our readers are extremely well identified with the moral, civic, and philosophical position and social position of this paper. That represents an important opportunity in the sense that the people believe in the newspaper. If somebody [does] not have [the] opportunity to study all the cases, or has doubts, and we recommend, due to the moral prestige that we have, we consider that could help this candidate. We administer it in the best way possible, our moral and civic influence [over] the people. In which way? In the way not to recommend persons that we consider dangerous for the community or without enough merit to be mayor or to be a representative or to be a senator.

Q: Looking back on forty-nine years as publisher and editor of this paper, what would you say have been your greatest contributions to the Hispanic community?

A: First of all, we have been developing the spiritual solidarity of them, not against other communit[ies], but in favor of their community from the base of culture, from the base of language, and from the aspect of traditions, always indicating that we have to serve the United States as a nation [that] has been receiving us with great generosity typical of this country. This is a country of the opportunities for the fallen people in the world. Naturally, we were interest[ed] in cultivat[ing] in our readers and in our community the spirit of solidarity, the interest in our culture.

Columnists and
Investigative Journalists

chapter 11 **Rick Bragg**

Rick Bragg gained fame as the southern correspondent for the *New York Times* and currently works as a national correspondent for the paper. Born in rural Alabama on July 26, 1959, he was the first of his family to graduate from high school. He took his first newspaper job at age eighteen and was winning national journalism awards by age twenty. After stints in Alabama at the *Anniston Star* and the *Birmingham News*, Bragg became Miami bureau chief for the *St. Petersburg Times*. He won a prestigious Nieman Fellowship to Harvard University in 1992 and has won forty national journalism awards, including the Pulitzer Prize for journalism in 1996.

Bragg claims he inherited the southern ability for storytelling, and he travels the South, the nation, and the world, writing stories about poor people and people in trouble. He has covered everything from tornadoes to the Oklahoma City bombing, and his stories have appeared in *Best of the Press* (1988) and in *Best Newspaper Writing* (1991). His 1996 autobiography, *All Over But the Shoutin'*, won wide acclaim as "a classic piece of Americana." He is also the author of the highly regarded *Ava's Man* and *Somebody Told Me*, a collection of his newspaper stories.

In this interview Bragg remembers his rural roots and how his early upbringing and life lessons influenced his writing. He discusses the beginning of his journalism career in Alabama and how each subsequent job led to his improvement as a writer and reporter. He talks about his time in Miami, his work for the *St. Petersburg Times*, and why he ended up working for the *New York Times*. He also reminisces about his adventures in Haiti, the Gulf War, and time at Harvard. He is particularly critical of what he perceives as the eroding quality of current newspapers.

Rick Bragg was interviewed by Kelly Benham on October 26, 1995.

Q: You have a reputation as being one of the best storytellers in newspapers today. Where did you develop that skill?

A: Well, I come from a long line of liars and storytellers. Much of my family was illiterate, but they were great storytellers in an oral sense. When I was a little boy, I would sit at the feet of my father, grandfather, uncles, and their drinking buddies and listen to them tell tales on the front porch of our old house after supper on Sunday night.

They were masters of drama and comedy and tragedy. They told stories about strange men in Korea who kept coming at them even after they had shot them twice; they told stories about dogs that could climb a tree; about mean women in Rome, Georgia, who kept a razor down the neck of their blouse.

The stories started out mostly true, but the more whiskey they drank, the more the truth was sacrificed to the story. All I try to do in my work is weave in all that tragedy, drama, and comedy, but stay true.

Some people say I write like a woman. I'm not sure what that means. But I do know that my father's storytelling was only half of my education. While he and the men would talk about blood and sport and fish as big as a bulldog, my mother and her sisters would hold court around my grandmother in the kitchen and tell gentler stories about babies born, funerals that were "beautiful," and the nicer, sadder, sweeter side of growing up in rural Alabama in the 1960s and 1970s.

Q: You answered that question like you were writing one of your newspaper stories.

A: I don't know any other way to talk.

Q: A lot of journalists today seem to come from the same middle-class and upper-middle-class backgrounds. But you didn't grow up that way, did you?

A: Not damn hardly. My momma was abandoned by my daddy three times, for months or years. He finally left us for good when I was ten or eleven, I think, and died from alcoholism and tuberculosis when I was in the tenth grade.

That doesn't mean he didn't have an influence, only that much of it was bad. He left me with a few skills. He taught me that if a batter gets a good hit off you, then the next time he comes to the plate, throw a fastball at his head. He taught me that if a man is kicking your ass in a fistfight, it is honorable to hit him with a rock or a bottle or to try to thumb out one of his eyes.

He also left me with some books. At a time when the kids my age were dropping out of school to work in the cotton mill or as a pulpwooder, my daddy encouraged me to read. He bought books by the pound and gave them to me in cardboard boxes. He had no idea what to buy. There would be a copy of *All the King's Men*, by Robert Penn Warren, beside sheer and utter trash, paperbacks with half-naked nurses and titles like *Young Surgeon in Love*. But there would also be the complete Tarzan series, or *Innocents Abroad*, or Edgar Allan Poe. When people ask me how did I learn to write, who were my influences, the truth is, everyone.

But while I owe my father for those gifts that probably altered my life, he was a thoroughly worthless man. He left my mother to raise three sons . . . and never seemed to care if we were going ragged or even hungry.

Q: What about your mom?

A: My momma took up the slack. She picked cotton for a living in a time just before the big mechanical cotton pickers took over, working in red-dirt fields with poor blacks and white trash who had no other skills and no other possibilities. She worked as a maid, and she took in ironing and washing for other people. She worked as a waitress in A. G. Baggett's Truck Stop. With the help of her sisters, she kept us in clothes and groceries.

Q: You won a national award for a story on her.

A: The story that won that award was more a tribute than anything else. I didn't really give a damn if anybody else read it, but I wanted her to see it.

It was supposed to be a column on Mother's Day, but the features editor at the *St. Petersburg Times* wanted to make it a centerpiece with pictures of my mom. When I sent her a copy of the story, and talked to her on the phone, her only comment was: "I didn't know that anyone ever noticed." I think what she meant was that no one thought that what she was doing was anything special.

Q: Tell me about the place you were born and how you grew up.

A: Believe it or not, I started to come into this world about halfway through the first-ever Calhoun County showing of *The Ten Commandments*. My momma and daddy were at the Midway Drive-In, about halfway between Anniston and Jacksonville, Alabama. My momma started going into labor, and they took the speaker off the window and headed the car toward Piedmont. There were hospitals closer by, but the one in Piedmont was cheaper. My momma blushes and refuses to talk about the details of my birth, but I have it on good authority that I was either born in the parking lot of Piedmont Hospital or sooner. Momma won't say.

I grew up in the little communities that lie in the foothills of the Appalachians. It's cotton-farming country, punctuated with mountains so green that they can almost hurt your eyes. Most of my life we lived in the communities of Roy Webb, Williams, and Possum Trot. Possum Trot's main distinction was that it was the place people went to take off unwanted dogs. They'd put the poor dog in the trunk of the car, drive out to this isolated community and dump them out, then drive away fast. It may seem inhumane, but it was better than buckshot. The one good thing about it was we were never short on dogs.

Q: What was it like being a child of the civil rights era?

A: I still remember going to Anniston, Alabama, and seeing George Wallace stand on the stage at the Anniston Auditorium and talk about "nigras" and if we, if my momma and daddy and aunts and uncles and cousins, would vote for him, he would protect our way of life. That always sounded kind of funny to me, seeing as how we lived in a shack and had virtually nothing except some raggedy-ass car and other people's throwaway dogs. I was only a child then, but I was smart enough to know that most of the people . . . , pipe shop workers, farmers, soldiers from Ft. McClellan, and other blue-collar folks, lived pretty much the same way that we did. Maybe their life was a few pegs higher than the black folks', but I'm not sure it was anything worth protecting.

Q: What were your own family's personal feelings about integration?

A: Back then, *integration* was one of those twenty-five-dollar words that the politicians in suits talked about. But, despite what people think, it was not a preoccupation with us. Until I was six, I had never even seen a black person, except on a few occasions we saw them when we went to buy groceries in town, and that was rare.

But something happened when I was six or maybe seven, when my daddy got a job at a body and fender shop in a nearby community called Spring Garden. He moved us out of the little house that I had grown up in, surrounded by my mother's relatives, and he took us about twenty-five miles away to this isolated little place—well, I guess it wasn't any more isolated than where I had grown up—and rented this tumbledown old two-story white house—what used to be the beautiful main house of a big farm.

There was a small colony of black folks who lived in the old sharecroppers' houses less than a mile away down a dirt road. And it was through their children that we had our first exposure and experiences with blacks. At first it was ugly. We threw rocks at them, and they threw rocks back. But then we slowly but surely—I guess out of curiosity more than anything else—got to know each other a little bit. One of them, I remember, had a head too big for his body, and we called him "Water Head." We would go swimming together and talked for long hours about why their hair was the way it was and why their palms looked just like ours. We operated out of ignorance, and I'm sure this might even sound a little insulting to many black folks in the current racial climate we live in, but it seems now that our innocent questions about our differences were kind of nice, kind of sweet.

Q: You have a reputation, even in a business full of liberals, of being even more so. Did anything else happen to you as a child to help shape your attitudes and politics?

A: Well, first off, I don't really have any politics, but I sure have some attitudes. That same year that we lived in the big old white house, my daddy decided to hit the road for a while, so he took every single penny we had in the house and just left. We didn't have any money, and my momma didn't have a job, and I think she was just too proud to ask any of her relatives for help. I remember we ate a lot of cornbread and buttermilk. I distinctly remember at least a few times being hungry. One of the old women—I think there were a couple of them in that little cluster of houses where the black folks lived—must have heard about it. Maybe it was something we said or did. And they started showing up at my momma's door with food. It wasn't much, sometimes it was just corn, but it was something. That will alter your attitudes about race, something that no amount of pontificating by the George Wallaces of the world will ever be able to change.

Q: It seems to me that the current racial climate would be disappointing to you.

A: It is, very much so. I hear Farrakhan [minister of the Nation of Islam] and David Duke [former Klan member and Louisiana politician], Al Sharpton [New York minister and civil rights activist] and that fat boy—what's his name again? You know, the loud mouth, . . . [Rush] Limbaugh [conservative radio talk-show host]—for some reason when I hear his name, it always makes me think of cheese. And I hear them spouting off in their own specific varieties of racism, and it makes me sick.

I realize that race is more complicated now than it was then, that affirmative action and other modern-day issues divide us, but it ought not to be that way. Part of the problem is the economy and the fact that there are just fewer plums on the tree for all of us to reach for, and that is naturally going to cause friction. . . . But I have seen the absolute worst in people of both colors—and the absolute best—and I believe we could all get along if a few divisive loudmouth peckerheads would try to find a new line of work.

Q: Tell me something about your education.

A: I went to elementary schools where your ability to spit a long way, or take a punch, was more important than the New Math. I loved to read, but I also loved to throw rocks, ride horses, go hunting, catch fish, swim naked, kiss girls, wreck motorcycles, and act a fool.

Q: Were you interested in journalism at all then?

A: I was an editor on my school paper in high school, because everybody knew journalism class was easy, and you could tell the teacher you were working on a story and instead go shoot basketball in the gym. When I edited the stories of my reporters, I was impressed by how deadly dull they were. At this point I had already started to read some Faulkner and Truman Capote and Tom Wolfe and more popular, modern-day authors like James Clavell, and I knew it didn't have to be that way. I knew that newspaper stories could have strong images. All we had to do was think a little, which is hard at seventeen. At seventeen, I am convinced, I was mildly retarded. I had no real plan for college. I remember thinking, as I neared the end of my senior year in high school, that driving a UPS truck seemed like a pretty good job.

Q: What happened?

A: I took one course in the fall of 1977, and it probably saved my life. I took a feature-writing course at Jacksonville State University in Alabama—we lived about fifteen minutes away—and as I was doing a solidly mediocre job in that class, I got a job offer from the weekly *Jacksonville News*. They wanted a young person they could pay virtually nothing to write the sports column. The only job I had ever really had up until then was pick-and-shovel work, so I thought I was in heaven. They paid me to write. It was like stealing.

Q: Did you ever feel like it hurt you, not having a degree?

A: I think it hurt me more in a personal way. I regret every day the four years I could have had learning some things. But even more than that, I regret the four years I could have had to extend my childhood a little bit. I think a lot of college students take for granted the fact that they have been given a four-year pardon from having to enter the real, harsh world of making a living. And I envy them.

When I was thirty-two and had been working for what seemed like half my life, I won a Nieman Fellowship to Harvard University, which I am sure made me the least-educated person to ever walk into Harvard. And as much as I loved the chance to study and to be part of that rarefied academic world, I still long sometimes for a Saturday-night football game in Jacksonville, Alabama, or drinking an illegal beer with people my age, talking about nothing more complicated than a history test or women. Well, okay, women are pretty complicated. But it didn't seem so back then.

But going back to your first question, I'm not sure what I missed in the classroom at a small southern college was more important to me in the long run than being able to experience life in a newsroom so early on. I guess it was a pretty fair trade.

Q: Let's move on to your Alabama jobs.

A: The ten years I spent with Alabama newspapers, before moving on down to Florida, gave me the best foundation for big-time journalism that I could ever imagine. I was a sportswriter at first, because it was the only job I could get. At the *Anniston Star*, I covered "Bear" Bryant [legendary football coach at the University of Alabama], "Shug" Jordan [football coach at Auburn University], and I covered Richard Petty [race car driver]. Richard Petty once ran over my big toe. He was whipping his car into the garage after qualifying at Alabama International Motor Speedway in Talladega, and I was standing with my foot stuck out right in his way. It only hurt for a minute, 'cause those cars have those big, soft tires. And he got out and apologized and told me I really ought not to have had my foot stuck out in the way.

But the great thing about being a sportswriter is that you get to write with imagination, with color and detail. And I think, I really believe, that made me a better writer further on down the road. I was working at a paper called the *Anniston Star* when I got into a mild skirmish with my sports editor. It involved everything short of me knocking his teeth down his throat, and the managing editor, to get me away from him, made me a real reporter. They moved me to the desk where I covered two rural counties. I wrote about speed-trap towns, cockfights, a triple murder, and a little place called Mars Hill and, just in general, had a ball. It occurred to my editors that I would probably be more valuable writing about these things in a news-feature, big-picture, front-page sort of way than it was to have me sitting in city council meetings growing calluses on my ass. . . . I have never made any apologies about being the designated pretty writer.

Q: What about your first big newspaper job?

A: The *Birmingham News*, a sadly conservative, consistently mediocre newspaper in the state's largest city, offered me a job in the mid-'80s, and it was just a little while until I was doing the same kind of stories there. I did series on the slow death of Alabama's coal-mining towns, on prison conditions, on truck drivers who were killing Alabamians by the dozens because of poor regulations. A series of stories I did on an Alabama preacher wrongly convicted of killing his wife cleared the minister's name, but that story, while it probably helped my career, is also probably my greatest failure, at least my greatest regret.

Q: Why?

A: Because it was only half done. I knew through my reporting who the real killer was, and we even raised his name in the newspaper, opening ourselves to lawsuits if I'd been wrong. But while I did point this man out in the newspaper, it wasn't enough to convince authorities, so he is still free, still living down in south Georgia. . . .

Q: Is Birmingham where you kicked in a locked door at a crime scene?

A: The door was not locked.

Q: No?

A: It was nailed shut. And the building supervisor specifically told me that if the door was not locked with a key, then it was okay for me to go inside. He didn't say a damn thing about no big old tenpenny nail holding it shut. And I didn't really kick it. I just sort of nudged it with my foot. Firmly.

Q: What did you find when you got inside?

A: There had been a killing by this man with a long history of mental illness. He had been in and out of institutions, and he had been released the most recent time for reasons that were not real specific. I could see through the window that he had spray painted what seemed to be a confession on the wall of the living room. It turned out that wasn't what it was, but since I'd already kicked the door down, I went on inside anyway.

Q: Is it true that you once kicked a Rubbermaid trash can all the way across the *Birmingham News* newsroom and took out the book editor?

A: Yes it is. I was nonplussed. I love that word, *nonplussed.*

Q: Are you prone to become hysterical and scream at editors and call them low-life sons of bitches?

Q: No, not a word of that is true. Okay, some of it is true, but not if I respect them. And just lately, I respect the people I work for. In St. Pete I worked for some of the best word-people I could ever imagine, and while the *New York Times* is full of frustrations, they're all little ones, and for the most part I've been allowed to write the way I like to write, pick my own stories, and be proud of what I do.

Q: It sounds like the frustrations in Birmingham were bigger. Why did you leave?

A: I worked for a conservative editorship that didn't like to take many chances . . . and I was always fighting with them. They killed a story or two, so I decided to quit. I sent resumés to several mid-sized papers—I had won a bunch of state and regional awards over the past several years, which mid-sized papers tend to like—and I was lucky. I had several places to pick from, including St. Petersburg, which at the time had a reputation as being a paradise for good writers.

I went and talked to Managing Editor Michael Foley, who said after a few minutes, "So are you a pain in the ass?"

And I said, "Yes."

And he said, "Well, I don't see any reason why we can't hire you. . . ." In March of, I think it was '89, I went to the Clearwater bureau of the *St. Petersburg Times.*

Q: They still talk about one story you did.

A: [Laughs.] What happened was, I had a run of some pretty good stories, page-one pieces on an old woman holding out against developers, serious stories like that, and the editors in St. Pete had already decided after just a couple of months that they were going to put me on the state desk. But— and I'm still not sure they didn't do this on purpose—there was still one last bullshit story that I had to do, the kind that makes you roll your eyes and shake your head, or just hang it.

In Dunedin there had been a rash of chicken maulings by a bobcat. The editor said, "Rick, go up there to Dunedin and get the skinny on this." I did it. I didn't whine. But I convinced myself that somehow I would make them pay. I went up and interviewed a chicken that had survived an attack, losing only a considerable amount of its featherage and perhaps its dignity, considering where those feathers were torn from. I went back to the paper and wrote this lead: "Mopsy has stared into the face of death, and it is whiskered." I thought that they would say, "Okay, we finally pushed the boy too far," but instead I got a note saying, "Great lead." I always have had an odd talent for diving head first into the septic tank and coming up smelling like roses.

Q: What was your first state staff job?

A: I was a state reporter covering southern Florida and had the freedom to roam around the southern half of the state, excluding Miami. I wrote about poachers, mercury poisoning in the Everglades, and the editors brought me back to St. Pete to write about the birth and death of Siamese twin babies.

Q: You won the American Society of Newspaper Editors award for that story.

A: That was the Distinguished Writing Award for nondeadline. Mike Foley called me up and said, "Well, Butt Plug, you've won a big one." Foley always had remarkable tact in situations like that.

Q: But most of your time at the paper was spent in Miami.

A: Yeah, at least three-quarters. I didn't speak any Spanish, and I'd never even been to Miami, but I begged them for the job. Miami in the early 1990s had to be the most exotic, dangerous, and weirdly beautiful city in the country, and I just had to do it. John Costa, the deputy managing editor, in announcing the move wrote: "One of them, Bragg or Miami, will have to give."

I rented a house in Coconut Grove, and the first night someone stole my stereo, but that was OK. I think for the first time in my life, I had found a home. I loved Miami the way some men love women. I wrote about Haitian refugees, anti-Castro guerillas, brutal cops, pitiful crack whores, riots—I still don't hear real good out of one ear because I got hit with a chunk of concrete during a riot in Liberty City—and black churches as a haven from the violence of inner-city Miami.

I traded my 1966 convertible Mustang for a 1969 Pontiac Firebird convertible. I worked my ass off on good stories and spent my weekends fishing or bobbing up and down in the water on South Beach. It was probably the happiest time in my life.

Q: But the *St. Petersburg Times* used you on stories that demanded more tough reporting than pretty writing.

A: Well, I think there's a bias in this business that if you're a good writer, you're nothing but a pretty pen, and if you're a good reporter, you can't possibly be a good writer, and that's kind of silly. There is no good writing without really, really good reporting. I know I'm not the first one to say that, but it's true.

As the buildup for the Gulf War began, the editors in St. Pete decided they should send me for a while, even just a little while, to write about it. . . . I wrote about Jewish soldiers who were forced to hide their religion; some of them even had to say their prayers in a closet and had the Star of David removed from their dog tags, so as not to offend their Saudi hosts. The U.S. military did not like that story worth a goddamn, not that I gave a shit, because I was going home anyway.

Q: At the time a lot of Americans didn't think any American fighting men should be there. How did you feel about it?

A: On the way to Saudi Arabia, I bumped into a middle-aged sergeant who was leading a platoon of men who would ultimately fight in the war . . . and he talked about how ridiculous it was for him to be risking his life in a war over cheap gasoline. He said, "I guess I'm here to protect the American right to drive a Cadillac." I know this man was not a coward, because he'd fought in Vietnam and was only months away from full retirement. He could have gotten out of his duty, but now, in a completely different time in his life, he was risking it again. I remember thinking that I was seeing what true guts was about. He didn't have blind devotion to his country or any cause, but he was doing it anyway because it was better, to him at least, than any job he would've had outside the military.

One more thing sticks in my mind about that sergeant. American journalists had been fond of reporting that this was a dangerous war for Americans because so many of the Iraqi soldiers were said to be zealots and not afraid to die. When I asked the American sergeant what he thought of that, he just laughed out loud: "Son, everybody's afraid to die."

Q: Why did they send you to Haiti?

A: Because I wanted to go. I had always had a moth-to-a-flame fascination with Haiti, and when President Aristide was forced to leave the country and they killed so many people that first night, I thought we had to go and explain it, somehow. Here is a nation just a few hundred miles off the coast of Florida . . . that was filling Florida up with refugees on rickety rafts. I just thought it was important. The story I wrote from Haiti I think is still one of the best things I've ever done. It's a little purple, but that's all right. I saw so much death that I foolishly thought I would never see anything like it again. . . .

Q: What did seeing that much death do to you?

A: It's not easy to talk about, but I can talk about it. You don't have to go to Haiti to discover what death is about. You see it in the breezeways of housing projects in poor neighborhoods in places like New Orleans and Birmingham and certainly Miami. Especially Miami. In Haiti it was just more common. And the commonness of it hammers at your shell.

The first night I spent in Haiti I spent in the city cemetery, where hundreds of thousands of crypts rise like a little city up out of the ground, where hundreds of thousands more are buried underneath. I remember interviewing this young man who had gone searching for his father's crypt—his father had been killed by Haitian soldiers on a lark, purely because he happened to be standing in a doorway, an easy target—but there had been so many burials in the past few days the crypt keeper could not remember where he had buried him. I wrote a line that said how the young man climbed to the top of a cross on one of the crypts, hoping he could spot his father's burial place from there, but all he could see was his own future: a life in the slums nearby ending in an anonymous death in this place. I guess the most accurate way to describe what Haiti did to me was, it broke my heart.

Q: Were you in any danger?

A: Not really. The danger is always that you'll be caught in the middle of the warring factions. Sometimes people just get in the way of a bullet. It happens in housing projects all the time. I got roughed up a little, a couple of times in crowds and once at the airport, leaving. But it was no big thing. I slept in a Holiday Inn, for God's sake, and if it hadn't been for the bodies outside in the street in the morning, I could have been in Fort Myers.

Q: So the Haitians you interviewed were in more danger than you. How did you get their stories without putting them at risk?

A: The great danger in a place like that is that you'll get somebody else killed because you're clumsy, because you assume that you're just slicker and smarter than you are. . . . I interviewed people in pitch-black rooms. I interviewed people by having them lie down on the floor of my Jeep as I drove in circles around the city. And I tried to do everything I could to protect those people. Well, let's put it this way. I can live with a lot, but I don't think I could live with the fact that I got somebody killed because I was just stupid.

Q: Were you criticized at home because you didn't name all of your sources?

A: The people who criticized me—one guy said I was personally responsible for the invasion of Haiti, because Clinton quoted from my stories in his State of the Union address—have never been anywhere even remotely close to that kind of story, or to that kind of danger. I'm not trying to make it sound melodramatic, because while I did get shot at there, I did not have, as so many Haitians had, some soldier walk up . . . , stick a pistol to my head and kill me at point-blank range.

I don't like unnamed sources, and I very rarely use them. I probably use them less than one half of one percent, probably much less than that. But in Haiti it was the only way to protect those people. . . . [I]nvariably the only people who ask those questions would pee in their pants and cry for their momma the first time some bad man started pumping a twelve-gauge shotgun into the crowd that surrounds you. I don't think those people have ever seen the sheer abject terror that comes into the eyes of people who realize if they don't run fast enough and far enough, they're going to die right there. And if they don't cover their face soon enough, somebody will come to their house later that night and rape their children, murder their wife, and drag them off to kill them. I hope this doesn't sound a little thin-skinned, but I have never had much respect for people in this business who are all mouth. My daddy would have said, "You don't have enough ass in your britches to say that about me."

Q: Who are you referring to? Someone in particular?

A: Pat Buchanan called me a liar on national TV. He said I had exaggerated the killing. Of course, the closest he's ever come to Haiti was—well, he ain't never come nowhere close to Haiti. But the editors of the New York Times liked [the stories], and they put them on the front page, and I respect the editors of the New York Times a hell of a lot more than I do some Republican punkinhead who thinks America would be a great place if everybody was just white, Christian, and belonged to the country club.

Q: What do you think your stories accomplished?

A: I think the stories did have an impact. I doubt seriously if they forced the invasion of Haiti. I think that a steady drumbeat of stories about human rights abuses in Haiti in the New York Times definitely influences policy makers. I think that's a given, and it's something I've never been really comfortable with. I'm still not really comfortable with it.

Q: What about it makes you uncomfortable?

A: Well, I guess it's a trade. We like it when our stories do some good. We like it when our stories bring about change in a good way. I liked it when the story I did about the old washerwoman in Mississippi resulted in hundreds of thousands of dollars in contributions for scholarships for poor children. So I guess I have to accept the fact that these stories can have other consequences. We put this stuff in the paper because we have proved as sufficiently as we can that it's true. At the *Talladega Daily Home*, if I misspelled a running back's name, all I was going to do was make his momma mad at me. If I get something wrong in the *New York Times*, well, let's just say the consequences are greater.

Q: Explain why Florida in general and Miami in particular had such an important place in your career.

A: I think it's just because this state, bar none, is the best place to be a reporter in this country. Hell, maybe in any country. The variety of people and the variety of problems coupled with geography make it the best state for stories. I believe that Florida is where I really flexed what little bit of literary muscle I have. And I think it made me a better writer, and it sure as hell made me a better reporter. And if you think about Florida as this very dysfunctional, dangerous, but mildly entertaining family, then Miami has to be the uncle they keep chained in the attic.

My very first day in Miami, Nelson Mandela was being honored by a union group there, and the town, which is split along racial lines in the best of times, had come apart completely over his visit. Black folks of course worshiped him for the obvious reasons, but the Cubans, angry that he had once embraced Fidel Castro, were seething. I drove out to Miami Beach, parked my car, and the very first thing I saw when I looked up was Cuban folks and black folks picking up dried horse manure from the street and throwing it at each other. The horse manure was there because the city had decided it was necessary to use mounted police officers to try to keep them from killing each other. I went and got myself a can of pineapple juice at a little bodega, walked back to the steps of the civic center, propped myself up comfortable, and settled in for the show. I thought to myself, "Lord, I have found me a home." This is the honest-to-God truth.

Q: So why leave it?

A: Well, I hadn't really planned to. I had mildly regretted leaving college so early most of my life, as I said before. And someone at the Nieman Foundation program at Harvard—I'm still not real sure who it was—mailed me an application and a blank envelope.

All my life I had carried a chip on my shoulder because of my lack of education, or at least my lack of a formal education. I had spent my career proving that I didn't need it. So it was kind of ironic that I would want it after I felt I'd finally showed I could do without it. To make the proverbial long story short, I applied for it and was one of the twelve American fellows selected for '92–'93. It took me out of Miami the same week that Hurricane Andrew slammed in. It destroyed my little house and many of my belongings. I don't believe in signs, but this would have been a pretty powerful one that it was time to move on.

Q: So how was Harvard?

A: Weird. And delightful. Here I was, in the best university in the whole world, and it was free and open to me for a whole year. Some people spend their Nieman years just hanging out, or writing their memoirs, but I studied. I studied African American history and culture, Latin American history and culture, Afro-Caribbean history and culture, women's history, U.S. diplomacy, religion, and I shot a lot of basketball. But mostly what I did was talk to [Bill] Kovich [head of the Nieman Foundation], the smartest man I know. We talked about newspapers and about writing and about life as we know it. I didn't know my own father all that well, but there were times when I wished he had been Kovich.

Q: So what did you do when you got back to the *St. Petersburg Times?*

A: Paul Tash, the new executive editor, made the decision to shut down the Miami bureau and promoted me—at least I guess that's what it was—to roving national reporter. What they said was: "Do whatever you want to, find the best stories you can, and we'll let you go." And that's what they did. I spent a month on the Navajo Indian reservation, writing about the hantavirus and about the Navajo uranium miners who were slowly dying of cancer. I went to a small town in Texas to write about the last black resident who was being threatened by the Klan and ultimately would be run out of town. I covered the floods in the Midwest.

Q: You were only there a few months. What happened?

A: Two phone calls that summer changed my life profoundly—one from the *Los Angeles Times,* the other from the *New York Times.* They offered me jobs at exactly the same time, leaving me with what some people called a delicious decision to make, but looking back on it, it was pure hell.

Bill Kovich and Howell Raines [author of *My Soul Is Rested,* editorial page editor of the *New York Times,* 1993–2001, executive editor since 2001], a fellow Alabamian, both told me that I should go to New York. They affirmed what the *Times* had told me, that the *Times* was changing, that they were letting at least some of their reporters write, really write, and were not trying to turn everybody into a good little *New York Times* reporter in a bow tie and horned-rimmed glasses. Kovich called me at home one night and said, "You only get one chance in life to pitch for the Yankees or sing at the Met." Raines just puffed up and said, "Boy, this train don't swing by people like you and me more than once." So I figured whatever decision I made was do-or-die. I decided to go to L.A., which would be one of many large mistakes in my life.

Q: What happened?

A: The short version: they didn't keep their promises. I knew immediately that this dream job would not work out in a practical sense. So I quit. After three weeks. I called the *New York Times* and said I had made a mistake. They left me waiting for seven minutes while they talked amongst themselves, I guess. Then the hiring editor called me back and said the same job was still open if I wanted it. So I took it and moved to New York in January 1994. Maybe I should point out here that this was the coldest winter they'd had in years.

Q: And how did you fit in?

A: From the beginning, it was almost like a dream. They let me chase my own ideas and let me write. I wrote about the homeless, about inner-city killings that left the walls of buildings covered with testimonials to the dead, and just in general wrote about the saddest, most poignant corners of the city. After six months of this, they sent me to Haiti to cover the human rights abuses and the buildup to the return of Aristide and the possibility of an armed intervention. Again, I wrote about the killing and worse the people there inflicted on each other. Got five, or got four, death threats and slept poorly.

Then, I got a call from the national editor, telling me not only that they were going to send me back south, to cover the Deep South for the *New York Times*, but that they would have done it even sooner except that I was preoccupied with Haiti. So in my first nine months, I'd worked on the metro, national, and foreign desks, had my stories nominated for Pulitzers, and won several smaller awards. I don't guess things could have gone much better.

I wouldn't trade a Pulitzer for my Nieman Fellowship, and the year of free and clear life it gave me, and I wouldn't trade it for the bully pulpit that I have at the *New York Times*, where my stories can actually alter people's lives for good. Stepping over bodies someplace kind of makes winning a plaque, even if it's this very special one—well, let's just say it puts it in perspective. I'd still love to win it [he did win a Pulitzer Prize for feature writing in 1996], but I wish I could have won it back when I was still young enough to use it to get women.

Q: I can't believe you just said that.

A: What? I've done waxed philosophical about journalism, got all het up. I could have said, "used it to snake babes."

Q: At your writing seminars, you talk about how newspapers are digging their own graves with short, cute stories. Does it bother you that you have devoted so much of your life to a profession that some people believe is dying?

A: It's only dying because it is so poorly managed. While it's true people read less, while it's true that it is difficult to marry up with technology, I think the main reason that so many newspapers are failing is because they're being run without imagination, with an eye only on profits and just generally stump-dumb and butt-stupid. You've got large newspapers like the *Atlanta Journal-Constitution* trying to compete with television with short, quick, dumb, piece-of-shit stories. And you've got small newspapers all over the country trying to emulate *USA Today*, a newspaper that, at its very best, is bad. Well, we can't be TV, and we ought not try to be. We've never really reached ignorant, vapid people with newspapers.

To read newspapers, you've got to want to read, and we insult those people every day with the crap we turn out. Good writing has given away to cute writing, and a clever turn of phrase seems to be worth more than an investigative piece or a heartfelt feature. I've had cabdrivers in Atlanta talk about how there was nothing to read in the *J-C* [*Journal-Constitution*], while doctors and other professionals won't even pick it up. My doctor, who is a gastro-whatever it is—what do you call a gut doctor? Anyway, he said very appropriately, "It don't have no guts." I thought that was funny. . . .

I got into this business at the time of Watergate, in a time when investigative journalism was entering a really great era. And I followed it through my whole youth, and now I'll ride it out into old age. And if I really am in the end of a dying business, let me put it this way: seeing the end of this business, then that's fine. 'Cause I'm not real sure it can go much further down the toilet. There is such a thing as mercy killing.

Q: So what would you do different?

A: That's part of the problem. I'm too selfish to ever want to go into management. A story is what it's all really about, and that's all I really care about. The thought of running some small newspaper somewhere, of trying to put together the kind of newsroom where reporters are excited about their work—you know, the kind of place where they slap high fives when they come back from pinning the city councilman up against the wall with their question, or writing a lead so good they have to get up from their terminal and walk it off—that is very seductive. But anyway, in a practical—or at least as practical as I can be—answer to that question, the first and most obvious thing is to turn the attention of your newspapers away from bar graphs and pie charts and all this other shit, away from what one paper refers to as "containables"—those little short pieces that don't have to jump from the front page—and line up every single copy editor or slot man or backfield editor who believes any story can be told in eight inches or less and slap the mortal shit out of them.

I'd encourage writers to take chances, not in their reporting so much as in their writing. Everybody is not a stylist. Everybody is not intended to write like Tennessee Williams after a half-bottle of whiskey. But one reason that there is so much damn deadly dull writing in this country is because writers are being told by their editors to "save it for your novel."

Q: You've lived in fourteen cities in about as many years. Do you like living that way?

A: I think I used to. I'm like everyone else when you get to be about thirty-six. I'd sort of like to have a puppy, but it would starve. I'd like to think about maybe buying a house, but I wouldn't get to live in it. It'll change someday.

Q: When?

A: When I'm old.

Q: What are you going to do when you're old?

A: I'm going to try to have a puppy.

chapter 12 **Carl Hiaasen**

Carl Hiaasen, a native Floridian, started writing his trademark satirical columns for the University of Florida student newspaper. After a stint at *Cocoa Today* (now *Florida Today*), he joined the *Miami Herald* in 1976. He served as a member of the investigative team at the *Herald* and also wrote for the Sunday magazine before switching to the Metro section as a regular columnist. He has won numerous awards for his exposure of corrupt politicians, avaricious land developers, and illegal business practices. Diane Stevenson compiled several of Hiaasen's columns in the book *Kick Ass* (University Press of Florida, 1999). Hiaasen has also authored wildly successful novels, including *Tourist Season, Skin Tight, Double Whammy,* and *Sick Puppy.* Author Tony Hillerman calls Hiaasen "the Mark Twain of the crime novel," and Donald Westlake says, "Hiaasen is so good he ought to be illegal." His fame extends to the musical world, where he has been immortalized in song by Warren Zevon, who put two Hiaasen-authored tracks on the album *Mutineer,* and by Jimmy Buffett, who based his song "The Ballad of Skip Wiley" on Hiaasen's *Tourist Season.*

The interview begins with Hiaasen's memories of journalism school at the University of Florida and his experiences writing for the student newspaper. He discusses the differences between being an investigative reporter and a columnist, drawing from his experiences at the *Miami Herald.* He reserves particular contempt for the corporate mentality that he feels plagues newspapers today. He addresses some of his favorite topics from his writings, including the environment, Disney World, Big Sugar and the Everglades restoration, Miami politics, Elian Gonzalez, and the 2000 presidential election. He also shares his thoughts about what makes a good reporter and about what he considers his greatest contribution to journalism.

Carl Hiaasen was interviewed by Julian M. Pleasants on May 21, 2001, in Islamorada, Florida.

Q: Talk about your time at the University of Florida and your journalism studies.

A: Well, I had transferred there in the fall of 1973 from Emory University, where I was an English literature major. . . . I knew I wanted to go into newspapers at the time, and Emory did not have a journalism program. Florida had one with a good reputation, and so I transferred there. I started doing some columns for the *Alligator* [University of Florida student newspaper] — political, kind of satirical columns. I don't know if the columns at that time would have qualified as journalism, but they appeared on the op-ed page a couple times a week in the *Independent Alligator*.

That was coinciding with my immersion in the journalism curriculum for the first time. I think I started out having some bizarre notion that I wanted to write for television, and I was taking some broadcasting classes the first semester. I also had a writing class with Jean Chance. At the end of it, I remember she took me aside and said, "You really do not want to go into broadcasting. You will be frustrated; you will not really get to write what you want to write; and you are really better suited for newspaper work." Of course, she was right. So I took her advice, and it was the best thing I ever did, I think.

Q: What impact did Buddy Davis have on your career?

A: He was tremendous. I don't know anybody in the business who [had] Buddy Davis [and] wasn't profoundly affected by working with him. Opinion writing was the course — I think that's what it was called at the time. . . . With Buddy, what he taught you was, if you are going to have the audacity to write an opinion piece, editorial column, whatever it happened to be, you better get off the fence; you better write what you say; you better have a target and say what needs to be done to fix the problem you are writing about, and hit home, have your research and your facts right.

Of course, all of us remember the brutal experience. You would submit your piece of writing to Buddy, and he graded it. You would get back a cassette. It was Buddy giving you an oral grade. You had to sit there . . . and listen to this cassette where Buddy would just sort of [give] a running monologue, a running critique, of your editorial piece. . . . At the very end of it, he would lay your grade on, you would hear the grade, and . . . you would be trembling in your chair, and you would be thrilled as punch if it was anything above a C; you just did cartwheels on your way out the door. But he drilled it into you. Some kids hated it, and they didn't make it through there, but that was his whole point, that if you are serious about being in the business, you got to be serious about expressing yourself in a way that people can understand it and backing it up with facts.

I think all of us left with an appreciation for how to be tough. There's nothing to this day more aggravating than to pick up, all over the country, when I travel, an editorial page and read a newspaper's editorial on a subject and not have the faintest idea where they stand at the end of the editorial, and you can tell it was a committee decision, and you can tell it was a committee writing job. You aren't doing anybody any service by that, and that was Buddy's point, . . . that this is an important privilege that you have, this opportunity to address the readers of your publication. You should use it to say what you think and deal with important issues, and if you can't make up your mind about something, you [have] no business writing about it. To this day a lot of editorial writers have trouble with that idea, that they don't want the phone to ring in the morning; they don't want the letters to come in. I think Buddy would tell them what he told all of us: "You are getting into the wrong business. Go do something else."

Q: You have never had that problem.

A: Well, you know, it's not easy. I mean, I have always been opinionated, and there's a lot about what is going on in Florida that always angered me. I never had any trouble finding the energy or the enthusiasm or the emotion to write, but there's a very specific discipline that goes with that, and some people don't have it. You can have all the right passion in the world and all the right feelings in the world, but if you can't express yourself or you can't win people over or at least get your idea across in a way that they understand, then it all goes to waste. But that's true for almost all kinds of writing. I mean, a novelist who can't keep readers turning the page, he may be as gifted as it comes in the use of the English language and descriptive abilities and his imagination, but if you can't tell a story, you're out of business.

It's the same with writing a newspaper story. . . . Gene Miller, the great reporter for the *Herald* who won two Pulitzer Prizes, . . . always liked to say, "There are no bad stories; there are just bad reporters who cannot write the stories." That's hyperbole, but his point was, if you do the work, you can turn almost anything into a readable piece, something that reaches out to the readers who ought to be concerned about it. Now, you're competing with the Internet, and you're competing with a jillion cable-TV channels; you're competing with all kinds of printed media, magazines that you didn't have to worry about. Newspapers should be more interesting now than they were. They should be better written and more creatively put together now than they were twenty-five or thirty years ago, and they're not. They're dumbed down. That was their solution to the competition, was to make it dumber, and they're missing quite a bit, in my opinion.

Q: Talk a little bit about your experience on the *Alligator*. I wanted to read one quotation from you about that experience: "Writing columns for the *Alligator* was a piece of cake. We had Nixon in the White House. Each day provided a wonderful new atrocity. It was a splendid opportunity for a columnist to learn the value of contempt, ridicule, and satire. It gave me a pile of newspaper clippings that continue to scare the hell out of editors years later."

A: It did. I was in an unusual position, because I had never worked really as a reporter. I was just in college, and I was writing these opinion columns that they were printing. Of course, my idea was that I could go right out of college and be a columnist, which is absurd and would have been the worst thing in the world for me, but because the columns were well received in Gainesville and the university, I thought about it. I still think some of them are pretty funny, but, again, the material was priceless. It was like shooting fish in a barrel. You had [Henry] Kissinger [Nixon's national security advisor and secretary of state]. You had the charade of the peace negotiations going on and [the] bombing [of] Cambodia. Then you had, of course, Watergate, which is what got a lot of us into the business to begin with. . . .

[In 1974] Richard Nixon is resigning after Watergate, after the third-rate burglary that nobody was supposed to pay attention to. It was an extraordinary time to be at that age in America, with the [Vietnam] war grinding down and kids being killed, and coming out of the era of assassinations of Bobby Kennedy, Martin Luther King, Jr., and John F. Kennedy. You had all that happening. Kent State was still fresh in everybody's mind. It was a very dynamic time, and it was a good time to be writing edgy, irreverent, satirical, and sometimes sophomoric stuff. There was an audience for it;

there was an appetite for it. I mean, we had a crook in the White House. It doesn't get any worse than that. We had a guy who was ordering and approving and paying for burglaries and breaking into people's psychiatrists' offices [a reference to Daniel Ellsberg, the Pentagon analyst who leaked the Pentagon Papers regarding the Vietnam War].

You know, it makes you laugh years later when you hear these droolers get up and talk about what an evil person Bill Clinton was and comparing that whole thing to Watergate. It's absurd. These people must have been under a rock during Watergate. We're talking about high crimes in Watergate, the destruction of incriminating evidence, the eighteen-minute gap on the tape. Every day, there was something new.

To me, it [satire] seemed a natural voice to write in. It was the way I looked at the world, the way I saw what was happening. It seemed to me perfectly reasonable. Satire, and sometimes a kind of lacerating form of satire, was the perfectly natural way to go at corruption and evil and the misdeeds of politics and all that. But there were people it made very uncomfortable, very nervous. I like to think it was all the things that Buddy Davis taught us, and others at [journalism] school, that you have this great privilege and you have this responsibility, the least you can do is say what you think and take the flak for it, take the heat for it. There are always going to be people who just disagree with you, but there's no sin in disagreement, and there is no sin in getting people talking about something controversial.

Even when I started the column at the *Herald*, there was a high degree of nervousness about it. I wasn't always a nice guy, especially if you were caught with your hand in the piggy bank and you were a politician—you know, your day was ruined if you read one of my columns about you, and they weren't used to that.

Q: Did you ever have any pressure from the University of Florida administration?

A: No, I would hear things, that they didn't like certain things, but I never got any pressure. I would have welcomed it, of course, . . . because it wouldn't have bothered me. You always like to think that you are hitting some sort of target. You hate to think you are firing into a vacuum. Honestly, and this is going to sound really odd, I really tried to work hard at making the columns funny, so that even if people didn't necessarily agree with me, the humor was there. That's because it's a very hard thing to be funny about serious subjects; it's one of the toughest things you can do, but I enjoyed making people laugh. That's certainly the same motivation for the novels, is that I enjoyed seeing [people] entertained by something I wrote.

That was the biggest high I had ever experienced, walking around that campus and having people I never knew—professors, people I didn't know—stop me and saying they liked the column I wrote. It just knocked me on my butt every time somebody said they had even read it. . . . It was such a big high, to be told that something made them laugh. Still, to this day, those are the best letters I get . . . [and] my favorite columns are the ones that are funny as well as poignant.

Q: You apparently developed your writing style very early.

A: Yeah, I guess. Again, I tell people it isn't so much a style as it is my voice, the honest voice that I go through life with. It's the same, very similar to the narrative voice of the heroes and heroines of the novels I write. It's the way I look at the world. It's very hard for me to divorce myself, even in fiction, from my point of view about certain things. It's so strong. At a very, very young age, I held very strong points of view, right or wrong. It seemed to me it is such a natural way for me to do it.

The most difficult time after I got out of school . . . [was when] I got on the investigations team, where, of course, you are heavily edited and heavily lawyered. Every shred of subjectivity is beaten out of that work, and it has to be, because you are dealing with many cases [with] high libel potential. You are dealing with serious allegations against people. You are disciplined and trained to take yourself out of every sentence in that story. Your point of view should be the last thing that hits the readers, but you should still be able to make a strong point. So I went from that experience for a couple of years, where it was almost a clinical detachment. You could be in even the worst scandal, and your adrenaline was going, because you knew you were onto something if it was a particular level of corruption, or you had a good story or something, but when you sat down to write, you wrote with the view that they are not going to know anything about how I feel.

Then you go from that to saying, "How would you like to try a column?" It's like having handcuffs cut off. It's a completely different muscle that you are using when you are writing opinion, as opposed to writing investigations, or magazine pieces even.

So . . . the biggest adjustment was that I had been away from it for so long. I got out of school in 1974, and I started the column in 1985, so it was like eleven years I hadn't done that kind of writing. [A]t that point, I was about halfway into *Tourist Season*, which is the first novel I tackled on my own. The hero of that novel was this deranged newspaper columnist [Skip Wiley]. Everyone thought that I had modeled it on myself, but the truth was . . . I modeled myself after Skip Wiley, not the other way around. But that was a hard thing, because it was just all of a sudden, "Okay, it's a completely different job; we want you to do this column; we want you to say exactly what you think about things; and if you raise a little hell, fine." That was what the pitch was. Then when it started happening, everybody got a little, "Ooh, not that much hell." But that didn't last. [T]hey got used to it.

Anytime you sit down and say, "I think I am going to write something funny," it's the hardest thing in the world. I think if you spoke with Dave Barry [syndicated humor columnist], who is a good friend of mine and one of the funniest guys on the planet—and funny in person as well—he's also the hardest-working guy I have ever known, and he agonizes and bleeds over every line. Almost anybody can write narrative, straight narrative, or, in the case of newspapers, can cover an event competently and make it fairly interesting, but if you say, "I'm going to set out to be funny, and not just funny, but currently funny, topically funny, sharp," it's hard to do. It's very easy to fall flat on your face. . . . It's the most challenging, I think, kind of opinion writing to do.

Q: There is a very fine line between satire and cynicism. How do you draw that line?

A: [P]eople . . . say, "Well, . . . you are such a cynic."

I say, "A true cynic is a person who doesn't think there is any hope, and if I were a true cynic, I wouldn't be wasting my breath, or all those dead trees that we publish the *Miami Herald* with, to bother putting a column in the paper." As long as there's a tiny little spark of outrage out there somewhere in the public, waiting to be kindled into something bigger, then you got to keep writing. A cynic is someone, I think, who gives up, says, "To hell with it." There isn't a day that goes by, especially living down here in the Keys and watching it change as radically as it has, where I don't think to myself, "This is a lost cause; it's time to bail out, or it's time to bail out of Florida; we're not getting better, we're getting worse." All it takes is watching the legislature in session, and you get that stomach-churning feeling that it's all a lost cause.

But then you also see things happening. In the letters I get from folks all over the state who are standing up finally and saying, "We have had it with this stuff, and we're not going to let them get away with it here. We saw what they did in Miami, we saw what they did in Key West. . . ." They may lose most of the battles, but they'll win every now and then. And then what do you do? Do you walk away from those folks and say, "To hell with it," quit trying? No, you can't do that.

So I don't see myself as a cynic. Certainly, satire has a cynical note to it. When you hear a politician give the most cockamamie story to explain something atrocious that they have done, he would look at the columnist and say, "You're just being cynical," and I say, "No, I'm being skeptical." After this many years, I would hope that I have some kind of instinct for when somebody is lying.

That's one thing, people say journalists are so cynical. They're not cynical necessarily; they're skeptical, because they have spent most of their careers being lied to. That's a fact. That's what we do, day in and day out. We go to the mayor, and we say, "Why did your friend get this contract?" and he says, "It's just a coincidence." That's a lie. Now the newspapers and the reporters can't call it a lie, but I can certainly in a column cast grave doubt on the veracity of that statement. If you get your facts right and you dig in a little bit, a lot of times it's just a question of connecting the dots. I call it for the reader . . . I say, "I will show you how it happened; follow the ball." And then it turns out to be right.

You're nuts if you aren't skeptical, but I don't see it as saying, "Well, the whole country is corrupt." I think there's a huge, especially in the state of Florida, . . . great engine of greed that has always been a dominating force in Florida. But the interesting thing that happens with that is the momentum builds to develop and exploit every square foot of this place, because it is a gorgeous and a very unique state. Well, I can't walk away from it. That's what a cynic would do, just walk away.

Q: Some critics say that journalists have abdicated their responsibility. William Greider [political and national affairs columnist] argued that reporters were often good on the facts but weak on the truth.

A: Absolutely. I couldn't agree more. But I don't think it's anything new. I think reporters today are more astute than they were fifty or sixty years ago. They're more intrepid than they were. They're more dogged. They're better educated. . . . Very good on the facts, but very weak on the truth.

There's this fraternity that develops. The best reporting about the White House generally ends up being done by people who don't have the White

House as a beat. The White House reporters in the *Washington Post* didn't break the Watergate story. If memory serves, they were somewhat resentful of these two city-side reporters [Bob Woodward and Carl Bernstein]. Greider [and] Seymour Hersh [uncovered the My Lai incident in the Vietnam War] and all these heavy hitters . . . came out of a generation where you had a whole government stitched together on lies, and on a daily basis. They [the government] would lie to you about how many boys died in Vietnam that day. What more despicable lie is there than that, that Johnson or Nixon or whoever was making? So, naturally, you've got that [skeptical] attitude.

Now it's a much more comfortable life. Although newspapers are shrinking and people are being laid off and quality is certainly not what it used to be, the fact is . . . we're much more a self-absorbed society than we were in the 1960s and even in the 1950s, I think. Now it's much more celebrity-driven. You pick up the paper, and you can find much more news about Madonna than you will ever find about the Nobel Prize winner for science or for genetics or for cancer treatments. That's the public appetite.

I'm not sure that the blame goes entirely to journalists for that, but I do think there are plenty of important things that aren't covered well. This is going to sound like a typical reporter. I don't lay it on the reporters so much as I do on the editors and the management of newspapers, because good investigative reporting costs money, and many, many times you get to the bottom, and you have a dry hole. You've spent thousands of dollars, and you've got nothing to put in the paper, and there are not any newspapers today that are willing to eat that kind of expense. Their solution has been in many cases to disband the investigative team or poach from it to the extent that they don't have the same number of full-time reporters. I think these decisions are trickling down, and then you take the steam and the heart [out] of the reporters themselves if you don't let them go out and do their jobs.

Q: Has the *Miami Herald* done that?

A: To some extent, although the great thing about being in Miami is that the news will not let you do that. The news will not let you abdicate that responsibility, because one scandal is on the heels of another scandal all the time. You can't ignore it; you have to dispatch resources. Morally, you have to do it. There are places that do not have the bizarre and constant news flow that we have, where it's very easy to just forget about your investigative team, and you have them pulled off to cover this and cover that, daily stuff. Here, we could have an investigative team ten times as large as we do now, and they would all be busy. My view is that we have way too few people doing this kind of work. But they will never be able to shut it down, because the nature of news and the preponderance of corruption down here just will not let them. . . .

We went through the happy phase of newspapering for a while, what we used to call "Jell-O journalism," soft journalism, because it's easy. Nobody writes you any letters—here is the mayor cutting a ribbon; here are the kids on the first day of school. Instead of putting hard news in the paper, you make it softer. But we went through our phase of that, we certainly did, at the *Herald*. Readers didn't like it, despite what they said in the focus groups.

What people say they want to read and what they read are two different things. We went through a period where we went from having a Pulitzer Prize–winning crime reporter, Edna Buchanan, and extensive and exhaustive crime coverage. We went through a period where it was perceived that we had too much crime. The chamber of commerce was [saying] we're scaring people off; we're overblowing the crime; we're exaggerating it; . . . so we went to this phase where crime was not covered as thoroughly. And guess what? The next group of focus groups said, "What happened to all your police coverage?" Then we scrambled back the other direction.

By ignoring it [crime], we're not doing anybody a favor. What we are doing is, we are depriving them of information that they're going to turn on Channel 7 and see. It's stupid, and they finally figured that out, but we went through that phase—all newspapers did, I think—of, "Oh gee, we are just bringing people down in the morning with all this." Well, guess what? Crime is now down. Homicides are way down in Miami. The attention brought results. Why are we writing about the tourists getting mugged and killed as they leave Miami International Airport—this isn't good for tourism? Well, it's even worse for the tourists getting mugged and killed, okay?

Those decisions are not made by reporters. Those decisions are made by editors and above. I don't know of any reporters who would not salivate at the chance to go after the big story . . . instead of being yanked off to go cover a craft show. Most reporters just hate that stuff; good reporters do. They would much rather be out digging through records and following up leads that come in. . . . Those are the ones we are out there digging for, not for our own glory, because nobody remembers the bylines; nobody remembers who writes these stories. It is folly to think that. It all goes into the birdcage.

Q: That is an interesting point. What makes a good reporter?

A: To some extent what makes a good cop, too. A good instinct for when something doesn't look right, doesn't fit right, doesn't sound right. A story just doesn't hold up. Secondly, an unfailing instinct for when you're being misled or lied to. Third, and probably most importantly, a real strong sense in what's right and what's wrong, that when somebody does something wrong, who is in a position of public trust, it should go in the newspaper. It's that simple. Let the readers decide whether it is worth throwing him out of office or not. The fun of it is just digging, digging, digging . . . ; nothing gets a good journalist going with more energy than the idea that somebody is covering something up.

You're not out there for yourself. The big high, the kick I always got, was knowing I had gotten hold of something, knowing they hated the idea that I got . . . hold of it, and they were going to get to read all about it on the front page on Sunday. The byline didn't matter. It was just the idea that you can't keep the truth from people, and as much as you want to try, we're going to put it in the paper, and they can deal with it.

Q: But the problem is partly what you mentioned earlier—haven't a lot of these reporters been co-opted? Has the media really protected democracy? I would imagine Thomas Jefferson would be very disappointed in today's press.

A: Oh, yeah, but I think the press has always disappointed people. I don't think that's anything new. I think they are much less co-opted today than they were in Jefferson's era, to be honest with you. . . . I also think that the disease isn't being co-opted so much as it is being dispirited, to the point of laziness sometimes. You know, you go where the facts lead you, and if you have to go crawling and begging and groveling, which is what pretty much it is at most newspapers now, . . . just to get what you need, that will take it out of you. What happens then is that you . . . start self-editing—"I don't want to go after that; they will never let me go chase that story"—and the result is that good stories don't get written.

[For] the vigorous free press in this country today, the big enemy is Wall Street, or the big enemy is the corporations that own these newspapers, who are now putting out newspapers for shareholders, not for readers, who are much more concerned with pleasing the stockholders than they are with meeting the real day-to-day needs of readers. So these papers are being shrunk by attrition. They're getting thinner. All this is being done without telling the readers, and they're just not supposed to notice that there is nobody covering the city council meeting for a few weeks because . . . somebody quit, and they're not going to replace them, to save money.

Meanwhile, something is not covered, and somebody gets away with something, and somebody's community is worse off for the fact that we're too cheap to keep a full payroll. It's absolutely the truth of the *Miami Herald*, and it's true probably to every paper in the country, if they're going to be honest about it. So that is a much greater danger to people's need to know than whether the reporters are too cozy.

The source of the problem is real simple: there aren't enough reporters, and there aren't enough good reporters. The pool is shrinking, not growing, because newspapers are shrinking. That's a far more disturbing thing to me. You know, you have a corporate culture now existent in many newsrooms that was never there when I started. I mean, you never heard about the business side. Now it's much different. Everybody in the newsroom is painfully aware of what the circulation numbers show . . . because they get posted. I never knew what the profit margin of [the] *Miami Herald* for Knight-Ridder was. I knew we made a lot of money, but I didn't know. Now it's emblazoned in the brain of everybody on every floor of the paper, that if the *Herald* does not make its twenty-two, twenty-three percent, whatever Tony Ridder [head of Knight-Ridder newspapers] has decreed for this year, we face cutbacks, layoffs.

You can't pollute the reporter's mind with these kinds of concerns. You want him to go out and kick over the rocks and give the people, that community, the most thorough possible coverage that is available. Yet you are telling him, "You can do that, but don't spend this; don't take this source to lunch; you can't go to Tallahassee." It's insane. That's a terrifically scary thing, but it's nothing new. Papers have always been cheap.

Q: But twenty-two percent, that is a pretty good return. They should have a little extra money to —

A: He [Tony Ridder] wants twenty-five percent this year. It's absurd. I always tell people I know heroin dealers who would be thrilled with that kind of profit margin. It's completely obscene. It's unrealistic. It will have a devastating effect on the quality of the journalism that is being produced, because it means getting rid of older experienced people to whom they can afford to offer buyout packages. It's very sad, and it's shortsighted. And it's not by any means unique to Knight-Ridder. The *L.A. Times* is going through it. Gannett has been famous for it for years. Gannett was the pioneer of journalism on the cheap. You know, I worked for Al Neuharth right out of college.

Q: Talk a little bit about your experiences in Cocoa with Al Neuharth.

A: I remember I graduated in March of 1974, and I think my first day was March 21, if I'm not mistaken, 1974, *Cocoa Today*, which was the precursor of *USA Today*. It was the tenth anniversary . . . of the founding of that newspaper, or some anniversary of it, and I just happened to arrive that day. Al Neuharth had assembled everybody in the pressroom for a big pep talk and congratulatory speech. I'm sitting there, and no sooner has he gotten started than he launches into an attack on one of the reporters, on, specifically, a series that had been done called "Confessions of a Used-Car Salesman," which I had seen.

It was fascinating stuff, these guys telling how they dolled up these wrecks and were able to get people to buy them. They put sugar in the tank and did all this horrible stuff to make it sound good for a minute, and then they would sell them. It was . . . also filled with comments of horror and contempt by honest car dealers who said, "We would never do that." It was a very balanced series. Well, the Used-Car Association of Brevard County, or whatever the hell they called themselves, had raised some hell and in their outrage had pulled some ads. Al was on a roll about how one-sided he thought the series was, a little too strong, a little too tough on everybody. Well, he never had the balls to come out and say it was because they pulled some ads. I thought, "This is my first day in the real world of journalism, and I've got the publisher of this newspaper chewing out a reporter for doing his job." So much for theory; so much for idealism.

[Y]ou talk about separating the ethical barriers between the newsroom and the business side. Neuharth lived on the beach in a big fancy house, and at the time he had just married a state senator named Lori Wilson. They lived . . . on Cocoa Beach, and there was some setback in zoning issues that the neighbors had raised about what Al was doing with the property. We dutifully . . . were writing about it. [T]here was a possibility Al was going to be cited for building below the setback line on the beach, which was a big environmental thing up there at the time.

I'll never forget, he called in from wherever he was traveling, and he had the story read to him word for word over the phone, and he said, "What is the headline going to be?" And he rewrote the headline himself. A complete violation. That's like having Nixon write the headline on the Watergate stories that you want to read. But he was the boss. There was a great deal of dissension and demoralization at the newspaper because of this. He was meddling in the story; he should've sat back and taken his lumps. The whole newsroom was just appalled that he would do this sort of thing. It was hard on the editors. I felt bad for them. They get the call, and what are they going to do? That's their boss; are they going to tell him to go pound salt? They would be out of a job. . . .

Management, it may be, isn't the enemy, but they're not necessarily your friends either, and they're not necessarily committed in the way that reporters and front-line editors are to putting out a complete and thorough and balanced newspaper.

Q: Then there is a lot of hypocrisy in publishing.

A: A terrific amount of hypocrisy, and I would go so far as saying, in some cases, corruption. I don't mean criminal corruption, but there's certainly a corruption of the unspoken bond between the readers and the newspaper. "We will always serve you first"—that's just plain bullshit. If we believed that, we wouldn't be laying people off right now at the *Miami Herald*. . . . We barely have enough photographers to cover the day-to-day news, and they want to lay off four more now. That isn't what a newspaper in a big, dynamic, growing community does for its readers. It's basically the same as cutting your police force in the middle of a crime wave. . . .

But, believe me, we're not alone; it's going on everywhere . . . , so I'm not singling out Knight-Ridder. We shouldn't even pretend that we are working hard for you, the reader. We're working hard to make that twenty-five percent for Tony Ridder, is what it boils down to, and the shareholders, so that he doesn't get yelled at, at the next shareholder's meeting. We aren't really doing journalism here; this is a franchise operation, and our job is to make money, and you got to understand that. And, by the way, we will put something on your front lawn every morning; some days it's going to be better than others; some days it's going to be real good; and some days it's going to be disgraceful, it will be so thin. At least be honest with them; say, "Lookit, we are getting hammered from corporate headquarters, [and] that's why the paper is getting thinner. It isn't because there is less news happening, folks. It's because we are printing less of it than we ever have."

Q: What is your view of USA *Today*? Is that the wave of the future?

A: No. Everyone said that. . . . I don't think it is. I think it's great for what it is.

... I read it when I can on airplanes. But I think most readers are sophisticated enough to know that you're just getting little M&M bites of news, and if you really want to know what's going on in the Middle East, you don't look it up in *USA Today*. You go to the *New York Times* and the *Washington Post*. Having said that, I also have to note that probably eight out of every ten readers, that's all they really want to know about the Middle East. . . . I don't think it's the wave of the future, but I don't think the future is all that bright either. *USA Today* . . . has gotten better, I think, over the years, the quality of the writing. They break stories.

Q: They do some investigative journalism.

A: They do, and they have gotten a hell of a lot better than when they first started. But I know everybody, all of us, went to color weather pages. That was our answer. Let's make the weather map almost real life-size, and that will show readers we really care about them. It's expensive putting all that color in the paper, and the same number of people looked at the weather page who looked at it before. So they abandoned that. . . .

I think there are plenty of times when shorter is good . . . [but] I think there are a lot of times that . . . the only way to distinguish us from the broadcast media and from the thinner newspapers and magazines is to be able to do what they call "interpretive journalism." A good paper can deliver something that TV, radio, and the Internet can't give you; depth and insight and basic investigative stuff can't be duplicated by TV or radio . . . to the devastating effect that it can have in a newspaper. So . . . that's really our only trump card over these other media. One thing we can do that they can't do is depth. More and more papers are shrinking away from depth—let's . . . be just like radio, only let's be it in print. It's insane . . . [and] they wonder why nobody is picking up circulation, why advertising is flat. Well, there are a lot of complicated reasons. One of the reasons is we aren't offering people anything they aren't getting anywhere else. We're failing in that regard.

The best newspapers, the ones that are making tons of money, are spending tons of money on the product. They're going through down cycles now because of the economy, but the fact is the *New York Times* remains a highly profitable newspaper—the *Washington Post*, a highly profitable newspaper—and also at the same time high-quality, and they spend a fortune covering the world. You know, we close all our bureaus outside of the United States; we do all this great cost cutting; and then we wonder, "Gee, I wonder why our circulation is flat. . . ." If it were Coke and Pepsi, they would be finding ways of getting more people to use their product and not just putting less syrup into the soda. But that's what we do in the newspaper business.

Q: Explain how your experience with *Cocoa Today* impacted your career.

A: I was there about two and a half years, and I had a great time. It was a great learning ground. I was very lucky to be surrounded by some talented people. . . . [T]he good thing about a small paper is if you got a little bit of ambition and a little bit of talent, they will let you try and do almost everything, which I did. They had a little Sunday magazine, and I worked for that. All kinds of different stuff. I would get a crazy feature idea, and it was, "Why not? Try it." There was not the level of bureaucracy that you get at a bigger paper, where you have to go through all these channels just to try anything new. That was the good part. I think the part I didn't like was it was small-town, and it did a lot of small-town stuff that drove me crazy. . . .

When you have a smaller paper like that, you have a lot of people on their way to somewhere else, and I was included. The only way to make any money was to change jobs, honestly. When you are getting $7.50 a week raises and told that is good—people with families, you know, you aren't going to hang in there.

I understand that people move around, and the same thing, of course, happens here at the *Herald* on a bigger scale. In the twenty-five years I have been here, if you just took the people who walked out the door to the *Washington Post*, to the *New York Times*, or *Time* magazine or *Newsweek* or L.A., you would have an extraordinary staff of talent. A certain amount of it is inevitable, that kind of change, but it is hard, because just when someone would get to know a community or get to know a beat—someone who was covering Cocoa Beach—just when you finally nail it down, you get moved to another beat, or they leave. . . . But the readers . . . aren't really aware that a whole re-education process now has to begin. Every time you change a beat, it sets the level of coverage back in the community. The result is a lot of smaller communities are not covered very well.

Q: Why have you stayed with the *Miami Herald* for twenty-five years? Did you ever have a desire to go anywhere else?

A: No, I didn't. I had some opportunities, but I didn't. First of all, I couldn't see myself living anywhere else. This is where I was born and raised. Florida is—really, it just is a character in the novels; it's a character in my life.

It's very hard to walk away from this place for any length of time, even as much as it has changed and as heartbreaking as it has been to watch some of the change.

[A]fter about two years at Cocoa, they called me up because I had won second place in some national award. . . . Two things changed my mind [about moving to the *Miami Herald*]. One is that I had a young family, and it was a lot more money than I was making or would ever make at Cocoa. . . . Then second of all, my father had just passed away, . . . my mom was alone . . . and I just thought it would be better if I would be around for my mom. It was much better for me, I think, for a lot of reasons to be writing about a place I cared about and at least had some roots. For me, it was a place I knew from childhood, so the learning curve was not nearly as steep for me.

Q: Was one of the critical factors in your decision that you would eventually get your own column?

A: [W]hen you join a paper, they always say, "What do you have [for] long-range plans?" and I'd written down, just whimsically almost, "Someday I would like to write a column again; I wrote one in college. . . ." I didn't actively go look for the column. . . . I [had] been on the investigations team. We just finished up a long investigation in the Bahamas. It was very grueling, about corruption involving the prime minister, and I had been away from home a lot. I was just fried; I was burned out for the time being. Not on all of it, but you always have a postpartum period after you spend a lot of months on something, and you finally get it all in the paper in the space of a week or six days. . . . Then . . . the executive editor at the time came to me and said, "Would you be interested in taking a shot at doing the column?" It was one thing I hadn't done at the paper. It was one of the few . . . writing jobs I hadn't had, and I said, "Yeah, I will give it a shot."

Then, once I got comfortable in the voice and comfortable doing that length—doing the same length every column, which was another discipline I had to learn—what I . . . found was you do get a sort of emotional connection with your readers, and the mail you get, a sense that they start looking for your column; they expect you to be responding and writing about certain things to get them angry. All of a sudden, you feel like it is your duty. It sounds odd; that's the last thing I expected. I go through periods all the time when I say, "To hell with it. I don't want to do it anymore. I'm tired; I can't do that and the books at the same time." But then you get this mail, and people seem to really depend on you in the morning over their breakfast cereal to at least say what they have been thinking and ranting and raving about.

Part of it gratifies your ego, but part of it is also, [and] I told them this, the only way I would ever leave is if I thought there was someone else with as strong a voice about especially the environmental stuff that I feel strongly about. . . . You know, I always feel like if I go, no one is going to do this. Not that I do it exceptionally well, but there will not be anybody doing it, because our pattern is, we're not replacing people who leave.

Then before you know it, the years pile up, and you are doing it, and the longer you do it, the harder it is to walk away from it. I certainly don't need to do it anymore. It's not a financial decision on my part. I've been so ridiculously lucky with the books. I've just been blessed with being able to do the novels and enjoy some success with that, but I do the column because it's important. I do the books because it's therapy. It's therapy for me, and it's fun. It's different. It's a very challenging kind of writing, to sit down and construct a whole novel. You have to use up a lot more tricks in your bag to do a novel. But the column is important because you write it, and it's in the paper the next day, and you're responding to something, hopefully fairly quickly, shining a little spotlight on this one thing before it gets too far in the legislature, too far with the county commissioner, before somebody's life is messed up because they do something stupid, or somebody's sitting in jail who should not be in jail.

So the immediacy of it, . . . this adrenaline rush of jumping on a big story, still is there. I think if it wasn't there, I wouldn't do it. I'm saying all of this, [but] six months from now, I could bag it. I don't know. For me, the tough part is going to be keeping the loyalty to the paper going while they are shoving good people out the door. There is almost a point of a moral line in the sand that you have to draw. This isn't affecting my life at all. I still get my paycheck, and they're still happy to get my column, but these are people I have worked with for years, good people who do not deserve to be treated this way. At some point, you say, "I can't sit by and watch this happen." I hope it doesn't come to that, but that would be one of the deciding factors, not anything to do with my own personal life.

Q: In your columns, I have been particularly interested in your descriptions of politicians: "pernicious little ferret," "worthless blowhard," and my personal favorite, "a veritable slag-heap of mediocrity." Do you get pressure from editors to modify your comments or phone calls from the maligned?

A: I think I used to get the occasional cringing phone call saying, "Gee, do we really have to say that?"

And I would say, "Look what he did."

"Yeah, but he's going to be on the phone tomorrow."

"Let him be on the phone tomorrow, so what?"

I don't relish or take any joy in knowing—I mean, these are folks with wives and husbands and kids, and I take it very seriously. As frivolous or as whimsical as some of those names sound, those are applied to individuals who did some really bad stuff and whose actions affected people. To me, they were perfectly accurate descriptions. But, yeah, they get queasy about it. Readers love it. I don't hear much from the politicians themselves, because they are always afraid if they write to me, I'll put that in the column too. . . .

But in the case of, like, the "pernicious little ferret," I think I was referring to Humberto Hernandez [former Miami city commissioner], who is now in jail for voter fraud and for money laundering and fixing an election. He first came to the public attention when the ValuJet crash happened in the Everglades. He has a law firm, and he sent someone in his law firm to infiltrate the bus full of relatives who were taken to the crash site, so they could hand out their business cards to try to get lawsuits against ValuJet. To me, I was easy on him. He's lucky that all I called him was a "pernicious little ferret." But, I mean, where on the food chain does a guy like that fit? There's no bottom. He's right where he belongs, jail. Good for him. I don't have any compunction about that at all.

Again, keep in mind that I save these sorts of little rants for people who have a public trust. I don't pick on the little guy; I don't pick on a gas-station owner or a grocery-store clerk who is rude to me or something. I never do that. These are people who have put themselves out there and said, "Lookit, I'm the best and the brightest. I'll do this for you; I'll do that for you; I'll represent you fairly; I'll be honest; I will not steal." Then they turn around and do everything they said they weren't going to do, to the detriment of government, the people they are elected to serve, their families, and everything else.

I wrote about this guy . . . , who's just slime from way back, back when he was in the City of Miami politics. This guy is a sitting member of the Miami-Dade school board, and he's getting money from the federal government to run low-income housing. He's taking a check to subsidize rents for older people, and at the same time, this one individual, he was going to her [his renter] every month and shaking her down for—I think it was—up to $350 a month, when she was supposed to be paying $28 a month rent, and the rest was paid by the government. . . . He's shaking her down for extra cash, so he's getting paid twice, by the feds and by the woman who the program was designed to help.

Now, my question is, what can you say about that individual? There's no way he's going to read that column and not feel sick to his stomach if I have anything to say about it, because it's a shameful and disgraceful thing that he did. . . . His lie was that he was just charging the extra money to rent the furniture in the apartment, except the only problem was she owned the furniture in the apartment. I don't care if [he] breaks down in sobbing, hacking hysteria when he reads the column. I don't care, frankly, if he throws himself off a building. At some point, if you put yourself out as a protector and a defender of the public trust, and this is how you behave, your number's up, as far as I am concerned. I have no sympathy whatsoever for him.

Q: Where do you get most of your information? Do you ever use inside informants?

A: Yeah, sometimes you get tips. . . . I really just read the paper and watch TV and just poach liberally and then check with the reporters and watch a story evolving. I have files of stories that I see evolving over time. They still like me to be on top of the news. That's also because it is a daily paper, and you want to be topical. But I do try to bounce off what is happening because . . . your readership level is highest for those stories that are making people talk. You know, you don't want to do Elian Gonzalez to death, but it was on the front page for months. I had to write a number of columns about Elian Gonzalez. The election fiasco, the recount fiasco—well, I had to bite the bullet after the first couple. Even when you knew which way it was headed, you had to do it. You knew the outcome; you still had to write the pieces. It's being timely and trying to find something original to say, if you can.

Q: Looking back on the Elian Gonzalez saga, what is your reaction to the story now?

A: The same. I think the outcome was absolutely the only morally acceptable outcome. When you have a living parent of a kid—I don't care if he's a communist or whatever—he's the kid's father. He belongs with his father. Any other civilized society, there wouldn't have been a question, but he became a pawn, [and] he was used shamefully in this country. He was held up like a bowling trophy and trotted around, "Look what we have got, nah-nah," looking at Fidel. Well, the whole world thought this was insane . . . ; give him back to his father, for God sakes. It wasn't like he was orphaned. If it had been an American boy who had washed up on Cuba's shore, what do you think America's reaction would have been?

And the other stupid thing was, it played right into Castro's hands. I mean, you could not have scripted it any better for him. He could not have done anything . . . else to get half a million people on the streets of Havana. They weren't marching at gunpoint; they were really pissed. I understood both sides; I understood their emotions, but right is right, and as a parent and a father, if I would've been that little kid's father, I would've been just as upset as he was.

But looking back, it divided the community. . . . [T]here were a lot of people in this community who felt that the obvious thing was not being said—and that is, he belonged [with his father in Cuba]—because they were scared. There's this fear that if you speak out, and especially if you are Cuban American, that you would be persecuted, or even worse things happening to you, for agreeing. I heard from a lot of Cuban Americans on my voice mail at work and letters, scared to give their names. It was very sad. You know, they hated Castro as much as anybody. This is not about Castro; it's about a boy and his father. . . . I just got tons of mail from people saying, "Thank God somebody finally wrote what should have happened in this case."

Q: Who won the presidential election of 2000?

A: Well, I think from the study the *Herald* did with *USA Today* and others, clearly the intention of most Florida voters was to vote for Al Gore. . . . Using the typical standards of judging these ballots, Bush would have won, or did win, but the intent of the voters, just looking at the numbers, clearly was to elect Al Gore, meaning, of course, he should be in the White House now. But the rules are the rules, and if your ballot is not proper, you cannot [be counted]. Whatever happened, if you're George W. Bush, there are all kinds of reasons to be extremely humble—not only losing the national vote by half a million votes, but knowing that the people of Florida did not pick you.

It was a mess, and kind of a dispiriting one, and I guess the only philo-sophical thing you can say was that it was always Gore's race to lose, not just in Florida, but nationally. The other thing you can say is that Ralph Nader, without any doubt, cost Al Gore the election. . . . In Florida he certainly did. Nader clearly had enough margin of votes, and the election was that close. So when they start plopping those oil derricks in the wilderness, the Arctic Refuge in Alaska, they ought to name one after Nader, because that's why it's happening.

Q: Let me ask you about Operation Court Broom. How did this corruption and bribery in the court system go on so long, and how was it uncovered? One judge said that he could not be blamed for taking a bribe because he was on drugs.

A: There was a whole crew of them. There was a little system going on, and I don't know how this story broke. . . . I do know that it went on because, as these things often unfold, there was a fraternity of judges and attorneys who were friends, and ex-judges who later became defense attorneys, and it could be done fairly quietly because they were all in on it. You know, wink, wink, they all knew, and it was pretty tight knit.

One of the reasons it went on so long, obviously, was because, again, the issue of changing [reporters]. You have a reporter who covers the courts for eighteen months, and he's off the courts. It would be very tough to break that story. You have to have someone who has been there a long time and knows all the players, unless you get a real big break. But, secondly, the reason it went on is because the state attorney's office has always been a political office; it's an elected office in this town. So they end up as friends or colleagues or golfing buddies of some of the judges, and there's an incestuous little thing. Not just in Miami-Dade; it's even more true in some of the rural counties in Florida. Everybody knows everybody else. You just don't spend much time investigating your friends.

And that's the function of a newspaper; you have to light a fire. The sad thing is that so many of our corruption [cases] down here are made by the federal government. The FBI comes in or DEA [Drug Enforcement Agency] or whatever it is, because they are not part of the local political network.

That's why the federal government has had to take such an active role down here, because there has been a general reluctance, going back to when Janet Reno was state attorney, to spend a whole lot of time on public corruption cases. The prosecutor's position will be, "Well, the feds have much better laws for that." And they do; they have RICO [federal anti-racketeering laws]; they have conspiracy laws. You can also make good conspiracy cases with the state of Florida law . . . but there is . . . a general reluctance and queasiness to go after somebody who contributed to your campaign.

You asked me before about Miami; is it more corrupt than other places? Yes, certainly, I think it is. I think there's corruption everywhere, and I think in a state as booming like Florida, I think greed is going to rule the day in small towns just as it does in cities, but I think Miami just has a history. It has a particularly bumbling form of corruption. It's egregious corruption. It's clumsy; it's not sophisticated. . . . You know, the FBI videotape is showing, and there's the guy taking the money, and he's giggling like a six-year-old and then counting the money on videotape. . . .[T]here's just no cool to it at all. Instead of just slipping it in their pocket and slipping out the door, they're just idiots. It's great for me, for my job; it makes it a lot more fun. . . . I'm firmly convinced that it exists everywhere. I think just the level of it and the sometimes bizarre nature of it is what makes Miami a little bit special.

Q: Yet the voters continue to reelect Joe Carollo and Xavier Suarez and all those guys to political office.

A: Yeah, it's really amazing. The other thing is these are folks with absolutely no charisma. . . . Alcee Hastings, one of our congressmen, was impeached from the federal judiciary, for God sakes, on corruption charges. He was acquitted in a criminal trial, but a panel of justices decided he was guilty; they booted him off the federal bench, which almost never happens, and we put him right back in Congress. Humberto Hernandez, whom I mentioned earlier, the city commissioner in Miami—they were well aware of what he did in the ValuJet crash; the voters were well aware that he was under investigation for money laundering and bank fraud; and they elected him resoundingly. Now, granted, the election was fixed, but he still had enough votes.

Q: In the *Miami Herald* today, they were listing the one hundred most lucrative corporations in the state, and Lennar Homes, which built homes destroyed by Hurricane Andrew, was near the top. I know you wrote about them in *Tourist Season* and in several columns. Does this kind of building still go on?

A: Well, I think they have to be more careful. I'm sure it does. We'll find out when the next big hurricane hits, won't we? Lennar certainly got their share of press, well-deserved, after Hurricane Andrew. Other companies did as well, but that's the largest home-builder. They got mad at me for doing some columns about some stuff they had done, and then they got caught in another development building houses on, basically, dump sites, tire dumps. . . . There's a long history of that kind of behavior in the building industry in Florida. Presumably, the new building codes will help. Presumably, the insurance industry is actually going to start paying attention to what kind of homes it insures now.

Q: Well, the adverse publicity hasn't seemed to hurt the company's bottom line very much, has it?

A: Not at all, no. . . . I was told they were unhappy and they were yanking some ads. Of course, I lost about thirty seconds of sleep over that; . . . you can't worry about that stuff. They were wrong. People's lives were completely disrupted and ruined because these folks couldn't build a house that stood up to ninety-mile-an-hour winds. . . . I'm not thinking about them. I'm thinking about the people and their kids who had to tape garbage bags over the holes in their house and huddle in the rain for three days . . . after Hurricane Andrew because they were living in a cracker box and didn't know it. Those are the people that I'm writing for.

Q: This is off the subject a little bit, but in several of your novels there is a character named Skink. Where did that character come from? Is he modeled on anybody?

A: No, certainly not modeled on any former governor. In the novels, he's an ex-governor who goes crazy and goes running into the woods and only comes out to wreak havoc and seek vengeance. He's just sort of a wild man. . . . Confronted with the kind of corruption that really exists, he couldn't deal with it, fictitiously. I have been asked, certainly, by ex-governors if they were models for Skink, and they wish they were, but, no, absolutely not. He's the sort of character I wish existed in real life, and it's one of the great joys of the novel, being able to turn him loose and have him kick some butt.

Q: Is he, in a way, your alter ego or conscience?

A: I think in those novels that he appears—if not my conscience, he really is the moral compass of those novels, and he was never created that way; he just sort of popped [up]. I needed a kind of a renegade character, and in an early novel called *Double Whammy*, I just invented him. . . . But it [Skink] was just supposed to be around, originally, for a couple chapters in that book, but he sort of took over. That is what happens sometimes in fiction. I liked him so much that I brought him back for a couple other books. But

I wish there had been someone like that who had been in the governor's mansion at some point.

Q: Well, there is a little resemblance to Claude Kirk.

A: Well, maybe physically. But politically . . . I think Claude is one of the ones who insists that he is modeled after him, one of his many delusions.

Q: Let me talk to you a little bit about one of the major topics in your column, the environment. I wanted to quote to you what Nathaniel Reed [a noted Florida environmentalist] said about your writing on the environment: "He takes no prisoners, whether they are black, white or human. If you are ludicrous, if you are droll, if you are an idiot or a bandit, he will either have a great deal of fun with you or he will absolutely skewer you."

A: That's high flattery from Nat. Nat knows more about the Everglades than any living human I think I know, so I respect his opinion on it. You know, I'm not a hydrologist, and I'm not a biologist, and I don't know all the intricacies of this program. All I know is that there's a whole lot of money to be spent on this [Everglades restoration], and that means a lot of it is going to get stolen and wasted. That's my concern, that it be spent doing what the intent of the law is and what the will of the people of Florida wants. It will never be the same Everglades. The Everglades are now broken up by two different highways and eaten up by subdivisions on both flanks, so it can't ever be the old Everglades, but the least they can do is put the freshwater back. If they got any brains at all, they will. Now it's complicated. . . . I don't pretend to understand it all, and even the environmental community is periodically at each other's throats.

I have to look at the big picture and sometimes remind people that twelve and fifteen years ago, nobody gave a rat's ass about the Everglades. You never heard a politician talk about it, except for Bob Graham. It wasn't popular. In his first run for governor, Jeb Bush had almost nothing to say about the environment or the Everglades. It's no accident that he got on this bandwagon in a big way, and I give him credit for it. I don't know whether he cares or doesn't care, but he did get involved. He threw his weight around in Washington, and he did what he had to do to get it rolling.

The point is we can spend the next fifty years arguing about how much acreage Big Sugar needs to give up or what the phosphorus levels should be coming into Taylor Creek, but it has to get rolling, because we don't have a whole lot of time. As the drought that we are now going through attests, it doesn't take much to throw the whole system out of whack and cause incredible upheaval in the wildlife community and in the demand and supply equation for both coasts . . . of Florida. I think it's a victory that the bill got passed. I think it will be a tragedy if people are allowed to loot it and scam it and milk it the way is inevitably going to happen at some level. I think that somebody has got to ride herd on it, and it would be a perfectly wonderful legacy for Jeb Bush. . . . But some politician needs to get on it, whether it is at the congressional level, to make sure that it happens and lean on all these people.

[I]t would be very nice to say, "Yeah, let us get Big Sugar to pay for fixing up the whole Everglades." Well, there are a couple things wrong with that. First of all, I'll be the first one to say that they treated the place as a toilet for four years, and it's atrocious what they did to the pine. But they aren't singularly at fault for what the Everglades has become. The problem, for instance, of what has happened in Florida Bay is a result of the freshwater flowing out of the Everglades. It can as much be traced to the south Dade avocado farmers and tomato farmers as it can [to the sugar farmers].

You want to look to blame; look at the people who developed from West Palm all the way down to Florida City. You are talking about massive sucking-up of water from Naples, everywhere. The municipalities and the government and the politicians who were running them were as much as looting the Everglades and doing damage as Big Sugar was and everyone else. There is no shortage of people to blame. . . . [T]he environmentalists need to understand you cannot expect the private sector to pay for all this; they aren't going to. Politically, they don't have a chance against the Fanjuls [Alfonso "Alfy" Fanjul, Jr., and Jose "Pepe" Fanjul, owners of Florida Crystals]. They don't, not a chance.

Q: How powerful are the Fanjuls?

A: I think they are powerful to the extent that, you know, as *Vanity Fair* suggested, can they affect the presidential recount? Probably not. I think they can suggest lawyers, but I don't think the Fanjuls are calling the election. . . . I think they give a lot of money to Republicans and Democrats, and I think they probably had as much access or more with Bill Clinton than they do with Bush. . . . I think all the press and all the anger about the Everglades has been good. It has certainly straightened them up a little bit. I have very little sympathy for the sugar industry, and that goes back to the virtual slavery in which they held migrant workers for so many years.

Their solution to that, instead of upgrading their living conditions, was just to bring in machines.

[Sugar] is one of the biggest welfare programs that the American people support, and they don't even know it. It's huge corporate welfare. Of course, the Fanjuls go nuts when you use that phrase, but that's exactly what it is. It's a handout; it's a big, fat, juicy handout. The sort of thing that politicians love to scream and yell about. If it's some unwed mother with three kids, they would be raising hell, but if it's two multimillionaires in Palm Beach, it's okay.

Q: Let me quote Nathaniel Reed again: "Hiaasen, with laughter and a rapier, has skewered most of the Everglades opponents more than once. He knows how to hurt, and he knows how to make you cry with laughter." I notice you have often applied that rapier wit to the sugar industry.

A: I did, and part of it was based on their reaction to the initial . . . stages of the Everglades movement . . . , [a] complete disavowal of any responsibility for what had been done. . . . Now, they got their thinking adjusted a little bit; they want to be good citizens; but at first it was complete arrogance. Complete arrogance. It was basically, "We can do whatever we want, [so] go screw yourself." At that point you have to go at them with both knuckles. A good bit of ridicule is something that they, of course, despise. They would rather be screeched at than made fun of, so whenever possible . . . I try to do that.

Every time I think [I see] a brief glint of some sort of conscience . . . — "Gee, have I been too tough on them?"—all I have to do is pick up the Palm Beach *Shiny Sheet*, the society pages, and look at the party rosters for the Fanjul social schedule. Again, this is money that the taxpayers have stuffed into their pockets to live this kind of a life, so that their crop will get sold at a guaranteed price and so that crops out of Jamaica and other poor countries that could use some capital don't get it. I mean, then all the sympathy evaporates in the world. They are just fine, and I haven't hurt them any. But the one thing that they do fear is that shift in public opinion. They could care less about whether I'm making fun of them, but they do care if the politicians start reacting to calls from constituents who are reacting to either a column I wrote or a speech Nat gives or whoever gets up and rants and raves.

Q: Are environmentalists stronger today in political and economic terms than they were ten or fifteen years ago?

A: Yes, absolutely. I don't think you would see [George W.] Bush [U.S. president, 2001–present] backpedaling on all his energy stuff already and mealy-mouthing about conservation. . . . Do I think they are organized? Not as organized as they should be. Are they effective? Sometimes. I think some groups are very good and effective. I think that there's so much work to be done in so many different places in this country, around the world, that it's very hard to expect them all to be marching to the same drummer or all on the same page. These are people who care, and they are vocal, and it's to be expected that they aren't going to agree on how to fix the Everglades. But at some point, political expediency has to sink in.

It [development] has made environmentalists out of the meek and mild electorate that normally would not even show up at a city council meeting or a zoning board meeting. Republican, Democrat, it doesn't matter; it's a quality-of-life issue, and I always tell people that. Here in the Keys, it's a big issue. If you make this as ugly as Hialeah, Florida, then your tourism is going to reflect that; it's going to go down, and everyone suffers. It has to come down to money, ultimately, people's pocketbooks, and then they say, "You are right; it's good economic sense not to destroy the beauty of a place, not to wreck the ecology of a place like Florida." It's stupid to destroy it, even for a real-estate sale.

There's definitely a bigger price to pay now for some of the most egregious kind of developments. At some point, some companies say, "You know what? This isn't going to be worth it. It's going to be ugly, and we're going to be in the headlines, and it's going to take a lot of time. Let's see if we can change this and don't do this, reduce the density." These things are happening more and more. I can't say I'm optimistic, because I think the general thrust of most development is to see a piece of property and envision how many people . . . we can cram in there.

Every year, they [Florida legislators] try to get away with more and more stuff. This is where it's so important to have strong editorial positions, strong columns, just good, strong, vigilant journalists who are watching, because so much of what happens in Tallahassee is done secretly, and you find out after the fact. Looting Preservation 2000 is just the beginning, I imagine. You have a couple of real jokers who are in positions of strong power in the [Florida] House and the [Florida] Senate. And this . . . is kind of dull day-to-day stuff that it's hard to get voters and readers interested in until it is something that . . . affects their life so directly, either visually or some other way, that then they are mad; then they want to raise a ruckus. By then, it's sometimes too late, so it's a challenge to keep people worked up about it.

Q: I was very intrigued by your book *Team Rodent,* about Disney World. What persuaded you to write that book?

A: Random House had this little series of books they were going to do for a Library of Contemporary Thought, [and] they called me and said, "We are trying to get a bunch of writers on board for this; anything you want to just rant and rave about—a short little book—think about it, just anything that ticks you off that you have not written that much about."

So I said, "Yeah, I could write about Disney," because I think they have had a tremendous impact on Florida, but I think they've also had a huge sort of financial and cultural and every way impact on American society. It's their philosophy that their way is the only way and the best way. I see Disney World as a metaphor for all of it, because of what happened in Central Florida, the phoniness of all of it, the fatuousness of it. The idea of putting this theme park, which I will be the first to admit is just an incredible technical achievement, in a place that could be anywhere. . . . [B]ecause it is so insulated and so alien to the true Florida experience . . . [it] is, for someone who cares about Florida, a source of some resentment. They transformed the tourist economy of Florida, and they certainly turned Central Florida into a parking lot, and a tacky one at that.

You mentioned about hypocrisy. That was one of the underlying themes in that novel, is that how they act and how they present themselves and how they really behave as a corporate citizen are two different things. Since then, the horror stories I have gotten from employees!

Q: According to your book, the Disney corporation is not a very good citizen.

A: Not in my view, no. They're just like any other big company. What's interesting, the subdivision—Celebration [a planned community]—to show you how they have captured, and successfully captured, the American myth—people go there and see it as a tourist [attraction]. It's a subdivision, and the tourists stop there and wander around expecting to see . . . Mickey and Goofy playing in the yards. I don't know, but it's such a problem that the people who really live there have these signs in the yards that tell people, "This isn't a tourist exhibit; we live here. Please don't come into our house." Because you had people walking in. . . . It's truly more about illusion than about the reality. For the employees, certainly, it's a different world. When they get involved in lawsuits, they are a big, bare-knuckled, hard-ass company. They really do have their own government, their own fiefdom. Extraordinary autonomy.

It's really an amazing thing to see basically the entire state system of law and order and government, judiciary, everything, roll over for one company, and that's what happened when Disney came to Florida.

Q: Let me conclude with a couple of broad questions. I realize you are still in the middle of your career, but when you look back on your time as a journalist and as a writer, what would be your greatest contribution to your community and the state?

A: I don't know. I mean, I honestly don't know. I would like to think I was really just another voice that raised the awareness of the public to certain issues. Really, if nothing else, I think the columns have served as a signal to, I hope, lots of readers and people living in the community that it's all right to get up and say what you think. . . . So when you write a strong column, suddenly people realize that it's okay to have strong opinions. This is what America is all about, and it's good to remind them of that. I think that's some value, that I take comfort in knowing that people might be less afraid to take a stand because they see it can be done without any dire consequences. In terms of . . . legacy, newspaper work is all transitory. I hope the novels are read. It would be lovely if they are read fifty years from now, and people laugh and say, "Hey, I know what he was talking about."

In terms of the newspaper work, I probably am most proud of a project we did that stopped a couple [of] big condo projects up on Card Sound Road in north Key Largo, where they were going to turn that into basically a huge city of condos and apartments. Card Sound Road . . . is a beautiful stretch of north Key Largo that they were perfectly prepared to rape and pillage until we wrote about them.

I'm just one person writing a column that may or may not be on the money, but if it's your life and involves your kids and your family and quality of life, if you turn out in enough numbers, you are going to intimidate the politician into listening to you. Otherwise, you aren't going to be heard, and that's the sad truth. And to the extent that the columns get people riled up enough to make them show up, then I feel good about it. I don't take credit for it, but I feel good about it.

Q: One reason for your success might be that your ripostes are not caustic, and they are tinged with a sense of humor so that, although you make a strong statement, you do not appear to be too judgmental. Is that a fair assessment?

A: That's a charitable assessment. I think that some of the targets of the columns would argue with that. I mean, there are times when I am very judgmental. . . . But I think what I do try to do is limit the scope of the column to some individual thing, an action, a vote, something that was done that was wrong that needs to be fixed. You know, I don't think you want to do a broadside; I think you want to be specific. And I certainly don't have any trouble saying something laudatory about Jeb Bush or whomever when they have taken a courageous stand on something. . . . By the same token, I don't have any qualms about kicking them in the knees when I think they have really sold the citizens down the river on something. But you have to have that ability, . . . if you are going to be tough on them for doing something you think is wrong, you also have to be fair.

[Y]ou have to be, and I've said it before, an equal-opportunity son of a bitch—that's my job. . . . It doesn't matter. Wrong is wrong, right is right, and, presumably, you are writing the column because you have a strong sense about that, strong feelings and positions about what's right and what's wrong, and, presumably, that's why they gave you a newspaper column.

Q: As a columnist, you always have to be something of a curmudgeon, do you not?

A: I think you do. . . . People have different visions of a newspaper column. Some are very comfortable writing about walking their dog or a funny thing that happened at the supermarket. That's never been my style. My mission has always been to get out there, mix it up, and be right in the middle of it, and be on top of the news. You're going to get enemies; you're going to get flak; but to be relevant and germane and topical and all that means getting off the fence.

Q: One final question. What do you want to accomplish in the future?

A: The only thing I want to do is to keep writing columns that mean something, about things that are important. When that becomes impossible to do, for whatever reason, then I stop. If you are realistic, you don't have any grand ambitions beyond that next sentence you're trying to write. You want every sentence to be better than the last one that you wrote, and as a novelist, that's what you do. Even as a columnist, you want every column to be better than your last column.

If you're a realist, you don't think in terms of making a difference; you think in terms of doing a good job, writing the best thing you can write, and then it's up to the readers and voters and citizens to decide how they want to react. That's all you can do. You aren't proselytizing; you aren't preaching; you aren't running a pep rally. It really is just keeping afloat and trying not to lose your love of the language and your skills and your sharpness. You know, I don't have any grand ambition except to keep the same sort of level of honesty up. I think staying angry is the most important thing to do if you write the kind of things I write. Even the humor — it all comes from anger . . . ; satire has always come from a sense of anger and injustice. Mark Twain, [Jonathan] Swift, whoever was writing it, they were all writing about something very serious and something that really upset them, and they were making people laugh at the same time, a tough thing to do. But [when] you lose that anger and you get a little too passive and mellowed out, then you are of no use at all to the readers, in my opinion, at least in my job.

chapter 13 **Lucy Morgan**

Lucy Morgan is the capital bureau chief in Tallahassee for the *St. Petersburg Times*. Born in Memphis, Tennessee, she grew up in Hattiesburg, Mississippi. She moved to Florida in 1960 and began her newspaper career with the *Ocala Star-Banner*, while working as a stringer for the *St. Petersburg Times*. She joined the *Times* staff full-time as a news staffer in New Port Richey and later as a statewide investigative journalist. In 1985 she took over as bureau chief in Tallahassee. She has covered a variety of state and local stories, including drug smuggling, corruption in law enforcement, Florida politics, and the Florida presidential election of 2000. In 1985 she won the Pulitzer Prize (with Jack Reed) for investigative reporting of the Pasco County sheriff's department.

Her work has received recognition from the American Society on Ageing, the University of South Florida's School of Communications, the Florida Society of Newspaper Editors, and the Florida Press Club. Morgan also received the LeRoy Collins Distinguished Community College Alumni Award.

In this interview Morgan first explains her reasons for coming to Florida and how she got started in journalism as a small-town reporter. She discusses being a woman in a traditionally male occupation and details her more fascinating investigations, particularly the drug-smuggling case that won her a Pulitzer Prize. She also talks about her methods, especially the use of public records as part of her investigative reporting. She shares her thoughts on Florida politicians, most notably Dempsey Barron, Lawton Chiles, and Bob Graham, and lobbyists in Florida generally. She concludes with her perspective on the "arrogance" that she sees as a problem among journalists today.

Lucy Morgan was interviewed by Jean Chance on February 6, 2000, in Tallahassee.

Q: What was your first job in journalism?

A: Let me start by telling you how I got here. I am not sure there is anything like it. I had three small children at home in 1965, and a woman knocked on my front door . . . [and] introduced herself as the area editor for the Ocala paper and explained that their local correspondent had been killed in a traffic accident and wondered if I might be interested in writing for the paper. I told her that, well, I had never done anything like that before, or even thought about it, and asked why she would come to my door with that kind of request. She told me that the local librarian in Crystal River had told her that I read more books than anyone else in town, and she presumed that if I could read, I could write.

I needed money and I decided, "Well, I will try it." After all, it was only part-time. . . . About two months later they put me on their full-time staff because, at twenty cents an inch and five dollars a picture, I was making more money than they wanted to pay me.

Q: Any recollection of particularly memorable stories that you covered at that time?

A: My assignment, at first, was to do civic clubs, city councils, traffic accidents, anything that happened in the Citrus County area. I remember one of the early city council meetings that I went into. All of the other people who covered governments back then were, like I, stringers who were paid by the story, and most of them had never had professional journalism careers. The city council in Crystal River would look over to the three or four of us who were reporters there at various moments in the meeting and say, "Now, do not write this," and these people would very cooperatively not write this. I very quickly ran afoul of the establishment because it did not seem appropriate to me. I had no training, but it just did not seem appropriate to let the mayor decide when we would write about what the city was doing, so that I was very quickly in trouble with the mayor and have probably never gotten out of trouble since.

But I tended to write what was occurring in front of me, and they took a very dim view of that in the Crystal River city council, although the citizens of Crystal River and most of the cops loved it. They thought it was great sport. [In] those early city council meetings, they were having a huge controversy over the police department and a sewer system, and I remember a lot of those early stories that were just sheer battlegrounds. It was a very colorful scene to cover.

Q: Were you using a tape recorder or pad and pencil? Obviously, no computers at that time.

A: I used a pad and pencil to take notes. I would then go home and type it up on an old portable typewriter and then read the story over the phone to an editor who took it down in Ocala. If it was a feature with less of a deadline, I might send it in by bus or mail, but most of the time back then, we had to read the story. Sometimes, you had to make up the story as you went along and read it at the same time, if you were filing at night for the next morning's paper.

Q: Any difficulties juggling being wife, mother, and newspaperwoman?

A: Always. Sometimes I took them with me to news stories. They have probably seen more fires and traffic accidents and things like that than most anybody's children. I was a single parent trying to juggle these two jobs and three children. I had a housekeeper, and either she or her daughter would sleep at the house in case of something happening at night. I was responsible for [covering] fatal traffic accidents in Hernando, Citrus, and Levy Counties, and we seemed to have a lot of them back then. So I would often be at one of these four A.M. accidents.

Q: Were most of the journalists that you worked with and competed against male at that time?

A: If they were staff, they were male. It was entertaining to work against them because most of the people that we covered were men, and it amused them to see me beat the men [reporters], so that often I would get a call from, say, a Levy County commissioner who wanted to leak a story to me. It would not be the best story in the world. By the stories I work on today, I probably would not even bother to write it, but at the time, it greatly aggravated the men I worked against that I would often beat them because of the largesse of men who were playing with them, and me too, probably.

Q: The year 1968 was a notable period in which you got attention in court circles, including a state attorney in Pinellas County, dealing with grand jury investigations.

A: Yes. By then our staff had expanded substantially, and we had been doing some stories on corruption in city government in Dade City. I was asked to go over and baby-sit the grand jury one day. The grand jury returned a sealed presentment. I wrote about that, speculating on the contents of that presentment, somewhat successfully, apparently. The state attorney, on the day the story was published, dropped a subpoena on me, demanding that I appear and give him the source of the information in the story. I refused and was immediately sentenced to five months in jail.

On that day we raised an objection to the state attorney's legal ability to do what he was doing, which he apparently decided might be correct. So he issued a second subpoena for me a few days later, ordering me to appear before the grand jury. I again refused to divulge the source, although I did give him a nicely colored copy of the story. I colored in blue the stuff that I had observed—you know, the state attorney walking into the grand jury room with the Dade City charter [and] the names of the witnesses. I painted in green the two paragraphs that came from a confidential source, and I painted in bright purple the information that had come from the state attorney himself. It made the state attorney very happy, and I gave that to the grand jury. I was subsequently sentenced to another three months. We appealed both sentences and ultimately won.

Q: Did you actually serve any length of time?

A: No, it was really kind of disappointing. I bought all these books to read while I was in jail—like the complete works of Tennyson. I have yet to read them. But they let me out on bail from the courthouse. I did not have to get locked in the cell.

At the *Times*, Gene Patterson was editor and made every court appearance and immediately said, "Lucy, we do not think you are going to have to go to jail, but if it ever happens, the *Times* will hire a housekeeper to take care of the children. We want you to write a daily column from the jail." So the *Times* was prepared to do whatever had to be done and certainly gave me all the legal support that I needed.

Q: Ultimately, there was a Florida Supreme Court vindication of the act you took to protect a confidential source.

A: Yes. Up until that time, there was no court protection in Florida. The reigning case was an old Miami case where the person subpoenaed had been forced to testify. In July 1976 the court came with a ruling written by Justice [Joseph] Hatchett, which said that only under certain compelling circumstances could a state attorney compel a newspaper reporter to testify. What he did was follow very closely the three-part test that was set out in *Branzburg* [*Branzburg* v. *Hayes*, 1972] originally, that there had to be a compelling state interest; they had to prove that they had looked elsewhere for the information; and they had to prove that I might be the only source of that information to subpoena [me]. They had done, of course, none of that, having subpoenaed me on the day of publication. So that became and remains the law today. It has been through a few curves since then, but was now reiterated just as recently as last year in a decision.

Q: In 1982 you investigated drug smuggling in Dixie and Taylor Counties. How did that come about?

A: At the end of 1979, my husband wanted to leave the job as bureau chief on the north Sun Coast and to take a job as editor of editorials. My youngest was almost turning eighteen, and I thought it might be a good time for me to quit working for the Pasco section and do something else. I sent a note to Andy Barnes, who was then ME [managing editor], saying that, if they ever would like to create a roam-around-the-state-and-cause-trouble job, that I would be interested in doing it. [Barnes] decided on the spot to create the job.

I started it by spending about a year looking, at about the same time Richard Kelly, the congressman from Florida, fell into Abscam [a national scandal stemming from FBI investigations into congressional corruption], and he was conducting his own investigation. I had covered him when he was a circuit judge, so I had a good road into both him and his attorney. I began that year by spending almost all my time on Abscam and covered the trial in Washington at the end of that year and the election that swirled around it.

I had been fascinated by some of the old Florida drug cases. I started looking at the statewide grand jury, which had been an early tool used against drug smugglers, to no avail. Every time I would go ask prosecutors or cops or drug people questions about drug prosecutions, inevitably someone would say, "You know, you should go and look at Dixie and Taylor Counties; the drug smugglers own the counties." I sort of tossed it aside the first few times that I heard it, but I was in Tallahassee interviewing the head of the Florida Department of Law Enforcement, who at the time was Jim York. He gave me a great quote that day. He told me they were never going to stop drug smuggling in Florida until they could drive a stake through the heart of . . . a drug smuggler in Dixie County of some renown. The state attorney for that area told me that a majority of the county commissioners from Dixie County had gone to a drug trial and testified for the smugglers. I knew there must be a record of this. The potential for a story, I could see there.

I really thought I was going to go there, write a few stories, walk out the door, and not spend a whole lot of time on this, but before it was over, I had spent several years. A chief deputy in Dixie County had come to me, offering to rat out all of his fellow deputies and wear a wire if I could turn him over to an honest cop; he didn't know any. I gave him to the U.S. attorney's people from northern Florida. Before I was able to finish there, a whole bunch of deputies, a school board member, a county commission chairman, and 250 other souls went to jail, because the feds took an interest in my stories and pursued the smuggling. It was a rather interesting chapter, where the smugglers had pretty well co-opted the local officials.

Q: Why do you think they felt so safe to be so openly corrupt?

A: Part of it, I think, is the lack of journalism. . . . I subscribed to the local weekly papers. There were three at the time, the *Dixie County Advocate*, which at one time was owned by the sheriff in Dixie County, and the *Taco Times*, . . . [and] the other one was another Perry paper; I think it might have been the *Perry News* or something. Of the three papers, only the *Taco Times* reported drug arrests as being real. The *Dixie County Advocate* would often not report them at all, or report them if some out-of-towner was arrested. They did have to report when the Cadillac owned by the Dixie County school board chairman was found parked next to thirty thousand pounds of marijuana in neighboring Taylor County. However, they ran a correction the following week, saying that Cadillac didn't belong to . . . the school board chairman. What they didn't tell you in the correction was that it belonged to his wife.

The guy at the *Advocate* told me that when he first came to Dixie County, he wrote an editorial about the illegal [hunting] of doe deer, denouncing it, thinking that he was on the side of motherhood in an area like that, only to wake up the next morning and find a dead doe's head on his doorstep. He subsequently wrote an editorial about illegal dumping of garbage, only to wake up the next morning and find his lawn strewn with garbage that had been dumped there. He said those were his only two efforts to get into journalism that was at all controversial. I think the lack of a daily newspaper in that area simply allowed those officials to run roughshod in any direction they wanted to.

In fact, the county commissioners who went to testify in Wakulla County on behalf of a convicted drug smuggler of some renown, urged the judge not to send him to jail, saying it would be an economic loss to the county if [he] was sent to jail. They apparently did not realize that the court reporter sitting in the front of the room was recording all these words. When I went up and read and bought the transcripts and went to interview them about it, they denied ever having said these things and kept telling their friends that none of this was true, only to have it hit them broadside when I wrote the stories. One of the most fascinating things about Dixie [was that] we did not sell a paper in Dixie County or Taylor [County]. We had no circulation. We had a truck that went through there every day on its way to Tallahassee. Often, the sheriff would stop our truck and demand a copy of the paper to see what was in it.

Q: That coverage was nominated for the Pulitzer Prize in 1982. I am interested in how you utilized public records in the kind of reporting you did. Would you be offended to have your type of reporting defined as investigative reporting?

A: No, not really. I have, at times in my life, taken offense at that word. I suppose I take less offense, having won a Pulitzer in a category called "investigative reporting." I think a lot of what many of us do is investigating. If you are going beyond simply walking out of a public meeting and writing what occurred in it, there is some level of investigative reporting. I think a lot of reporters see that title as rather pretentious. So, yes, I would not label myself that if someone were to ask me what I was, but, clearly, a lot of the work I have done over the years that has been well received has been investigative in nature, because I have gone beyond taking what was given to me on the surface. I have gone into every conceivable record.

If I am going to take a project, I will isolate the principal names that I know in the beginning I am dealing with, and that is essentially where I start. I strip the public record of every record that is there. Nowadays, it's almost too easy to start, with the electronic systems that are there. You give someone the results of, say, an AutoTrack, and you have there your Social Security number, date of birth, the property they own, the vehicles they own, the accidents they had, their driving records, their criminal records—all kinds of different records just handed to you in the space of a few seconds. However, experience tells me [not] to trust those as being all that is there, or as even being correct all the time. But I would strip the records that are available [and] go to wherever those people have lived in their lifetime, if I am seriously looking.

Q: The purpose for the searching of public records has to do with litigation?

A: Well, it is twofold. First of all, you bulletproof yourself from an attack. You have the record in front of you. Secondly, if you look at a deed that was recorded twenty years ago, and you see that the subject of your story bought a piece of land somewhere and paid x amount of money for it, that might be the focus of what you are looking at, at that moment, but down the road, it may be that one of the people who witnessed that deed is a figure in the rest of what you are doing, and you are looking to establish a relationship between that person and another person. Also, in the moment that you get sued, you are not scrambling around trying to prove what you have already written; you have the documents there. I am a big advocate of keeping very good files. I can go . . . back to files of virtually any project I did, including that Dixie County drug project in the 1980s, and pull the files. . . . I can go back and pull them and confirm or find a fact from many years ago.

Q: How important is meshing public records with human sources?

A: I think it is important to also talk to the people. If what you have is a public record trail, you have a pretty dry account. People can add information and context to that record. For instance, in the Dixie County series, a lot of those smugglers were people who had never made more than thirteen or fourteen thousand dollars in their lives, but they were paying cash, twenty thousand, thirty thousand dollars for vehicles and things.

   I went to interview the car dealer in Dixie County who had sold them all these vehicles, and he put that in a lot of context in talking about them. [About] . . . the notorious smuggler, [the car dealer] said, "You know, Lucy, you need to get to know the whole [man]." He taught me one of the best lessons I have ever been taught. He said, "You know . . . the drug smuggler, who makes a lot of money and pays cash for cars, but you do not know the guy who buys a boat for his neighbor when his boat sinks, pays for surgery for a neighbor's child when the child is ill, or builds a church with the money he has made from it, and unless you know all of those things about him, you do not know the whole [man]." From that moment on, I have realized how important it is for us to know the whole [person], in anything that we are looking at.

Q: Back to 1982, the Dixie County investigation is fairly well completed, and attention to the *St. Petersburg Times* coverage merited a lot of national review at the time it was nominated for the Pulitzer. The next three years, you are working in another county with reporter Jack Reed on Pasco County corruption charges.

A: In the beginning, I was working on it myself. All during the Dixie-Taylor [stories], I lived in Pasco County. And I kept running into people at home who would say, "Quit going out of town. You need to be looking at the local sheriff." And I had covered that department years before; I knew it fairly well. [In] February, early March, of 1983, I accepted a speaking engagement at the local police academy—which trained sheriffs, deputies, local police, and anybody around there, and it was run through the junior college—to talk about press relationships. I just had assumed in accepting it that this would be raw recruits getting their initial police training and didn't think much about it, but when I got to the class, it was about fifty veteran police officers. It was a refresher course of people who were already in jobs.

Our paper, in just that week, committed a rather egregious sin in their eyes, and actually in mine, too. One of our reporters had quoted an anonymous spectator at the scene of a police shooting, saying that the police murdered this guy, which was against our policy and certainly not conducive to good relations between reporters and police. So this whole audience was ready to fry any reporter they could catch in their grasp.

I spent the night defending—although I did not defend that conduct; I told them I agreed that it was wrong—but discussing police relationships, in an atmosphere that was first very hostile. By the time we got to the end, I think most of the guys in the audience were at least cordial to me on the surface.

The next morning at about seven o'clock, I got a call from one of the men who had been in that audience. I had known him for years and knew him to be very close to the sheriff in Pasco County, and I would have considered him to be totally the sheriff's person, but he called and said, "I would like to talk to you; I have come to the conclusion that the sheriff here is quite corrupt, and somebody needs to do something about it."

I said, "Well, I am not sure I am your person. . . ."

[He said] . . . , "You would be the only one I would really trust, because to do this, I am trusting my job, if not my life."

So I agreed to talk to him that day, and he and his wife came to the house that day, put their car in our garage so nobody could see it, and they spent the entire day telling me, with some documentation, of the broad outlines of what they thought was going on there.

Q: Did she also work for the sheriff?

A: No, she just came along with him. In fact, she became an important part. She became a conduit. As things developed and got hot, she and I would often both go shopping at Belk's at the mall, and when we went to try on clothes, she would pass under the booths in the fitting rooms, in the ladies' room, the documents that he would need to get to me, or I would hand back stuff to him, because most of the people that the sheriff assigned to follow me were male. We just found that was a good way to circumvent them.

Q: Was that your idea?

A: Yes. It sort of came to pass because she was supposed to meet me at the mall to give me some documents he was sending, and we realized I was being followed when we got there. So I just got out of my car and went into Belk's, and she came in behind me. We saw the guy come in following us. I don't know whether he knew who she was or not, but we did not speak to each other. I picked up the first item of clothing I came to and went into the fitting room, and she followed. I don't think they ever caught on to what we were doing because we never acknowledged each other's presence, but we did it a number of times over the years that passed.

We had all kinds of ways of trading documents. Sometimes he would drop them in my mailbox at night and put the flag up to let me know he had been by, so that when we went out to get the paper in the morning and saw that the flag was up, we would know there were new documents in the mailbox.

There was one hilarious incident where he was trying to deliver an entire box of documents that he had come upon, to me. I had parked my car and left it unlocked in a K-Mart parking lot and had gone in the store. I was tooling around the store and, usually, whoever was following me would follow me into wherever I went. So the guys who were following me had come into the store. I looked out the window of the K-Mart and saw that as he was transferring this box of documents from his car to mine, he dropped the whole damn box and was scampering around in the parking lot getting them picked up. So we had some near hilarious misses.

I warned everybody from the beginning that we were dealing with a sheriff who absolutely hated me, and the minute he were to see me on his tail, he would assume the worst and be the worst. So they decided that I should follow the story, primarily because of the source that was there.

This was March of 1983, and I thought any story that was done should be finished and in the paper before the end of 1983, because 1984 was an election year, and I didn't want whatever we did to be perceived as an election attack. I still think that is a very important part. It is a real problem for journalists. You get the most negative information on a public official during an election campaign, [but] it is absolutely the worst time to unveil it because the politician can say, "Oh, those are just my political enemies after me," so that [the story] gets, in a sense, the least credibility at that time.

About this same time, the captain of that department was indicted with Santo Trafficante [mob boss from Tampa], and one of his allegations was that a lot of the members of that department had organized-crime ties and that the department had done inadequate backgrounds on them. I went over, with this original source, the entire three hundred or so men who worked for the department, in a roster of them which he had provided, and identified the ones he thought had a problem of some kind. I decided that I would have to do background, certainly on these that [were suspicious]. I began working in Tallahassee on police standards. At the time, they had to file with the state a copy of the officer's birth certificate, training records, employment history, a number of various pieces of information that included any prior arrest record and their fingerprints, and they ran them. I was able to get a basic look at each sworn officer by doing that.

Then I took the ones who were either in leadership positions, had rank, or had been in some sort of trouble or who had been identified to me as potential trouble sources and did a more thorough background on them.

What I found by doing that was that one in every eight officers had a criminal arrest record. More than half of them had lied about that arrest record to get certified as cops. That didn't include things like DUIs [driving under the influence arrests]. I took only criminal arrest records, non-traffic and non-DUI. And [nothing] juvenile. One of them, in particular, had been arrested by some of the officers he was now working side by side with, for theft-related [reasons], like stealing stuff that he was caught in possession of. One of them had been a Hernando County deputy. . . . At the time he went to work in Pasco, his driver's license was suspended; he had an arrest record for theft—and he was given a badge and gun and a green light to drive in Pasco County.

My favorite of the deputies was a guy who had been the wheelman in several armed robberies in Tampa, and the Tampa cops had given him immunity from prosecution because he ratted out his coworkers in several armed robberies. When he was caught, he tried to kill himself, missed, and shot out a hole in the side of his trailer. So he was a guy who ratted out his codefendants, was an armed robber to start with, or the wheelman for them, and a bad shot. He couldn't even kill himself when he tried. He was wearing a badge and gun in Pasco County. One of them had an outstanding grand theft arrest warrant for stealing the police dog when he left a similar job in the Keys. He had stolen the dog. I mean, most of them were funny if you weren't thinking of the liability that the department was creating for itself there.

One of them had been a sheriff's deputy, in the Keys, who had been drunk and high on cocaine and had a minor traffic accident and pulled a gun on an elderly couple who were involved in the accident. The couple fled into a Holiday Inn. A trooper arrived on the scene and had a dramatic description of this deputy holding a gun out at the crowd. The trooper called on him to drop the gun, and he turned toward the trooper, aiming this .38. The trooper, just at the moment he was about to fire, thinking that he was going to have to kill this guy, recognized him as a local sheriff's deputy and managed to get him to drop the gun, rather than simply shooting him. But they let him resign and go on his way, and Pasco picked him up without ever determining that about his background, although it was clearly in the public records of Monroe County.

Q: That kind of drama is a Lucy Morgan trademark that pops up in your stories.

A: Yes, he [Jack Reed, assigned to assist Morgan by the *St. Petersburg Times*] was a Pasco reporter covering the county commission in Pasco. So what I did was assign him the financial side of it. You can get an idea when you are looking at public officials. This was a sheriff who had been a city police chief, [and] he had been in the public arena most of his adult life. He had come into office with a net worth of, say, seventy thousand dollars [and] within a few years, earning nothing more than the salary we knew about, he had become worth three or four hundred thousand dollars, net worth, and acquired a lot of property. He had not inherited any; his family was very poor. He had been through three divorces, I think. So, just looking at his financial disclosures, you knew there was something going on in this, other than him being a law enforcement officer. . . .

We found, as a matter of fact, that he would put the departmental money in a bank. Often on the same day, he would get loans of four or five hundred thousand dollars from this bank to invest in private property schemes. He got himself extensively involved in the ownership of a small shopping mall, of a funeral home, of a lot of property. He was way overextended and making a bunch of money on the side. Some of the people who worked with him, like his partner in the funeral home, was the guy he assigned to be his administrative chief in the office, who was supposedly doing backgrounds and did such a poor job with backgrounds.

We also found . . . a part-time deputy who bought his own patrol car and his own gun and his uniform and put himself on the road and directed a lot of investigations, some of them against his enemies. This was an eccentric millionaire, who was almost running the department, or at least running the things he wanted to run, and the sheriff was letting him. He gave the sheriff a house and a lot of other things. I knew he hated me because I had caught him with his pants down before. But I also knew, because of that dislike for me, that everything we wrote better damn well be exactly right and documented.

Q: And he did sue.

A: Oh, yes, but I required from the very beginning that nothing go into print that did not have a paper document to support it or a taped interview, that there would be no unnamed sources — there would be nothing we could not simply prove in a court of law. I had covered the courts for years, so that became my standard, that it had to be something that would pass muster as evidence, and we did that. Nothing in that series, which began running in December of 1983 and wound up in April of 1984, was unsourced. I mean, you could use it as a textbook case.

He did ultimately sue us. We itemized and numbered . . . fourteen thousand and some documents. . . . We won a jury trial. [It is] very rare to win a jury trial in a libel case, but the jury came back and said each and every fact challenged was absolutely true. It cost us a fortune to defend it, but we won it in the end. I suspect that is a deterrent to a lot of other people who might file libel suits. . . . We won the legal fees back out of it, and we always give legal fees to charity when we win. It was a great victory.

Q: What was it like to learn that your work had won the Pulitzer Prize, in 1985?

A: It is interesting. I had never even thought about a Pulitzer. I had never thought about contests. I had never entered one myself. I didn't know that the Dixie County stuff was heading in that direction. I remember when he was editing the Dixie County stuff, Rob Hooker had jokingly said, "Lucy, this stuff is either going to win you a Pulitzer or get you killed. . . ."

I had been through so much torment in that project. Not only were the stories good and it was fun to report, it was a tremendous strain to report on a sheriff in a county in which you lived. He waged a vehement attack against me, us, the *Times*. He had bumper stickers out that said, "Screw Lucy Morgan" and "I do not believe the *St. Petersburg Times*." I mean, he waged a lot of personal attacks. His friends threatened and were very aggressive toward my daughter-in-law and her baby, who lived there at the time, threatening her, terrified her several times. On occasion, they would give me a description of what my grandchild had worn to day care. There were just all kinds of threats that came with that project.

Anyway, the day after the Pulitzers were announced, I came into work, and Dick said, "A source wants you to meet for lunch and asked me if I would come with you. [He] has something to [say] about the sheriff's thing."

I thought, "I really don't want another source on this sheriff's department; I am tired of this story; go away." But I went to lunch, and when we got to Pappas [Greek restaurant], Gene Patterson and Andy Barnes, our then executive editor, were waiting with champagne to tell me. . . . The *Times* gave me an immediate pay raise, I think of one hundred dollars a week. The editor I worked for spent the rest of the week beating the weekender [story for the Sunday paper] I had promised him out of me, because there are so many distractions. You learn quickly that it is the next story that is important, not the one you just finished.

[In 1985 Lucy Morgan became head of the Tallahassee bureau of the *St. Petersburg Times*.] So I went from looking at drug smugglers and public corruption and organized crime into state government and politics. Somehow, it seems like a natural transition. The drug smugglers were more candid than the state officials to deal with. But it has been an easy transition, and it has been a lot of fun, because I have been able to take the investigative techniques that I developed along the way and apply them to state government. It is amazing how much you find when you don't take what comes to you at face value.

Q: What are your observations about the various governors and administrations that you have covered?

A: It has been interesting. Graham [Bob Graham, governor of Florida, 1979–87] was by then very comfortable as governor. He was very open. Of all the governors that have come along, he was the most accessible. We had free run of even his office, except for his own office. We could go down and talk to the top of his staff without having to go through a gatekeeper. In fact, we were invited to the mansion more than we wanted to go. We always paid. We still do that; when we are invited to the mansion, we go and eat or drink—whatever is going on there—and make a donation to the mansion fund . . . to pay for it.

Our policy at the *Times* is, we take nothing from nobody, and, believe it or not, that is sometimes hard to do. I adhere to the policy. Sometimes, I simply am in the position of handing cash to a lobbyist who has picked up the tab. I don't have a clue what he is doing with it, but I know that I have paid my share. In the case of a governor, you can usually make a donation to somebody. I recently went to Israel with Governor [Jeb] Bush [Florida governor, 1999–present], and I was faced with a situation where Holland and Knight's [law firm] Israel office was paying for some of the meals we were having. I didn't want to be rude, but what I did when we got back was make a donation to Holland and Knight's Holocaust Fund. You usually find some appropriate way to repay the money. . . . Where possible, we buy our own tickets. I recently went to the Sugar Bowl to tag along with [Talbot] Sandy D'Alemberte, the FSU president [1994–2003], and there were a number of functions—one, a dinner which we paid $150 to get into, which was not worth $150. I paid for my game ticket, $125.

Q: You were chosen to be a member of the *St. Petersburg Times* board of directors. What does that mean to you? What does that represent?

A: It was interesting. My whole career, I have been overly frank with everybody everywhere. It's just my nature to be too frank. I had always assumed that there would be a day when I would get fired for being too frank, that I would call some editor a shithead who had really been a shithead. I had been really fortunate over the years at the *Times* that most of the editors I had worked for had been people who could take it when I dished it out. I had just assumed that trait in me would get me fired some day. Well, Barnes calls me in, in the summer of 1991, and says . . . , "I want to put you on the board of directors."

To my knowledge, there is no reporter anywhere in anybody's organization that has crossed over that line and been put on a board like that. My immediate response was to say, "Andy, I do not think you are ready for anybody who is as frank as I am to sit on that board."

He swelled up like a toad and said, "You really do underestimate me; that is why I want you on this board."

Q: Talk about your observations of Lawton Chiles's administration and your coverage of his funeral.

A: I think [when] Chiles came into office, all of us had great hope that this was sort of [a] dream governor. You had a governor and a lieutenant governor, with Buddy MacKay, who were enormously experienced, had good reputations, and came back from the dead, so to speak, to run this state — and did nothing with that.

Q: Did you think he was going to win that election [gubernatorial contest of 1990]?

A: Yes. I thought from the moment he entered, he would . . . win. Martinez was not a charismatic governor. I think that Martinez would have won reelection if Chiles had not come in, that Chiles essentially came in and saved the Democratic Party from itself. In a sense, he also killed it. . . . But Chiles had this sort of mystical quality about him that made people just worship him, just lots of charisma. I think the liberals saw him as a guy who would be willing to pass taxes and to do the uncomfortable things that needed to be done to govern. The conservatives saw him as still sort of a good old boy. Actually, I think the conservatives were more right. I think Lawton Chiles was basically a good old boy from Polk County who was most comfortable around his own cronies. The people he appointed to jobs were generally his cronies, not necessarily the people best qualified for the job.

I think he made a lot of mistakes. I think he generated a lot of goodwill, and that may have been his best asset. I think much of his time as governor, he wasn't interested in the day-to-day job of governing. I think he liked being governor and liked using that role for things he was really interested in, but there was not a whole lot that interested him.

The biggest disappointment that I had in Lawton [was] I had always assumed him to be very ethical. When he went in, he established this rule for his staff that nobody could take anything valued at more than, like, $2.50 from anybody, which was a great standard to establish in government, where you had, for contrast, legislators taking expensive meals and trips and bottles of wine and everything from lobbyists and [coming] under fire for [this]. So it was a great contrast, but Chiles did not himself adhere to that standard. He took free hunting trips, free trips to games. He took free shotguns and things from sugar interests. So it was a disappointing contrast. I think he saw himself above the fray. There was a sort of arrogance to him, where he thought, "These things do not influence me, so I do not need to have a rule." The standard that he set for the people who saw that happening was poor.

Q: What about the cast of characters in the legislature that you have observed during the time you have been bureau chief? Dempsey [J.] Barron, for example, president of the Senate?

A: I enjoyed Dempsey a lot. Unlike many people in the legislature, Dempsey was pretty frank about what he was doing and where he was going. You could disagree with what he wanted to do, but he knew how to use the process to reach an end, probably better than anybody since then has ever achieved. Dempsey knew how to horse-trade and how to get something done. He knew what everybody wanted, and he knew how to trade what one senator wanted for what another senator had and how to use that to get a bill through the system.

He and I had a great relationship. When his office would get too filled with lobbyists wanting something, Dempsey would call me and say, "Would you drop by?" Of course, the minute I would come and start to spend a little time in there, the lobbyists would leave, so I was the periodic cleaner-out of lobbyists who didn't want to ask for favors in front of me.

When there was a huge power struggle in 1986 over who would become the Senate president, Ken Jenne had thirty-nine signed pledges from members of the Senate to make him president of the Senate. He never achieved that position because Dempsey overthrew him. I was sitting in Dempsey's office when I realized that it was final because the sergeant-at-arms delivered to Dempsey the parking cards for the chairman of the rules committee and the leadership positions for Dempsey to distribute to whoever he wanted to have them. The key to all power in Tallahassee is the best parking spots.

I watched him bring all of the [legislative] process to a halt in the final week or ten days of a session because an elderly retired teacher from FSU—Ms. Fay Kirtland was her name—was lobbying for a group of retired teachers who had been left out of a benefit by some sort of timing problem. They had retired in a certain year, and there were a few years where they did not get adequate health insurance. So it appealed to Dempsey not only to give Ms. Fay an appointment, but to bring the whole budget process to a halt until somebody was willing to put the item in that would fix this little problem for Ms. Fay and her retired teachers, most of them elderly women spinsters who contributed a dollar to Dempsey's campaigns each time. Dempsey was perfectly capable of using his power for that kind of person as he was for the head of St. Joe Paper Company or somebody. I think it probably amused him more to use his power in moments like that than it did for the big-deal people.

I think that's part of what made him such a charming political character. He learned how to deal with the powerful people in this world and the little people in this world he had once been part of. Early on, when I first came here in 1986, I was appalled by the free stuff that legislators took from lobbyists—including Dempsey. I mean, they could eat every meal, just constant gifts of things. They [lobbyists] took them on trips, hunting or golfing or whatever else they wanted to do.

Q: Did you write about it?

A: Yes. In 1987 I decided to compare the gifts that legislators reported getting with the gifts lobbyists reported giving. The law required a legislator to report any gift valued at more than twenty-five dollars. The lobbyists were supposed to report the aggregate, but they didn't have to identify who got the gift. I know you would be shocked to know that there was a difference of several million dollars in what was reported given against what was reported gotten. I kept notes during the course of the year when I saw a legislator leaving on a trip with a lobbyist, or something like that, so that I had some basis, but I did a story. At the time, it was a criminal misdemeanor for a legislator, or any public official, to violate that law. Well, the legislature's reaction to the stories I wrote in 1987 on this problem was to go back into the law in 1988 and eliminate the criminal penalty from the law and raise the amount of the gift they could take to one hundred dollars.

Dempsey always preached that a trip was not a gift, that you couldn't make that comparison, which, I think, even Dempsey knew that was a ludicrous position to take. But, one morning in the midst of all my reporting and questioning the legislators about this, Dempsey calls me at the office about nine-thirty, and he says, "Lucy, you are right." He said, "Last night, I went out with a bunch of lobbyists, and they bought this huge steak dinner with a big baked potato with all this sour cream, and I drank all kinds of whiskey throughout dinner, and after dinner, they bought me all these fancy after-dinner drinks, and I drank all this brandy and stuff. And," he said, "this morning, I feel like a bouquet of dog-asses; I should not have taken those [gifts]. . . ." That's the way Dempsey was. I also think that Dempsey, somewhat like Lawton Chiles, saw himself as unreachable by this largesse. He felt that everybody gave him things and that none of them bought him by doing it, that it was an entitlement.

Lobbyists at that time were, I thought, tremendously demeaning of themselves. You would see them cleaning up the garbage or serving drinks or slicing the ham, doing things like this at events that Dempsey or other legislators had. . . . The successful lobbyists were those who could drive them around, extricate legislators from drunken incidents, pave the way for them to get from point A to point B, or, if it was a legislator's birthday, stage a party for him.

Q: What are lobbyists like in 2000?

A: At the turn at the century, the best lobbyists are those who thoroughly know the issue, know the process, and know the member. . . . But, as term limits impact [politics], the one underlying influence that is always going to be there is the lobbyist who has contributed money to the campaign and has gotten his clients to do it. [A good lobbyist] . . . will help them raise money, help them run whatever campaign functions they need done. He cultivates the secretaries everywhere in the building. He will be sure they get an appropriate gift at times, nothing lavish, flowers or candy at the right moment.

[Morgan discusses finding hidden items in legislation]. . . . I love to find those little buried treasures in a bill. Unfortunately, I fear that we find very few of them. These things are put into complex bills that relate to insurance and very dull issues and things that you think aren't interesting at all. I think a lot of things get into law that you just do not realize until later, way down the road, you see the impact, if you see it at all.

Q: Are the legislators also more overwhelmed the closer you get to the end of session?

A: Yes, you have so many bills and so many issues floating around that it is very easy to technically tweak a bill to greatly benefit one business or another. Most legislators do not have the time or the expertise to understand what a little tweak here or there does on the other end, once something gets into law. In these last-minute amendments, you don't have any staff to analyze them most of the time, so that it gets onto the bill, usually in the final week of session or the final day of session, and it gets into law without anybody really having looked at the consequences of it. . . . Ideally, any change in the law ought to go through that process where it is heard at public hearing, and staff can analyze it, and you know what it's going to do at the other end. In fact, that doesn't always happen.

Q: Do you see yourself, as a journalist, as having a leadership role, a responsibility?

A: I have always felt that a reporter had to set an example, that if I am going to throw rocks at a public official who misbehaves, I need to be behaving. I can't establish a different standard of behavior for myself, so that I have always expected to be arrested if I broke the law, to have a listed phone number, to meet the criteria that I would expect of a public official. I have always tried to live by a standard that is, if not above reproach, as close there as I could get.

Q: One of the quotations attributed to you was, "It has been an enormous benefit being a southern woman dealing with good old boys." When they hear that Hattiesburg accent, they think you do not have a brain in your head.

A: When I open my mouth and speak southern, it is disarming to the average man who has been in control of the world and not expecting women to play much of a role in that. They assume I have no brain when they hear this southern brogue, until it is too late. Many times, I have had men just walk themselves out on a limb, terribly, and get caught out there lying to me or being dumb, because I am smart enough to catch them doing it. And they just haven't realized it. I would much rather be underestimated than overestimated.

Q: Are a lot of your sources uneasy or on edge, just because you are Lucy Morgan and you have the reputation? Are they wary of you?

A: Yes, people are wary of me. People tell me, the worst thing in the world is to come in your office and have a message that Lucy Morgan is looking for you. But I think the people who have a reason to be wary are wary of me if they have done something they know that I could catch them doing that is wrong. People who have gone about their business in an honest fashion, and have done the best they could, don't worry about me. They understand that I will be fair. . . . Public officials get shot at from every angle all the time, and I know that. I don't want to be guilty of picking on them for minor offenses. When I shoot at them, I want to load the gun, and I generally have that reputation. Generally any public official who knows me well knows that when I call, it's serious. They better return the call; there is a reason to call me back.

[Being a journalist means] you have to develop a tough hide. People are going to yell at you when they are caught doing things wrong. Usually, the lower they are in the food chain—the city councilmen will squeal the most, because they are the least experienced at having bad things written about them. I can go into almost any town and tell you whether there is a good newspaper there, because if it's easy to get public records, if public officials are responsive and appear to be candid, odds are there is a pretty good newspaper working there.

[Having worked for the *St. Petersburg Times* for thirty-two years], . . . I cannot imagine working for a company that was . . . restrictive on whether you could spend money or what options you could take. I think I would have a lot of trouble there. Those are the kind of horror stories I am hearing out of the chains these days, and it frightens me terribly for the future of journalism, because those people who work for them are very disheartened. There is no esprit de corps. There is no fun for them in what they are doing. The *Times* has let me pursue stories and things that are fun. Why should I look anywhere else?

I mean, the *Times* is often branded as being arrogant. Well, I think we are different and, in many ways, we are better, because of our independence. We can make decisions fast, and a lot of our people can make decisions.

Q: Can you think of anything that having a journalism degree or a bachelor's or master's degree or a law degree would have added to your capability in doing this job?

A: I am sure it would have made me better educated. Most of my education has come from the two-year degree and the reading I have done, . . . but I would have liked to have had it. I think that it gives you credibility that you don't have without it. I guess I have a Pulitzer instead of a degree. That gives me some credibility. But I think a basic education is now a requirement. I probably couldn't get a job at the *St. Petersburg Times* with my basic credentials now. The competition for jobs, for good jobs, is so high that I think you have to have that basic degree to have the credibility to go beyond it.

Q: What have we not talked about that is of interest about Lucy Morgan?

A: It may be clear, but I think that reporting becomes a highly personalized thing, whether you want it to or not. There are lots of people in the Capitol who will tell their secrets to me but not to my staff. So I think reporters most of all need to be nice to people, need to develop that line of contact so people feel free to talk to them. If I fail to teach that to people I speak to, I have failed at everything. I don't think there is any need for the arrogance I see among some reporters and journalists. I think we need to be nice to people, respectful of them, and ask them for information rather than demand it. Only in that way can we be successful in getting to the bottom of what we are doing and finding all the information. Nothing turns off the average person who possesses information like the arrogance of a reporter who comes in demanding something.

Editorial Cartoonists

chapter 14   **Don Wright**

Winning a Pulitzer Prize is the pinnacle of most journalistic careers. Don
Wright, editorial cartoonist, has two of them (1966 and 1980), in addition to
scores of other awards. Combining "a rare intelligence and a sense of moral
outrage," said one newspaper, Wright "uses his space with crystalline preci-
sion, capturing in a single frame the essence of a half-dozen windy op-ed
articles." His cartoons are on permanent display at Syracuse University, and
he has mounted several one-man art shows across the country. He began his
career with the *Miami News* and has been at the *Palm Beach Post* since 1989.
"Don Wright is unpredictable, not compartmentalized, free-spirited—beyond simple or traditional categorization," as one writer put it. "And that is a
trait of genius."

Wright begins his interview by recalling his early experience in newspapers, straight out of high school. Originally a photographer and graphics
editor, he recounts how Bill Baggs, editor of the *Miami News*, pushed him
into trying editorial cartooning. Wright also comments on being syndicated
and how he feels about the numerous awards that he has garnered throughout his career. He discusses his daily work process, the characteristics of a
good cartoonist, and how newspaper competition with television has altered
the profession. He concludes with thoughts about his future and that of editorial cartoonists in general.

Don Wright was interviewed by Julian M. Pleasants on December 12,
2001, in Palm Beach, Florida.

Q: Give me a little bit of your background, mainly your newspaper background.

A: [I] jumped right into the newspaper business after high school; . . . [I]
didn't go to college. What I wanted to do initially, more than anything
else, was to become a cartoonist. I wanted to do a comic strip along the
lines of *Steve Canyon*, which was very popular at that time. I was told by
my high school art teacher that the way to find out all of the things you
had to do in order to become a strip cartoonist was to work for a newspaper. So . . . that is basically how I started in newspapers, as a copy kid at the
Miami News, way back in 1952.

Q: Then you worked your way up to be staff photographer?

A: Yes. I was lucky enough to be offered a job in the photo department as an
apprentice, and I took it from there. The editor of the art department,
where I originally wanted to work, decided I wasn't qualified. . . . I was
extremely fortunate to get the chance to try photography.

Q: Did you like it?

A: I loved it. It was my liberal education. It forced me out of the naive, teen-
age cell I was living in. All those fantasies about becoming a great strip
cartoonist just went away. I began to understand what life was all about,
because I was forced into situations I had never dreamed of—covering
bookie raids, seeing mutilated bodies. I came in contact with shocking
events most people my age would never have had to confront. . . . In a
sense, it really shaped me.

Early in my career as a photographer, there was a reputed serial killer
running loose across the country. His name was Dennis Whitney. . . . [H]e
wound up in South Florida in the early 1960s. His technique, as best I can
recall, was to go into an empty, or nearly empty, service station at night,
rob it, take the attendant into a back room, and shoot him in the head.
Eventually, Whitney made it to Miami and, indeed, committed that same
type of crime against a service-station attendant. They rushed him [the
victim] to the hospital, where he was treated, and in spite of the severity of
his wounds, he hung on and managed to survive. It occurred to Jim Bel-
lows, then the editor of the *News*, that the attendant might be able to give
. us a description of the killer. . . . [He]. . . agreed to see me. The idea was
that I would try to get the killer's likeness down on a sketch pad, drawing it
as this poor guy described it.

To be perfectly honest, in my opinion the likeness really didn't resemble
Dennis Whitney that well. But he apparently saw the drawing and cut and

ran. In the process, [he] hijacked an automobile, killing the woman who owned the car, but they chased him down and caught him. That was probably the first time anything I had drawn really had much in the way of impact. I think about that a lot and wonder if perhaps in some way I contributed to the death of that woman. Also, I'm puzzled as to why he ran in the first place because, to me, that drawing really did not establish a likeness at all.

Q: Did you ever have any formal training?

A: No, none whatsoever.

Q: When did you discover you had an affinity for drawing?

A: I don't know whether you discover that, or you just simply love it so much that you do it until you get better and better at it. . . . It was just an inclination I had that never left me.

Q: In 1958 you became graphics editor at the *Miami News*. Tell me exactly what that entailed.

A: The graphics editor is pretty much what the photo editor is today on most newspapers. He . . . is basically in charge of the photo department, choosing photographers for special assignments. . . . [The job] also involved laying out pages, and, when I did it, the back picture page, which was one of the highlights of the newspaper at that time, and pretty much coordinating the photo department operation with the rest of the news desk.

Q: Did you enjoy that job?

A: I did. It taught me a lot about editing, and it taught me a lot about the responsibility of putting out a newspaper every day, which involves a lot of people working together after coming to some sort of consensus. Sometimes there were arguments and debates about what should lead the paper and which picture should go with what. It's the kind of procedure you would actually want, because it encourages the contribution of the entire staff. I think newspapers today are terribly formula-ridden, even bureaucratic. In those days you argued things out, and, generally, I think by the time the newspaper came out it represented the very best combined efforts of everyone involved. I thought we were very successful doing it that way.

Q: At some point, as I understand, Bill Baggs persuaded you to do some political cartoons.

A: He didn't just persuade me; he kept on me all of the time. When I went into photo, my priorities changed. I kind of lost interest in cartooning as a way of making a living. . . . I was getting so much out of photography and learning so much about the crazy area I was growing up in. The newspaper business in general—all of its facets were exciting to me, and becoming a cartoonist was now the last thing in my mind. . . . But Bill always wanted his own staff editorial cartoonist and always thought I could do it if I really wanted to, so he kept after me and he kept after me and finally, circumstances dictating, I tried it.

I was young and kind of hotheaded and decided that on the news desk, as photo editor, I was probably a heck of a lot smarter than I really was. I quit one day in a petulant fit over something that hadn't gone my way, figuring there were other newspapers just dying for my services. Instead, Baggs stepped in and, again, made the editorial cartoonist pitch. He asked me if I had another job. I said no. He convinced me to try it. He said, "If it doesn't work out, you could go to the [*Miami*] *Herald* or do whatever you want."

I liked Baggs an awful lot, but I reminded him that I wasn't really prepared to do this. I wasn't one of those people who kept methodically current on crises and issues of the day.

He said, "Well, you will, you will." I finally agreed to give it a try, but viewed it as something temporary—just to get me through—until I found something else to do. And here I am.

Q: Was there a trial period? Did you have to start drawing right away?

A: He didn't indicate, in any way, that this would be a trial period. Baggs really believed in me, believed that I was going to succeed. To this day, I wonder why he thought that, because I didn't think that. And when I go back and look at some of that early work, I wonder why in the world he ever thought I could do it, because some it was God-awful. I mean, not drawn well and simplistically thought out. As a matter of fact, in some ways I caused them a great deal of pain because I developed some very conservative attitudes, often finding myself at odds with the editorial page. Baggs, to his credit, left me alone. At no point did he step in and say, "You cannot draw those cartoons"—cartoons that were sometimes a direct contradiction of what we were saying on the editorial page.

Q: How would you assess Baggs's term as editor of the paper? He is legendary in Florida circles.

A: Well, he deserves to be a legend. We're talking about a different breed of newspaperman. . . . Bill Baggs was a courageous, bigger-than-life individual who walked with a swagger and who believed newspapers ought to serve the community without surrendering themselves to powerful interests within those communities. He had a marvelous way of leading a dual life—being an approved, active member of the chamber of commerce, downtown development authority, and all those organizations . . . and then, after leaving their rarified air, allowing the paper to blast these same people who were oh-so-chummy with him. He actually encouraged it, while maintaining their friendship and respect.

They constantly complained to him, "Bill, look what your editorial page said today."

Baggs would say something wry like, "You know, I just can't seem to control those guys. . . ."

He understood that, at its heart, a newspaper should tell the truth, no matter how hard.

Q: It seems today, from what I have learned, the bottom line is most important for newspapers.

A: To say that the bottom line is the chief concern of newspapers today is a common observation and, certainly, has some validity. But I think the biggest threat to newspapers is that they really have lost their identity and don't know exactly what they are anymore. First, television was the bogeyman. As television became more and more popular and subscribers started to fall away, newspapers seemed confounded. [T]hey began to do strange things like adopting sort of garish magazine formats and deciding that if a newspaper front page looked a lot like a television set—splashy colors and very short stories—that this would get readers, thus advertisers, back. Well, it didn't work. Frankly, this kind of approach has caused those of us who still believe in newspapers a lot of anguish.

The Cox organization pretty much lets each newspaper run the way it wants to. We can call the shots here. The *Palm Beach Post* is a good newspaper, and we're lucky to have people running it who are a lot like the people I grew up with.

Q: Have you ever gotten any negative reaction from Cox, or from the headquarters, about any editorial cartoon you printed?

A: Never, in all honesty, never. . . . I sometimes worry about that. Where are they? Do they care? No, they have never pressured me about anything I have ever drawn. . . .

Q: Have you ever wanted to be with the *New York Times* or the *Washington Post*? I know Rick Bragg worked at the *St. Petersburg Times* and never anticipated he'd get to the *New York Times*.

A: Shortly before Bill Baggs went to Hanoi, North Vietnam, on a peace mission, he was offered and had accepted the editorship of the *New York Times*. One day he sat me down at one of those fancy, members-only clubs downtown and asked if I would be interested in coming to New York with him to become the first editorial-page cartoonist the *Times* had ever had.

I said, "Damn right, I would."

He said, "I am going to bring you there. . . ."

But not long after that, following his travels abroad and his efforts to help end the Vietnam War, he contracted pneumonia and died.

Q: The *New York Times* still does not have an editorial cartoonist.

A: No, they do not.

Q: When did you first become syndicated, and was your first syndication with the *Chicago Tribune*?

A: No, my first syndication was with the *Washington Star*. . . . I considered myself somewhat of a purist in that I never really sought syndication. I wanted to be able to do work that was qualified to be reprinted nationally. But syndication, I didn't really pursue that. Of course, most cartoonists want to get syndicated right away and make a lot of money. I didn't think I was ready, nor consistent enough, to be syndicated, frankly, although I had started to be reprinted nationally fairly regularly.

Signing on the proverbial dotted line was the biggest mistake I ever made, because Elmlark [Harry Elmlark, head of the syndicate], as it turned out, was pretty much a one-man operation. . . . His idea of selling was to occasionally phone newspaper editorial departments from his office, wherever it was, and say, "Would you like to take him?"

Jim Fain, a man I admire tremendously, took over as editor of the [Miami] *News*. He asked if I was syndicated. When I said, "Yes, with the *Star* syndicate," he insisted they were doing a terrible job representing me and offered to help me find a better syndicate. . . . Fain helped me find a lawyer. We sued the *Star* in federal court for restraint of trade and, after two years, won. . . . Soon after that, the [*Chicago*] *Tribune* moved in; we had discussions; and I've been with them ever since.

Q: In how many papers are you currently syndicated?

A: We mail out 375 every day to newspapers in the United States, Canada, and abroad.

Q: How does that syndication process work? How are you paid?

A: Every newspaper, depending on size and circulation, pays the syndicate a certain fee, and, basically, we split that. Rates are set and raised by the syndicate.

Q: Have you ever wanted to be a writer?

A: Everybody wants to be a writer. Everybody thinks he is a writer. Writing is tough. I have known some very, very fine writers, and I know how hard it is to do it well. I'm not sure I could be the kind of writer I admire and respect—for their intellect and turn of phrase. I don't know that I can meet those standards. But I might be willing to try.

Q: You were able to evolve into an editorial cartoonist.

A: Yes, and I'm continuing to evolve. . . . I'm still very interested in what I'm doing, digesting events and telling people what I think about them. I like to think my cartoons are a legitimate, valuable form of commentary. . . . God help me if I start doing what a lot of other cartoonists are doing these days—reducing everything to useless, humorless quips.

Q: Do you consider yourself an artist or a journalist?

A: Am I an artist? That's for others to judge. I've tried hard to be an artist. Sometimes, something latent forms on the paper, leading me to believe that, with practice, I might qualify as an artist. There are other times I do stuff I can't believe I did and would like to have back.

Q: You have had a one-man art show at the Lowe Art Museum in Miami and at New York's Syracuse University. Syracuse has a collection of your work. Other people consider you an artist.

A: Yes. Sometimes I think they're wrong, though.

Q: I wanted to talk to you about two important events in your career, the winning of the Pulitzer Prize in 1966 and 1980. In both cases it was awarded for general excellence. What was the key factor in the 1966 award? Did you send them a collection of your cartoons?

A: I think it's hard to know why the Pulitzer board does some of the things it does. The 1966 entry included a number of cartoons, the number the entry specifies must be included. They did say the award was for the body of my work, but the cartoon they cited was a drawing of two antagonists standing in the middle of a bombed-out wasteland, one here and one over there. Obviously, they had just survived mutual destruction, and one was saying to the other: "You mean you were bluffing?" That's the one they lauded as a representative of my work. If you are asking me what the criterion is, I'm not really sure.

Q: Were you surprised at the 1966 award? You had not been an editorial cartoonist very long.

A: I had not, and I was shocked, as a matter of fact. Newspaper people used to gather around the Teletype to find out who was winning what. . . . But I was at the water fountain in the middle of the city room. I used to clean my brushes in the water fountain because I didn't have a sink. I was standing there, and suddenly everybody screamed. I looked up, and all these people were running at me. They told me I had won the Pulitzer. I said, "Shit." Or something like that. That's how it happened. Stunned, I was stunned.

Q: What was your reaction to the 1980 award?

A: This time, I was properly grateful. So many things had happened to the *News*. The *News* was gradually being whittled away to nothing. . . . Advertising was disappearing. It was obvious this couldn't possibly go on. We weren't going to survive if we didn't find some way to turn the paper around and negotiate a better arrangement. So, to me, it meant a lot for the paper to get the Pulitzer, to help put it back on the map, to reassert our identity.

Q: You won a lot of other awards: Sigma Delta Chi, Overseas Press Club, Kennedy Memorial Journalism Award, David Brinkley Award, among many others. Which other awards are meaningful to you?

A: Well, of course, they are meaningful to me on a temporary basis. . . . I have been in this business long enough to know that the only thing that matters is how you are judged on the cartoon that's in today's paper. Fame is fleeting. I don't think I want to attach too much importance to having done some work that a lot of very nice people thought deserved an award. I would rather be judged on what I do every day and on my consistency.

Q: Discuss the process you go through every day to produce an editorial cartoon.

A: The process varies from day to day. The question that puzzles me the most and I almost resent, but the one that most people invariably ask, is, "How do you get your ideas?"

Q: Notice I did not ask that.

A: Bless you, sir. I have never been able to answer the question adequately and, honestly, do not even know why it is being asked. How does anyone get an idea? The fact of the matter is that it happens sometimes in a different way than it might have happened the day before. It's all contingent upon luck, passions, feelings, pressure of deadlines, and, maybe, even what you had for breakfast. Constant pressure causes you to tackle every day in a different way.

Sometimes, you come in, and you don't have a thing in your head. The closer you get to deadline, the more frantic you become, knowing full well you have to do something, anything. Then your head says, "Okay, you have got this idea, but you did something like that four or five years ago. Are you just recycling an old idea? Isn't that creatively dishonest?" Those predicaments, I think, are the real test of the cartoonist. Can he maintain some kind of quality and get a thought across in a coherent matter on that kind of deadline?

There are other times when the issues are so acute and, to you, so clear-cut your engine's running flat out on all cylinders. You get five, six, seven ideas tumbling one over the other. You know every one of them has merit. That's a wonderful feeling, being able to select from one of those seven or eight idea bursts and then go at it.

Q: Do you always get the idea first and then start drawing?

A: Get the idea first? Yes.

Q: Do you doodle?

A: Sometimes I doodle. I mentioned the pressure of deadlines. When it gets close, I sit down and start doodling and hope, somehow, the hands will come up with an idea. You do other things, too. You start scratching your head, you get up, you sit down, sometimes you swear, you walk around the room, you sit down and doodle some more.

Q: What time do you normally come in, and do you always work here in the *Palm Beach Post* office?

A: Yes, [I] try never to take it home with me. I'm mainly a night worker, so I come in around 1:00 P.M., then start getting the cartoon out. Usually, I've started the cartoon the day before, because of the deadline pressures here . . . ; this is a morning newspaper. . . . I try to get my drawing started the day before, then when I come in at 1:00 P.M., finish it. Sometimes I come in and start over. It depends on whether something more important has occurred, on whether or not I feel I can start fresh and not shortcut the artwork to the extent that I might deprive the cartoon of its impact.

Q: What time is your deadline?

A: 3:30 P.M. every day.

Q: Do you work fifty-two weeks a year?

A: No. Forty-eight or forty-nine weeks. Five days a week.

Q: That is a lot of cartoons. What would you say are the characteristics or qualities of a good editorial cartoonist?

A: Independence. I think it's critical. Being allowed to say pretty much what you want within the bounds of good taste. I don't believe, as I used to believe, that an editorial cartoonist should be allowed to do whatever he damn well pleases, no matter what. There's got to be some mutual understanding that the editor is always going to be held responsible for what you put in the paper. The trick is maintaining independence of thought with a proper sense of maturity.

Q: Is too much text a problem?

A: It can be a problem, yes. Sometimes what you call too much text, or just a lot of text, is quite necessary. Change of pace in the format of the cartoon is quite necessary. I'm doing a lot of panel cartoons and changing the approach so that I don't become too predictable. Holding readers on the editorial page is the hardest challenge of all.

Q: Someone else I talked to said that the reader needs to recognize who the people are and what the issue is. The cartoon has be drawn well enough so that when a reader looks at it, they recognize that it is [Richard] Nixon [U.S. president, 1969–74], for example.

A: I think each cartoonist develops their own caricatures of key figures. For example, [Bill] Clinton [U.S. president, 1993–2001]. If you looked at all of the cartoonists doing Clinton, you would see that none of the caricatures really matched up very much. Their readers eventually got to the point where they accepted these interpretive caricatures, whether they were remarkably close to the way Clinton actually looked or not.

Q: The reader knew it was Clinton.

A: The reader knew it was Clinton, even though technically, as a legitimate caricature, it really wasn't on the mark. We all develop our own stylized Clinton, Nixon, or George W. Bush [U.S. president, 2001–present]. Some cartoonists are better at caricaturing than others. . . . Someone like Mike Peters does some of the most grotesque, insanely funny caricatures that you not only accept them, you like them. . . .

Q: Is humor an essential quality for an editorial cartoonist?

A: A terrific sense of humor is essential, but I think the big problem in editorial cartooning today is that most of the young cartoonists think all they're supposed to do is be funny. . . . For some strange reason, a lot of editors have come to believe that humor is all there is to editorial cartoon commentary, and they're reprinting this vapid, spineless stuff. Consequently, the relevance of editorial cartooning is slipping away. . . .

Q: Critics say what they would like to get from editorial cartoonists is truth, but what does that mean?

A: Yes, what does it mean? My truth may not be the same as your truth. I would like to think that any cartoonist studies his issue carefully and is prepared to defend it once he takes a volatile position that upsets a whole lot of readers. When they call, is he prepared to defend it in detail? If not, I think to some extent he's cheating. . . . You have to be able to tell them why you've interpreted the crisis this way, why you think George W. Bush's role in it was not up to snuff, and where you think he made mistakes. Some readers who call in are livid, beyond the point of recognizing anything you say as legitimate. They just want to hammer you as quickly as possible and get off the line. But if you succeed in getting them involved in a conversation, they begin to accept this whole idea of differing with one another as part of a democratic process, and that actually works.

Q: I would guess that you hear, "You have gone too far this time," a lot.

A: Yes. But if you manage to keep them on the line, they sometimes realize that the two of you have differences and may never agree, so they promise to pray for you. They may also feel you aren't completely beyond hope, and they will come back to the paper the next day.

Q: Would you feel like you are not doing your job if you did not get any responses?

A: There is nothing worse . . . than being ignored, believe me.

Q: What do you read in preparation for your opinions?

A: I am a news junkie. I keep this horrible thing [television] on most of the time.

Q: CNN.

A: I have the wire services, all of them. I read the *New York Times*, the *Wall Street Journal*, the *Miami Herald*, the *Sun-Sentinel* and my own paper. In between, I've got *Time* and *Newsweek*. . . . My recreational reading generally leans toward current events.

Q: Once you have done all your preparation, and you come up with an idea, do you at any point run this by somebody else, ask them what they think?

A: Well, I've been doing this a long time, and I'm allowed some latitude there. When I was coming up, of course, it was customary to submit an idea first and get an okay. Now, what I do is work out a cartoon I want to go with, after sorting through a lot of different ideas. I check it out with my wife, mostly. I show her the sketch and ask her what she thinks. She will critique it and, sometimes, say, "No, that is not you." So I'll go back and start all over. By the time I come in, at roughly 1:00 P.M., I'm pretty well set on what I'm going to do.

Q: It seems to me, from viewing some of your cartoons, that you are very concerned about deflating pomposity and exposing hypocrisy. You are particularly good at providing satirical comments on current events. Is that a fair assessment?

A: I think it's a fair assessment of any really good cartoonist. You're talking about those character flaws that run rampant throughout our religious leaders and our politicians, once they gain a position of power. Sure, it's my job to go after them. What hurts me is when they ask for [a copy of] the original [cartoon].

Q: What sins are most abhorrent to you?

A: Hypocrisy, I think, is probably at the head of my list. One of the phrases that makes me cringe, when used by a politician, is "The American people want" or "The American people think." I don't know what the American people want. Sometimes I don't think even the American people know what they want. But I do know that most politicians, polls aside, have no idea what the American people want.

Q: I have noticed, in viewing your cartoons, that you have always had a very strong interest in the environment.

A: When I grew up as a kid playing in the woods, and I did a lot of that, I was always totally mesmerized by nature. It makes me angry when we take it for granted. I have very profound feelings about that, and every chance I get to say something in defense of the planet, I try to do it.

Q: Do you see your job more as a catalyst or as someone trying to educate people about issues?

A: Good question, probably some of both. . . . I think today's editorial pages have trouble getting younger readers to drop by. I think part of my job is to try and be stimulating enough to get them hooked, maybe, on paying us a visit. That's a tough order, and I don't know that I am really achieving it, but I see it as one of my responsibilities.

Q: Do you see your cartoons as some kind of a competition with the thirty-second sound bite on television?

A: Absolutely, I do. When I was growing up, the newspaper was the information hub of the family, particularly on Sundays. . . . Not anymore. . . . Television is experiencing its own problems. Viewership continues to fall. . . . Newspapers are probably missing a good bet and ought to go back to doing what they do best. This includes beautiful writing with details, beautifully described, telling people the truth, no matter how hard it might be.

Q: Tom Fiedler [executive editor, *Miami Herald*] mentioned that everybody was watching the 2000 presidential election on television, but the newspapers were the ones that made sense of what was happening. The next day, it was newspapers' responsibility to explain what had happened.

A: We were filling in the holes, no doubt about that. Television is a medium of the moment. The trouble with newspapers is that for some reason, and for the longest time, we believed we had to compete with the helter-skelter of TV news coverage. But television can't cover news completely. That's our job. If we do it the way we should do it, newspapers would be more appealing to readers as well as advertisers.

Q: What is your opinion of *USA Today*?

A: I didn't approve of *USA Today* at first, because I thought it was going to be more of the same old garish, spastic approach to journalism. Colored boxes and glitzy this and that plastered all over the place. But *USA Today* has evolved into a newspaper that, at times, does a pretty good job of reporting and, occasionally, some good investigative reporting. They seem to have transformed themselves, quite gradually, into a substantial newspaper.

Q: When you produce your editorial cartoons—let's say an editorial on the Everglades—do you hope it impacts Governor Jeb Bush [Florida governor, 1999–present] or the Florida legislature? Do you expect to have some shift in opinion as a result of it?

A: Of course you do. But I think one of the mistakes editorial pages make is that they appear to be writing solely to the governor [and other politicians], . . . trying to pressure him, or her, into whatever position the editorial page wants. Instead, we ought to be talking clearly . . . to the people who elect those officials. I think that's a better way to go after them.

Q: Do you think readers read the editorial pages?

A: Not enough of them. . . . So, again, we're back to the stimulus thing. In the *Wall Street Journal*, its editorial column down the left side of the editorial page reflects the paper's position and is beautifully written. It also has an edge to it. . . . [Y]ou cannot take your eyeballs away, whether you agree or disagree. We have got to be able to do that on all our other editorial pages.

Q: I noticed you have had an interesting time drawing cartoons of Richard Nixon, as did most editorialists.

A: Everyone had a great time with Richard Nixon.

Q: You miss him terribly, do you not?

A: We have John Ashcroft [U.S. attorney general, 2001–present] now.

Q: You indicated that you are pretty liberal in your views. How do you assess Richard Nixon as president?

A: I think Richard Nixon was, personally, a very troubled man who lacked confidence. I think his nature, his instinct, led him to believe that no one around him really could be trusted. I think he was paranoid beyond belief. In summing up Richard Nixon, I would say his presidency was one of our biggest personal tragedies. It's not that Nixon wasn't capable of being president; it was just that he wouldn't allow himself to be president. His entire time seemed to be spent trying to figure out who was going to do what to him and how he could get even. He didn't even trust his own aides.

Q: What is your view of Ronald Reagan [U.S. president, 1981–89]?

A: My problem with Ronald Reagan is that the media kept calling him the Great Communicator. Every time someone says that, I think how low the standard of communications has plummeted. Very few politicians, today, use the English language well, either written or spoken. I will, however, give him credit for having had better speechwriters than George W. [Bush]. Other than that, he was a nice enough man. I disagreed with him most of the time.

Q: What about Bill Clinton?

A: Interesting man, great cartoon subject. A man I wouldn't trust as far as I could throw him, of course. If you want me to talk about Bill Clinton, that would take probably an hour and a half. But, as a cartoonist, I have to tell you I really miss him.

Q: Why are there not many female editorial cartoonists?

A: There are a couple of reasons. I used to maintain that if a really good female cartoonist came along, one who was independent and willing to work really hard, she would become an overnight success, instantly wealthy. We were ready for a strong female viewpoint on the editorial page. . . . I don't think we ever really got someone with that kind of commitment. There are some female editorial cartoonists out there, but if you ask me their names, I couldn't tell you.

Q: Could you discuss some of the other editorial cartoonists you admire?

A: Jeff MacNelly, I guess, would be right up at the top of the list. Jim Borgman. I like Mike Peters. Revere Pat Oliphant. My general feeling is that editorial cartooning, in terms of quality, has fallen off precipitously. But I try not to worry about something I can't change.

Q: What was your assessment of one of the giants of the industry, Herbert Block [Herblock], who recently passed away on October 7, 2001?

A: I admired Herbert Block for a lot of reasons. He was, for one thing, a good writer. He was an excellent student of politics . . . and he was tough. . . . No matter what you say about all the other cartoonists and the stuff they did, Herblock was the guy who got Richard Nixon.

Q: Herblock's cartoons had a huge impact on the public view of Joe McCarthy [U.S. senator from Wisconsin, 1947–57; held hearings to root out communists in America]. He presented McCarthy as sort of an ape man.

A: I give credit to the *Washington Post*. Herblock was magnificent and the paper backed him up.

Q: When you look back at your career as an editorial cartoonist, what do you consider to be your most important contribution?

A: I don't think I have made my most important contribution yet, and if I thought I had, I would stop doing it. I keep hoping that, somehow, I can make some sort of big difference, without having the vaguest notion of what that difference might be. A worthy contribution would be influencing some kid, somewhere, to become a really good, kick-butt editorial cartoonist.

Q: What is the future for editorial cartoonists? What will happen once Oliphant and Mike Peters and the rest of the current group are no longer doing their work?

A: The trouble with tackling that subject is you come off like some kind of old fart, complaining about the way things used to be. I do think we've lost our way. Editors are putting up with junk and running it because they think that's all there is. We ought to be providing them with something better. Editors ought to be demanding something better. Syndicates ought to be offering something better.

Q: It seems to me that this state has a large quantity of outstanding newspapers.

A: I believe Florida has more really fine newspapers than any other state in the union.

Q: Why and how did that happen?

A: Why did that happen? Burgeoning population probably demanded it. We get people from all areas of the United States who, from whence they come, demand good newspapers. Competition for readership creates good newspapers.

Q: What is the future of newspapers? Are we going to eliminate the handheld document that we have now?

A: I have never believed it. People prefer something tactile. The printed page will never disappear. But I do think that newspapers have to drastically improve their quality.

Sportswriters

chapter 15 **Edwin Pope**

Born in Athens, Georgia, Edwin Pope was raised on sports and began his journalism career as a newspaper typist at the age of twelve at the *Athens Banner-Herald*. After early jobs with the *Atlanta Constitution*, the *Atlanta Journal*, and United Press International, he moved to the *Miami Herald* in 1956 and has been there ever since. He became sports editor at the *Herald* in 1967 and began collecting a steady stream of accolades, including the Red Smith Award (the highest honor for sportswriters in the nation) and induction into the National Sportscasters and Sportswriters Hall of Fame, the Florida Sports Hall of Fame, and the National Football Hall of Fame. His books include *Football's Greatest Coaches*, *Baseball's Greatest Managers*, *Encyclopedia of American Greyhound Racing*, *Ted Williams: The Golden Year*, and *On the Line*. Many of his columns are compiled in *The Edwin Pope Collection*.

In this interview Pope talks about growing up in Athens, Georgia, during the depression and his entry into journalism. He was, at age fifteen, the youngest sports editor in the country. He reflects on the usefulness of his journalism degree, in contrast with the amount of practical experience he gained over his career. He discusses the qualities important to being a good sportswriter, how sports serve as escapism for fans, and how television has altered sports over the past decades. Drawing upon his long tenure in Miami, Pope shares at length his thoughts on college sports, particularly college football, and on the importance of sports to Miami as a city. He also weighs in on issues such as coaches' salaries and academics and reminisces about some of his favorite sports memories, such as the 1980 Olympics, when the American hockey team defeated Russia.

Edwin Pope was interviewed by Julian M. Pleasants on February 16, 2002, in Key Biscayne, Florida.

Q: Discuss your early life in Athens, Georgia, and tell me how you got interested in sportswriting.

A: My early life in Athens, Georgia, was paradise. I don't know how anybody could have had a better place to grow up, because we had the University of Georgia there and all the attendant sports. Everybody in town was a football nut, but times were tough. We had a standing saying that we had no coal for the stove, no food for the kitchen, holes in the roof, holes in our shoes, and no socks—then came the depression. But everybody was poor, so nobody knew the difference.

I learned to type when I was about six, and when I was eleven, he [his father] gave me an old, used Underwood. I'll never know where he got the ten dollars to buy it, because ten dollars was a lot of money. I just turned on the Georgia Tech–Missouri Orange Bowl game of 1940 and copied down every word that Ted Husing, . . . a very famous sportscaster, . . . said, including the commercials. It was about twelve pages single-spaced.

In my ignorance I got on my bicycle the next morning, rode it down to the *Athens Banner-Herald* and looked around for a guy who looked powerful and authoritative, and kept asking everybody, "Who's the editor? Who's the editor-in-chief here?" I was eleven years old; I'm barging around this office.

It got to be a joke. They'd say, "He's over there; he's over there."

Finally, I got the editor-in-chief. I said, "Do you need a running story on the Orange Bowl?"

He said, "Well, what do you mean?"

I said, "Here it is." I thought copying over the radio was a running story because I'd read them in the *Atlanta Journal* and *Constitution*. I didn't know from anything.

He looked at it, and he said, "No, we don't need a running story, but who typed this?"

I said, "I did."

He said, "You want a job?"

I said, "Yes, sir."

He said, "We can't pay you anything, but we'll give you a lot of good experience," and they did. He kept his promise on both counts.

Q: At one point you were supposedly the youngest sports editor in the country.

A: Supposedly, and there was a reason for that. It wasn't because I was the most expert by any means. [In] 1943 every able-bodied man was in the service, and nobody ever heard of a woman sports editor. That would have been laughed out of the town, it was so outlandish, although they are all over the country now. Everybody was either drafted or gone off to work in the big town. They made me sports editor when I was fifteen.

Q: Tell me about your journalism courses at the University of Georgia.

A: Frankly, I took journalism because they would excuse my classes when I would go off with the football and basketball and baseball teams and that kind of thing. We had a great journalism school. I don't think I got nearly as much benefit out of it as I could have and should have, because I was getting up to go to work at six o'clock in the morning at the *Banner-Herald*. I'd have to make the fire and then light the fire. In the wintertime it gets cold in Athens. It would be so cold, I'd have to type with those old cloth gloves on. Just about the time the office was getting warm, before anybody else came in, I'd have to run off to school.

Q: Do you think it's necessary for people in sportswriting or newspaper work today to have a journalism degree, or is it just as good to learn by experience?

A: It hurts me to say this, but I don't think it's necessary to have a journalism degree. In a lot of cases, you can learn just as much in six months, a year, out of college about practical journalism as you could have [if you had] taken your major in [journalism]. I don't regret the journalism [degree]. I regret that I didn't apply myself more to it. I wish that I had taken more English and history, English literature, political science. . . . When you get out of college, you can learn the journalism, but once you get out of college, you're not going to learn the other stuff. You can't go back and get the other stuff.

Q: Was working for the *Red and Black* [campus newspaper] good training for a journalism career?

A: I think so, yes it is. It's really on-the-job training, where you have to make up and lay out and really get down to the nitty-gritty of reporting who, what, when, where, why. . . . I was working on the *Red and Black* while I was working on the *Banner-Herald,* and I was also sports editor of the *Pandora,* which is the yearbook. Then I was stringing for about five or six papers: the Albany paper, *Macon Telegraph, Atlanta Constitution* and *Atlanta Journal, Augusta Chronicle.*

Q: What kind of athlete were you in high school?

A: That's an interesting question. I wasn't any kind of an athlete in high school. When I was little, at the Athens Y [YMCA], until I was about twelve or thirteen, I was a pretty good athlete, but I just didn't grow. When I got to the university, I was on a boxing team. I did have a wonderfully tragic-comic experience as a boxer, though. While I was boxing, I was also juggling all these other jobs [and] going to journalism school. Then the season rolled around and I happened to be up in . . . the information director's office one day, leisurely opening a letter [which said] . . . undefeated NCAA champion Doug "Little Adam" Ellwood [was] slated to make his 1947 or 1948 . . . debut. Unbeaten in 250 fights. I realized that was who I was going to have to fight. I said, "Oh, God." They had just had a little article about me in the *Atlanta Constitution* about the fighting writer or the writing fighter, whatever. I was trapped.

I went down and went to work out that afternoon. I told our coach, who was an old professional lightweight, . . . [and he] came over to me, and he said, "Edwin, I don't think you ought to fight Saturday night. This guy's had a lot of fights." He was like twenty-nine years old, and I was about eighteen. I'd never fought anybody, except around town, a couple of college bouts. To say I was pedestrian as a fighter would be giving me all the best of it.

I said, "Pete, I know I shouldn't fight this guy, but they've had this story in the paper. If I don't fight now, everybody will say I'm yellow." I said, "I know I'm yellow, and you know I'm yellow, but we don't want all those people out there to know it."

He says, "Okay." Then he said something which greatly added to my self-esteem. He said, "It's your funeral," and walked away.

I was the smallest guy on the team, so I always had to spar with somebody bigger than me. I arranged to spar with a middleweight first, trying to get myself incapacitated. Failing in that, I asked for the heavyweight who happened to be a good friend of mine, but he had a terrible temper, and I hit him as hard as I could upside the head, while he was just toying with me. [He was] so infuriated with me, he just launched this right hand and hit me in the nose and blood started pouring everywhere. To make a long story less long, they took me to the hospital and X-rayed me and found my nose was broken, and it was the happiest day of my life when they told me. The guy comes out and he says, "Mr. Pope, . . . I'm afraid you won't be able to fight Saturday night."

I said, "Oh, that's too bad."

Q: Some professional athletes claim that many sportswriters are frustrated athletes, and when they report on football or professional basketball, they are not as knowledgeable as they should be because they haven't played the game. How do you answer that charge?

A: First of all, I would say that they're right in that almost all the sportswriters I know are failed athletes. I have seldom run into a sportswriter in sixty years, . . . who didn't either try to be an athlete or want to be an athlete or had some ambitions thwarted. As for the professional athletes saying they [sportswriters] don't know what they're doing, I mean, a doctor doesn't have to have cancer to diagnose it. That's my answer to that. A lot of times the people who are the sportswriters know more than the athletes do about what they're doing.

Q: Did you always write about sports?

A: At the UP [United Press], I had to do a little bit of everything. There was no such thing as just a sportswriter then. . . . I'd . . . have to rewrite all the news from all over the South. I was like the southern overnight editor at the same time I was southern sports editor. But that was good; that was a great learning experience, and it was tough. . . . That's the most beneficial thing, career-wise, I've ever done. I was only there for a couple of years, but then a new sportswriter came to town, Furman Bisher. . . . I was just so taken and enchanted by his writing. I had never read anybody who wrote that well. I just threw out all of my ambitions to go on with the wire service, and I decided that's what I wanted to try to be.

Q: In 1950 you went to work for the *Atlanta Constitution* and worked for Furman Bisher?

A: I did. . . . I meant to tell you one thing that was sort of funny in a nostalgic way about the *Athens Banner-Herald*. It was an old wooden building, and the editor was a fellow named Hugh Rowe, and he was sort of a distant figure. He didn't truck with the guys on the second floor. [The] second floor was sort of second-class. He had his own office downstairs. . . . Hugh Rowe wrote a column called *A Little Bit about Everything and Not Much about Anything*, which I thought was a great title for a column.

Everything was so technologically backward. The composing room was on the first floor; we were on the second floor; and to get copy down, they sawed a hole in the floor and had a rope with one of these big huge paper clips on the end of it. If you had copy, you'd pull up the rope, put the copy on the paper clip and let it down, and then lean on the bell, to the great distress of the head of the composing room. They'd take it and spread it out among the Linotype operators. Then, when they'd have proofs for you to read, they'd send them back up to you by putting them on the clip at their end and leaning on the bell until you felt like going down there and killing them. That's how we got the copy from the so-called newsroom to the composing room.

As ancient as it was, it was fascinating, and it had a romance that's pretty hard to attach to journalism today. Every Saturday night I would go down and watch those old flatbed presses run. I was absolutely enchanted, just in rhapsody watching that. The whole thing was a great adventure.

Q: When you were at the *Atlanta Constitution*, were you still covering the University of Georgia sports?

A: Occasionally. [I] covered everything—Georgia, Georgia Tech. I was doing stunts like riding with stock-car drivers and going up on flagpoles with flagpole sitters. Anything that came along. As I say, it was the last thing from specialization. It was a small staff; we only had, I'd say, maybe ten people on the whole staff. Now a comparable paper would probably have at least forty, with all specialists.

Q: In 1956 you left Georgia for the *Miami Herald*. Given your affection for Georgia and Athens, why would you leave the state to go to Miami?

A: First of all, I had just written a book called *Football's Greatest Coaches*, which turned out to be surprisingly successful, largely because Ed Sullivan [newspaper columnist and broadcaster, host of radio and television variety shows] plugged it on his television show one night. I called up Ed Sullivan—again in my youthful ignorance, just about like when I took that radio account down to the *Athens Banner-Herald*. . . . I call[ed] him up, got him on the phone, which you could never do today. I said, "Look, I got this book; . . . why don't you bring about twenty-five of these coaches from all over the country around and have them on the stage at one time. It would be a first. Nobody's ever done that. . . ."

He says, "I'll tell you what, send me a copy of your book and . . . maybe I can mention it next Sunday night."

I made sure the publisher in New York sent him a copy of the book. I was sitting at home, watching *The Ed Sullivan Show*, [and] . . . I said, "Aw geez, he's never going to get around to it. . . ."

But with about five seconds to go, he says, "I want to show you a great new book by a friend of mine." Of course, he didn't know me from Adam's off ox, and [he] held up the cover of the book. The next day it really took off. The reason I mention that is because it gave me a grubstake to come to Miami.

Also, I was very irritated over something so small you can't believe it. The *Journal* and *Constitution* were not benevolent employers, to put it bluntly. At one time, I put in a requisition for . . . a manual pencil sharpener. . . . [W]e only had one pencil sharpener in the entire newsroom, [and] you had to walk about seventy-five yards to it. By the time a guy would walk out there and shoot the bull with everybody on the way there and back, you would lose ten minutes of valuable time, so I put in for a pencil sharpener, which I was going to screw down to my desk. The requisition came back with a big "X" . . . and a "No" on it.

I went in there and said, "Is this a joke?"

He said, "No, that's not a joke. That's what I'm in here for, to prevent unnecessary extravagances."

On top of being redundant, that was very insulting to me. I said, "Hey, you're talking about a $1.75 pencil sharpener."

"No, no," he was adamant.

I said, "When are you going to pay me for excerpting *Football's Greatest Coaches?*"

He said, "I'll either give you a voucher, and you can go down to the cashier and get it, or I'll put it on next week's paycheck."

I said, "How about a voucher?" so he gives me a voucher, and I go down and collect the $250. Then I went back in the sports department and called the executive sports editor of the *Miami Herald,* who I knew, and said, "Can you use a man?"

He said, "What man?"

I said, "Me."

He said, "When can you be here?"

I said, "Tomorrow, . . . I'll be there." We didn't have to go through all this battery of psychiatric tests back then like you do now, else there wouldn't have been any newspapers back then because everybody was crazy that worked for them back then.

Then I walked back in and told the managing editor, "I got the $250, and, by the way, I quit. . . . I refuse to commit my career, whatever it may be, or my life, to a paper that won't supply me with a $1.75 pencil sharpener," and I took my stuff out of the desk and left.

Coming to the *Miami Herald* was the luckiest thing that ever happened to me, and it was sheer luck. The *Miami Herald* has treated me as well as my own family would have if they could have.

Q: If you look back from the perspective of the year 2002, who would you select as the greatest college football coach?

A: The popular answer would be Bear Bryant because he won so many games, although Joe Paterno has passed him now. But Bryant had much more charisma. Bryant had this amazing stage presence where, when he walked into a room, everything got quiet, and he had this gruff stentorian voice, and he was much more physically impressive with a great deal more presence than Joe Paterno has, although Paterno is a great man, I think. Those would probably be the popular choices.

I'm not sure but what Eddie Robinson, the coach at Grambling for all those years, given the resources he had, wasn't the best coach that ever lived. The truth is, we'll probably never know. The best coach that ever lived could have spent his life at East Muscogee High School . . . for fifty years, and nobody ever heard of him. It's just a concatenation of luck and resources and timing. Bryant was at the right school with all the resources and great recruiting resources.

Q: As sports editor would you go out and cover sports?

A: Yes, [and] I would write a column. I had very few other duties than writing a column. I was writing a minimum of five columns a week for thirty-five years.

Q: What makes a good sportswriter?

A: A lot of things. I think obviously the first thing that makes a good sportswriter is just raw, natural ability. I certainly can't lay any claim to that, because I think I had a lot less raw, natural ability than a lot of my peers. I tried to make up for it by working harder and working longer hours. I'd [also] say attitude. You have to take for granted that a guy is willing to put in some murderous hours. Sometimes they're murderous; sometimes they're very easy. You've got to be ready to pull up stakes and take off and leave your family and everybody else and cancel every kind of social obligation you might have or even family obligations. I find that there are fewer and fewer who are willing to do that. I can't say that I blame them, because flying is not what it used to be.

Q: Would it be more difficult to write about sports or to write about something like politics?

A: Well, it evens out, I think. Sports is easier to write about because there's always something you can see and put your finger on, and there's always a final score up there. In politics, it's so subjective. Half of it is guesswork. You don't know which are the crooks, which are the bad guys. You're pretty sure ninety percent of them are crooks, but you don't know for sure. In sports there's always a winner and a loser.

On the other hand, a sports columnist almost always has to go somewhere. That's the killer part of it. Not many days when you can just sit in the office and write off-the-wall like the political columnists or the general columnists do. That's the great advantage they have over the sports columnists, but I think what balances out the other way is that they have to scrounge for ideas. Being a sports columnist can be physically very wearing. It's not a healthy job.

Q: You won the Red Smith Award, which is generally considered the highest award for sportswriters. What was your reaction to winning that award?

A: I was just stunned. . . . I was just absolutely blown away because I never thought, never even dared think about it or dream about it.

Q: In your book *The Edwin Pope Collection*, James Michener wrote a very laudatory introduction. Michener earlier had written a book, *Sports in America*, in which he tried to explain the importance of sports in American life. How would you make that assessment?

A: It amazes me that there are so many people that take sports so seriously. But I really should not be amazed because sports, to most people, now more than ever, is pure escapism. . . . It is entertainment; it takes your mind off whatever—terrorism, bad marriage, bad job, not being able to pay the mortgage. You can just leave your work-a-day world and walk into another world. That is what sports is. It is understandable to me that there are so many people hooked on it. [It is] still hard for me to absorb the intensity with which some people approach sports as fans.

Q: As you know, if it's Georgia versus Florida, and your team loses, for some fans it is devastating.

A: Absolutely.

Q: In some cases they are not even graduates of the university. Why do they take it so seriously?

A: Well, that is like Sigmund Freud said that he spent thirty years searching for the answer to one question, what do women want? So I would put your question in the same category as Freud's, what do sports fans want? I like sports fans, and I think they are a lot smarter than most writers give them credit for being, especially with all the new ways to see sports. . . . It still baffles me and befuddles me . . . as to why are they that way. I guess that everybody needs something outside of his everyday life to attach himself to, or devote himself to, or to be fanatical about, whether it is your church, charity, philandering, stealing money, hating someone, or whatever.

Q: How has television changed sports? Now you have ESPN, ESPN2, the Golf Channel, and you can see everything from pro football to curling twenty-four hours a day.

A: One way it has changed sports is that it has created a lot more millionaires because every time those TV shows come on, they have to pay fees to somebody. Those people that get those fees pay a lot of those fees to the players. In dealing with the players, [it] is entirely different from what it used to be.

Q: How important are professional sports teams for Miami?

A: That is something that we are endlessly debating in this go-round about whether they are going to get a new . . . stadium for baseball, which they desperately need. My contention is that people who don't have any inter-est in baseball or going to the games shouldn't have to pay a penny of their tax money. Of course, the baseball owners think that the public should pay for everything. I think that the teams themselves and, even in some cases, the players and certainly the owners should pay for all the stadiums. They have been getting a free ride forever.

Q: Certainly, Wayne Huizenga [owner of the Miami Dolphins] would have enough money to build a new stadium.

A: He would, but my question would be, if Wayne Huizenga is worth one and a half billion dollars, is it fair to ask him to spend a third of that to build a dome stadium, to give up a third of his net worth just so a lot of people could enjoy it? That is the attitude of people who want a new stadium. . . . They say, "Well, Huizenga has the money." He does have the money, but I don't see that he has an obligation.

Q: Do you think when the city or state builds a professional sports stadium, that it is economically profitable for the community? Does it generate enough tourist dollars and tax revenue to overcome the costs of building it?

A: Time and again, it has been shown by expert economists that it doesn't have a commensurate economic benefit to the city. Baseball doesn't bring anybody into town. It's just a huge nontaxable white elephant sitting there that very often brings down the quality of life around the stadium. You don't see any baseball or football stadiums in upscale neighborhoods. It doesn't really create very many jobs, except minimum-wage people who sell beer and popcorn.

No, I don't think it even comes close to equaling the public output. As you can see, I'm not supportive of the public paying all the freight for a pro franchise. There is no question that pro sports add to the quality of life. It's an adornment to the lifestyle of the people who live in towns, but it also takes its toll on other things. It is taking a huge toll on college and high school sports and other amateur sports. Everybody talks about [how] the entertainment dollar only goes so far; that's no doubt true. But there is also the question about the entertainment hour; how many hours people have to spend. Where are they going to choose to spend them? Are they going to go out and do something that benefits everybody, like the Optimist League or a high school football game or a little neighborhood basketball game, or are they going to pay fifty-eight dollars for a seat at the hockey game?

Q: I noticed in the paper today that the Dolphins have just raised their ticket prices.

A: For the fourth straight year.

Q: It now costs something like forty-three dollars for a good seat. If you have two boys, and you want to go to a Dolphins game, with parking and hot dogs, it has to be a minimum of $150. Who can afford to do that?

A: Well, I ask myself that question all the time. I see these people going in there that I know aren't rich. They do without or borrow the money. It has gotten way out of hand. Baseball is particularly a game of fools, both players and owners.

Q: Why is baseball not as popular as it used to be?

A: My personal opinion is that life has gotten so much faster—every movie you see wants to be so much louder than the last one; the cars to go faster; the explosions . . . noisier; the fatalities . . . more numerous—life has gotten to be so much faster that, especially young people, demand everything at a fever pitch, and baseball isn't played at a fever pitch. Baseball is played at . . . [an] even slower pace than it used to [be] because they have ever more commercials. The World Series game has forty-five minutes [of commercials]. You can just about count on them lasting three and a half hours. That just doesn't tie in with the pace of American life.

Q: I know some rabid baseball fans who resent the fact that a shortstop who hits .230 gets five million dollars a year. They see this as an extraordinarily high price to pay for average baseball players. Also the players' attitudes seems to have gotten worse—they are arrogant and won't sign autographs—and this has turned fans off. Do you think that is a fair assessment?

A: I don't blame the players for taking the money. That is why I say that it is a game of fools. The players ruined it by insisting on so much money, but the owners didn't really have to submit to their demands, but they did. So it is a question of who are the biggest fools? The owners or the players?

Q: Should Pete Rose be in the Hall of Fame?

A: I don't think so. I think he bet on baseball. I think the evidence is incontrovertible that he bet on baseball, or otherwise he would have gone to court, which he never has. He has never been tested in court. It is generally thought that Bart Giamatti [former commissioner of Major League Baseball] knows and has evidence that he bet on baseball. I don't think that there should be a place in the Hall of Fame for anybody who ever bet on baseball. If you bet on baseball, it follows that there is a chance that you might have bet on your own games. The way that Pete bet, I wouldn't think it unusual, because Pete is sort of—not so much a scoundrel or saint as he is amoral; he doesn't see the difference. No question that he loves baseball and was a wonderful asset to baseball.

Q: I presume that college football is still your favorite sport. How have the athletes changed in the years that you have been reporting college sports in general, but college football in particular?

A: They have changed negatively. There are reasons. The demands by the media have increased almost exponentially. You used to go out to a University of Miami practice or press conference, and there might be four people there. You go out there now, there are thirty-four people. If a guy is a good football player it's a heavy burden on him, dealing with the media. Although this has always been the case in some way, it has been more marked in recent years. If a kid has athletic ability, he has a free pass in life, just about from the time that he is six or eight years old on. He can get away with anything.

Q: Both in and out of school?

A: Oh, yes, absolutely. This always [has been the case] to some degree, but not like it [is] now. If some fourteen-year-old kid gets in trouble, and the high school coach knows that he is going to be a great football player, he will intervene, and a lot of times [it is] with the sufferance of the teachers. Let's say that they are much less humble than they once were. A lot of them are pretty arrogant, but they are still much better to talk to than any of the pro athletes, except for hockey players, race-car drivers, and horse-racing people.

Q: Those people are easier to talk to?

A: The three pro sports I mentioned are the easiest. Horse racing—trainers, owners, and jockeys. Hockey players mostly, but coaches too. Automobile racing—those guys would let you ride on their fenders if it wouldn't slow them down. They are terrific, but I notice that the hockey players, as the salaries go up, the hockey players' tolerance for media demands is going down.

Q: Are college athletes today less intelligent, less articulate than in the past? More articulate? How do you assess them?

A: The athletes today are much more media savvy. They give you better answers, in part because the journalists ask better questions, and a lot more of them. They give you better answers than they would have ten years ago, twenty years ago, forty years ago, [because] nobody even asked them any questions. People didn't go to the dressing rooms after the games, you wouldn't have thought of it. Personally, I think the biggest waste of time and space on a sports page is all these innocuous quotes from athletes, few of whom ever say anything worth repeating.

Q: The athletes often say, "Somebody has really got to step up for this game"; "We've got to focus."

A: "We didn't execute." Yes. "We just got to regroup." We print all that garbage.

Q: Are there more clichés in sports than in other areas of society?

A: Clichés are clichés because they are so true. But now you hear them—like the one, "we control our destiny." You can't control your destiny; destiny is destiny. Or fate, "we control our fate." You cannot control fate. Fate is fate; it is preordained. . . . We compound the felony. They are bad about clichés, but I don't blame them as much as us for printing them.

Q: One thing that disturbs a lot of academics at universities is this rather lax attitude toward athletes' irresponsible behavior. Without getting into specifics, there were wide receivers at Florida State University and the University of Florida who were caught stealing. Not only were they not kicked out of school, they remained on the football team. They were suspended for one or two games. What is your reaction to that?

A: Well, I look at that in the context of society as a whole. Now when I grew up in Athens, Georgia, about the worst trouble that you could get into was knocking out a streetlight with a rock. You couldn't be drunk, because you couldn't buy anything to drink. You couldn't be drugged, because there were no drugs. There were much fewer opportunities to be a bad guy. As a result, we didn't have much misbehavior. I don't know how we would have reacted if we would have had the opportunity for misbehavior that they have today.

I think that there is a great division of how the coaches handled this. For example, I think Spurrier [Steve Spurrier, former football coach at the University of Florida]—even though I don't care much for him personally; he is too arrogant and thin-skinned for my taste—is a pretty good disciplinarian. And just the opposite, I love Bowden [Bobby Bowden, football coach at Florida State University] as a person, but I think Bowden is a bit too light on the players. If you ask him about it, his answer is, "Well, that is the way kids are these days." Well, that's not the right way to confront this.

Butch Davis at the University of Miami was a chronic liar. Football coaches in college and pros are the world's biggest liars, except for politicians. It would be a dead heat if you had a lying race between head football coaches and politicians. Maybe . . . they have to lie. All I know is that they would climb a tree to tell a lie. Butch Davis is the worst of the whole field of worst. Yet he was a wonderful disciplinarian, a very decent and honorable man in every other respect.

Q: That reminds me. I want to go back to the Miami football team, 1986, when they wore fatigues, had gotten in fights, and had been accused of other indiscretions. They cultivated this bad-boy image.

A: Actually, the severity of their malfeasance was overrated. Most of the things that they did wrong were not terrible, but their attitude was so arrogant, and they taunted and showboated and hotdogged, and I thought it had reached its apex, of course, at the Fiesta Bowl, the 1987 Fiesta Bowl. That is an insult to all of football, to me, the way that they acted there. . . . [T]hey were cursing the Penn State fans from the door of their locker room before the game. Jimmy Johnson let them get by with it. Actually, I think Jimmy Johnson encouraged them to do it. I thought it was shameful, and I wrote columns to that effect. I wrote that Jimmy Johnson should apologize or be fired. His answer to that was to go in and offer to resign to President Tad Foote [president, University of Miami]. As it happened, the athletic director, Sam Jankovich talked him out of it at the last minute. . . .

The whole scenario of the Fiesta Bowl was a blight on college football and just shameful. It was everything that college football shouldn't be. I know that there are a lot of abuses in college football—anybody would be terribly naive to think that there are not—but it also does a lot of good. The way that it unifies alumni—I think that it's very healthy.

Q: Do you think that there is a lot of cheating going on in college sports, particularly in recruiting? I noticed that sanctions have been recently handed down against Alabama and Kentucky for violating NCAA rules.

A: You know, I really don't. I know that a lot has gone on, but I think that is just the fear factor.

Q: Fear of the death penalty [stringent NCAA sanctions]?

A: Right. It stops a lot of this. I don't doubt but what hundreds, maybe thousands, of coaches, including some of whom I am absolutely positive of, kept stacks of tens, twenties, fifties, and hundreds in their desk drawer. And if a guy needed a new suit, he would go by the coach's office, and he would dip in there and hand him the money. The money was furnished to him by affluent alumni. I don't think that happens near as much any more. I think that the University of Miami now has four compliance officers. They didn't use to have any. Now they have four people who do nothing but to see that they are in compliance [with] this tangle of NCAA regulations.

I'm sure there is a lot of hanky-panky going on, but it's not . . . as open and as wild as it was, like when Max McGee [Green Bay Packer wide receiver who caught seven passes in Super Bowl I] told me, when he went to Tulane, he had any kind of car that he wanted any time that he wanted it. When SMU [Southern Methodist University] got the death penalty, one of the higher officials told the athletic director he had to do something about these abuses. The athletic director's response was, "I don't have time or the resources to do that; . . . we have a payroll to meet."

Q: What about financial stipends for college athletes?

A: It's not financially feasible. If you had to pay, first of all, you couldn't just confine it to football players; you would have to pay every athlete. . . . Say [there were] five hundred; you paid them all; nothing less than two hundred dollars a month would even make a difference these days. Do the math; it wouldn't work. Besides, they are already getting paid. At the University of Miami, you are getting $35,000 tuition free. So they are getting paid, basically for four years, $140,000.

Q: When we examine college sports, it is an expensive proposition. Should coaches and players accept money from Nike for wearing their shoes and athletic equipment? I know that they get million-dollar contracts.

A: I see a lot of flaws in the coaches' accepting the money. It compromises the university and makes it even more commercial. But the colleges themselves aid and abet this by using this as part of the coach's compensation. When you get into the pros, it's just business to me. I don't really see anything wrong with it in the pro sports. The only thing that I see wrong with pro sports is it enables thieves like Nike to charge kids from the ghetto $160 for a pair of Jordans [shoes].

Q: Are you disturbed by players turning pro early after one or two years of college?

A: Absolutely, I think it's terrible. Now we are seeing that they don't redshirt nearly as many players, because they know that they are only going to have them for a short length of time. That is not all that disturbs me. . . . I think that the pro leagues should compensate the colleges for every player they use. I'm not just talking about the guy turning pro early. I think that if, let's say, Dan Morgan, who went from the University of Miami linebacker to the Carolina Panthers. In effect, the University of Miami is a factory that produced Dan Morgan for the larger company, the Carolina Panthers. I think that the Panthers should have to pay a fee. . . . The pros get such a free ride from the colleges.

Q: What about coaches' salaries?

A: Oh, that is a sore point with me. I think that it is just absolutely ridiculous to pay a college coach two million dollars like Spurrier was getting, or one million like Bowden. Two million is getting to be the going rate for top coaches like Bob Stoops [head coach, University of Oklahoma]. As soon as Bob Stoops hit two million, Butch Davis hit the ceiling and started thinking that he was a two-million-dollar coach. That was part of the reason that he left the University of Miami to go to Cleveland. I think that is a terrible abuse. Doesn't bother me about the pro coaches; I mean, it's gross, crass.

Q: I wonder also if there needs to be more NCAA control about grades. I know that some schools have very low admission standards; some schools have higher admission standards. Should there be some sort of national standard?

A: I certainly think it should be standardized and higher. I don't think you should take a complete academic washout, accept him as a regular student. I think this should be done on an NCAA level, and I really don't understand why it hasn't been done that way. We could sit here and agree that there should be a national standard, [but] I can see an immediate holdup, where the president of the University of Florida would say, "It's wrong for you to try to hold us to the standards of Princeton or Yale or Harvard or MIT or Tulane. Our function is as a public university; we shouldn't be that elitist as to demand these high admissions standards such as the Ivy League schools and others."

Q: How about graduation rates for college athletes? You rarely hear that from sports announcers.

A: Well, you see, those figures are released pretty often. The ones that have high graduation rates rush into print with them. Miami has increased its graduation rates tremendously in the last ten or twelve years. I must say, in all honesty, that I think, and it's quite patently obvious to me, that the teams that don't have very high graduation rates don't put a very high premium on character or academic ability when they're recruiting. I don't think—with all due respect for Bobby Bowden—I don't think he's going out looking for many Rhodes scholars or anything approximating it. All he's interested in is whether they run a 4.3 or 4.9.

There are other coaches, . . . Larry Coker [Davis's replacement as head coach of the University of Miami football team] would be one of them, . . . who believe the two go hand in hand. A good student is a better football player, and . . . you have far fewer problems with a guy who has shown through high school that he is an honorable person who does his best academically.

Q: Let's talk about the University of Miami football; you've covered them for a long time. When you look back, there have been some rather extraordinary coaches at that campus. Almost every one, Jimmy Johnson, Dennis Erickson, Butch Davis, etc., went on to a successful pro career. Who was the best coach?

A: That's a great question. Oddly enough, I've never been asked that question, and I'd be hard pressed to give you an answer. I probably would have to say Howard Schnellenberger . . . , [who] came in and built it up from almost nothing to a national championship. I'm convinced had he stayed, he would have won . . . just as many national championships as other coaches there wound up winning.

Q: I know you mentioned how you feel personally about Spurrier, but how would you evaluate his career as a head coach at Florida?

A: Spurrier's career at Florida? Fabulous. . . . It's hard for me to imagine anybody doing any better job at any college over the same period of time, except maybe Tom Osborne at Nebraska, and Osborne had advantages involving academics that Spurrier didn't have, and they have a system at Nebraska, a very sinister system there, . . . where they use walk-ons as scholarships. Say there's a player in West Big Nose, Nebraska, that they just don't have a scholarship for. The local 4-F club or something like that will pay his way. It's a very organized network. He effectively has a scholarship, so they have an unlimited number of what amounts to scholarships, which gives them a huge advantage. Osborne was also a fine coach. Other than that, I don't see how anybody could have been a better coach for the period of time than Spurrier.

Q: How influential was Spurrier's style of play on the SEC [Southeastern Conference]?

A: Often imitated, but never replicated. I think people tried to do what Spurrier did, but they can't do it, because they just don't have the knack for it and the mental quickness that Spurrier has for it. The things that Spurrier has been doing at college, I'm not all that convinced that he's going to be that successful in the NFL. Those guys have seen all of that stuff. That's not going to cut any ice up there. Besides, I think Spurrier's thin skin and super-sensitivity to criticism and his aversion to doing outside things—part of the reason, I think, he didn't like dealing with the alumni, going to alumni functions. Didn't like recruiting—can't blame him for that. I don't think he'll stay very long. I don't think he'll last five years in the NFL.

Q: What's the greatest or most exciting sporting event you've ever attended?

A: No question, the 1980 Olympics at Lake Placid; the U.S. victory over the Russian ice-hockey team. I don't know much about hockey now, but I knew even less then. There was a transportation strike . . . so a lot of the guys just left. Only about half the media were still around for this wonderful, wonderful event. I went and sat beside a fellow [from Boston] . . . and he explained to me what was happening during the whole thing, and then

I went as crazy as everybody when the U.S. got the winning goal. I remember I got so excited, I apparently threw a very expensive pair of prescription glasses into the air. It was just the most riotous, ecstatic event. Nothing else could even come close.

Q: Because it was so unexpected?

A: Unexpected and patriotic. They weren't given . . . any chance whatever. . . . The second most exciting would be Jack Nicklaus winning the Masters when he was forty-six years old in 1986. . . .

Q: What's wrong with boxing?

A: It's just wall-to-wall sleaze, always has been. It's no worse now than it's ever been. They keep saying that it won't last; it will sleaze itself out of business.

Q: Is it the promoters?

A: Yes, mostly, but [also] the managers. Managers are just as crooked as anybody else. The fighters are the victims. Any sport in which the object is to maim or kill the other person couldn't possibly have very many redeeming virtues.

Q: How have sports reporters changed since you started in the business?

A: The main way they've changed is you hardly ever used to see a sports reporter who wasn't a drunk. Now you hardly ever see one who will even take a drink. Standards are much higher these days. They're much, much more knowledgeable about sports because of TV. They start watching TV when they're five or six years old, and they know everything there is to know about a sport by the time they're twenty years old, when we had to see it all firsthand.

Q: When you are writing, you are trying to get an audience that is essentially wedded to television or listening to the radio. How do you get people to read your column and read the newspaper?

A: I think the thing I try to do mostly is address and deliver an opinion on what the people have found most interesting on television. I want to be writing about what they're going to be talking about when the column comes out the next morning. You used to be able, . . . a long time ago, [to] go to an event and more or less tell them what happened. Now, you have to tell them why it happened, more why it happened than what happened.

Q: What do you think of USA Today?

A: I think USA Today has had a salubrious influence on sports journalism if for no other reason than the emphasis is put on tight, bright writing and the proper use of graphics, not this helter-skelter all-encompassing hunger for gigantic space-eating photos.

Q: Have you ever had any problems from either Knight-Ridder [publisher] or an editor about anything you've written?

A: I had two problems, which is not very many for forty-five years, I think. One time I wrote something rather cutting about Hialeah Racetrack when it was starting to go down way back in the '60s, late '60s. I referred to it as a rich folks' country club, and I got a note from John S. Knight that said I was being arrogant. He took issue with what I said because he was one of the rich folks whose country club it was. Naturally he took issue. He was a great man; there's no question about that.

Q: At that time, he was publisher, right?

A: He was publisher. I think that was before we were Knight-Ridder. I wrote him back that if he just wanted a sports editor who would be a mirror for his own opinion that he was going to have to find somebody else. I wasn't going to do it. I never heard a word back from him. That's the kind of guy he was.

Q: You mentioned that in the beginning of your career you could never have had a female sports editor. Now there are an increased number of female sportswriters. Are there many female sports editors?

A: Yes. They're all over the place. Philadelphia has had several of them. The *New York Times* has had at least one. It's not at all unusual to have a female.

Q: What about African Americans and minorities in the profession?

A: We don't have near as many of them as we should have. Obviously, the ones who do come in and are very good rise to the top very quickly. Most of the newspapers I know, certainly Knight-Ridder and Gannett, are very diversity conscious and are always looking for minorities—African Americans, Hispanics, although Hispanics aren't a minority in Miami. For some reason, [it is] hard to find gifted Hispanic newspaper writers.

Q: We need to talk a little bit about the Dolphins. Give me your assessment of Don Shula. Do you see him as the greatest pro coach?

A: All things considered, I think Shula was the greatest pro coach. Even though he didn't win a Super Bowl his last twenty-two or three years, they were always right there. In thirty-three pro seasons, he had two losing seasons. That is truly incredible. . . . On sheer persistence—and you have to give some weight to longevity as a coach. Not only that, but to maintain the quality of teams, despite the fact that they almost never got a premium draft choice, because they always did so well. I think he was the best because he was so consistent.

Q: How would you rate Dan Marino among NFL quarterbacks?

A: I wouldn't rate him as the best quarterback who ever played. I think there have been several other quarterbacks. Joe Montana [former San Francisco 49ers quarterback], Johnny Unitas [former Baltimore Colts quarterback]. Without any question at all, Dan Marino is the greatest pure passer who ever picked up a football. No question about that.

Q: When you look back on your career, are you satisfied with your accomplishments?

A: No, no.

Q: In what sense? What would you rather have done?

A: I think I could have been more ingenious or innovative. I will have to say that innovativeness and departure from the general line of thought is more encouraged now than it was thirty, forty years ago. It's hard to pick out one thing. I . . . probably should have been more interested in basketball and maybe a little more interested in baseball.

A problem that I had was that I was . . . never as much a fan of sports as I was of writing. If I quit tomorrow, I would never go to any other sports event—except maybe a tennis match or a horse race or a college football game, if I could get in the press box. I'm not a big sports fan. A lot of times I would have to crank myself up in the morning to get interested about the subject I was writing about. I never had to crank myself up about the writing, because I loved to write, and I still do. I would have been better. All these guys you hear on sports talk radio and most of the outstanding sportswriters are real sports [fans]. That's their life. That's not my life. I never wanted it to be. I would have been a better professional if it had been my life, but I wouldn't have been as happy as a person.

Index

Julian M. Pleasants is the director of the Samuel Proctor Oral History Program at the University of Florida. His most recent book is *Buncombe Bob: The Life and Times of Robert Rice Reynolds.*

Books of Related Interest

The Values and Craft of American Journalism: Essays from the Poynter Institute, edited by Roy Peter Clark and Cole C. Campbell

The Changing South of Gene Patterson: Journalism and Civil Rights, 1960–1968, edited by Roy Peter Clark and Raymond Arsenault

Maximum Insight: Selected Columns of Bill Maxwell, by Bill Maxwell

Kick Ass: Selected Columns of Carl Hiaasen, by Carl Hiaasen

The Wide Brim: Early Poems and Ponderings by Marjory Stoneman Douglas, edited by Jack E. Davis

Orange Pulp: Stories of Mayhem, Murder, and Mystery, edited by Maurice J. O'Sullivan

Al Burt's Florida: Snowbirds, Sand Castles, and Self-Rising Crackers, by Al Burt